P9-DGL-722

The Presidency of
ABRAHAM
LINCOLN

AMERICAN PRESIDENCY SERIES

Donald R. McCoy, Clifford S. Griffin, Homer E. Socolofsky
General Editors

George Washington, Forrest McDonald
John Adams, Ralph Adams Brown
Thomas Jefferson, Forrest McDonald
James Madison, Robert Allen Rutland
James Monroe, Noble E. Cunningham, Jr.
John Quincy Adams, Mary W. M. Hargreaves
Andrew Jackson, Donald B. Cole
Martin Van Buren, Major L. Wilson
William Henry Harrison & John Tyler, Norma Lois Peterson
James K. Polk, Paul H. Bergeron
Zachary Taylor & Millard Fillmore, Elbert B. Smith
Franklin Pierce, Larry Gara
James Buchanan, Elbert B. Smith
Abraham Lincoln, Phillip Shaw Paludan
Andrew Johnson, Albert Castel
Rutherford B. Hayes, Ari Hoogenboom
James A. Garfield & Chester A. Arthur, Justus D. Doenecke
Grover Cleveland, Richard E. Welch, Jr.
Benjamin Harrison, Homer B. Socolofsky & Allan B. Spetter
William McKinley, Lewis L. Gould
Theodore Roosevelt, Lewis L. Gould
William Howard Taft, Paolo E. Coletta
Woodrow Wilson, Kendrick A. Clements
Warren G. Harding, Eugene P. Trani & David L. Wilson
Herbert C. Hoover, Martin L. Fausold
Harry S. Truman, Donald R. McCoy
Dwight D. Eisenhower, Chester J. Pach, Jr., & Elmo Richardson
John F. Kennedy, James N. Giglio
Lyndon B. Johnson, Vaughn Davis Bornet
Gerald R. Ford, John Robert Greene
James Earl Carter, Jr., Burton I. Kaufman

The Presidency of
ABRAHAM
LINCOLN

Phillip Shaw Paludan

UNIVERSITY PRESS OF KANSAS

© 1994 by the University Press of Kansas
All rights reserved

Published by the University Press of Kansas (Lawrence, Kansas
66049), which was organized by the Kansas Board of Regents and is
operated and funded by Emporia State University, Fort Hays State
University, Kansas State University, Pittsburg State University,
the University of Kansas, and Wichita State University

Library of Congress Cataloging-in-Publication Data

Paludan, Phillip S., 1938–
The presidency of Abraham Lincoln / Phillip Shaw Paludan.
    p.   cm. — (American presidency series)
Includes bibliographical references and index.
ISBN 0-7006-0671-8 (cloth)   ISBN 0-7006-0745-5 (pbk.)
1. Lincoln, Abraham, 1809–1865. 2. United States—Politics and
government—Civil War, 1861–1865. I. Title. II. Series
E457.P18 1994
973.7'092—dc20   93-46830

British Library Cataloguing in Publication Data is available.

Printed in the United States of America

10 9 8 7 6 5 4 3

The paper used in this publication meets the minimum requirements of the
American National Standard for Permanence of Paper for Printed
Library Materials Z39.48-1984.

For Marty
For the years

What doth the Lord require of thee,
but to do justly, and to love mercy,
and to walk humbly before thy God?

Micah 6:8

CONTENTS

Foreword		xi
Preface		xiii
Acknowledgments		xix
1	The State of the Union: 1860	3
2	Assembling the Cast: Winter 1860–61	21
3	To Sumter: January to April 1861	49
4	Congress Organizes, Lincoln Acts: April to December 1861	69
5	Forging the Resources of War: January to February 1862	97
6	Northern Power Emerges: March to June 1862	119
7	Leaving Old Moorings—McClellan and Emancipation: June to December 1862	137
8	Cabinet Crisis: December 1862	167
9	Emancipation and the Limits of Dissent: January to June 1863	185
10	Union Power Affirmed: May to July 1863	203
11	The Meaning of War: July to December 1863	217
12	Reconstruction Beginnings: May 1862 to December 1863	233
13	Lincoln Affirmed: January to June 1864	259

14   Louisiana and Reelection: June to November 1864   275

15   The Reconstruction Proposition: December 1864 to April
     1865   297

16   Conclusion   315

Notes   321

Bibliographical Essay   363

Index   379

FOREWORD

The aim of the American Presidency Series is to present historians and the general reading public with interesting, scholarly assessments of the various presidential administrations. These interpretive surveys are intended to cover the broad ground between biographies, specialized monographs, and journalistic accounts. As such, each will be a comprehensive, synthetic work which will draw upon the best in pertinent secondary literature, yet leave room for the author's own analysis and interpretation.

Volumes in the series will present the data essential to understanding the administration under consideration. Particularly, each book will treat the then current problems facing the United States and its people and how the president and his associates felt about, thought about, and worked to cope with these problems. Attention will be given to how the office developed and operated during the president's tenure. Equally important will be consideration of the vital relationships between the president, his staff, the executive officers, Congress, foreign representatives, the judiciary, state officials, the public, political parties, the press, and influential private citizens. The series will also be concerned with how this unique American institution—the presidency—was viewed by the presidents, and with what results.

All this will be set, insofar as possible, in the context not only of contemporary politics but also of economics, international relations, law, morals, public administration, religion, and thought. Such a broad approach is necessary to understanding, for a presidential administration is more than the elected and appointed officers composing it, since its work so often reflects the major problems, anxieties, and glories of the nation. In short, the authors in this series will strive to recount and evaluate the record of each administration and to identify its distinctiveness and relationships to the past, its own time, and the future.

The General Editors

PREFACE

The oath is a simple one, made all the more austere because there is no coronation, no anointing by priest or predecessor. The office has passed from one person to another months before, first by popular election and then by a ritualistic casting of votes by presidential electors, whose names are forgotten if anyone knew them in the first place. The only requirement on the day the president takes office is an oath or affirmation: "I do solemnly swear that I will faithfully execute the Office of President of the United States, and will to the best of my ability, preserve, protect and defend the Constitution of the United States."

Each president in the history of the nation has tried to protect and defend the Constitution—some with more dedication than others. Each responded to the challenges and the opportunity that his time gave him. No president had larger challenges than Abraham Lincoln, and the testimony to his greatness rests in his keeping of that oath, which led him to be responsible for two enormous accomplishments that are part of folk legend as well as fact. He saved the Union and he freed the slaves.

He preserved the unity of the nation both in size and in structure. There were still thirty-six states at the end of his presidency; there might have been twenty-five. The population of the nation when he died was 30 million; it might have been 20 million. The constitutional instrument for changing governments was still in 1865 what it had been in 1861—win a free election and gain the majority of the electoral votes. Another option might have existed—secede from the country and make war if necessary after losing the election. A divided nation might have been more easily divided again—perhaps when angry westerners felt exploited by eastern capitalists, perhaps when urban minorities felt oppressed by powerful majorities. And there were lasting international consequences from Lincoln's achievement: Foreign oppressors of the twentieth century were not allowed to run free, disregarding the two or perhaps three or four countries that might have existed between Canada and Mexico.

Because of Lincoln, 4 million black Americans gained options beyond a life of slavery for themselves and their children. Men, women, and children were no longer bought and sold, denied their humanity—because of Lincoln, but certainly not because of Lincoln alone. Perhaps 2 million Union soldiers fought to achieve these goals. Women behind the lines and near the battlefields did jobs that men would not or could not do. Workers on farms and in factories supplied the huge army and the society that sustained it. Managers and entrepreneurs organized the resources that helped gain the victory. But Lincoln's was the voice that inspired and explained and guided soldiers and civilians to continue the fight.

Black soldiers, too, preserved the Union and freed slaves. And these black soldiers were in the army because Lincoln wanted them there, accepted the demands of black and white abolitionists and growing numbers of soldiers and sailors that they be there. Hundreds of thousands, perhaps millions, of slaves, given the chance, walked away from slavery and thus "stole" from their masters the labor needed to sustain the Confederacy and the ability of those masters to enslave them. No one would ever again sell their children, their husbands, their wives; no one would rape and murder and mutilate them, control their work and much of their leisure.

Lincoln kept his oath by leading the nation, guiding it, insisting that it keep on with the task of saving the Union and freeing the slaves.

Too often historians and the general populace (which cares very much, and may define itself in vital ways by what Lincoln did and means) have divided his two great achievements. They have made saving the Union, at least for the first half of his presidency, a different task from freeing the slaves. They have noted that Lincoln explained to Horace Greeley that he could not answer Greeley's "Prayer of Twenty Million" and simply free the slaves. His prime goal, he told Greeley, was to save the Union, and he would free none, some, or all the slaves to save that Union. But before Lincoln wrote those words he had already decided that to save the Union he would have to free the slaves.

This well-known incident illustrates the major premise of this book:

xiv

Freeing the slaves and saving the Union were linked as one goal, not two optional goals. The Union that Lincoln wanted to save was not a union where slavery was safe. He wanted to outlaw slavery in the territories and thus begin a process that would end it in the states. Slave states understood this; that is why they seceded and why the Union needed saving.

Freeing the slaves, more precisely ending slavery, was the indispensable means to saving the Union. In an immediate practical sense, those 180,000 black soldiers were an essential part of the Union army in the last two years of the war. They made up almost 12 percent of the total Union land forces by 1865, adding not only to Union numbers but subtracting from the Confederate labor force. Moreover, those black soldiers liberated even where they did not march. Their example was noted throughout the South so that slaves far from Union occupation knew that blacks could be soldiers, not just property, and they began to march toward freedom.[1]

Ending slavery also meant saving the Union in a larger sense. Slavery had endangered the Union, hurting black people but also hurting white people, and not only by allowing them to be brutes, as Jefferson had lamented. Slavery had divided the nation, threatening the processes of government by making debate over the most crucial issue of the age intolerable in the South and, for decades, dangerous in the Congress of the United States. To protect slavery the Confederate States of America would challenge the peaceful, lawful, orderly means of changing governments in the United States, even by resorting to war. Lincoln led the successful effort to stop them and thus simultaneously saved the Union and freed the slaves.

Why does it matter that Lincoln linked saving the Union and the emancipation of the nation from slavery? First, it is necessary to get the historical record straight. It matters also because in understanding our history Americans gain access to the kind of faith that Lincoln held that our means, our legal processes, our political-constitutional system work to achieve our best ideals. Too many people, among them the first black justice of the United States Supreme Court, Thurgood Marshall, have doubted that respect for the law and the Constitution can lead to greater equality. "The system" too often has been the villain, "institutional racism" the disease that obstructs the struggle for equality. The underlying premise of this book is that the political-constitutional system, conceived of and operated at its best, inescapably leads to equality. Lincoln operated on that premise and through his presidency tried to achieve that goal.[2]

But how did he do that? One of his accomplishments, the one that took most of his time, was fighting and winning a war. He chose the generals, gathered the armies, set the overall strategy; he restrained the dissenters and the opponents of the war; he helped to gather the resources that would maintain the Union economy and that would enable the Union military to remain strong and unrelenting. He kept himself and his party in office, the only party that was dedicated to saving the Union and ending slavery. And he kept an eye on foreign affairs, seeing to it that Great Britain remained willing to negotiate and to watch the conflict rather than joining or trying to stop it. This book examines how he and his government and his nation achieved victory.

But I am particularly interested in what Lincoln said, for the most important power of a president, as Richard Neustadt has argued, is the power to persuade.[3] Thus it is vital for a president to inform and to inspire, to warn and to empower the polity, to bring out the "better angels of our nature"—better in the sense of allowing the nation to achieve its best aspirations. "Events have controlled me," Lincoln said, but what he did most effectively was to define those events and to shape the public opinion that, he noted, was "everything in this country." In the 1840s a Whig newspaper came close to the mark I am admiring in assessing Lincoln:

> Put the case that the same multitude were addressed by two orators, and on the same question and occasion; that the first of these orators considered in his mind that the people he addressed were to be controlled by several passions . . .the orator may be fairly said to have no faith in the people; he rather believes that they are creatures of passion, and subject to none but base and selfish impulses. But now a second orator arises, a Chatham, a Webster, a Pericles, a Clay; his generous spirit expands itself through the vast auditory, and he believes that he is addressing a company of high spirited men, citizens. . . . When he says "fellow citizens," they believe him, and at once, from a tumultuous herd they are converted into men . . . their thoughts and feeling rise to an heroical heights, beyond that of common men or common times. The second orator "had faith in the people"; he addressed the better part of each man's nature, supposing it to be in him—and it *was* in him.[4]

At their best American presidents recognize that their duty as the chief opinion maker is to shape a public understanding that opens options and tells the truth about what the people can be and what their problems are. Appealing to the fears we have, manipulating them to win office or pass a law or achieve another goal, does not so much *reflect* who we are as it in fact *creates* who we are. It affirms us as legitimately fearful—afraid of something that our leaders confirm to be frightening—and as being citizens whose fears properly define us.

Appealing to better angels is more complicated—it requires calling on history for original aspirations—reminding Americans for example that the basic ideal of the nation is that "all men are created equal." Equally vital, such an appeal also requires reminding Americans that they have in fact established institutions that work to that end—not only reminding them of their aspirations but also reassuring them that their history, their lived experience, reveals legitimate paths to achieving those goals. History thus acts to recall the nation's best dreams, but it also restores faith that the means to approach the dream live, abide in the institutions as well as in the values that shape the nation.

I believe that a history of the presidency of Abraham Lincoln can show how Lincoln managed to shape a public understanding, how at times he failed, but how he usually succeeded. Thus he set a standard that makes it legitimate that we, when the better angels of our nature prevail, define ourselves in important ways by who Lincoln was, by what he did, and by what he said.

ACKNOWLEDGMENTS

I have learned much from other Lincoln scholars, especially those with whom I disagree. Our debates have been conversations, not arguments, and I am the better for my exchanges with them. The notes to this book show in detail just how dependent I have been. Roger Bridges, Lloyd Ambrosius, Don Nieman, Gabor Boritt, Tom Schwartz, Frank Williams, and Mark Neely have provided invitations to speak and thus to develop ideas about Lincoln and his age. Neely also deserves special thanks for an insightful reading of the manuscript.

I learned to care for history from Raymond Lindgren when he was chairman of the department at Occidental College and from Andrew Rolle and Cliff Kroeber and the late Merlin Stonehouse when they taught there. I learned to understand the Civil War era from Harold Hyman and Robert Johannsen when I studied at the University of Illinois. I am grateful for all their lessons.

Fred Woodward, who directs the University Press of Kansas, knew when not to express his anxieties about my progress and when to encourage me in other ways. I have also benefited from knowing Don McCoy and Cliff Griffin, who aren't supposed to be mentioned as editors of the series, so I mention them sincerely as nurturing friends and colleagues.

My colleagues in the University of Kansas History Department have provided a stimulating and nurturing environment for my scholarship. I'm especially grateful to my chairmen, Norman Saul and Daniel Bays, during the period that I was writing this book for their support and understanding. I thank the General Research Fund of the University for its support of early chapters and the Hall Center for the Humanities for providing a semester for research and writing.

I've been blessed with excellent research assistance, especially from Brian Dirck and Bill Young.

My personal debts are less easily expressed. My mother encouraged me constantly with her eagerness to learn more about everything. Her memory is green. I am blessed with two daughters who have nurtured my work and my life. My wife, Martine Hammond Paludan, has listened on countless walks and over morning coffee and evening cocktails to every idea I've had about "The President," and she has questioned and cared about it all.

I am grateful to this assembly of colleagues and friends and family for making this book possible. I hope Lincoln's many colleagues and friends in the abiding conversation about America's best hopes are equally grateful.

1860

★★★★★

The great debate took place in the afternoon on the open square, where a large, pine-board platform had been built for the committee of arrangements, the speakers, and the persons they wished to have with them. . . . In front of it many thousands of people were assembled, Republicans and Democrats standing peaceably together, only chaffing one another now and then in a good natured way.

As the champions arrived they were demonstratively cheered by their adherents. The presiding officer agreed upon by the two parties called the meeting to order and announced the program of proceedings. Mr. Lincoln was to open with an allowance of one hour. . . . His voice was not musical, rather high-keyed. . . . It had an exceedingly penetrating, far reaching quality. The looks of the audience convinced me that every word he spoke was understood at the remotest edges of the vast assemblage. His gesture was awkward. He swung his long arms sometimes in a very ungraceful manner. Now and then he would . . . bend his knees and body with a sudden downward jerk, and then shoot up again with a vehemence that raised him to his tiptoes and made him look much taller than he really was.

There was, however, in all he said, a tone of earnest truthfulness, of elevated, noble sentiment, and of kindly sympathy, which added greatly to the strength of his argument. . . . Even when attacking his opponent . . . there was still a certain something in his utterance making his hearers feel that those thrusts came from a reluctant heart, and that he would much rather have treated his foe as a friend.

—Carl Schurz, *Reminiscences, 1858*

1

★ ★ ★ ★ ★

THE STATE OF THE UNION:
1860

It was happening in the United States as it happened nowhere else in the world—peacefully, but solemnly or boisterously as they chose, every white man in the nation over twenty-one eligible to take part if he wanted to—the people were changing their government. In this election over 81 percent of the eligible voters turned out, scattered throughout cities, towns, and villages across the land, arguing, talking, picking up their ballots (marked clearly with party designation), then publicly dropping them in wooden boxes or clear glass bowls, cheered by their friends, jeered by their opponents. It was a celebration, a ritual, fun as well as serious, and the two feelings manifested a passion for this clear demonstration of how free people governed themselves. They had been arguing about their future for decades now—whether that future would encompass slavery, how they could, if they could, reconcile keeping millions of people slaves while still revering liberty. That argument was larger than the soul-troubling issue of the injustice of enslaving people—enough of them believed that blacks (they usually called them "niggers") were inferior by nature to whites. The argument also included the impact of slavery on the lives of white people. Some people feared that they would have to share the frontier with blacks and with masters who could not tolerate open debate or free elections. They worried that they would have to compete in Kansas, Nebraska, Colorado, New Mexico—the huge million-square-mile region stretching from Missouri and Iowa to California and Oregon—with an economy that de-

graded self-disciplined white labor and rewarded self-indulgent aristo-
crats who whipped their laborers instead of paying them to work.[1]

Some people were troubled by other forms of slavery's expansion—
politics seemed paralyzed by the issue even as civil liberties were under
attack. As antislavery feeling grew and candidates and officeholders began discussing slavery, proponents demanded new rules—Congress
had enacted gag rules in 1836 and 1840, restricting the ability of the national legislature to debate the issue. Massachusetts senator Charles
Sumner had been beaten almost to death for making a speech against
slavery. The proslavery legislature in Kansas Territory had passed laws
that punished antislavery speakers with sentences ranging from two
years at hard labor to execution, depending on the nature of the speech.
The Supreme Court had struck down state laws that protected local citizens from the outreach of the federal fugitive slave law—slavery's influence was reaching into Wisconsin, Iowa, Massachusetts. That same
court had declared the major plank of the Republican party platform
unconstitutional—slavery could not be kept out of the territories. Armed
legislators challenged each other on the floor of Congress over the slavery question. The electoral process itself seemed at risk. Threats of secession were staples of the campaign—if Lincoln was elected, Southerners claimed, then the Union was finished. The will of the voters would
be trumped by secession. Changing governments by balloting would be
stymied by abandoning that government entirely.[2]

Then the election was over; the people had made their choice—for
the nation's sixteenth president but for something deeper as well. In the
eighteen previous presidential elections Americans not only passed
down the office; they changed their leaders, expressed their wishes,
and showed their commitment to changing governments quietly, peacefully, regularly. They voted for their candidate and their party, of course.
But they also voted for the process established in Philadelphia in 1787,
modified slightly by constitutional amendment in 1804, opened to involve them in burgeoning numbers in the Jacksonian years, and now
more than seven decades old. Unintimidated or unpersuaded by secessionist rhetoric they had expressed their faith in that process.

This time it appeared that such faith might not be enough to hold
the Union together. The election results confirmed the divisions over
slavery and offered little hope to Southerners that the process would
work to their benefit. The most ardent proslavery candidate, John
Breckenridge, had carried the vast majority of the Deep South. Stephen
Douglas had offered a more moderate choice there and was rejected.
John Bell, running on the Union party platform, also offered a compromise position but he persuaded large numbers of voters only in the bor-

der states. Douglas showed some strength in the Middle West, but Abraham Lincoln, the "Black Republican" candidate, as Southerners called him, swept the North.

The six-year-old Republican party had carried every Northern state, and its candidate gained 180 electoral votes to the 123 gathered by his combined opposition. Lincoln was indisputably the constitutionally elected chief executive, chosen by one of the largest voter turnouts in United States history. If participation was the sign of commitment, American voters had shown their commitment to the process. But the Republican victory was entirely sectional. Lincoln won every county in New England, 109 of 147 counties in the mid-Atlantic states, 252 of 392 counties in the old Northwest of Ohio, Indiana, Illinois, and Michigan. In contrast seven Deep South states cast no votes at all for Lincoln; he won only 2 of 996 Southern counties. Further clouding the mandate was the fact that only 39.8 percent voted for Lincoln although he was still 10 percent above his nearest challenger.[3]

But slave states were not interested in the statistics of the victory. The candidate most hostile to slavery had been chosen by Northern voters, and slave states feared that a dangerous new course had been charted. Seven of them did not even wait for Lincoln's inauguration to see if their fears were justified. Within the space of three months the Gulf Coast states had seceded. Eight others were watching intently to determine if they should follow suit.

Yet faith in the process endured. The nation had weathered threats of secession in the past. This was simply another cry of wolf, many thought. "Humbug, nothing but folly," Lincoln had called it in 1856. Four years later during the campaign, Republican Carl Schurz bantered about prior secession attempts, "one, the secession of the Southern students from the medical school in Philadelphia," a ridiculous charade, and "the second, upon the election of Speaker [of the House] Pennington [in 1859], when the South seceded from Congress, went out, took a drink, and then came back. The third attempt . . . would be when old Abe [was] elected. They would then secede again and this time would take two drinks but come back again." Other influential Republicans echoed his response: "Mumbo-Jumbo," "as audacious a humbug as Mormonism," "a game . . . nothing but a game." Some observers argued that the system would find a solution through compromise. Most people in the North expressed their faith in their government with a simpler, more instinctively conservative reaction: The proper response was to "enforce the laws," editorial after editorial proclaimed.[4]

But secession threatened the orderly operations of self-government. Here was a challenge that asserted that the process would not continue unless one side won, that votes peacefully registered could be trumped by men carrying guns who would not wait until the next election to have their way. They would demand it now, take it by force if necessary. The most promising experiment in self-government in the world would have failed.

It would be an enormous reversal of fortune for a country that in recent decades had grown prodigiously. Population had increased from 23.3 million in 1850 to 31.5 million in 1860. No state had lost population, although Vermont's growth was almost stable in the decade. Southern states were growing most slowly, but even the slowest-growing, South Carolina, was gaining. Virginia experienced a healthy 12 percent increase, and Missouri, exceptional among the slave states, grew nearly 74 percent. The North, in contrast, was really taking off. The area the census called the "Middle States," including New York, Pennsylvania, and Ohio, gained 3 million people, an increase for that region of 25 percent, Illinois more than doubled its population, reaching 1,712,000 and making the 36 percent gain in neighboring Indiana look almost puny. The Northwest of 1860, Michigan, Wisconsin, and Iowa, grew impressively too, profiting from the fact that they were becoming the granary for Europe. In an age in which population growth was equated with prosperity and strength, the increase in the nation's population between 1850 and 1860 was greater than the total population in 1810.

These figures had an impact on national affairs. Since most of the population increase occured in the North the percentage of Northern representatives in Congress increased. By 1861 slave states could elect 83 of the 233 members of the House of Representatives—only 37 percent. In the past the South had been able to protect its besieged peculiar institution from national laws by controlling the presidency through the region's influence in the Democratic party. Presidents Pierce and Buchanan were Northerners, but they knuckled under when Southern Democrats insisted. Presidential vetoes could shield slavery if necessary. Southern control of important congressional committees also gave the South power. But with Republican power growing, potential veto overrides and growing numbers of rebellious committee members forecast danger.

Southerners were used to scenting danger on issues remote from slavery itself. Since the early days of the republic slave states had felt threatened by any outreach of national power that did not protect slavery. From the Bank of the United States, through the "tariff of abominations," to federal control over commerce, Southern congressmen, presidents, and judges had opposed laws that used federal power to shape the economy. Stalled in the Congress as of 1861 were proposals, backed by Republicans and many of those promoting economic development, who were concentrated in the burgeoning North, to raise the tariff, improve rivers and harbors, provide homesteads in the West, begin building a Pacific railroad, and provide federal support for higher education. Threats of vetoes and legislative maneuvering by Southern legislators had held back these expansions of national power, but demographics, economic development needs, and antislavery hostility were building pressure to break the dam. Population figures were driving national politics.

The racial and ethnic nature of that population also had potential to shape Lincoln's America and his war. There was a greater proportion of foreign- to native-born Americans in 1860 than at any previous time in the nation's history. Over 4 million—20 percent of the nation's 31 million-odd—were foreign-born. Of the 8.2 million increase in population in the prewar decade, 2.7 million consisted of immigrants who had come to the nation since 1850. Because many native-born were children of immigrants the influence of the foreign-born was even greater than the numbers suggest. Although the immigrant population generated fears among many Americans, others believed that immigration in such numbers was "a fact which may justly enhance rather than detract from the satisfaction wherewith we should regard this augmentation of our numbers." The people were "seeking homes for themselves and their children," and that said something positive about the nation.[5]

Because far more immigrants came to the North they built voting and representation majorities for that region, adding to its strength and influence. They provided muscle for its growing industries. Other immigrants grew the crops that fed the flourishing population. Most important, because so many immigrants were young men, they offered the potential of half a million soldiers; predominantly Irish and German but also French, Polish, Swedish, Mexican, Danish, Hungarian, Welsh, and Scottish, most of them were eager to show their loyalty to their new nation.

Almost 4 million of the 4.5 million black Americans were slaves, and thus did the nation stand on the brink of civil war. Preserving slavery was the nonnegotiable imperative of the slave states. Limiting or destroying the influence of slavery over their lives was the insistent demand of Northern majorities. One group of white people would win this contest, but until the fighting started blacks could do nothing to affect the outcome. They were chattel—they could be sold, individually or in groups, separated from parents, children, husbands, wives at the whim of their masters. They could be whipped, branded, threatened, even killed "if necessary to secure discipline," as several slave codes put it. Because the law forbade blacks from testifying against whites, slaves faced rape and torture and murder without defense so long as no whites witnessed the act. Some Southern states in the 1850s passed laws protecting slaves from extreme cruelty, and whites generally encouraged blacks to live in families, providing comfort and community amid slavery's brutality. But no white person in the South made any effort to end the institution. The South paid for and controlled a race it considered inferior and so had brutalized. Self-interest and self-preservation combined to promise that so long as Southern white men held power slavery would abide forever.[6] "Man's foulest crime," Herman Melville called slavery. Across the Atlantic an eccentric Danish philosopher, Søren Kierkegaard, was writing that the only unforgivable sin was the conscious destruction of the human spirit. Somehow that judgment had yet to echo in the South, and most Northerners managed to escape the thought even though militant abolitionists spoke similar words.

There were many other events to claim attention, events easier to watch. A fantastically burgeoning economy was a powerful distraction, and that wealth rested in considerable measure on the work of slaves. While slavery nurtured and shaped Southern society and fed its prosperity it simultaneously provided wealth for the whole nation: Cotton manufacturing was the leading industry, and cotton exports were by far the largest of any product. The national economy was growing at rates that for the most part evoked celebration and awe. Per capita wealth grew remarkably, placing the United States in the front rank of the world's nations—on a par with Britain and France. Real wages increased in the prewar years, growing decade by decade. The director of the 1860 census was inspired to declare, "And who can justly estimate the influence upon the general happiness and prosperity—upon the progress of civilization of the sum total of effective labor, capital, and skill represented by such an aggregate?" The credits rolled on, pointing to gains in farm implements, pig iron, rolled iron, machinery, coal, gold, silver, copper, clothing, lumber, printing presses, sewing machines, cabinet furniture, jewelry, watches, chemicals, salt, fish, petroleum. Only whaling and cod fishing had declined, but Americans could rely on "that beneficent law of compensation which pervades the economy of nature, and when one provision fails her children, opens to them another in the exhaustless storehouse of her material resources, or leads out their mental energies upon new paths of discovery for the supply of their own wants." When oceans were exhausted of whales presumably another resource would serve the nation's purposes. Another species might perhaps arise to replace the 800,000 bison slaughtered in 1860 (that foreshadowed the deaths of 15 million). But such ideas rarely intruded to dampen the celebration. The census director could count only greater and greater growth: a total value in domestic manufacturing alone of nearly 2 billion dollars: *"An increase of more than eighty six (86) per centum in ten years!"* he gasped.[7]

These figures were even more impressive because they represented growth in less than half the economy. The nation was still predominantly a nation of farmers. Almost 59 percent of the labor force worked in agriculture, compared to 18 percent in manufacturing and construction. Almost three-fourths of the country's exports came from farms. Over 75 percent of the people lived in rural areas. And the census of 1860 displayed the expanding bounty of the farms: wheat production was up nearly 70 percent in ten years; corn increased by 40 percent; wool, dairy products, meat production, hay, orchards showed similar increases. And Southern-based crops, cotton, tobacco, sugar, increased equally well. In the North, however, this great growth increasingly linked shop, factory, and farm. "In nearly every department of rural industry mechanical power has wrought a revolution," the census declared. Agriculture was also connected to larger vistas by a growing emphasis on education, on learning from farmers in other countries and regions. There were at least forty magazines and newspapers in the nation focused on agriculture. When Lincoln addressed the Wisconsin State Fair in 1859 he described an interrelated economy of farm and shop and store, of new inventions increasing the output of educated farmers who enriched and improved themselves and the nation with their knowledge, their new tools, and their hard work.[8]

The North was thus prospering, and that prosperity built upon a diversity and an integration of the nation's economy that could be witnessed on a page of the manuscript census. There on Schedule 1, page 740, for Springfield, Illinois, were Abraham Lincoln, fifty-one years old, lawyer, owner of a $5,000 home, $12,000 in personal property, born in Kentucky, and with him his wife, thirty-six-year-old Mary, no property listed, born also in Kentucky; sons Robert, sixteen, Willie, nine, Thomas, seven, all born in Illinois; two servants, M. Johnson, "18. F," and Phillip Dinkell, "14. M." Above the Lincolns on the list were Lotus Niles, a forty-year-old "secretary," born in New York, worth $9,500, and his family; Edward Biggs, a forty-eight-year-old teamster from England worth $4,300, married to Nancy who had come from Virginia, and the father of nineteen-year-old Hamilton, an apprentice carpenter; fifty-year-old Harry Corrigan, born in Ireland, the richest man in the neighborhood with $30,000 in real estate, his wife and two Illinois-born sons, one of whom ran the livery stable that his father owned. Just next door to the Lincolns lived D. J. Snow, his wife Margaret, and two sons, four and two. The only property listed for him was $350 "personal estate," and the census taker provided no occupation. Next to Snow lived widower William Burch and his two children; like Lincoln he was from Kentucky, but his children had been born in Illinois. Burch was a clerk worth $2,200. Beside Burch was Richard Ives, bricklayer, born in New York but who had come to Springfield via Missouri where he had acquired a wife and stayed long enough for a daughter to be born. Bricklaying allowed Ives to acquire $8,000. And right next to him was the old farmer Lyon, who owned $12,000 in real estate. Born in Virginia, he had lived in Kentucky, where a son had been born. His widowed sister or perhaps his daughter (she was eighteen years younger than Lyon) lived in the household, and with the help of two sons, a daughter, and a hired man, all from Illinois, she took care of things.[9]

Looking up from that census page observers could envision the economic cost of a successful secession. If the seven Confederate States of America and their 5 million people attracted even four more states and 4 million more people to their side the United States would lose one-third of its population, almost half of its territory. And the open and integrated economy that had pulled the Lincolns from Kentucky and the Lyons from Virginia and brought them material success would be imperiled. Successful secession would deprive the nation of its most valuable export crop. The huge and prosperous Mississippi and Ohio valleys would surrender New Orleans, a major port from which they shipped their cash crops. Northern banks, which had loaned nearly $300 million to Southern farmers, plantation owners, and entrepreneurs would face forfeiture. The vast free-trade zone that had fostered perhaps the most prosperous marketplace in the world faced the prospect of an iron curtain dividing it in two.[10]

The prospect of such a fate threatened the hopeful in the North, those people who believed in a glorious future for an expanding economy. There were other threats as well. The great wealth generated in the prewar nation impressed many observers, but that wealth was concentrated in the hands of a declining number of people. In the South this was clear in a single statistic: About 33 percent of families held slaves in 1850, but a decade later the number was down to 25 percent. In the North statistics pointed to similar economic inequality; thirty percent of the population owned 92 percent of the wealth. In the cities economic inequality was even more stark and, because rich and poor jostled each other on crowded streets, more obvious. One percent of northeastern urbanites owned almost half the property in their cities.

Census takers spoke predominantly of prosperity and hope, but some dark signs appeared. The increase in real wages had declined to about 1 percent in the years between 1850 and 1860. A recession that began in 1857 had put thousands out of work in the nation's major cities. The largest strike in the nation's history had taken place in Lynn, Massachusetts, in 1860. Southern critics were attacking the North for its materialism and for the costs of industrialization, which allegedly were turning that region into Charles Dickens's Britain—filled with beggars, paupers, oppressed workers, greedy factory owners. Although Republicans answered with claims that "the interests of the capitalist and laborer are in perfect harmony with each other," as Henry Carey put it, some party programs contradicted the assertion. Lincoln's party advocated territories open to free soil as a "safety valve of our industrial and social engine." Leaders such as Lincoln and William Seward worried publicly that the search for wealth had corrupted moral values.

The leading intellectuals of the North also suggested that something was wrong. Emerson, Thoreau, Hawthorne, and Melville wrote of the dangers of industrialization: "Things are in the saddle," "The railroad rides on us," Ethan Brand's satanic furnace, the brutalized factory workers of "Tartarus of Maids," Ahab, whose "fixed purpose is laid with iron rails, whereon my soul is grooved to run." Popular fiction echoed this anxiety. *Uncle Tom's Cabin*, the most popular book of the age, condemned slavery but indicted both North and South for a wealth-worshiping culture in which human beings were treated as commodities. The most consistently popular author of the age was Dickens, exposing, condemning, lamenting an industrializing Britain. Among the Northern elite feelings grew that the burgeoning of wealth had come at the cost of moral character. William Ellery Channing, one of the leading New England ministers, charged, "Our present civilization is characterized and tainted by a devouring greediness. . . . The passion for gain is everywhere sapping pure and generous feelings." *Harper's Weekly* began the year 1857 with a series of articles on a swelling venality that sent men away from public service toward making money and a government that was itself corrupted. In the midst of the secession crisis, New York lawyer-aristocrat George Templeton Strong wrote of a North that was "timid and mercenary . . . spiritless, money worshipping." Northerners tolerated the expansion of slavery, one writer explained, because "gross materialism . . . the progress of gain, an external expediency is preferred to . . . lofty ideal aspirations and spiritual truth." The North was an economic colossus, but many people wondered if its moral core had been lost.[11]

The secession crisis thus had the ironic impact of frightening and thus energizing both the hopeful and the doubtful in the North. The hopeful looked at what would be lost in a nation divided. Yet anxious Northerners perceived that the challenge of secession reflected a moral crisis that would have to be addressed if the nation wanted to save its soul from its wealth-worshiping instincts.

There was less ambiguity about the constitutional system. Perhaps that clarity, in addition to the profound political interests of the people, helped focus attention on political and constitutional flaws. The demands of the South for protection of slavery had expanded the reach of slavery at the very time that Southerners proclaimed small-government ideals. The 1857 *Dred Scott* decision gave constitutional legitimacy to slavery wherever the nation expanded. By taking away the power of Congress to stop slavery from entering national territory Roger Taney's Supreme Court promised that human bondage would spread wherever the flag advanced. When John Breckenridge ran for president in 1860 one of his promises included a slave code for the territories that would have expanded national power over free speech and the press. Northerners feared that slavery also would reach into free states. In 1859 the Supreme Court struck down a Wisconsin state law that impeded the catching of fugitive slaves. Republican lawyers such as Lincoln predicted that the Court would follow these rulings with a decision that would force slavery into Northern states, an extreme view but in the environment of the time not unthinkable.[12]

Supreme Court decisions threatened politics, flying in the face of growing Northern public sentiment that was hostile to slavery. *Dred Scott* simply denied the legitimacy of the Republican party as an antislavery party. It also undercut Northern Democrat Stephen Douglas, who argued that the people of a territory could reject slavery. Supreme Court benchmen became proslavery henchmen, telling the Northern populace that the only answer to the outreach of slavery was acceptance. Unless Northerners wished to repudiate their Constitution, no political solution existed to the most threatening of challenges to the nation's existence. Voters could not elect men such as Lincoln or even Douglas unless such men gave up their basic principles. If they wished to remain true to their fundamental law they could choose only a proslavery future. This was the logic of the highest court in the land, the considered judgment of the nation's "forum of principle."

The Supreme Court built crisis upon crisis by shoring up Southern determination, thereby energizing secession. Since the highest bench had endorsed the proslavery constitutional argument, Northern opposition represented lawless extremism, further evidence that the North would never respect Southern rights. "This sectional combination for the subversion of the Constitution," as the South Carolina secession convention called it, therefore made secession just and imperative.[13]

The new Lincoln administration thus faced the challenge of reclaiming the Constitution, rescuing it from the proslavery theorizing of its highest court. The president had allies in the enterprise. First, Taney's position was a shocking innovation; *Dred Scott* marked the first time that the due process clause had been used by the Supreme Court as a substantive doctrine upholding slavery. Taney's innovations lacked the secure authority of precedent. Second, his arguments were extreme in a world where slavery was in decline; that extremism was compounded when the Confederacy adopted Taney's ideas to challenge the Union. Third, the idea that only Supreme Court justices could declare the meaning of the Constitution had not yet been established. Lincoln had summoned the ghost of Andrew Jackson during the debates with Douglas to argue that Congress and the president had equal authority to define the fundamental law. The people themselves, by casting their votes and thus instructing their representatives, could shape constitutional directions. That argument still resonated, especially in the context of Taney's prorebel leanings. Lincoln and national legislators were free to offer and implement antislavery constitutional alternatives.

An experienced and attentive republic was watching. Constitutional questions were the basic diet of democratic politics, and politics was the passion of Northern citizens. They voted in numbers that reached 90 percent in some elections, 81 percent in 1860. They voted for candidates who lectured them on constitutional law and history—the great clashes between state and national authority that echoed throughout the nation's history were debated in town squares and farmyards as well as in statehouses and in Congress. And the voters were also lawmakers and law enforcers themselves—they staffed local governments and rotated offices regularly. They sat on juries and made court days public carnivals. Every expansion of the country required that new governments be made, temporary ones such as those that organized wagon trains, mining camps, and claims clubs to protect land titles, permanent ones with sheriffs and town councils and county commissions and even with posses and vigilantes to preserve the public order.

This vast experience with the theory and practice of self-government offered options and potential strength to Lincoln's task of shaping the Constitution. First it committed Northerners passionately to the enterprise. It also provided constitutional options that might be called upon—a range of responses promising flexibility in making the Constitution fit changing needs. The vital and abiding tradition of self-government gave Northerners personal experience in knowing that constitutional ideas were matters of debate and discussion, keeping them open to persuasion at the same time it made them repudiate changing government by any other means. That experience promised a willingness to preserve their government by violence if necessary. A citizen of such a self-governing republic, one observer wrote in 1859, "watches with eager interest its course and whenever difficulty or danger impends, with something more than a sense of duty or spirit of loyalty, acts boldly and greatly in its service."[14]

In the four years before the confrontation at Fort Sumter the nation's politics had interconnected these strands to generate the crisis that developed in the aftermath of the election. The anxieties of industrialization and the transformation of the Northern population had helped bring about past political movements that spoke of dark conspiracies eating at the foundations of the republic. Jackson's Democrats feared economic plotters manipulating a "Monster Bank," corrupting politics, and stealing the fruits of labor's honest toil. The Antimasonic party warned of a mysterious "Illuminati" corrupting democratic government to its own sinister ends. The Know Nothings' reaction to the huge increase in immigrants to the nation also conjured up conspirators, this time Catholics, ranging from parish priests to a usefully distant foreign pontiff. These movements not only intensified political discussion; they had energized partisanship, lending to politics the passion of a moral crusade. Antimasons had created the first political conventions, Jacksonians organized politics on both local and national levels, Know Nothings drew religious fundamentalist organizations to their cause and added appeals that attracted young men eager for some kind of crusade. And the Republicans learned from this. Northerners were well-schooled in the rhetoric of treachery and the tactics of political organization when the Republican party began to speak of the "Slave Power Conspiracy" and to organize young "Wide Awakes" to march in massed torchlight parades against the foe. Such passion helped to intensify the crisis the nation was undergoing and provide recruits to fight against the devils of the age.[15]

Yet if the passion of such politics built party enthusiasm it scared people who believed in orderly change, wanted secure progress toward economic growth, and were committed to preserving a government that provided both. Republicans had to be morally inspired, economically progressive, and devoted to the rule of law.

By 1860 the Republican party had managed this balancing act and thus had become the major alternative to the Democrats through its increased conservatism on issues other than slavery. No one doubted that between the two parties the Republicans were the antislavery party;

Democrats did not even contest that prize. Republicans knew that in order to add to their voting totals they would have to reach out for votes in states that were more moderate on the slavery question than their solid bloc of states in the upper North (New England, New York, Michigan, Minnesota, and Wisconsin). Pennsylvania had gone Democratic in 1856 (Buchanan had won his home state), but the totals were close if American party votes were added to Republican. Republicans also hoped to take either Illinois, Indiana, or New Jersey; if they could take Pennsylvania and only one of those states they would win the presidency. But voters there were conservative on the slavery issue, and so ambitious Republicans moved to the Right, reaching out to other voting blocs. Horace Greeley described the strategy privately: "I want to succeed this time, yet I know the country is not Anti-Slavery. It will only swallow a little Anti-slavery in great deal of sweetening. An Anti-Slavery Man per se cannot be elected; but a Tariff, River and Harbor, Pacific Railroad, Free Homestead man may succeed although he is Anti-Slavery." Greeley thought that Missouri's Edward Bates had the right stuff, but Bates was sixty-seven years old, clung to the Whigs into 1856, and had been an open nativist. He also had equivocal views on the issue of slavery expansion. William Seward, seasoned by his governorship of the nation's largest state and by two terms in the Senate, was the other possibility, but he had such strong antislavery credentials that when he adopted moderation no one believed him to be anything but an opportunist.[16]

That left Lincoln, whose political assets were clear. He was from Illinois, one of the critical states in the 1860 election. He was known as a tough debater who had held his own with the champion of the Northern Democrats. This would not be an asset in the campaign (presidential candidates had never campaigned personally for the office), but the fight with Douglas showed Lincoln's talents and had given him a reputation. He had clear and solidly founded antislavery credentials, staked out in the 1858 debates. But he also had other long-standing testimonials on internal improvements, supporting them in Illinois as early as the 1830s. Lincoln was not well known in the East, but he remedied that political disadvantage to a large degree by going to New York City in February 1860 to deliver a major address at the Cooper Union and then by traveling throughout New England for a couple of weeks, gaining friends and making himself known to the delegates to the convention, scheduled for Chicago. There he was nominated on the third ballot, and the campaign began.

Lincoln was the nominee in part because the Republicans had moved away from the extremes of their moralistic wing. The old New

England reformers who wanted to stop people from drinking, to make them respect the sabbath and to attend public schools as well as to force slaveholders to emancipate their slaves did not have enough political clout to take the presidency. Now the Republicans had Lincoln, a man of different temperament. Lincoln had attended public schools only as a child, and had done little to support public education in Illinois. He held vague and personal religious ideas. He had even been attacked for "infidelity" in a political campaign. He did not drink, but he had rejected coercive prohibitionist tactics in favor of using reason and gentle persuasion in helping drunkards to reform. In lauding the Washingtonian Society he rebuffed the religious imperialists who had once dominated the antiliquor crusade. He rejected nativism with its implied coercion of immigrants. When Republicans adopted Lincoln they moved to a man who seemed to have little disposition to make anybody do anything, even the right thing.

Lincoln did have steel within him, however, and that steel was shaped and hardened not by a desire to make anyone do the right thing but by a commitment to the political-constitutional system that would itself move the nation toward its highest ambitions. He believed in the political, economic, and legal institutions of his age because he was a successful product of them. He had made his career as a lawyer and as a politician—on both paths he learned to negotiate and to persuade and to use the system. He gained personal satisfaction in being among other lawyers and politicians, hearing their laughter at his stories, noting their respect for his ideas, taking pride in being chosen by them for leadership. His success made him one of the wealthiest men in Springfield and soon made him its most prominent citizen. His first major speeches, given at a time when he was defining his public identity, extolled the legal order, called for "making respect for the laws, the political religion" of the nation. He counterpoised respect for the law with the mob rule generated by Jacksonian Democracy, and he made these assertions just as Alexis de Tocqueville published his criticisms of the tyranny of the majority.[17]

Temperamentally Lincoln believed in restraint and control. He urged that reason replace passion in facing the changes of the age. "Mind, all conquering mind," he insisted, was the anchor of self-government and reform. Personally, he feared losing his reason, losing control of himself above all else. The memories of seeing his young companion Matthew Gentry go insane before his eyes haunted him. He drank no alcohol because it made him feel out of control; he studied Euclid to sharpen his reasoning capacities. Lincoln was a man who harnessed his own passions and who admired the institutions of a land that needed discipline as much as it wanted liberty.[18]

These experiences and ideas set the framework for his response to slavery. Devoted as he was to the order of law Lincoln accepted the protections that the Constitution gave slavery. He supported the fugitive slave laws, the right of states to establish slavery, and even during the secession winter he endorsed a constitutional amendment that would protect slave states from federal interference with their "peculiar institution." He spoke against abolitionist societies as well as against slavery in his first public statement on the issue. His "beau ideal of a statesman" Henry Clay, earned Lincoln's admiration in his July 1856 eulogy because Clay had rejected the extreme abolitionist position that would "shiver into fragments the Union of these States; tear to tatters its venerated constitution." At the same time Clay had upheld the ideal that all men were created equal. Moreover, Lincoln condemned Seward's "higher law" speech if it was an "attempt to foment a disobedience to the constitution or to the constitutional laws of the country," and he denounced John Brown's violence and lawbreaking. Lincoln ever insisted that the Republican party was a conservative party.[19]

Lincoln's strongest opponents replied that indeed they were the real conservatives. Taney asserted that his court was interpreting a Constitution that was "not only the same in words, but the same in meaning . . . and intent with which it spoke when it came from the hands of its framers." Stephen Douglas charged that Lincoln was trying to change "the government from one of laws into that of a mob." Fundamental to both conservative claims was the assertion that the clause "all men are created equal" did not apply to black people. Taney said that the Constitution excluded that concept; Douglas agreed and added that popular sovereignty was the fundamental idea of the nation and therefore that white majorities could deny equality to others.[20]

These arguments effectively polarized the political and the constitutional discussion by wrapping the mantles of "constitutionalism" and "democracy" around the powerful racism of the age. They appealed to the worst angels of the American nature in the name of two of its most respectable ideals. Under the doctrines of Taney and Douglas defenders of equality for "all men" had been denied both the Constitution and the idea of political self-government. Democratic rhetoric threatened to push believers in equality to the position held by abolitionists such as William Lloyd Garrison and Wendell Phillips that the Constitution was an agreement with hell and that private conscience, not respect for law, must guide all people.[21]

Lincoln, faced with this challenge, appealed to better angels. Relying on ideas that Salmon Chase and other former Liberty party members had been advancing, the future president offered a reconciliation between ideals of equality and the constitutional system. Although the Republicans were a conservative party, he argued, they were simultaneously the party of egalitarian ideals, ideals inimical to slavery that were grounded in the Declaration of Independence: that "all men are created equal" was the basis of a self-governing nation. Lincoln insisted in many ways that the ideals of the Declaration were part of, inherent in, the Constitution itself. When he wrote about the beginnings of the nation he did not discuss separately the two Founding documents. None of the speeches and letters he wrote ever noted a difference between the promises of 1776 and the government organized in 1787. Arguing against the proslavery constitutionalism of Taney and Stephen Douglas's amoral popular sovereignty, Lincoln demonstrated that the Founders of the nation, even though they had accepted slavery in 1787, wanted to place slavery in the course of ultimate extinction. They showed their intentions in several ways. They never mentioned slavery in the Constitution, and they outlawed it from the Northwest territories: "The earliest Congress, under the constitution, took the same view of slavery. They hedged and hemmed it in to the narrowest limits of necessity."[22]

Constitutional government in the nation also threatened slavery because the principle of equality was built into the ideal of government itself. "At the foundation of the sense of justice there is in me," he said, lies the "proposition that each man should do precisely what he pleases with all that is exclusively his own." That concept was at the core of self-government. "No man is good enough to govern another man, *without that other's consent*." And this principle, "the sheet anchor of American republicanism," rested on the ideals of the Declaration that "all men are created equal," which meant that governments had to rest on the consent of those men. "Allow all the governed an equal voice in the government, and that, and that only is self-government." The ideal of equality was manifested in acts of self-government. Thus the ideal depended on process, and expanding slavery imperiled process and ideal.[23]

Equality was built into government also in the economic ideal that Lincoln and his party treasured: the right to get ahead based on one's own labors. Republicans reassured voters and affirmed their own principles most fundamentally in their belief in the equal right to rise. The clearest fusion of economic ideals with self-government came from Lincoln on 4 July 1861 as the new president defined his war goal: "This is essentially a peoples contest, on the side of the Union, it is a struggle for maintaining in the world, that form and substance of government, whose leading object is, to elevate the condition of men—to lift artificial weights from all shoulders—to clear the paths of laudable pursuit for all—to afford all, an unfettered start, and a fair chance in the race of life."[24]

The Declaration's assertion that "all men are created equal" was thus inalterably woven into the economic, political, and constitutional institutions. Lincoln was not *either* a constitutionalist *or* an egalitarian; he was a "process-based" egalitarian. He believed that equality would be realized only through the proper operation of existing institutions. And slavery threatened that orderly evolution. Lincoln always believed that slavery was wrong and that its wrongness lay in its corruption of the realization of ideals of equality as they were manifested and given life within the entire economic-constitutional-political process.[25]

But Lincoln had to do more than assert that existing institutions accommodated equality; he had to demonstrate that process in a difficult and practical way. The difficulty arose because the state he lived in had a strong antinegro bias, and it also feared disunion. When Lincoln said that all men were created equal his rivals shouted "nigger equality" and "the Union imperiled." They tried to make voters see William Lloyd Garrison or John Brown instead of Lincoln himself.

To escape the comparisons Lincoln tacked, backing away from full equality. He did not seek black jurors, black voters, black officeholders, he told audiences. The equality he was most interested in was "the right to eat the bread, without leave of anybody else, which his own hand earns." He also retreated on the explosive issue of miscegenation: "Because I do not want a black woman for a slave does not mean that I want her for a wife." But even while accommodating prejudice Lincoln also had the courage to challenge racism by attacking slavery and by opposing nativism. He insisted, "There is no reason in the world why the negro is not entitled to all the natural rights enumerated in the Declaration." Yet he was not in the vanguard for racial justice in the prewar era. Few men who wanted to be elected by Illinois white male voters, or by most of the North's white male voters, could be.[26]

Thus Lincoln had to meet the powerful popular prejudice of his day with a new vision for realizing the Declaration's promise. Jefferson's Declaration had proclaimed equality a self-evident truth, but any politician who hoped for success in the mid-nineteenth-century United States could not embrace equality as an immediate truth. Lincoln therefore devised a means to make that promise conform to institutional realities: Equality became a "proposition." (The word would wait until Gettysburg; idea preceded word by five years.) It was a "standard maxim for a free society, which should be familiar to all and revered by all; constantly looked to, constantly labored for, and even though never perfectly attained, constantly approximated, and constantly spreading and deepening its influence, and augmenting the happiness and value of life to all people of all colors everywhere."[27]

By turning equality into a promise for the future Lincoln had resolved several conflicts. On the negative side his process-based equality pushed the achievement of that equality to a distant future. In August 1858 Lincoln promised that should voters accept his argument that the nation's constitutional commitment was to equality, "the crisis would be past and the institution might be let alone for a hundred years, if it should live so long, in the States where it exists, yet it would be gone out of existence in the way best for both the black and the white races."[28] Slaves and abolitionists might legitimately believe that time could erode hope for liberty as easily as it might achieve it.

But in a positive sense Lincoln had offered a means for people to embrace both their ideals about equality and their commitment to their institutions. He offered an escape from the cul-de-sac in which politicians had to pander to the prejudice of their constituents. Full equality, "freedom now," was impossible in antebellum America. Nevertheless, given that reality, the answer did not have to be "freedom never," as Roger Taney and Southern leaders proclaimed. There was now the promise that within the institutions the people treasured, institutions that had helped build their awe-inspiring, if anxious, prosperity, lay promises of expanding equality. Lincoln had pointed to the process of politics and the constitutional system as an imperative means to defining and achieving that ideal. The political-constitutional system was not a covenant with death; it provided the forums and the opportunities for moving society closer to an ever-expanding ideal. In providing this linkage in the prewar era Lincoln had made possible a future connection between saving that system and destroying slavery. A war, employing the prodigious resources of an expanding North and focused on saving those institutions against a confederacy resting on slavery, might bring equality much nearer, much faster. These possibilities impended as Lincoln moved toward his inauguration.

2
★★★★★

ASSEMBLING THE CAST:
WINTER 1860–61

For a week it had been hot and dusty, but that morning a shower cooled the air and tapped down the dust; the weather seemed perfect as the sun lit the carriage. Through the huge and noisy crowds that lined Pennsylvania Avenue James Buchanan and Abraham Lincoln rode toward the Capitol and exchanged pleasantries. Buchanan spoke of his happiness at leaving office. Lincoln said he did not enter the White House with much pleasure but promised, ambiguously, to maintain the standards of his "illustrious predecessors." (Meanwhile in Charleston Harbor Maj. Robert Anderson counted his supplies and nervously watched the ammunition being stockpiled near the insurgents' cannons.)

A guard of honor from the marines and the army marched closely beside the two presidents, so close that spectators caught only glimpses of them. On surrounding side streets cavalry patrolled and platoons of soldiers assembled should they be needed. Hidden on the rooftops along the route sharpshooters looked nervously at the crowds below. Ahead, riflemen looked out from darkened rooms in the Capitol and awaited the arrival of the carriage. Two batteries of artillery stood ready nearby. General in Chief Winfield Scott was making sure that no coup would stop the presidency from changing hands.[1]

Off to their right, behind the crowds, the two men could see the Washington Memorial. Begun in 1848 it now stood less than one-third of its promised height. Funds had run out in 1854, and so it had stayed in its unfinished condition; blocks of granite, stones sent from states and citizens groups throughout the nation lay around the base waiting for construction to begin again. No one could be sure when that might be.

Ahead of the carriage was another uncompleted structure. In 1850, even as Congress was arguing about the Great Compromise, plans were approved to expand the Capitol by adding a dome and extending the wings of the structure. Now the dome stood open, scaffolding exposed, beams of wood arching to meet at a center where a large statue representing liberty would stand. The statue rested nearby waiting for the completion of its pedestal. The two men rode up the hill; crowds cheered, their admiration mixed with their hopes that the future would bring their nation a less ominous outlook than the one it now faced.

The future looked grim in part because of the legacy Buchanan was passing to Lincoln. Many people had feared that the outgoing chief executive would not hand Lincoln a unified nation. Several factors contributed to the public concern. Extensive corruption had surrounded Buchanan's administration from its beginning. The election of 1856 had seen widespread voting fraud as wealthy men bought government contracts in return for campaign contributions. Buchanan's cabinet appointments replaced Democrats of good reputation with known spoilsmen who soon lived up to their roles with crooked land sales in Minnesota and New York, corrupt issuing of government contracts for the Washington aqueduct and for army supplies in the West, and the embezzlement of an Indian trust fund—and these abuses occurred in the War Department alone. When Secretary of War John B. Floyd resigned in 1860 he claimed it was for the nobility of the secessionist cause, but many observers in the North and the South saw an example of how the ever-growing search for wealth sapped the government's moral authority.

Conflicts over slavery were entangled with these questions of government morality, and the crisis involving Kansas revealed more than the dangers of expanded slavery. When Buchanan sought votes for the Lecompton constitution, passed because of massive vote fraud in Kansas, he bribed legislators with offers of jobs and with contracts to firms owned by congressmens' relatives. Then the administration supported the English bill, which offered a land grant if Kansas voters, given a second chance to vote on the constitution, accepted it. To get support for this bill the Buchanan administration walked the lobbies and aisles of the House, alternating bribes of government contracts with threats of loss of patronage. In June 1860 a committee of the House, the Covode committee, reported corruption ranging from Kansas to the navy yards in the East, including instances of promises of offices to congressmen and of offers of printing contracts to editors for political support. The

22

Republican-controlled committee evaded implicating Republicans with shady reputations—people like Simon Cameron in Pennsylvania and William Seward's longtime friend Thurlow Weed avoided the spotlight—and the overall effect was to brand the Buchanan administration as "the Buchaneers," more interested in spoils than in principle.[2]

Buchanan also had other burdens to bear. Not only did corruption weaken his administration, but the corrosive power of slavery in the republic also played a fundamental role. Long known for his Southern sympathies, surrounded by a cabinet dominated by Southerners, leading a party torn in two between Douglas and Breckenridge, hobbled further by his lame-duck status, attuned to Southern fears of a slave uprising, and presciently aware that Southern states were deadly serious, Buchanan faced the secession crisis with little room to maneuver and with a divided mind. His 3 December message to Congress exposed his turmoil. Secession was unconstitutional, the president argued, but the North had driven the South to it by generating fears of a race war. Still, the South was in no real danger because Lincoln would be restrained by Congress. The president would have to follow the dictates of federal courts, which sustained slavery in the territories and the fugitive slave law. But if the South did secede the president lacked the constitutional power to stop it. Perhaps a constitutional convention to pass an amendment protecting slavery in any state that now had it or should later want it would calm things—and also an amendment that nullified all Northern personal liberty laws—that would probably help, too. As Elbert Smith summarized, "The president defended the Southerner's own excuses for secession, denied them any such right, announced his unwillingness to coerce them, and declared that secession would be prevented only by concessions that every Southerner knew would never be made."[3]

Pro-Lincoln newspapers responded with dismay. The *Jersey City Daily Courier and Advertiser* saw "an elaborately contrived excuse for pusillanimity; and evasion of confessed obligation." New Haven's *Morning Journal and Courier* spoke of Buchanan's "weakness, imbecility and inconsistency which proves him utterly unfit for the emergencies of the times." Even the Douglas-supporting *Cincinnati Daily Enquirer* called the message "absurd . . . bare and idle abstraction . . . lame and impotent." Leading businessmen from New York went to Washington to demand action and expressed frustration at the president's lack of firmness. There were calls for Buchanan's impeachment and attacks on "the old public functionary" in the White House. Thus were there immediate pressures on Lincoln not to be another Buchanan.[4]

Northerners hoped that Lincoln was no Buchanan but it was not yet clear who he was. They understood the principles he advocated, knew that he represented standing up to slavery in some way, but what was that way? And how long would it take him to do it? Could he winnow good advice from bad and forge a policy and a will and, if necessary, the resources to save the Union? They might have been more hopeful if they could have seen an experienced leader as the new chief executive, but they saw something else.

Even those who knew him personally saw qualities that seemed anything but bold. He was a deliberate man who had learned to control himself and to move quietly and cautiously toward his goals. His speeches were carefully crafted, and he thought deeply about the problems he faced. His profound thought about the meaning of liberty and law and equality came not from flashing genius but from long and careful pondering. That manner of thinking nurtured and fed on his political skill, which also required weighing options, seeking ways to balance contending opinions. He was a prudent lawyer and a skilled operator of the political system. He was a man who studied and thought and drafted options for himself before acting. He came carefully to his judgments, waiting for circumstances to ripen, knowing as he read his Shakespeare that "the readiness is all," knowing as he read the Bible that "for everything there is a season." He would later explain (and boast?) that events had controlled him. On the surface these were hardly promising personal qualities for a nation in crisis.[5]

Moreover, Lincoln lacked administrative experience. He had held no significant military command, no leading position in industry or business. He had been a legislator, not a governor. Unlike his Southern counterpart, Jefferson Davis, he had not administered any government department. Most notably he had not been trained to command, as Davis had been at West Point. He was an outsider to Washington and its political culture. His last visit to the city had been twelve years earlier when he had served one two-year term as congressman. And, just as for all new presidents, everything about the office would feel strange for a while. He would have to learn the presidency in the midst of its greatest crisis.

Yet Lincoln had skills that might serve the nation and the office well. The standards of twentieth-century presidents, which visualize bold leadership of the Congress and of the Western world, distort Lincoln's presidency. Congress created most of its own agenda and was jealous of its authority. The United States had a minimal international position. On the entire domestic front, with the exception of warmaking, Lincoln would have to share authority and persuade, not command. And even in fighting the war he worked with Congress. He was well prepared for such cooperation. He was an excellent political leader at a time when parties provided unity and direction for governmental behavior and were sources of intense interest throughout the polity. He knew how to organize political strength, how to encourage his supporters to achieve his ends. The undisputed leader of Illinois Republicans, he became his party's first president. During the war when lawmakers began to question and at times to challenge decisions he had made or to intrude on executive prerogatives, his political skills would find important uses.[6]

But there was a much deeper level to Lincoln's political skills than his ability to maneuver and to balance factions; there was the quality of the man himself. He possessed a basic self-knowledge and security that allowed him to negotiate and discuss and converse with friends and political foes while respecting their intrinsic integrity. Lincoln had an ego, a sense of self. "It is absurd to call him a modest man," his secretary John Hay noted. "No great man was ever modest." But Lincoln's ego was not merely strong; it was secure. It did not arise from a self so vulnerable that it had always to be defended. It was not at risk in every political contest. Lincoln did not *have* to be right.[7]

Few great leaders, and certainly not Lincoln's nemesis, Jefferson Davis, so frequently mentioned their own failures and limitations. Lincoln deprecated his looks, his upbringing, his education, his political prospects, and even his most awesome enterprise—the war itself. His early life reflected "the simple annals of the poor." His sketch for a political biography was short because "there is so little of me." He apologized to McClellan, who had insulted him publicly, and offered to hold McClellan's horse if the general would win a victory. Despite his profound disappointment after Gettysburg, he apologized to Meade. "I wish to make the personal acknowledgement that you were right and I was wrong," he told Grant after Vicksburg. When Thurlow Weed complimented him on the Second Inaugural Address he replied, "Men are not flattered by being shown that there has been a difference of purpose between the Almighty and them. . . . It is a truth which I thought needed to be told; and as whatever of humiliation there is in it falls most directly on myself, I thought others might afford for me to tell it."[8]

A religious fatalism underlay much of his thought. "Why should the spirit of mortal be proud?" ran the opening line of his favorite poem, and he told Congressman Isaac Arnold, "I have all my life been a fatalist. What is to be will be, or rather, I have found all my life as Hamlet says, 'There is a divinity that shapes our ends, Rough hew them how we will.'" Such fatalism fostered an unwillingness to make unalloyed moral judgments about the failures of others. As bitterly as he con-

demned slavery he admitted that slaveholders faced a complex di-
lemma, one that he would not know how to resolve "if all earthly power
were given to me." His fatalism prompted a wry response when ministers came to the White House to tell him exactly what God wanted: He
wondered why God would talk to them and not to him about his job.
But foundational to his humor and to his awareness of the complexity of
experience was a frame of mind that opened inquiry, that suspended
judgment, that therefore allowed politics to operate at its most admira-
ble level in the effort to reason together with people who sought different ends.[9]

This frame of mind and temperament had practical consequences.
It helped keep inevitable party divisions within bounds, shaping unity
and keeping men's eyes on making the system work rather than on the
wrongs they had suffered. His secretary John Hay reported in late 1864
that "the president's favorite expression is 'I am in favor of short statutes of limitations in politics.'" Lincoln warned subordinates not to let
personal passions propel their politics. "It is much better not to be led
from the region of reason into that of hot blood by imputing to public
men motives they do not avow," he told one partisan. Accusatory letters
from politicians were seen as part of the problem in any political fight,
not a solution. When Henry Raymond wrote a letter "breathing fire and
vengeance against the Custom House," Lincoln responded to Hay that
"it was the spirit of such letters as that created the faction and malignity
of which Raymond complained." These sentiments revealed the maturity of his early admonitions to let reason and the "all conquering
mind" shape politics. His protestations against impassioned radicals as
devils reflected not just anger at their opposition but frustration over letting their hearts control their minds.[10]

An inspirer of loyalty and a manipulator of the ambitions of others,
a man who made few personal enemies and yet, through sharing his
true feelings with few people, maintained his independence of action, a
man who had learned to wait for the tide to sweep or for events to turn
his way, Lincoln may have been exceptionally well prepared to lead a
nation resting on the consent of the governed.

Yet these strengths might be weaknesses as well. If he was a master
at compromise, an open-minded politician, did that mean he would
compromise once more with defenders of slavery? If he avoided passionate quarreling might he lack the moral core to stand up for his principles? Was he so committed to the status quo that he would preserve
most of the world that Buchanan presented to him? Some hope glim-
mered because he was an outsider and uncommitted to the ways of
Washington. But might not that innocence make him the tool of experi-

enced men? There were many doubts about this Kentucky-born compromiser.[11]

Lincoln's preparation for the presidency was ambiguous; the existing power of the office he had won was not. The last vigorous president, James Polk, had left office twelve years before, and four subsequent administrations espoused and carried out a philosophy of limited executive power. Although Democratic tradition looked back to Andrew Jackson's vigorous eight years, Democratic practice had seen relative inaction with the exception of Polk's four years. But the opposition Whig party was no proponent of executive energy. Their birth cry had been a wail against President Jackson's "tyranny." Lincoln's roots were in a world where warnings against unrestrained executive authority were party gospel. Lincoln himself had cautioned against the dangers of a tyrant, had attacked Polk's authority to begin war, and had supported Taylor's limited view of the veto power.[12]

On the other hand it was not clear that Lincoln would have to fight a war or quarrel with Congress or control the legislative agenda or exercise the veto to influence or impede unwanted legislation. Lincoln came into office with large Republican majorities. The party gained five senators in 1860, and though its number of congressmen declined, the Republican party still controlled the House. Once secessionists were gone Republicans comfortably dominated Congress. Despite disagreements over means the party was remarkably unified in its ends: Government influence should encourage economic growth, and the expansion of slavery had to stop. If war came the usual patriotic pressures would rally Republicans behind their commander in chief even more passionately.[13]

Still, the man himself would be responsible for how quickly the government would act, and an apparent conflict obtained over the vision of what a wartime leader should be—bold and aggressive, controlling and marshaling resources and men—and the reality of Lincoln's temperament and strengths. That contrast provoked accusations throughout the war that the president was too careful, too slow, incapable of handling events, of making decisions. Observers wanted a Napoleon, bold, aggressive, shaping history to his purposes; instead they had a Kutuzov, using the resources that his nation provided, relying on the ongoing tide of history to bring him victory. They also found in Lincoln, to shift the image, a Tolstoy who called onto the scene men who would try to employ the resources available. McClellan played Napoleon happily, then Pope tried, then, reluctantly, Burnside, then Hooker and Meade, then finally Grant and Sherman. But behind them stood the president, who decided who would play the role and on what stage. And, like Tolstoy, Lincoln knew the importance of providing the story, the meaning, the interpretation of events that would determine how people understood the history that was unfolding. He began his interpretive task even as president-elect.

Even before it was official, Lincoln's election was expected. In October Pennsylvania, Indiana, and Ohio went Republican, practically guaranteeing that Lincoln would be the new president. By 6 November it was official, and Lincoln's party—now certainly Lincoln's party—began its celebrations. Yet while Republicans celebrated, South Carolina marched to secession, then Mississippi, Florida, Alabama, Georgia, Louisiana, and finally Texas. The first wave had finished and seven Deep South states claimed that they were no longer part of the United States.

They had been threatening the nation with such a move for decades, but after John Brown's raid and the support that the abortive slave insurrection had received in the North, secessionists began to plan for action if Lincoln won. Now they had acted and the problem was Lincoln's to face. Although Buchanan remained in the White House everyone knew that the real response to secession—the one that would halt or accelerate the process—would have to come from Lincoln. The president-elect would have to determine the size and character of the nation he would begin to lead some four months in the future.

Lincoln faced several ominous questions. Would there be further secessions? How many states of the new Confederacy would there be, and where would the border of the alleged nation be? At the North Carolina/South Carolina line, then south of Tennessee and over to Texas? Or would the border stand at the Pennsylvania/Virginia state line? Would it contain 5 million or 12 million people? Did the constitutional authority exist to stop secession and preserve the nation? Was the president, Congress, anyone capable of taking charge of the government?[14]

Answers to these questions depended on less specific considerations. What would public sentiment demand in the North and what would it tolerate in the slave states? The North gave Lincoln conflicting advice—some of it predictable. Conservative Democrats said to let secession happen. The states were sovereign and retained the legal authority to stay in or to get out of the Union. Radical abolitionists came to the same conclusion by different reasoning: Good riddance, Garrison and Phillips said. The presence of slavery in the nation corrupted its moral stance before other nations, demanded moral compromise of American citizens, eroded the capacity of the nation to purify itself of sin. Furthermore, these abolitionists argued, slavery depended upon the power of the national authority to survive; secession therefore cut off that necessary support. There was also a feeling that the North was so corrupt or cowardly that it lacked the moral fiber to stand up for a cause that was not selfish and materialistic. Thus letting Southern states leave and predicting their eventual return seemed the only solution to hope for. Some people advocated inaction as a means of chastening the South. Charles Sumner imagined the Gulf states facing a world hostile to slavery, cut off from the benefits of Northern strength. A few months of isolation and impotence might teach the "petulant children" some humility; furthermore, while they were gone, Congress could pass laws that would ensure the advance of liberty.[15]

But other voices argued that backing down from the secessionist threat would bring only a temporary peace. It was time to stand and show the people of both sections that blackmail would not defeat an election. Buchanan was damned by Republicans for telling Congress that although secession was unlawful and wrong, no governmental action against it was legal. Republicans had campaigned as the party of energy, of action, of backbone; now it was time to act. Republicans throughout the North emphasized standing up to Southern threats, and most Northern Democrats agreed. William Cullen Bryant's *Evening Post* asserted, "If a state secedes, it is revolution and the seceders are traitors. Those who are charged with the executive branch of government are recreant to their oaths if they fail to use all lawful means to put down such rebellion." Michigan senator Zachariah Chandler summoned the spirit of Andrew Jackson, who knew how to deal with South Carolina secessionists: "By the eternal, I will hang them." The *Springfield Republican* had the same vision: "Oh for one hour of Jackson!"[16]

Lincoln listened to the advice that counseled caution. He decided that not reacting would be the best reaction. As early as 15 October he was responding to a letter asking him if he would "countenance radicalism to the extent of embittering the feelings of our Southern brethren." He found no purpose in embittering those feelings, Lincoln wrote, but "my published speeches" would show his intentions better than "anything I would say in a short letter, if I were inclined now, as I am not, to define my position anew."[17] Silence was not Lincoln's idea alone; most of his party agreed that keeping quiet was the proper strategy. From Washington Sen. Lyman Trumbull had written Lincoln on 4 December 1860: "The impression with all, unless there be one exception, is that Republicans have no concessions to make or compromises to offer, and that it is impolitic even to discuss making them. . . . Inactivity and a kind spirit is, it seems to me, all that is left for us to do, till the 4th of March." Thurlow Weed's *Albany Evening Journal* told readers that "those who ask Mr. Lincoln to say or do something" are responding to "their fears rather than their judgment." An Ohio Republican told Salmon Chase that he hoped Lincoln "will not open his mouth, save only to eat, until March 4th."[18]

Lincoln thus avoided bombast to proclaim his toughness or the firmness of his views or the ability of the North to prevail. He refused to explain or repeat opinions he had already expressed many times. People repeatedly asked the president-elect to make some statement that would calm the waters, that would reassure the secessionists that he would not endanger them, but Lincoln refused generally to issue public statements. He was already on the record fully and clearly. Anything he might say in the midst of the crisis would serve only those people "who would like to frighten me, or, at least, to fix upon me the character of timidity and cowardice. They would seize upon almost any letter I could write as being an *awful coming down.*" People who had listened to him would not need to be told again; opponents who had not listened would simply use his remarks against him. To repeat his views would be "wanting in self respect, and would have an appearance of sycophancy and timidity, which would excite the contempt of good men, and encourage bad ones to clamor more loudly."[19]

Lincoln was not just trying to save face; he had a larger motive than avoiding the appearance of backing down or of anxiety about or reconsideration of past views. His actions would reflect on the viability of the constitutional system itself. The people had chosen a president through legally constituted means. They had had access to his opinions on the major questions. They had read and discussed party platforms. They had voted for the Republican ideas and platform. Was he supposed to "shift the ground upon which I have been elected?" he asked the North Carolina Unionist John Gilmer. Continuing explanations and reassurances would "make me appear as if I repented for the crime of having been elected and was anxious to apologize and beg forgiveness. To so represent me would be the principle use made of any letter I might now thrust upon the public. My old record cannot be so used and that is precisely the reason that some new declaration is so much sought."[20] "We have just carried an election on principles fairly stated to the people," he told Congressman James Hale. "Now we are told . . . the government shall be broken up, unless we surrender to those we have beaten. . . . If we surrender it is the end of us. They will repeat the experiment upon us *ad libitum.*"[21]

Yet as time passed Lincoln was clearly troubled by the constant calls to say something. He wrote privately and confidentially to a few people, explaining that he would not interfere with slavery where it existed, would favor the end of opposition to the fugitive slave law, had no intention of using the power over interstate commerce to touch slavery, considered raids into state or territorial soil "under what pretext, as the gravest of crimes." "The South would be in no more danger in this respect, than it was in the days of Washington," he reassured Alexander Stephens. He even bowed to pressure by writing a passage for Lyman Trumbull to use in a speech in Springfield promising that "each and all of the States will be left in as complete control of their own affairs respectively and at as perfect liberty to choose, and employ, their own means of preserving and protecting property, and preserving peace and order within their respective limits, as they have ever been under any administration." Lincoln sat on the platform as Trumbull spoke.[22]

In the nation's capital pressures for compromise grew. Southern radicals, even some Southern moderates, were asking for reassurances that Republicans probably would not grant. Still, no one had a clear picture of how deep secessionist sentiment might be. Given the fact that border slave states remained in the union, bargaining over terms might keep them there. Even if compromise ultimately failed, being on record as having tried would provide a moral high ground that could rally public support. Besides, Washington insiders were weathered veterans at bargaining and negotiation, and so they proceeded to do the things they knew how to do—hoping that something might turn up.[23]

Each house of Congress established a committee to deal with the crisis. The House moved first, setting up on 4 December—the day of Buchanan's message—a committee containing one member for each of the thirty-three states. Two weeks later the Senate joined the compromise efforts. The Senate's Committee of Thirteen included most of the important national figures in the Senate: Stephen Douglas, Jefferson Davis, John J. Crittenden, and William Seward. Although the two committees seemed to operate independently their efforts were linked by a desire to find proposals that would appeal to as much of the disaffected South as possible. Northern Democrats and border slave-state legislators were most active with plans, but interestingly enough the most well-known Republican in the country had a major role in the process.

William Seward served only on the Senate committee, but he worked intently on shaping policy in both houses. He was a constant visitor at the Washington home of Charles Francis Adams, perhaps the most important member of the Committee of Thirty-three. Seward encouraged proposals that emerged from both committees in the attempt to reassure the South while maintaining Republican support.

From the Senate committee came proposals under Crittenden's name: slavery within the states to be protected from national government interference; the revival of the Missouri Compromise line—no slavery above 36° 30' north latitude, slavery permitted below that line in territories currently held or to be acquired later; no cessation of slavery in the District of Columbia unless Maryland and Virginia agreed; no interference by Congress with interstate slave trade; slaveholders who lost runaways to Northern states to be compensated. Slavery was thus to be protected from every imaginable use of national authority and would be secure in existing Southern states. Most important, if the United States expanded into Central America and the Caribbean, slavery would expand too. For some time Seward let people believe that he might favor this "Crittenden Compromise."[24]

From the Committee of Thirty-three came more moderate proposals with a twofold purpose. First, to settle the crisis the South was promised that the fugitive slave law would be enforced and that the state personal liberty laws, which conflicted with slave catching, would be repealed. In addition came a nonamendable constitutional amendment protecting slavery in the states from any form of federal interference. The second purpose was to divide the South if it could not be placated, to detach the already seceded lower South from the upper South, where secession was still being debated. The divisive proposal rested on the admission of New Mexico to the Union as a state. No mention was made of slavery, but the territory had a small number of slaves and a slave code to protect them. Because the climate and soil forecast a bleak future for slavery, however, many observers believed that slavery would soon die there. The lower-south legislators opposed the New Mexico measure, but the upper-South lawmakers supported it. Lincoln allowed the New Mexico idea to flicker.[25]

Lincoln accepted most of these measures with one crucial exception. Enforcement of the fugitive slave law, repeal of the personal liberty laws, even a constitutional amendment promising that slavery would abide undisturbed in Southern states he accepted. Yet the key was Republican bedrock—no expansion of slavery into the territories. When word leaked out that such a proposal might be offered, Lincoln acted quickly and forcefully. He wrote Lyman Trumbull on 10 December, William Kellogg the next day, Elihu Washburne two days later, Trumbull again and Thurlow Weed on the seventeenth, and John Defrees the next day with one thundering message: "Let there be no compromise on the question of *extending* slavery"; "There is no possible compromise upon it . . . hold firm as with a chain of steel"; "I will be inflexible on the territorial question"; "If any of our friends do prove false, and fix up a compromise on the territorial question, I am for fighting again—that is all"; "Stand firm. The tug has to come, & better now, than any time hereafter."[26]

Saving the Union had grabbed the headlines, and it was probably inevitable that the nation's leaders should be seeking some way to placate the alienated South. But the crisis, by demanding attention to preserving the Union, the Constitution, and the order that both symbolized, endangered the moral core of the Republican party. It pressured Republicans to diminish their commitment to equality in order to purchase order and stability. More specifically the crisis threatened to uncouple commitment to the order of the constitutional system from the goal of equality that was its major purpose. As party leader Lincoln felt those pressures, but since his major accomplishment had been to connect equality and the constitutional process, 1776 with 1787, he was unlikely to succumb to demands to divide them.

Faced with calls to respect and preserve order, Lincoln replied by reminding people of the moral principles of antislavery; thus he would not compromise on slavery in the territories. He pointed out to correspondents that the major issue dividing the nation was the question of the good or the evil of slavery. Yet even as he kept the moral question in mind he wrote out a fragment on the Constitution noting the interconnections between the ideal of equal liberty and the constitutional order. The Declaration, expressing the principle of "liberty to all," was the "apple of gold" within the Constitution's "picture of silver." "The picture was made not to *conceal*, or *destroy* the apple; but to *adorn*, and *preserve* it. The *picture* was made *for* the apple—*not* the apple for the picture. So let us act, that neither *picture*, or *apple* shall ever be blurred, or bruised or broken."[27]

While men all over the country were emphasizing the Union and seeking constitutional arguments and amendments somehow to resolve the crisis, Lincoln worked to keep equality within the discussion. Promising to protect slavery where the Constitution protected it, he still insisted that dissent over the basic idea of equality divided the sections. Holding firm, in addition to respecting the results of the election, meant defining the Republican party: It must hold firm on the territorial question because the issue was between those people who believed that slavery was wrong and those who believed that slavery was right. Although he told John Gilmer that that difference should not be a source of conflict, it clearly was the reason that the crisis was upon them. But Lincoln thought that the issue could and should be settled through constitutional means that included elections in which people chose one side or the other. His party agreed; despite talk of compromise by Seward, when votes were taken on Crittenden's compromise measures not a single Republican vote was cast in Congress in their favor.[28]

The majority of the Republican party understood that they could not abandon their moral core. Indeed most party leaders reported that their constituents passionately opposed caving in. One person wrote from Pittsburgh, "The public mind is so enflamed against Compromise and so bitter against all efforts at concession. . . . It amounts almost to a fury." Republican congressmen refused to vote for any measure that allowed slavery to expand. James Russell Lowell explained their feelings: "The fault of the Free States in the eyes of the South is not one that can be atoned for by any yielding of special points here and there. Their offense is that they are free, and that their habits and prepossessions are those of Freedom. . . . It is time that the South should learn . . . that the difficulty of the Slavery question is slavery itself—nothing more, nothing less. It is time that the north should learn that it has nothing left to compromise but the rest of its self respect."[29]

Furthermore, compromise might have been impossible. Even before compromise measures reached the floor of Congress two-thirds of the delegates from the Deep South had signed a letter to their constituents proclaiming "all hope of relief in the Union, through the agency of committees, Congressional legislation, or constitutional amendments is extinguished." There remained some hope, however, that the upper South might be appealed to. Yet even this was tentative, for throughout the South men were watching for any sign that the new government might act to coerce the secessionists back into the Union, and their definitions of coercion were broad.[30] Lincoln had firmly set the Republican party on a course that Southerners rightly feared. Southerners had listened to his ideas for years. They understood that he had integrated promises of equality within a commitment to the constitutional process. To ask their commitment to that process meant essentially to urge them to accept the ultimate death of slavery. To demand that they stay in the Union forecast a future in which their world was lost. Inspired perhaps by a contemporary insistence on immediate equality many historians have missed this point. To fight for the Union of March 1861, says James McPherson, echoing legions of Lincoln scholars, was to fight for a Union with slavery preserved. But that view overlooks the very foundation of the secession crisis—the belief by seven Southern states—soon to be eleven—that slavery was endangered by the Union Lincoln would now lead.[31]

The Union that Buchanan and Pierce led certainly preserved slavery for the foreseeable future. But Lincoln had been arguing for many years that the Democrats' perception of the nature and meaning of that Union was wrong. Now he would, if he could, implement the proper meaning for it—a meaning that sent panicked slave states running for the exits.

Thus Lincoln's challenge to slavery was already in existence in 1861. To save the Union as of 1861 would of course save slavery in the states, but it would have killed it in the territories so long as Republicans kept the power they had shown in 1860. And most Southerners and Northerners believed that slavery had to expand or die. The war accelerated the death of slavery, but it was already in danger even before war began; that danger was why it began. Lincoln's constitutional ideals were coming to fruition, advancing the Declaration's assertion that all men are created equal. His conservative liberalism was unraveling slavery slowly within the constitutional process.[32]

Meanwhile, Lincoln was trying to put a government together, trying to bring to life the political philosophy his party espoused. Basic to the process was patronage, staffing the new government with Republicans, thus creating the glue that would hold the nation together. Patronage was so important that even during the Sumter crisis Lincoln was still making appointments, not only for major posts such as the ministries to Great Britain and France but also for such jobs as receiver for the federal land department in Olympia, Washington.[33]

Patronage clearly built party loyalty. Party workers expected support for their work in getting Lincoln and his colleagues elected. The process of letting cabinet officers who represented the factions of the party control most of the patronage in their departments ensured that the range of party opinion would be heard. Patronage also inserted Republicans at every level of government—providing to some degree a unified philosophy for how the government was to operate and making the government theirs in a personal sense. Patronage was thus of a piece with voting, with holding of town-, county-, state-elected offices, with widespread jury duties—instances that gave citizens personal experience with self-government. It also provided incomes for personal friends and not a few relatives of cabinet members and nourished scores of Republican newspapers with government publishing contracts or by appointing their editors to government offices. "Editors seem to be in very great favor with the party in power," the *Baltimore Evening Patriot* noted, "a larger number of the fraternity having received appointments at its hands than probably under any other administration."[34]

Lincoln rewarded Republican supporters very well. He removed Democrats from practically every office they held, replacing 1,195 out of the 1,520 presidential appointees he personally controlled. Reflecting the largest turnover in history, the appointments were part of an enormous growth of government employment demanded by war. Building allegiance, providing salaries for political friends, patronage increased enormously. In 1861 there were 40,651 civilian jobs to fill in the federal government. Nearly 22,700 post offices led the list, but there were over 4,000 treasury jobs, nearly 9,400 Navy Department places, and around 1,900 each in the War and Interior Departments. By 1865 the number had increased almost fivefold. Nearly 195,000 civilians worked for the federal government—most of them in the War Department's Quarter-master Corps.[35]

Patronage also integrated the two governing branches of the national government. While separation of powers gave the executive and the legislative different roles to play, patronage brought the two together and built communication between them. Communication was required because the Senate had to ratify most presidential appointments. But the appointments of most of the subcabinet-level positions did not wait for the final ratification; the president made them after consultation and negotiation with legislators. Legislators played major roles in apportioning important positions, such as collectors and naval officers for major ports, and they practically controlled the smaller appointments, such as post offices. The *New York Tribune* told applicants to go directly to legislators and not to waste time contacting the postmaster general's office: "Applications addressed to them will receive attention earlier than if sent to the Department and save much delay and trouble." The president had some maneuvering room when party factions recommended different candidates, but even then he listened carefully to lawmakers' arguments and forged alliances through his appointments. He built similar alliances by consulting with state governors about local appointments.[36]

The patronage system that Lincoln built began with the cabinet. Given the diverse elements that made up the Republican party it was vital that all factions be heard. Only six years old, the party was an amalgam of former Democrats, former Whigs, Free Soilers, Know Nothings, further mixed according to a geography that found border-state members bedfellows with Bostonians and Oregonians linked to New Yorkers. These divisions were entwined with divergent economic views as well: Free traders joined high-tariff supporters, greenbackers associated with specie advocates. Still, they called themselves Republicans and shared a vision of economic growth and development and a hostility to the expansion of slavery.

When Lincoln organized his administration he learned from Buchanan's mistakes even as he escaped the older man's political shackles. Slavery had undermined effective government in Buchanan's cabinet. Proslavery men feared strong Northern influences; Northern Democrats distrusted powerful Deep South advisers. Fearing to lose his Southern base Buchanan had ignored and then attacked the patronage claims of his most forceful rival, Stephen Douglas. He thereby alienated the most important counterweight to his own pro-Southern views and lost crucial constituents in the North. Lincoln's Republicans were less divided, of course; party conflicts did not promise the catastrophe that Southern Hotspurs could threaten. But Lincoln still reached out to every element in his party and thereby helped strengthen party union.

His advisers surpassed Buchanan's in their abilities. Buchanan's most prestigious post, secretary of state, went to Lewis Cass, who was almost in his dotage. Howell Cobb of Georgia was the most able of an undistinguished group who had been appointed almost because of their lack of distinction; they were men whom more able men had suggested. Buchanan would hardly get the best advice available from his cabinet after buying party peace at the price of executive feebleness.[37]

Lincoln did not, and probably could not, make the same mistake. The new party had generated energetic and strong leaders along with factions that contended for dominance. Party unity required that faction leaders be brought to Washington to govern. The first man Lincoln chose, and for the most prestigious position, secretary of state, was his strongest party rival, William Seward. He was the obvious choice, the favorite for the nomination that Lincoln had received and still the best-known and probably the second most powerful Republican. Lincoln could be effective only if he unified the six-year-old Republican party; Seward's support was indispensable.

Seward knew it. He had thought of himself as the leader of the Republican party for some time. He was eight years older than Lincoln, much better educated, had four years of executive experience as governor of the biggest state in the Union, had served twelve years in the Senate compared to Lincoln's mere two years in the House. Seward knew the important national figures of the 1850s and had become the best-known Republican in the nation by 1860. He had a reputation as a radical man—his insistence that a higher law than the Constitution would doom slavery allowed his enemies to link him to Constitution-burning abolitionists. But he had moved to the Right in the party, and Republican leadership of the antislavery Left was by 1860 in the hands of Salmon Chase. Chase's forces were working to get him in the cabinet to give the administration a radical direction. Thus a battle was shaping up over who would control the cabinet.

If Seward could not win the nomination he certainly meant to win the cabinet battle and so fortify his control of the Republican future to compensate for not being the candidate in 1860. He took the failure of the party to nominate him hard. When an associate complained that people would be disappointed if a potential placeholder did not get an office, Seward exclaimed: "Disappointment! You speak to me of disappointment. To me, who was justly entitled to the Republican nomination for the presidency, and who had to stand aside and see it given to a little Illinois lawyer!"[38]

Seward was not just a disappointed nominee. He represented a perspective within the Republican party that helped define its response to slavery within the fabric of the society. Seward shared with other members of the party a desire to oust slavery from the republic, but his view was Burkean in its gradualness. Unlike Chase, and to an extent, Lincoln, Seward thought that time was on the side of freedom—events and forces larger than human efforts would end slavery: "The laws of political economy, combining with the inevitable tendencies of population are hastening emancipation, and all the labors of statesmen and politicians to prevent it are ineffectual." When Seward spoke of a higher law that would doom slavery or of an "irrepressible conflict" between slavery and freedom he was referring to an inescapable process of history that would at once provoke a clash between the two and would ultimately give victory to freedom.[39]

Seward, of course, advocated the ideas of free soilers against any significant expansion of slavery. He was hardly silent on the issues of the day, believing that a statesman's task was to speak out against backward tendencies. When the 1850 Compromise was debated he spoke passionately against adding any slave states. Yet his faith in freedom's ultimate victory left him free to compromise and negotiate, and when the disunion crisis came he could envision the possibility of bargains made to conciliate the South. It was impossible to bargain away freedom's ultimate victory. If the South could be kept in the Union the Union would inevitably evolve toward freedom. He saw the victory of free soil in Kansas by 1860 as evidence for his hopes. He supported Republican economics as a means to accelerate the progress of settlement and the use of the nation's bounty. He advocated expansion to enlarge the domain of prosperity and freedom that would inspire and shape the wider world. This enthusiastic dream for America allowed Seward flexibility in the disunion crisis: to emphasize union rather than free soil— union at almost any price—since if extremists did not derail the process, the price would never have to be paid.[40]

Seward's vision of the disunion crisis thus offered the Republican party an escape from the precipice of disunion—if it calmed its moral enthusiasm and thought of the ultimate triumph of an expanded, rich, powerful and still free nation. It was a beguiling vision for those individuals who sought peace in their time, who could be happy with a hope that someday slavery would die.

But there were members in the party less languid in their views about the victory of free soil. Salmon Chase, Lincoln's ultimate choice for secretary of treasury, was the best-known voice for that position. Although only a year older than Lincoln, Chase, like Seward, had more impressive credentials. A graduate of Dartmouth, he had been a two-term governor of Ohio and twice elected to the Senate. He also had purer antislavery qualifications than the president did. A year before twenty-eight-year-old Lincoln gave his first significant speech—an argument for making respect for the laws the political religion of the nation—Chase had begun his career attacking the constitutional power of masters over fugitive slaves. By 1841, as Lincoln celebrated the election of William Henry Harrison, deemed safer on slavery in the South than his rival Martin Van Buren, Chase was moving into the newly organized Liberty party and developing a theory that challenged the power of slavery in the constitutional system.[41]

Chase first developed his position in his 1839 defense of the runaway slave Matilda, an argument in which he began crafting ideas he would later elaborate into the constitutional theory that undergirded much of the Republican party's principles. Basic to his argument was a belief that slavery violated the idea in the Declaration that all men are born "equally free"; the natural right to human liberty applied to all people. Yes, Southern states had slavery and laws to uphold it. But the natural law reflected the natural condition of human beings—created free and equal. Only positive law could impose slavery. Where no law established slavery, then freedom prevailed. Accordingly, since Ohio was a free state, Matilda's freedom was hers by natural right, but it was also affirmed by the Northwest Ordinance of 1787. Moreover, Chase used the federal system to defend freedom. The Constitution and congressional law provided a fugitive slave law. But that was a federal law—only federal officials could enforce it. The state officials who held Matilda were not empowered under that law, and therefore she should be free. Unimpressed, the judge gave the woman back to her owners, who immediately put her on a boat to New Orleans to be sold.[42]

Chase did not save Matilda, but he did establish a Republican constitutional vision that reconciled the party's desire for freedom with the nation's constitutional system, a way to have liberty and order, to be lawyers and politicians as well as antislavery advocates. Chief Justice Taney's "slavery follows the flag" and William Lloyd Garrison's "burn the Constitution" were not the polity's only options. Chase's argument respected states' rights even as it expanded the domain of freedom. It was a constitutional argument first of all, premised on the belief that the Founders of the country were against slavery, viewing it as a necessary but temporary evil. The Constitution they created did not mention the word slavery, a sign of their repugnance to bondage. Their policy toward slavery "was one of repression, limitation, discouragement; they anticipated with confidence the auspicious result of universal freedom." "By the convention which framed the Constitution, the irreconcilable opposition of slavery to freedom, and of slave labor to free labor, was well understood, and the solemn pledge given in the Declaration of Independence was freshly remembered. The soil wet with the blood of freedom's martyrs was hardly dry, and the echoes of devout thanksgiving for the great triumph of American liberty yet lingered throughout the land."[43]

The Founders left slavery in the states where it existed; they feared too strong an outreach of federal power to strangle it there. But wherever the national government's powers extended, national power should destroy slavery—in the territories, in the District of Columbia, in interstate slave trade. It should admit no new slave states to the Union. And where some obligation to recognize slavery existed—the fugitive slave provision of the Constitution, for example—the national government should stand aside and let states decide if they would return runaway slaves to their masters. Such a program would put slavery in the course of ultimate extinction—exactly where Jefferson and Washington and Madison wanted it. It would also, therefore, separate the nation from its most corrupting influence.[44]

Both Seward and Chase operated within the political-constitutional system—they were after all lawyers and, most crucially, politicians. But Seward's philosophy reflected the sense of security and well-being that a heritage of relative wealth provided, not just a well-considered political theory. Seward liked people, moved easily among them, accepted the foibles of men—shared them and somehow knew that life would work out well. After passion had done its worst, people would come to their senses, work their differences out, and see the victory of liberty achieved with the inevitability of gradualness. At the end of the day they would sit beside the fire, smoking their cigars, swapping stories about the follies of their youth and feeling satisfied with how it all turned out.

Chase somehow never felt at peace with the world around him. Even as a young man he felt that play and relaxation wasted his time. He was stung by immorality of slavery and motivated by a duty to end it as quickly as possible. His sense of personal moral responsibility meant that he made few friends, kept himself aloof, studied and prayed to achieve moral perfection, seldom told a joke or understood one. He was angered by Lincoln's pleasure in humor and defended himself after the president accepted his resignation with the remark that, unlike Lincoln, "I have never been able to make a joke out of this war." Some things were too important to joke about.[45]

Lincoln, for his part, tried to stay on good terms with Chase but gradually grew to dislike him. Chase may have earned Lincoln's enmity by his willingness to speak ill of and spread rumors about men whom Lincoln respected. Chase did not share that respect, and the damage was done when he tried to undermine these men behind their backs. Chase would be in the center of the great cabinet crisis of late 1862 after his attempt to get Seward removed by spreading rumors about the failings of the cabinet. Chase also spread rumors in early 1863 that Grant was an incapable drunk.[46]

Despite his later failings Chase held firm on the issue of compromise over slavery expansion. While Seward dallied with the Crittenden measures Chase reassured the South only that slavery would not be attacked where it existed; after that concession he demurred. Believing that Northern opinion rejected returning runaways, he was willing to compensate owners for their losses but thought the fugitives should be left free. And he was firmer than Lincoln in two specific areas: Lincoln agreed to return fugitives to their masters, and the president would later acquiesce in allowing New Mexico to have slavery (perhaps as part of the strategy of dividing the South). Chase held his ground, not without results. His commitment to free soil strengthened Lincoln's position, but also placed in the national view another voice for advanced antislavery measures. And it built into the cabinet a contest between Seward's conservatism and Chase's egalitarianism, each side struggling for the president's favor (perhaps his soul), that would last throughout the war.

Chase and Seward were the powers in the cabinet in the early days, and when war broke out the secretary of war would join their ranks. Yet with war seen as more bluff than reality Lincoln kept building a cabinet to satisfy political needs. In contrast to Buchanan, he did so by adding, even to lesser posts, men with influence. Postmaster general, secretary of the interior, secretary of the navy, and attorney general were filled generally on the bases of geography, party allegiance, and influence. Postmaster Montgomery Blair came from the best-known political family in the North, perhaps in the nation. His father, Francis P. Blair, had been an intimate adviser to Andrew Jackson and then had gravitated toward Lincoln after Fremont's loss in 1856. He favored Missourian Edward Bates at the Chicago convention in 1860 but easily shifted to Lincoln. His younger son, Frank, quickly became useful by campaigning for Lincoln in 1860 and would become a pivotal figure in keeping

Missouri in the Union. Father and younger son pushed the older son, Montgomery, for the cabinet, calling upon their antislavery credentials. Even though "Old Man Blair" kept slaves until the Thirteenth Amendment freed them, the family had fought slavery expansion prominently—Montgomery acting as counsel to free Dred Scott, Frank publishing a newspaper and stumping for Republicans in 1856 and after. With connections in both Maryland, where Francis Blair lived, and in Missouri, where his sons had gone to make their fortunes, the Blairs were important anchors among border-state antislavery Democrats.[47]

Caleb Smith was the least distinguished of Lincoln's cabinet appointments. He became secretary of interior because he was a longtime friend of Lincoln who had served in Congress and then worked for Taylor's election. He had seconded Lincoln's nomination in Chicago and seems to have been placed in the cabinet in part simply because Lincoln liked the man. The president had not needed to bargain for Indiana's support in Chicago; Smith and most of the state delegation were already for him. Still, he represented midwestern Whigs, as did Lincoln, and had other credentials as a persuasive political speaker.[48]

The border states and even the upper South may have persuaded Lincoln to put Edward Bates into the Justice Department. Bates came to Missouri in 1820 from Virginia where he had spent his first twenty-eight years. His attitudes toward slavery reflected those of the generation that ruled the Old Dominion as Bates grew up. He believed blacks to be inescapably inferior but thought that slavery was an evil that in time should be eliminated. By 1860 at sixty-seven he had earned a reputation as "a sage," known for his conservative opinions (reflected perhaps most strikingly in his belief that the Republican party was a passing entity; he thought that one day it would fade away to be replaced by his beloved and revived Whig party). With Bates as attorney general extreme constitutional views were hardly likely, a further comfort to Southern sympathizers.

Bates was also sound on the economy, so far as Lincoln was concerned. Both men believed in economic development with government support. Bates had earned enthusiastic endorsement from western economic developers with a resounding speech at the 1844 Rivers and Harbors convention. And he believed in an enduring Union, knit together by the Mississippi. Bates also would appeal to Know Nothings, for he had supported Fillmore in 1856 on the American party ticket. Thus Bates could voice the views of border conservatives and western economic developers and stabilize a party widely criticized for its radicalism.[49]

Other elements of the party still needed representation. From New

England came Gideon Welles, a former Jacksonian Democrat and a newspaper editor with excellent contacts in Washington, gathered partly from earlier service under Polk in the Navy Department. Welles had a glowing reputation for honesty—he once resigned the presidency of a life insurance company because he refused to pay lobbyists. He also stood against the reported corruption of the New York state legislature by Thurlow Weed, William Seward's closest ally. Widely respected throughout New England, Welles had been the pivotal player at the convention in keeping crucial New England votes from Seward. An aloof and austere man, Welles nevertheless had a sharp insight into character and a puritan's obsession with hard work. His appointment gave New England, which had gone almost unanimously for Lincoln, a well-respected voice that, combined with Vice-President Hannibal Hamlin, ensured loyalty from that section of the country.[50]

Welles's reputation was needed in the cabinet largely because Simon Cameron was there. Cameron brought a different cast to the Lincoln cabinet. He was the most successful politician in one of the most crucial states in the 1860 election, Pennsylvania. The Cameron machine shaped the state legislature through effective use of patronage and when that failed, bribery. The state's large number of electoral votes made it important; so did the fact that Pennsylvanians voted in October—a victory there would influence November voters. At the Chicago convention Lincoln's managers promised that Pennsylvania would be well-represented in any Lincoln cabinet but did not make any specific promise to Cameron. Still, Cameron was that state's leading Republican.

An influential man, yes, but Cameron's reputation for corruption was notorious. Three past presidents—Jackson, Polk, and Buchanan— had their opinions: Cameron was "not to be trusted by anyone in any way"; "a . . . tricky man in whom no reliance is to be placed"; "an unprincipled rascal." Thaddeus Stevens reputedly told Lincoln, "I don't think he would steal a red hot stove." When Cameron heard of the remark and complained, Stevens recanted: "I apologize. I said Cameron would not steal a red hot stove. I withdraw that statement."[51]

Lincoln nevertheless offered Cameron a cabinet post—either secretary of war or treasury. Cameron wanted treasury, but his reputation counseled caution. Seward's presence in the cabinet already tainted the new party with charges of political expediency, and Seward gave Cameron strong support. When news of Cameron's appointment leaked out, protests flooded in, raising the old charges of corruption against the Pennsylvania boss. Lincoln thus withdrew the offer, but since Cameron had already broadcast the news Lincoln could not take the office away so easily. Moreover, Seward warned of the costs of turning Cameron's many influential friends into enemies. An enormous number of letters arrived from Cameron's supporters, and even some of his accusers changed sides. Lincoln then demanded proof of corruption; when that proof was not forthcoming he reluctantly gave the Pennsylvanian the War Department. The protariff economic development forces that had helped to build the Republican party now had a voice in the new administration. That economic vision, however, was strongly tainted with corruption and with a widespread sense during the prewar years that the morality and self-denial necessary for a republic was eroding. Cameron would be watched closely.[52]

With the appointments of Seward and Cameron, the former linked to corruption secondhand through his friendship with Thurlow Weed, the "Wizard of the Lobby," and the latter a hands-on manipulator, the presence in the cabinet of men of undeniable public rectitude was important. Welles and Salmon P. Chase were there for that purpose. As John P. Hale wrote Chase, "Your being in the Cabinet would go far to dissipate an anticipation which has involuntarily been forcing itself upon my mind that the only ultimate result we have obtained at the recent Presidential election, is to turn one set of public robbers out of the Treasury to let another in."[53]

The cabinet thus served many purposes. Chase and Seward stood for the two most important policy options on the most compelling issue Republicans faced; the other cabinet members represented more political and geographic needs. It was a unity cabinet with Cameron, a former Democrat from Pennsylvania; Bates, a Whig from Missouri; Blair, a Democrat from another border state, Maryland; and Smith, an antislavery Whig from Indiana. The divergent voices would be heard, and Lincoln would get solid soundings on the feelings of Republicans throughout the North. He tried to impose some national unity on the cabinet as well. Several Southerners were considered for one post, but they turned him down; the unity would be Northern only. There were four former Democrats and three former Whigs, but as Lincoln reminded observers, he was a former Whig himself so the "sides" were even.[54]

It was a cabinet of influential men—men of maturity, Blair at forty-eight the youngest and the average age fifty-six—four years older on the average than the president himself. Certainly one man and possibly two were potential rivals for the office in the future, but all were able and important men in their own right. Lincoln needed such men as anchors for the new party because the institutional tradition was not yet established for the Republicans. Leaders were not practically interchangeable but were the magnets of party cohesion. Thus Lincoln surrounded himself with the prominent party rivals. The group might have proven un-manageable to a president of lesser talents. It wasn't. That would be clear later, but Lincoln had to prove himself first.

Historians have emphasized that many of the men in Lincoln's cabi-net gained their positions as a result of deals his managers had made at Chicago to win the nomination. It is certainly true that Lincoln had some political debts to pay from the Chicago convention, but paying those debts was important predominantly because the creditors were the other leaders of the party. These were not people simply to be "paid off" for supporting Lincoln at the Wigwam; they needed to be rewarded because of who they were. They represented the elements of the re-cently organized party—elements whose allegiances needed and de-served cementing. Their voices needed to be heard, and the factions needed to believe that they would be. A cabinet dominated by former Whigs would alienate former Democrats; a cabinet of conservatives would estrange radicals. The party needed unity as desperately as the Union did, and having all factions share the government provided that unity. A Seward presidency would have included almost all these men or certainly men acceptable to the individuals Lincoln chose. The unity of the party and the potential disunion of the nation required that strong men of diverse perspectives be ready to lead the country.[55]

The cast were taking their places: Republicans gathering the active roles, a president committed to using the constitutional and political system to end slavery and thereby secure a more perfect union, a party finding the means to that end in active debate because it included fac-tions from throughout the North—a broadly defined North that reached into Missouri and Maryland, the Midwest, and New England. Self-in-terest and the spoils of office drew many of the players, but they were also inspired by a sense of purpose: In the last six years they had built an institution able to grasp and ready to govern the national govern-ment as it faced its most compelling crisis.

1861

★ ★ ★ ★ ★

One day, John Sherman took me with him to see Mr. Lincoln. He walked into the room where the secretary to the President now sits, we found the room full of people, and Mr. Lincoln sat at the end of the table, talking with three or four gentleman, who soon left. John walked up, shook hands, and took a chair near him, holding in his hand some papers referring to minor appointments in the State of Ohio, which formed the subject of conversation. Mr. Lincoln took the papers, said he would refer them to the proper heads of departments, and would be glad to make the appointments asked for, if not already promised. John then turned to me and said, "Mr. President, this is my brother, Colonel Sherman, who is just up from Louisiana, he may give you some information you want." "Ah!" said Mr. Lincoln, "how are they getting along down there?" I said, "They think they are getting along swimmingly—they are preparing for war." "Oh well!" said he, "I guess we'll manage to keep house." I was silenced, said no more to him, and we soon left. I was sadly disappointed, and remember that I broke out on John, d——ning the politicians generally, saying, "You have got things in a hell of a fix, and you may get them out as best you can," adding that the country was sleeping on a volcano that might burst forth at any minute, but that I was going to St. Louis to take care of my family and would have no more to do with it.

—William Tecumseh Sherman, *Memoirs*

3
★ ★ ★ ★ ★

TO SUMTER:
JANUARY TO APRIL 1861

Lincoln stayed in Springfield selecting the cabinet that would assemble in Washington and filling hundreds of other positions. Hordes of officeseekers poured into town, jamming hotels and boardinghouses, some sleeping in Pullman cars brought in to handle the overflow. People stood in lines for hours to see the new president, to have their pictures taken in front of the modest house on Jackson Street. Letters of advice, of supplication, of abuse rushed in, so much so that Lincoln took on two secretaries, John Nicolay and John Hay, to handle the mail and to organize the large receptions that Lincoln held on the second floor of the state capitol building. In rare moments of leisure Lincoln was seen reading a history of the nullification crisis of 1832, learning what Jackson had done years earlier. He took time out to say some goodbyes—one to Coles County to visit his stepmother Sally and other old friends, telling his law partner Billy Herndon that he would be back in Springfield to practice law after his presidency was over.[1]

Meanwhile, Seward handled matters in the capital. Seward had asked Lincoln to come to Washington soon, but the president-elect decided not to go early. It is difficult to know why. He replied to Seward, discussing possible times that would be most likely to counter plots to interfere with his taking office, but beyond that he offered no direct explanation for delaying. Perhaps he was satisfied to let Seward take charge, to act as a sort of public spokesman for the new administration without committing Lincoln to any plan of action. Equally possible is that staying away was part of a general strategy to avoid following a course that could be misinterpreted as retreat or panic in the face of threats. So president-elect Lincoln would stay in Illinois and Seward would stay in Washington, working with the power brokers, looking for options that might preserve the Union and yet satisfy growing antislavery and anti-Southern opinion.

Being left in charge in Washington fit Seward's self-image. He was used to the idea of being the nation's leading Republican, and it was fitting that he be on the scene where major committees were in action trying to resolve the secession crisis. He knew the participants, and they knew him as the most important Republican within earshot. With Lincoln in Springfield Seward had the chance to free-lance a little. He did have a proposal that Lincoln had given to Thurlow Weed, designed to produce some compromise: a constitutional amendment guaranteeing that Congress would not interfere with slavery in the states; recommendations to Northern states that they repeal personal liberty laws conflicting with the Constitution; an amendment to the fugitive slave law giving alleged fugitives a jury trial.[2]

Seward was not content simply to introduce Lincoln's proposals. Even after congressional compromises had failed, he kept in touch with Southern representatives and kept alive the promise that somehow compromise might be reached. He was buying time, believing, as did Lincoln, that delay worked against the hothead minority that had provoked secession. And Seward was taking charge of Northern readiness as well: telling governors in New York and Massachusetts to get troops and supplies ready just in case, urging New York city moneylenders to keep interest rates low on loans to the government, supporting strong pro-Union replacements for Buchanan's cabinet as Southern sympathizers resigned.

Seward was also making speeches about ways to resolve the crisis: Lincoln's three proposals were included, but there were also suggestions for building railroads, for adding two states (with or without slavery was not clear) after Kansas came in as a free state, and for laws safeguarding states from raids such as John Brown's. Congressmen applauded him although some wondered at the vagaries in his proposals. When he attended parties and dinners Seward tossed off suggestions—perhaps Anderson and Scott should resign, perhaps there was something to be gained in a little war with Britain, France, Spain—patriotism might reunite the dissolving Union. Seward promoted a Peace Convention in Virginia, which met to work out another compromise. Letters poured in urging him to save the Union. It was heady stuff: "It seems to me that if I am absent only three days," he wrote his wife, "this Administration, the Congress, and the District would fall into consternation and despair." Lincoln of course would play an important role in the proceedings—the inaugural address would be crucial, he told Weed, and "I shall write him about that."[3]

As Lincoln prepared his inaugural address in Springfield crisis seemed balanced with opportunity. Between 20 December and 1 February seven Southern states had passed ordinances of secession, but on 4 February the tide appeared to ebb. Even as the seven met in Montgomery, Alabama, to write their new constitution, voters in the most important Southern state of all, Virginia, defeated delegates who favored secession. In the next four weeks Tennessee voters refused even to call a convention; Arkansas rejected secessionist candidates for a convention; Missouri chose delegates who later voted eighty-nine to one against secession. North Carolina rejected a convention that had secession on its agenda. Delaware, Kentucky, and Maryland were clearly going to stay in the Union. Seward had predicted that "we shall keep the border states, and in three months or thereabouts, if we hold off the Unionists and disunionists will have their hands on each others throats in the cotton states."[4]

That was Seward's hope. But this time he misunderstood the stakes of compromise. Prior secession threats had produced compromises that let slavery expand, and once more Northerners were being pressured to give in to Southern "grievances." More crucially, in the past compromises had come within the legislative process and had challenged no clear or widespread popular mandate. This time, however, any retreat would be a betrayal of the victory of a president elected on the very issue of slavery's expansion; such a retreat would be a stunning challenge to self-government and the Constitution. Perhaps too absorbed in casting balances and trading votes, Seward had minimized this distinction. Lincoln, however, saw the crisis as a challenge that had to be met. His party clearly shared his resolve, for even as he set out from Springfield congressional compromises had fallen apart.[5]

Balancing hopes for peace with a willingness to preserve the Union by other means should that be necessary, Lincoln left Springfield on 11 February, one day before his fifty-second birthday. His route took him through much of the North, where he could test public opinion and help shape it. One of his approaches emphasized that the crowds he drew were there out of respect for the office he held, not for Lincoln the man. Another appeal drew attention from party passion to political unity. He noted often that many of his listeners had voted for other candidates but that now they stood together to save the country. He emphasized that saving the Union was not the enterprise of any individual but of the people as a whole. It was their "business to rise up and preserve the Union and liberty."

At times he sounded threatening: "I may have to put the foot down firmly," he told New Jersey legislators, and they erupted in cheers. He also spoke in a more moderate voice that seemed to counsel calm: "There is no occasion for any excitement"; "There is nothing going wrong—nothing that really hurts any body." At the same time these words indicated that secession was not founded on real grievances. Southerners retained the rights the Constitution granted citizens; fugitive slaves were being returned. In that sense the crisis was "artificial. It has no foundation in facts. It was not argued up, as the saying is, and cannot, therefore, be argued down. Let it alone and it will go down of itself."[6]

He spoke often of preserving the peace, promising Southerners that there would be no use of force unless they struck first. "All we want is time, patience, and a reliance on that God who has never forsaken his people," he told a crowd in Columbus, Ohio. Yet while promising the possibility of peace he prepared a justification for whatever course he might take. At Indianapolis he spoke of the meaning of coercion, and though doubting it would be necessary, still denied that holding government forts or "retaking those that belong to it" or collecting import duties constituted coercion.

Lincoln also denounced the legal right to secede and raised the stakes with regard to the current Southern challenge. If the Union was not saved on this occasion, "nobody will have a chance to pilot her on another voyage." Furthermore, the Union itself was the basis for preserving the ideal of equal liberty, not just for Americans but for "the world for all future time." And if the country could not be saved without giving up the principle of equal liberty—"I was about to say I would rather be assassinated on this spot than to surrender it."[7]

These were preliminaries to the inaugural that Lincoln had worked on for months. They provided guideposts for the path that lay ahead. They revealed a man expecting trouble, hoping for peace but ready to face a conflict to preserve the Union and the vital principles it stood for. Lincoln promised to replace Buchanan's inertia with bold direction.

That image, however, was eroded rather precipitously when the nation discovered that Lincoln had to sneak into the capital in disguise late at night on George Washington's birthday. Apparently the remark about assassination was more than hyperbole. Threats against his life had been frequent, and with Washington so near Lincoln listened to advisers and entered the city secretly. He would have to recapture the initiative with the inaugural address, explaining what was at stake, what he would tolerate, what he was willing to do to preserve the government and the Union.[8]

Lincoln began by placing his taking of the oath of office within the abiding traditions of self-government, "a custom as old as the government itself." But he knew that this process was in danger because Southerners feared the effects of his election on their lives. Their fears were unfounded, he assured them. Nearly all his own speeches, the platform of the Republican party, contained promises that slavery would not be assailed where it existed. Furthermore, he would "cheerfully" enforce the fugitive slave law and other constitutional provisions that protected Southern property rights. He was taking his oath to defend the Constitution with no mental reservations. He would not construe the constitutional protections by "hypercritical rules" that would deny Southern rights, and he wanted officials to enforce the laws whether they approved of them or not.

The South was safe within the Union. But the Union itself could not lawfully be divided. It was perpetual both "in contemplation of universal law, and of the Constitution" itself. History showed that the Union was older than the Constitution and hence history spoke for a perpetual Union. No state therefore could lawfully leave the Union "on its own mere motion. Resolves and ordinances to that effect are legally void." "I shall take care," he added, "as the Constitution itself expressly enjoins upon me that the laws of the Union be faithfully executed in all the States." Should the South act despite his reassurances it would be challenging the law, and he would uphold the law.

Yet at the moment when Lincoln seemed to throw down the gauntlet he drew it back. There would be no invasion. In the interests of maintaining harmony, he would not send "obnoxious strangers" to enforce federal laws in the South. The mail would run unless rebels stopped it. He would not enforce the laws that he had every right to enforce. But at the same time he would "hold, occupy, and possess the property and places belonging to the government and collect the duties and impost": thus his policy and the legal arguments that would sustain it. He had told the South what it could expect from the new administration.

Then came a move to a different level and to a larger audience. Certainly Lincoln knew the immediate political impact of his words, but he also understood, in a way uncommon to other presidents, that definitions and descriptions of larger contexts might offer new directions, options, visions of the consequences at stake. A move to the theory of constitutional democracy might set standards and ideals that would allow the nation to survive the ordeal it seemed about to face.

He knew that there were "persons in one section, or another—who seek to destroy the union at all events, and are glad of any pretext to do it." They would not hear him; they could not be influenced or ennobled or fortified with a sense of direction. Yet those with minds still open might consider how the "national fabric" worked.

The Constitution protected the rights of minorities in plain words, "by affirmations and negations, guarranties [sic] and prohibitions." There had been no denial by any majority of any "clearly written constitutional right." If a majority did violate a vital right revolution might be justified. The nation did not suffer from such a situation, however. It suffered instead from differing interpretations of certain phrases: returning fugitives (was the state or the national government responsible?) and congressional duties toward slavery in the territories (may Congress prohibit it, must Congress protect it?).

Differences over these issues divided the nation into minorities and majorities. Majority rule would have to prevail or the nation would face continuing minority demands that would unleash counterdemands by other minorities; the result would be anarchy. "All who cherish disunion sentiments are now being educated to the exact temper of doing this."

The only "sovereign of a free people" was "a majority, held in restraint by constitutional checks, and limitations, and always changing easily, with deliberate changes of popular opinions and sentiments." The country belonged to the people, of course. They could change their government by revolution or by constitutional amendment, Lincoln noted. Ignoring the revolutionary option, he spoke of constitutional amendment as the acceptable method and urged that any proposed amendment be generated by state conventions rather than by Congress—the more democratic method was preferable. The authority of the government thus rested on the people, in whose "ultimate justice" he urged confidence. They had created a limited government, changed often enough that no administration could "very seriously injure the government." The "great tribunal, the American people" would surely provide the right judgment in a debate between North and South.

The political process thus stood as the ultimate authority in the issues before the nation, a belief basic to Lincoln's vision. His reliance on this process increased in part because the Supreme Court had lost its credibility as an unbiased arbiter of constitutional dispute. The *Dred Scott* decision had led Lincoln to adopt a view of the polity that limited the role of courts in deciding constitutional questions. Over twenty years a lawyer, he was committed to the judicial process, but when Taney's Supreme Court in effect declared unconstitutional the major plank of a political party, Lincoln chased the judges back to a more confined position. Judges' opinions deserved respectful hearing from other members of the polity, but their rulings were binding only on parties to the suit and perhaps as precedent in parallel cases. In such cases law-abiding citizens obeyed judicial ruling. Nevertheless, "upon vital questions affecting the whole people" American citizens could not "resign their government into the hands" of judges.

Thus Lincoln's polity relied on a faith in popular government. Yet Lincoln was not a Jacksonian Democrat. He stepped into politics attacking Jackson, remained loyal to a Whig party that challenged Jacksonian philosophies, rebutted the political philosophy of popular sovereignty. If he believed that the people were the ultimate source of authority he also understood that liberty as well as order demanded that they exercise their sovereignty through the political and the constitutional processes.

With its emphasis on the constitutional system, Lincoln's inaugural highlights an important point about the secession crisis. Lincoln believed that the system had already been assaulted—secession was an attack, one that could be embellished, made more stark and drastic by gunfire, but the attack was under way. Once rebel guns fired on Sumter the challenge was clearly inescapable. Lincoln's position, however, was not a strategy to make the South attack Sumter—it had already initiated conflict in Charleston and in the capitals of the Deep South in the aftermath of his election. In addition, hundreds of federal installations were being taken over by Confederate authorities. Lincoln did not need to set up a situation in which the South was the aggressor; the seceders had already attacked. Lincoln's reactions, both promised and executed, were an effort to limit the impact of that attack by keeping other states from joining it.

Practical matters continued to inform the argument against secession. "Physically speaking we cannot separate." Relations between North and South would continue, and peaceful dealings between friends were better than negotiations between alien nations, especially nations that had been at war. He asked for calm and serious thought about the course ahead, for reason to replace the passions of the moment. The "momentous issue of civil war" lay before them. The government would not "assail" the South if the Union was not assailed, but both sides needed to note that he had taken the most solemn oath "registered in Heaven" to preserve, protect, and defend the Union.

"I am loth to close," Lincoln told them, as if he thought that if he could keep talking and they could keep listening then all would be well. He evoked friendship, memories of past battles and dead forefathers, and called on the "better angels of our nature" to keep the nation together, to "swell the chorus of the Union." And then he was done. He had tried his best to define his course, what the people need not fear, and what they had to remember.

It was a plea for the status quo, but the status quo was not only temporal, not focused only on who held which forts and territory as of 4 March 1861; the status quo also respected the constitutional process, the rule of law, the oath of office, and the endurance of the Union. He would accept constitutional means to change the status quo—if the people were to amend the Constitution, then even disunion was possible. But unless or until that process occurred, and a long and problematic process it was, he would not allow the Union to slip away. He would do everything he could possibly do to preserve the Union. Those people who attacked that status quo faced "the momentous issue of civil war."

There were gaps in the address, topics avoided or not considered. As a presentation of the constitutional issues in the largest sense it was excellent—a powerful brief and a compelling argument. Lincoln's years at the bar had honed his profound intelligence; he had trumped Confederate arguments over secession. Yet two questions lay waiting, unanswered in the address. First, where was the moral element, the injustice of slavery that had been so compelling in his prewar speeches? His one reference to slavery was a statement that the debate itself over the good or evil of slavery divided the nation: "One section of our country believes slavery is *right*, and ought to be extended, while the other believes it is *wrong* and ought not to be extended. This is the only substantial dispute." Did this minimal reference suggest that Lincoln was shifting his thought toward means and away from ends? Would he be captured by the idea of protecting process while forgetting purpose? Was he ignoring the balance between equality and order that he had emphasized when his party was defining its ideals?

The second question was more subtle, though related, and also concerned balance. It raised the issue of Lincoln's particular understanding of the conflict and of his ability to provide for posterity a complex vision of the war's meaning. He had framed the conflict as a debate in which one side or the other must be right. Was seeing the conflict in this way appropriate for the awesome, brutal, indiscriminate leviathan of war that was emerging? Perhaps a sensitivity was needed to the possibility that God might judge both North and South as guilty for the sin of slavery and that the punishment would be equal to the sin. Four years later Lincoln and the nation might be ready for such an understanding. Time and the mountains of dead would tell.

The inaugural address gained strong approval. Even before Lincoln spoke the *New York Evening Post* was impressed by his "calm confidence in the good sense of his hearers and in the peaceful and recuperative workings of the institutions of his country." Opinion in Boston declared, "We cannot see how any right minded man, having in view the enforcement of the laws and the good of the country, can make any objection to it," and "the plainness and frankness with which he speaks must commend him to every mind."[9]

But praise was hardly unanimous. A judgment from Philadelphia deemed it "one of the most awkwardly constructed official documents we have ever inspected. It abounds in platitudes, incoherencies, solecisms, illogical deductions and is pitiably apological for the uprising of the Republican Party. " An Iowa paper flunked the work: "It is a wishy washy, unscholarly affair—unworthy of an undergraduate, to say nothing of a statesman." An Albany journal saw "this rambling, discursive, questioning, loose jointed stump speech . . . itself a symptom of the pending revolution and . . . its downward tendencies."[10]

His friends approved and his enemies disapproved. It was much as he had predicted: Those people who wanted to hear did, and those who did not, did not. There was sure to be conflict over any policy he followed. Yet in the North he could count on many more supporters, ranging from people at least willing to wish him well to those who would make every effort to help him in any way they could. Everyone who read it with an open mind would have learned how democracy, law, and the Union were intertwined.

Once the reaction to the inaugural died down Lincoln had to turn his words into action. Had the situation remained stable this task would have been less of a challenge. His policy portended watchful waiting, waiting to be assailed if it came to that, but in the most optimistic scenario, waiting for passions to cool, for Unionists in the South to gain influence as it became clear that Lincoln was not the harbinger of more John Browns. Then the growing public sentiment that since 1854 had eroded slavery's power slowly but surely would work its way out within the political-constitutional process.[11]

The day after the inaugural Lincoln received a message from Maj. Robert Anderson, commanding officer at Fort Sumter, that changed the picture dramatically. The constitutional process was not going to work its way peacefully toward a solution. Something was going to have to be done in an arena where every spotlight in the nation was focused. Careful consideration and rational calculation were going to be even more severely tested. The new Republican administration would have to do more than promise not to assail the South and to protect slavery where it existed. Lincoln was being pressed to define more precisely, not just in theory but in fact, what he meant by holding and possessing the property of the government.[12]

These factors perhaps underlay his decision to act alone in facing the crisis at Fort Sumter; there was certainly no other reason why he could not have engaged Congress. Although the full Congress had adjourned 3 March there was still time to bring together congressmen remaining in Washington when, on 5 March, Lincoln first heard from Anderson. The major had written that supplies were running out and that he needed 20,000 men. The Senate was meeting in special session as late as 28 March to confirm Lincoln's cabinet appointments even as Anderson's news came to the president. With the exception of those legislators living on the Pacific Coast, the most distant of them could have been in the capital within ten days. What was on Lincoln's mind? He knew there was a major crisis; he had spoken in the inaugural about having a conflict forced upon him, yet he was not gathering the nation's leaders to face the challenge.[13]

One explanation for his behavior is that Lincoln was not ready for a crisis because he did not initially see Fort Sumter as a real crisis. In his mind, the situation offered an opportunity to end subsequent threats of disunion by standing firm. Believing that the majority of the Southern population were Unionists he did not foresee civil war; only recently had he been able to conceive of war at all. Perhaps Lincoln did not gather the government because he was persuaded, or had persuaded himself, that the crisis was artificial.[14]

On the other hand, the new president may have clearly recognized the threat: a rapidly deteriorating situation that required action, maneuvering, weighing alternatives that as commander in chief he alone might have to execute. Fearing that congressmen could escalate the crisis, therefore, he wanted to handle events carefully by keeping the situation in his control alone. If he orchestrated the response he could play to Unionists in the South by exposing the poverty of Southern radicalism. Thus he would follow the sentiment of the inaugural address: an iron fist and an open hand. As the need for iron escalated he would still keep open the chance for unionism to assert itself: thus the call for a mere 75,000 troops on 15 April, three days after Fort Sumter was fired upon, and the call to the Southern states to join him in putting down the rebellion. As late as July 1861 he was still speaking of unionism among the majority in the South—and he stayed alert to Southern unionism throughout the war.

His interest in Southern unionism did not preclude using force to hold the Union together. Many Northerners believed that Southerners favoring disunion assumed that the North was too spineless to oppose Southern militants. Therefore by showing the mass of people in the South that extremists would meet firmness, their extremism would collapse. Montgomery Blair, speaking with some authority because of his border-state ties, especially endorsed this view. Thus even as Lincoln sought to appeal to Southern Unionists he had also thought of using force. During December 1860 the president-elect had written to four correspondents that federal forts would have to be held or retaken, asking one of these men to tell General Scott to be ready "to either hold or retake the forts." Yet as Lincoln traveled to Washington he made a special point of promising the people of Kentucky that he would treat them in the same way that they had been treated by the first three Virginian presidents.[15]

Only two forts of any significance remained, Pickens in Pensacola, Florida, and Fort Sumter. Almost everyone in both the North and the South was watching Sumter. Charleston's reputation as the seat of secession guaranteed that people would notice events there. Furthermore, in January gunfire had riveted attention on the harbor when Buchanan tried to send supplies to Major Anderson's troops via the *Star of the West*. Shore batteries surrounding the harbor opened up on the ship and forced its return to port. Some observers thought war had begun, but caution took over and the rush toward conflict slowed. Still, people kept alert to news from Fort Sumter. Lincoln sent trusted observers to Charleston to assess the situation and to determine if he might somehow appeal to unionism there.

Fort Sumter was a symbol; by comparison Fort Pickens was only a place. Much more secure than Sumter, Union forces could land supplies at Pickens beyond the reach of rebel cannon. Given a choice, anyone would have preferred to uphold Union authority there. Unfortunately, Pickens was secondary in the public eye—a place that had to be held, of course, but much less vital than holding Sumter, where honor was at stake and the world was watching. Lincoln wanted to hold Pickens; he readied an expedition to the fort, with instructions to "reinforce and to hold" it. And he wanted to hold Sumter, but holding a fort within range of Confederate cannon was a more delicate job. Lincoln moved carefully here. He ordered that steps be taken to organize an expedition to Charleston. But while the expedition to Pickens was ordered to proceed the Sumter expedition was told simply to be ready.[16]

For Secretary of State Seward waiting was the goal—a long wait that would ultimately bring Virginia and the rest of the South back to the Union. He apparently had been in contact with members of the outgoing Buchanan administration on Sumter and had worked out an agreement that the fort would get no reinforcement and no new supplies. He continued his insider's game, playing for time—promising Southerners that the Charleston fort would be evacuated, negotiating on when and how. Using his numerous contacts in the capital he had had two Supreme Court justices, John Campbell and Samuel Nelson, and two senators, John Gwin and Robert Hunter, tell Confederate commissioners who were trying to negotiate peaceful disunion that resolution was possible—Sumter would be given up—a bargain that Seward had heard from Southern friends would lower the heat, frustrate Southern hotheads, and allow Unionists in the South to restore calm and reunite the nation.[17]

While Lincoln was in Springfield, Seward had his way, and even after the new president arrived in Washington the secretary maintained some control. But gradually control was slipping from him into the hands of "the little Illinois lawyer." He had been able to get Cameron into the cabinet and had accepted Bates, but his influence was threatened as Lincoln named Welles, Blair, and Chase, Seward's potential enemies, to the administration. Still, Lincoln had asked for comments on the inaugural—a good sign—and Seward had moderated some of Lincoln's rhetoric and generally emphasized conciliation. The secretary of state also liked the general respect, almost reverence, that Lincoln had shown for the rule of law and tradition—the tone was right.[18]

Yet elements in the address troubled Seward, and the presence in the cabinet of more radical enemies also provoked him. Fighting back, he managed to get a letter published in the *New York Evening Post* just after Lincoln arrived in the capital, which described how the enemies of both Seward and the president were trying to defeat compromises with the South and wanted Seward out of the cabinet. The day before the inaugural Seward played a major card—he asked "leave to withdraw" from the cabinet. "I can't let Seward take the first trick," Lincoln told his private secretary. The president asked Seward to reconsider, and Seward agreed to stay.[19]

There may have been no connection between the reading of Lincoln's ideas and Seward's offer to resign. The secretary, fighting to have his views dominate the cabinet, was discovering that Lincoln wanted a balance, one that Seward could not control. But it is intriguing to note that Seward had read Lincoln's draft of the inaugural in late February; perhaps the combination of a more radical cabinet and a more militant president suggested to Seward more trouble than he felt he could handle—hence the offer of resignation. He withdrew it when Lincoln asked him to, but he would fight to keep as much influence as possible to guide the inexperienced president.[20]

Meanwhile, Lincoln was looking for a policy even as Union forts, ships, and money fell into rebel hands. (As the days passed after the inaugural and the new president sought advice, thirteen Texas forts, one by one, surrendered peacefully; Louisiana gave over $500,000 from the United States mint in New Orleans to the Confederate government; the USS *Isabella* was seized.) And all the while the Confederacy continued to create its government, appointing cabinet officers, so secure in its new status that its congressmen were legislating about post offices, lighthouses, and liquor control as state after state ratified its new constitution.[21]

Lincoln called the cabinet to almost daily meetings to ask what could be done. He also asked General Scott for military advice: How long could Anderson hold on? Could the army reinforce Sumter in that period? Scott had already told a gathering of officers that only the navy could relieve Sumter, but he answered that Anderson had perhaps a month, it was hard to say exactly. But one thing was certain: The army could not reinforce Sumter for "many months," and then it would take "a fleet of war vessels and transports, 5000 additional regular troops & 20,000 volunteers."[22]

Given such a hopeless picture it is not surprising that when Lincoln asked cabinet members for written opinions on Fort Sumter, five of the seven men advised against trying to supply it. Chase was not much more aggressive—he advised trying it only if it would not provoke a war. Only Blair insisted that the fort had to be resupplied, arguing that "measures which will inspire respect for the power of the Government and the firmness of those who administer it" would strengthen unionism in the South.[23]

Meanwhile, pressures grew in the North to do something—"Wanted: a Policy," a headline declared in the *New York Times*. Northern businessmen who previously had wanted Republicans to back away from coercion now were for "anything rather than *inaction*." The *New York Evening Post* noted the widespread criticism of Lincoln's "seeming inactivity," behavior that resembled "the disgraceful policy of his predecessor." Charles Francis Adams wrote in his diary, "The President is drifting the country into war, by [his] want of decision. Everywhere at this place is discouragement. . . . I see nothing but incompetency . . . the man is not equal to the hour."[24]

This apparent drift, especially apparent to Seward because he was not in charge, finally became too much for the secretary of state to bear. On Sunday 1 April he sat down and wrote out a series of ideas, "Some Thoughts for the Consideration of the President," describing the path policy should take. It was time to do something, Seward wrote; inertia seemed to have taken over the administration. Yes, there was some excuse for it—so much patronage to dispense, so much to do with the Senate still in town—but now the time to move had come, to stop the drift and take the reins.

First, the stakes had to be defined. Instead of discussing slavery, which only exacerbated angry feelings and divided the nation, the president should emphasize the primacy of the Union and hence stress patriotism over party. Since many people—most?—had come to see holding Sumter as a party question, Seward would advise abandoning Sumter, holding on to Pickens, reinforcing and defending the other forts on the Gulf of Mexico, and calling the navy in from foreign waters to prepare a blockade. Except for giving up Sumter Lincoln would follow these suggestions.

In foreign affairs Seward was more controversial and challenging. A few days earlier Spain had annexed Santo Domingo and with France's support was about to take Haiti. Here was a chance to forge "a vigorous spirit of independence on this continent against European intervention" that might be useful in coming days. Seward advised Lincoln to demand explanations from the two powers, and if the answers were not satisfactory Congress should be convened for a declaration of war. Seward also suggested getting "explanations" from Great Britain and Russia about their intentions. These were ambiguous ideas, but Seward clearly hoped that a little foreign crisis might diminish the disunion crisis, nor would it hurt to let the major powers know of Union touchiness should the crisis escalate. But it is likely that the secretary was reacting as he sometimes did in foreign affairs, assuming that a little unthinking belligerence would let the United States proceed on its bold and vigorous way.

Certainly Seward was tired of the days of apparent indecision and inaction. He had been at the center of the action for years, had even been in the front lines in the days before the inauguration. Now he had to wait on the untried new president who had introduced unfriendly voices into the cabinet and who seemed to be inclined to more radical views than Seward entertained. Thus Seward concluded his suggestions with his hand outstretched. Any course of action would have to be taken energetically, and every cabinet member would have to agree to it. "It is not my special province," he finished hopefully, "but I neither seek to evade or assume responsibility."[25]

Whatever the motivation, the memo to Lincoln was followed by Lincoln taking the reins. The president ignored Seward's offer to assume responsibility. Indeed it is likely that he ignored the letter itself insofar as responding to Seward. He wrote out some thoughts in the form of a reply: He was following a policy of holding the property owned by the government—as he had promised to do in the inaugural, with Seward's approval. Their only major difference was over Sumter. Lincoln paid little attention to the suggestion about a foreign adventure. He was a little annoyed with the inference that someone else might take over. Whatever policy that was adopted he would execute it, and he would continue to ask the advice of his cabinet and would handle the question of when to end the debate. But he probably never sent his response to Seward. He may have spoken directly to the secretary of state, or he might simply have let the note pass unnoticed so far as Seward was concerned. He had more important things to do than exchange memos with a colleague whom he had appointed about who was in charge.

What to do about Sumter overshadowed all other questions. North and South were watching, and doors to compromise were closing. Lincoln's two personal observers in South Carolina reported that in Charleston there was no Unionist feeling at all. S. A. Hurlbut, from South Carolina, talked to as many people as he could and reported on 27 March "Separate nationality is a fixed fact, . . . there is an unanimity of sentiment which is to my mind astonishing. . . . There is no attachment to the Union. . . . There is positively nothing to appeal to."[26]

Then General Scott unleashed a thunderbolt. He had been dubious about being able to hold Sumter, but Lincoln had instructed him to hold all forts still under Union control. Pickens was perhaps the best protected of them. Scott, however, the day after Hurlbut reported his findings, announced that both Sumter and Pickens should be abandoned. At end of the first state dinner given by the Lincolns in the White House, 28 March, the president called the cabinet members together and broke the news to them.

Lincoln must have been shaken by Scott's statement. He had relied on the general's years of experience, his great reputation, and now Scott advised retreat. The cabinet was also shocked by the prospect of another withdrawal. It was enough to be told that Sumter was unholdable; they had figured that out already, and even then some were determined to try to keep it. But when Scott said to give up Pickens their frustration mounted and then compounded after they heard his reasons. Scott was not making military judgments. He said that both forts should be yielded to "instantly soothe and give confidence to the eight remaining slaveholding states and render their cordial adherence to the Union perpetual." Yet there was reason to suspect that Scott was speaking for Seward. Their association went back years, and at least Blair believed that the general was voicing Seward's policy. Apparently this military leader was ready to back down and to follow the secretary of state's path.[27]

Whatever its origins, the cabinet rejected Scott's advice. When Lincoln asked on 29 March for their opinions, a majority favored relief for Sumter, and everyone, even Seward, said to protect Pickens. Seward agreed with Scott that Sumter was best abandoned, and Smith agreed. But Chase and Welles had joined Blair in favor of holding Sumter as well as Pickens. Bates simply said it was time to do *something*. The cabinet had swung toward action.

Lincoln may have hoped for concilation, but Blair threatened to resign. Then he called in reinforcements in the form of his father, still an influential voice in the vital border states and an adviser to Andrew Jackson in the nullification crisis. Francis Blair came to the White House and lectured Lincoln on the need for strength in the presidency, calling it "treason" to abandon Sumter. Furthermore, yielding to the South now would destroy public confidence in the administration, make secession seem constitutional, and could lead to Lincoln's impeachment. The senior Blair had summoned Old Hickory back to the White House.[28]

Lincoln now took the helm more clearly. Seward's memo of 1 April helped galvanize him, and his disillusionment with Scott further suggested the president's need to take charge. The Blairs had reminded him of the costs of retreat, of the imperative need to listen to a popular opinion that demanded an end to years of yielding to blackmail. He sent orders to get the strongest ship available, the *Powhatan*, ready to sail for Sumter. Confusion in orders, and perhaps Seward's deception, sent the ship toward Pickens, but Lincoln was in charge now. On 4 April, Lincoln wrote Anderson at Fort Sumter that he was to try to hold out until supplies reached him, possibly by the eleventh or twelfth. If those supplies were resisted the expedition would "endeavor . . . to reinforce you." Lincoln was getting ready to force the action.

The president still kept up contacts with Virginia Unionists; he believed that even now some major weakening of secessionist momentum might stay the acceleration toward war. On the same day that he wrote Anderson to be ready, at Seward's urging Lincoln met with one of the members of the Virginia state convention. Lincoln knew that Fort Sumter mattered profoundly to Virginia and that if he used force against South Carolina then Virginia might go to that slave state's side. The secession convention, with its majority opposed to immediate secession, stayed in session, watching. So the president promised that if the Virginia convention would disband he would evacuate Fort Sumter: "A state for a fort is no bad business," he mused.[29]

But no one in Virginia was willing to promise anything, and Anderson was given his instructions. Still, Lincoln kept his options open. If the Confederates permitted the resupply of Sumter there would be more time for Unionists to gain support. At the same time, the president was not offering the option of federal inaction, for even while suggesting that Sumter might be yielded he knew that the Pickens expedition was in progress. Should the Virginia Unionists be impressed with the promised retreat in Charleston Harbor they would still have to swallow the reinforcement of Pickens.[30]

But without a concession from Virginia Unionists, Lincoln was not going to give up Sumter. He had indeed promised not to "repossess" lost forts, but Fort Sumter still was in Union hands and he meant to keep it there. On 6 April Lincoln sent a message to South Carolina governor Francis Pickens that "an attempt will be made to supply Fort-Sumpter [sic] with provisions only . . . if such attempt be not resisted no effort to throw in men, arms, or ammunition will be made, without further notice, or in case of an attack upon the Fort." The supplies were on their way. Southern leaders might let the fort remain in Union hands, keeping a national presence there. It was a thin hope, but Lincoln was ready to act on it.

Serious events were unfolding, and Lincoln knew it. He conferred with the governors of Indiana, Maine, Ohio, and Pennsylvania on the same day that he alerted Governor Pickens. He ordered troops to be landed to reinforce Fort Pickens. Two days later he sent a short note to Governor Andrew Curtin of Pennsylvania: "I think the necessity of being *ready* increases. Look to it." And two days later he told Secretary of War Cameron to send Curtin a drill officer; Pennsylvania troops would be among the first to arrive in Washington after Sumter was fired upon.[31]

Lincoln's Fort Sumter policy had balanced contending options and had tried to keep as many of them alive as possible. The Republican party and its supporters—a party that had just won almost 49 percent of the popular vote in nonseceding states (1,866,000 of 3,825,000) and a huge electoral college majority—were almost unanimous in insisting that standing up to secessionist threats was imperative: otherwise, more blackmail would follow. As the party of backbone, giving in was intolerable to most of them. Senate Republicans, led by Trumbull of Illinois, had passed resolutions on 28 March: "It is the duty of the President to use all the means in his power to hold and protect the public property of the United States." Seward had initially miscalculated this sentiment, but as the crisis grew even he came to recognize its power. Lincoln had never forgotten it.[32]

Lincoln wanted to keep the support of more moderate Northerners, and especially border-state Southern Unionists, if possible, without losing more militant Northerners. Sending only supplies to the fort was the most restrained way of balancing the two forces. The implacable rebels would naturally interpret the act as aggression, but people with their minds and hearts open would see that Lincoln was not the unthinking revolutionary that his enemies described. After the first passion had passed they might still be open to discussion. Charleston would seethe and South Carolina would rage and hotheads in the Confederacy would join them. But calmer Southerners might be open to reason, especially those in Kentucky and Missouri and Maryland, perhaps even some deeper in the South.[33]

Lincoln's actions handed the decision to fire to Jefferson Davis. The rebel president, who had been claiming that his nation stood for traditional and conservative ideals, would have to calculate the cost of beginning a war. Did Lincoln expect war? Probably. His letters to his military leaders and to Northern governors suggest that he did. He had asked General Scott on 1 April to begin sending him reports on troop locations and movements throughout the country. His discussions with the cabinet seemed to assume that attempts to provision the fort would create a crisis, and he tried to send the *Powhatan*, the ship that Assistant Secretary of the Navy Gustavus Fox called "the fighting portion" of the expedition, to help with the provisioning. His firmness about Fort Pickens suggested a willingness to risk the use of force somewhere in the South. But except for surrendering the forts, and doing so not after but before negotiations, he had chosen the course least likely to alienate the Unionists in the South and in the border slave states while keeping the loyalty of Northerners. Whatever Southern Unionists might do, Northerners would certainly support their government more fervently if the Confederacy started the shooting, after having created the crisis in the first place. Indeed, newspapers in the North had speculated for weeks that Lincoln was trying to get the rebels to fire the first shot.[34]

The president later boasted that his 1861 strategy had worked: "The cause of the country would be advanced by making the attempt to provision Fort Sumpter even if it should fail . . . our anticipation is justified by the result." His plan of "send[ing] bread to Anderson" and of notifying the governor of South Carolina that only bread would be sent put into Confederate hands the choice he had once posed: "Shall it be peace, or a sword?" "The plan succeeded," he told Senator Browning; "they attacked Sumter—it fell, and thus did more service than it otherwise could."[35]

But if he expected war, Lincoln did not expect the Civil War. He did not know, nobody knew, that war would mean four years of bloodshed, 620,000 dead, another 500,000 wounded, 30,000 amputes, billions of dollars of lost property, wives and children and parents and siblings and friends shattered by grief. No one knew, either, although some hoped and millions prayed for it, that slavery would die, not a gradual death over decades but a comparatively swift death, executed by the terrible swords and guns of white and black men. What everyone knew was that constitutional government was at stake and it was time for action to save it.

4
★★★★★

CONGRESS ORGANIZES, LINCOLN ACTS:
APRIL TO DECEMBER 1861

With the surrender of Fort Sumter only five days in the past, the violence was escalating. Three days after Sumter, a small unit from Pennsylvania had had stones thrown at them; now, the Sixth Massachusetts Regiment was trying to get through Baltimore, and the crowd was growing every minute. Men carrying Confederate flags in one hand had rocks in the other, and the rocks were flying—then the large paving stones from the streets. Young soldiers, hardly remembering their training, the din from the crowd growing, were frightened. Inevitably someone fired a shot, then others, and by the time the day was over four soldiers and twelve of the mob were dead; thirty-one people had been wounded. At Sumter the only death had come by accident, when a soldier fired a final salute to the flag after the surrender. But here was bloodshed between soldiers rushing to save the Union and those who sought to divide it. Civil War was an hour away from the capital and moving closer every minute.[1]

The guns at Sumter, the riot in Baltimore, confirmed Lincoln's determination to preserve the nation's political-constitutional system. Presidential elections would be settled in polling places, by voters and the electors they chose. Threats to destroy the process by secession and armed blackmail would meet a resolve that balanced respect for Southern fears with a determination not to allow that fear to uproot the processes of peaceful change toward equal liberty. Lincoln would not abandon the decision by voters that slavery expansion had gone far enough, nor would he give up their right to choose that result in a process that had abided for over fourscore years and eighteen presidential elections.

When war began these general questions about the operation of the polity as a whole were replaced with more specific ones: What processes could be used to stop secession? What means were available to stop men who attacked the government? As commander in chief, having taken "the most solemn oath" to "preserve, protect and defend the Constitution of the United States," Lincoln looked for the weapons that the Constitution gave him to uphold his promise.

"In your hands and not mine rests the momentous issue of civil war," Lincoln had said in the First Inaugural Address. But once war came conditions changed and the president stepped forward. He had acted deliberately, carefully before the gunfire at Sumter began to keep the guns from firing. But once they fired he acted more boldly. On 15 April he declared the existence of a rebellion and called up 75,000 members of state militias into national service. Four days later the president announced a blockade of the ports of the seven Deep South states. He also called an emergency session of Congress, but, clearing a wide space for executive initiative, he set the date for congressmen to return over two-and-a-half months away—4 July 1861. For almost its first three months the Civil War was the president's war.[2]

His swift actions did not fully unleash war since he called a limited number of men. He knew he could get thousands more—Northern governors complained that they had ten times the number he asked for. Horace Greeley thought that 75,000 would march out of New York City alone. Lincoln called men not just from Northern states, however, but also from Southern states; he announced that "the utmost care will be observed, consistently with the objects [of repossessing places and property seized from the United States] . . . to avoid any devastation, any destruction of, of interference with property, or any disturbance of peaceful citizens in any part of the country." It was a measured response, testing for pro-Union sentiment that he continued to look for in the South, even in the early days of the war, ever conscious of those people who might be lured back into the Union.[3]

The early restraint gave way as the crisis escalated. The railroad line between Washington and Philadelphia was the fastest and most crucial path for transporting troops and supplies to the capital. Meanwhile, Maryland was alive with prosecession plots and protests, and Baltimore's loyalty remained in doubt. After the 19 April riots, outraged and frightened leaders of the city ordered the destruction of telegraph lines and bridges leading into the city. Rumors flourished that the Maryland legislature would arm the state to fight against the Union, and independently, some Marylanders organized local militia to fight for the Confederacy. Clearly something had to be done. Lincoln responded by suspending the privilege of the writ of habeas corpus between Philadelphia and Washington, D.C. Military authority replaced civilian courts and peacetime procedures there in meting out justice.[4]

Things continued to come apart. Just two days before the Baltimore riot, Virginia, the most crucial of the upper South states, seceded. Meanwhile, Southern governors responded to Lincoln's call for militia with scorn and defiance. He quickly recognized the need for more vigorous moves, moves that took him into constitutional terrain that no president had seen before. The Whig attitude toward the presidency, born of the attack on Jackson as "King Andrew," faded so rapidly that within weeks Lincoln was being called a dictator and his government a despotism.

With Congress away from Washington Lincoln reached for power wherever he could find it. He had the lawful authority to call up the militia, a 1795 law used by George Washington gave him that. But then he took a leap, claiming powers that the Constitution gave to Congress. His blockade proclamation implied a declaration of war that only Congress could provide, a minor misstep since nations can close their own ports and the flaw here arose from his use of the word "blockade." But other actions were clearly constitutional innovations. As May began he closed the mails to "disloyal" publications; he told generals to begin raising new armies; he paid $2 million out of the treasury to private citizens in New York to expedite recruiting; he pledged government credit for $250,000 million. He had no authority to do these things; Congress clearly did.[5]

Less clear but more immediately important was the meaning of the Constitution's statement, "The privilege of the writ of habeas corpus shall not be suspended unless when in cases of rebellion or invasion the public safety may require it." Lincoln's other actions, the blockade, the raising of men and money for the army and navy, unfolded gradually, and portended great changes but were so general in their impact that they lacked personal drama. The suspension of the writ raised in immediate and personal terms the fundamental question of the power of the commander in chief to control the liberties of a people so suspicious of national power that civil war had broken out. The writ had traditionally been used by judges to protect citizens from unlawful or arbitrary arrest. Why should such protection be abandoned now? The president had some serious explaining to do as he ventured into this new and poorly mapped ground.[6]

Experience provided frail guidance. For decades Americans had lived under the weakest government in the world. The ideology of states' rights, indeed state sovereignty, was dominant in the prewar years, and national authority had waned. Thomas Carlyle spoke of the United States as "the most favored of all lands that have no government."[7] State involvement in everyday life was limited to encouraging more private action, whether that meant economic development or removing inhibitions on growth. Only slaves, criminals, and Native Americans felt the power of governmental authority. Some states stifled opinions that threatened public morality, but in politics Americans spoke loud, often, and, as the highly politicized newspapers of the period demonstrated, with very little restraint.

The vast general liberty of most white Americans generated few reasons to define specific freedom under habeas corpus. The writ at the Civil War's beginning had a minuscule history. There were few federal crimes and hence few occasions to use it in federal courts; state judges, often elected, used the writ infrequently. When it was discussed most Americans probably recalled the outcry of abolitionists when fugitive slave laws denied alleged runaways access to it. A few lawyers and historians might have remembered British tradition, which established habeas corpus to protect citizens from the monarchy, but average citizens throughout the nation had no such memories. So far as they were concerned Lincoln's suspension was an unusual and unprecedented outreach of federal executive power.[8]

Action was imperative, however, as Baltimore demonstrated. Throughout the nation the possibility for similar disloyalty was woven into demography and politics. Here again the corrupting hand of slavery was ever present. In border states in particular but also throughout the North, who was loyal to the Union? People had migrated from slave states to free and vice-versa, leaving family and friends behind. They shared attitudes about and experiences with slavery, held them deeply, though living in different parts of the country. Would anything counterbalance them? Political loyalty linked Democrats North and South through racism, antipower rhetoric, and memories of anti-Republican struggles. Which Democrats would take that linkage to extremes? In the midst of a civil war, government needed to act when such questions threatened.

And who determined whom to watch, warn, jail? Every community had its watchdogs, some of whom were even constables and sheriffs. But should state authorities, national authorities, decide who were the public's enemies? Should state courts, which had for decades handled these matters, be allowed to act? Wasn't it time for national power to be asserted since state prerogatives were so often the source of arguments for disunion? Since no one had ever been to civil war before answers came from imagination, not experience.[9]

At the national level, Lincoln spoke the final word: Civilian justice and due process had ended where the writ was suspended; national power ruled. But it was unclear which executive department would assume control or what "control" would mean. The War Department was overwhelmed with its task of gathering supplies, weapons, horses, mules, and men. Simon Cameron was hard-pressed to handle his own affairs, and Lincoln distrusted him. Chase's Treasury had a growing number of field agents, and Chase had the energy and ambition to reach out into internal security operations. But Seward was faster and had more of Lincoln's respect than did the others; thus the secretary of state became the hub of early internal security actions. He set up a special bureau in his department with three clerks assigned to handle the filing and recording of internal security activities.[10]

Using federal marshals and attorneys and judges, employing postmasters as informants and spies, Seward began to gather information. Once it was known he was interested he attracted grievances and warnings from crackpots as well as from serious citizens. Seward was sent "disloyal" poems, "disloyal" songs: "Maryland in Chains," "The Banner of the South," "What Flag Shall We Wave?", and "The Times," described as a "splendid production but of highly treasonable caste." Other "poetry" was less "splendid." The endless, mind-numbing verses of "The Wagon" began, "And so our southern sisters / Are sitting side by side / In the new secession wagon / To take a glorious ride."[11]

Men and women with Southern connections were spotted rather quickly, usually by interdicting their mail. Policemen and postmasters opened letters with Southern addresses and sent suspect material to Seward. Some letters clearly revealed treason. N. B. Means received a letter from Baltimore from Tucker Smith asking for as much Maryland money as Means could obtain and announcing that "we are preparing upon the most extensive scale to resist the northern fanatics when they again visit our city." Smith wrote other letters asking about buying guns and referring to "cheerfully and willingly" joining the rebel army in its "hour of need." Means was sent to Fort Lafayette, the usual place for persons of suspect fealty, but he was allowed to sign an oath of loyalty in late March 1862 and was released.[12]

Other individuals were not treated so well. Bethel Burton was arranging to sell guns to rebels when arrested on 12 September 1861; he stayed in jail for most of the war. Richard Freeman was in New York City when the war began and was caught trying to buy machinery to ship to the South. Parker French, alias Carlisle Murray, alias Charles

Mascyn, trying to buy ships for the same purpose, was also caught. French admitted that his behavior looked suspicious but claimed that because his reputation was already so bad "unfavorable constructions were put upon all his acts." Felix Wyatt also stayed in jail after his arrest in September for selling ammunition and telegraph wire to the rebels.[13]

There was not much pattern to such imprisonments. Robert Walker was charged with sending guns to the South but was released after taking an oath of loyalty in October. So was William McKernan, who was accused of gathering troops for the rebel army. Robert More was caught in New York City with dispatches to Europe seeking support for the Confederacy but was released on his oath in October also.

Men with important friends were treated better than those without them; friends could attest to the loyalty of suspects and get them out of jail. Maurice Mayer, "Jewish lawyer said to be disloyal," in Seward's words, had relatives in Natchez to whom he wrote that he was neutral in the presence of Unionists, but among "those he could trust he does what he can to strengthen the hands of the Confederates," as the police report noted. New York police chief, J. P. Kennedy, a vigorous prosecutor of suspected rebels, arrested Mayer on 19 November 1861. But when his friends, including Mayor George Opdyke, petitioned Seward, vouching for Mayer, he was released with the explanation from Kennedy that his letters to his Southern relatives were probably designed to appease his family. This did not keep his wife, Rachel, from being arrested when she returned from a visit to Canada allegedly bearing secession dispatches. Yet she was released within two weeks. Still, Mayer was required to request permission to correspond with Southern relatives, and only family matters could be discussed.[14]

Newspapers were targets for strict surveillance. Large New York papers such as the *Journal of Commerce* and the *Brooklyn Eagle* were closed for a time, but even a small weekly in upstate New York felt the reach of Seward's long arm. When the *Franklin County Gazette* announced that the war was wrong, that it threatened American liberties, cost too much treasure, was gotten up by fanatics to make Republicans rich, its editor Francis Flanders felt the force of federal power. Marshals confiscated his private correspondence, Flanders was thrown in jail, and the paper was expelled from the mails, cutting into circulation and income drastically. When Mrs. Flanders kept on publishing, she came close to jail herself. Still, knowing important people continued to help. Mrs. Flanders contacted Governor Edwin Morgan, who wrote to Lincoln as preparatory to a visit by Mrs. Flanders and her sister-in-law to the president. After that visit, Flanders was released from jail although the paper was not allowed in the mail.[15]

The security system caught major public figures, too. The members of the Maryland legislature who tried to take that crucial state out of the Union were arrested, then released on parole from time to time. Some of them, though not all, were permanently released after taking an oath of allegiance. At least one of the leaders of the movement, S. Teakle Wallis, was still in jail on 15 February 1862 when the War Department took over the security program, even though Maryland was securely in Union hands by then.

Cranky generals could push the program to extremes. When attorney Dennis Foley served a writ of habeas corpus on General Porter, Foley was arrested for "attempting to embarrass the military authorities . . . by serving an illegal writ." This farce was quickly undone and Foley released. But the point had been made: The generals were watching; they might act arbitrarily or responsibly; and they would define which was which, subject to later review by their commander in chief.

But especially at the beginning of the war the administration was not fully in control, even in the suppression of opposition. Seward's early activities were essentially reactive; he and his three clerks spent much of their time trying to find out what some local Dogberry had done to suppress opposition. Given the increasing duties of the executive branch many minor matters slipped by unnoticed. Civilians in areas where the war was not raging frequently persuaded local authorities to put dissenters in jail. Seward often let them stay there—and Lincoln did not object.[16]

Some guidelines about civil liberties were needed in this chaotic situation—if only to persuade the people that the government was being steered by a hand stronger than partisan caprice. Lincoln insisted that the war was being fought to uphold constitutional authority, but he had to argue the point, not just announce it. John Merryman's case provided the forum.

Merryman, an officer in the Maryland militia, was using his position to recruit and train Confederate sympathizers. Part of their training included burning the bridges and cutting the telegraph lines between Washington and the North in the aftermath of the Baltimore riot. At two in the morning on 25 May 1861 Merryman was arrested at his home and confined in Fort McHenry by Gen. George Cadwalader, acting under Lincoln's suspension order of April. Merryman was only one of hundreds who had been arrested for similar activity, but his fate would determine the process of military supervision of loyalty and provide a justification for the outreach of federal power.

Merryman's case came under intense and widespread public scrutiny; Roger Taney saw to that. The chief justice picked a public fight with the president on the whole question of suspension. Taney, still formidable at eighty-three, raised the issue of whether the military was free to arrest suspicious Marylanders without asking permission of local judges.

Acting in his role as chief judge of the circuit court in Baltimore Taney made a special trip to take Merryman's case. The town still echoed with the recent clash between soldiers and pro-Southern mobs as Taney issued a writ of habeas corpus to General Cadwalader at the fort, telling him to bring the prisoner into the judge's court for a hearing. Word went out that Taney was challenging the president; perhaps federal authority would back away from the nation's premier jurist if not from the protests of Baltimore citizens. But Cadwalader refused to deliver Merryman. By the time that the court's marshal told Taney of the general's response, a crowd of nearly two thousand people had gathered to watch Taney's reaction. Taney played to the crowd by receiving the marshal on the steps of the courthouse, and, after announcing that the general had defied the law, the judge turned toward his courtroom and remarked that even he, the chief justice himself, might be arrested soon.

It was grand drama, but Taney was not in danger. Indeed he wrote a blistering lecture to the president and the American people warning that Lincoln's action threatened despotism: "The people of the United States are no longer under a government of laws; but every citizen holds life, liberty and property at the will and pleasure of the army officer in whose military district he may happen to be found."[17]

At the root of Taney's argument were two questions: Could the president, rather than Congress, suspend the writ, and could a judge stop the president from deciding to act on his own? Taney insisted that only Congress could suspend. Looking everywhere but at the reality around him, the judge summoned precedent, syllogism, textual analysis of the Constitution. He gave no reason for his argument that legislators were preferable to presidents as suspenders; he did not discuss their closeness to popular opinion, their greater opportunity for discussion, debate, or compromise. He did not even reason that since Congress has the authority to declare war it ought also to have the power over wartime limitations of liberty. Angry that his beloved Maryland was filled with growing numbers of Union troops, anti-Republican to his marrow, on record openly with proslavery constitutional opinions, Taney looked into books and precedents written in times of peace to proclaim the limits on a president in times of war—the judge even denied that conditions in Maryland were disruptive enough to require military involvement. And he insisted that unless Congress had suspended the writ the president had to await a call to action from the courts before he could perform any act suppressing the rebellion. The chief executive could act only when a court told him that someone had disobeyed a court order.[18]

Taney was trying to extend recent constitutional history—a time when the president had let judges control the meaning of fundamental law. He remembered that Buchanan had told the nation that Dred Scott's case would define the place of slavery in the territories and the status of black people in America. Lincoln answered that the president could define the meaning of the Constitution and that the people themselves, in electing the president, also made constitutional law. There was too much at stake to leave the meaning of the Constitution and the polity it helped define to nine justices. After the Civil War the Supreme Court would become the final authority on fundamental law. But at the beginning of that war Lincoln held to an older view—the Constitution was too important to be left to judges, especially judges who tried to spread slavery even as they paralyzed the authority of the president to preserve the Constitution's Union.[19]

Lincoln took Taney's challenge seriously, demonstrating his belief that the war involved preserving the law and the Union. His Fourth of July address to the reassembled Congress consisted almost a third of constitutional argument. He answered Taney by looking up from the text and showing that the Constitution was adequate in war as well as in peace. Major legal thinkers of the age supported him, including the professor of constitutional law at Harvard, the leading constitutional lawyer in Congress, and leaders of the American bar. At times Lincoln would stretch his powers beyond constitutional limits, but not in this instance.[20]

Taney had claimed that Lincoln violated his oath that "the laws be faithfully executed" because he had stolen congressional authority over the writ. But Lincoln asked lawmakers and the nation to consider the reality they faced as a test of that oath: "The whole of the laws which were required to be faithfully executed were being resisted . . . in nearly one third of the states." Would he have broken his oath if he had allowed one law to stand in the way of enforcing the others? He denied breaking even one law. The Constitution did not specify which branch could suspend the writ; it did maintain that in cases of rebellion suspension was authorized. Lincoln had faced that emergency. Was it plausible that the Founders intended that he should stand by as the danger ran its course, waiting for Congress to gather? Clearly if forces favoring rebellion triumphed Congress might never gather at all.[21]

Though slightly disingenuous, Lincoln's argument reflected realities. Some response to the disruptions near Washington was necessary;

Maryland's loyalty was suspect. It was unclear whether the state's legislature would bark secession louder than it would bite and whether it wanted neutrality or Confederate allegiance. The prospect of appealing to Maryland courts to legitimize the arrest of Maryland citizens promised at least long delays while secession gathered strength. Lincoln's position gave the national government a mandate to act; it showed the Constitution to be an instrument for action, not paralysis. Moreover, it provided justification for gathering most questions of loyalty under one umbrella, thereby regularizing restrictions on liberty. Lincoln's defense weakened the force of the opposition's accusations that Union supporters were motivated by partisanship rather than by the Constitution they claimed to be defending. It demonstrated that the government could legally fight a war for survival.[22]

Sometimes the demonstration involved chicanery. On one occasion, in Minnesota, Seward managed to sustain the image of due process while keeping the suspect in custody. Justice James Wayne had issued a writ to the secretary of state on a soldier's claim that Lincoln could not call for volunteers without a congressional act. Seward responded that he would comply only if he was assured that the justice would rule for the government. Wayne let him know that he would; Seward then complied with the writ, and Wayne kept his promise.[23]

More often the government broadcast its influence in bold language. Seward, then Stanton, when the War Department took over military arrests, both declared allegedly that they could "ring a little bell" and have anyone in the nation arrested. Throughout the war Lincoln's rhetoric was threatening, subduing dissent when the nation seemed in peril. But in practice the Union government exercised remarkable restraint. Few orators or editors were arrested for their attacks on Lincoln. The most notorious case, that of Clement Vallandigham, did not occur until May 1863 and was a rarity. The authorities arrested suspects and then released them after they took an oath of future loyalty, a practice that served two purposes. It warned protestors about the consequences of going too far, and it let the government avoid the political hazards of trials in which antiwar judges might repeat Taney's performance. As Seward told Police Chief Kennedy, a few arrests would "produce a proper effect." Although local authorities did threaten and jail large numbers of "wrong thinking" people, the national government's record refutes accusations that Lincoln was "a dictator."[24]

Even in places where the government and its soldiers faced dangers far greater than mere words, the rule of law soon prevailed. When war broke out Lincoln and Seward were too busy with eastern problems to guide western warmakers. In the bloody and often chaotic bear pit of

Missouri, Union generals, such as Ulysses S. Grant and his commander at the time, John Fremont, on their own authority closed down newspapers and arrested the suspicious. "I am entirely without orders for my guidance," Grant announced. By September 1861, however, military commissions were established to handle disloyalty.

The dissent these commissions confronted almost always went far beyond critical speeches or editorials. Union soldiers and supporters faced men with weapons, not speeches, in their hands; barns, crops, livestock, and bridges were being destroyed. Civilians were murdered frequently and soldiers' lives were often in danger. Yet even in such terrorized areas concern for legal restraint existed. When the military courts tried guerrillas or rebel soldiers (part of the problem was determining their roles), regular procedures were followed: Witnesses were required to confront the accused, who was allowed counsel (although these lawyers could not address the commission), and sentences were reviewed by department commanders. The president himself reviewed all death sentences. About 15 percent of the accused in Missouri were acquitted, others had their sentences reduced, some pleaded guilty to lesser charges and thereby were allowed to escape the death penalty. It was a severe form of legal proceeding but not an arbitrary one. With the arbitrary arrests by frightened volunteers and the random, uncontrollable violence in the state, Missouri was, in Mark Neely's words, "a nightmare for American civil liberties." Still, there would be other cases in the nation's history—for example, the imprisonment of over 120,000 Japanese Americans during World War II—in which civil liberties would be more thoroughly and arbitrarily restricted by the national government.[25]

Lincoln's defense against Taney's charge of dictatorship told his subordinates in the military as well as his commanders among the populace that law would rule this conflict. The "frictions of war" and the limited reach of federal power meant that the law would not rule absolutely, but it would be the standard to guide the saving of the government from the anarchy of secession and the havoc of war.

The president's argument was disingenuous in that Congress was not in session because he kept it at home. Except for an unlikely order from courts in the area, the executive was the only branch of government available to act. If the argument for executive suspension rested on the need for action, then Lincoln had stacked the deck. Yet action was imperative, and the Constitution did not stand in the way of the president acting to save the union. Clearly, as one of Lincoln's able defenders said, if Taney's views prevailed, then "judicial power may be . . . quite . . . effectual to overthrow the government in time of war." Lincoln had shown why rulers that the people had elected should trump appointed judicial obstructionists.[26]

Thus the opening days of the Civil War brought a new and unprecedented strength to the presidency, largely because the war itself was unprecedented, unparalleled in American history. Moreover, the executive gained power because only executive action was possible between the fall of Fort Sumter and 4 July. Still, Lincoln's expansion of power was not above the law. War demanded new authority, and Lincoln ensured that it would be constitutional authority. Furthermore, he would not exercise authority alone. This became clear when Congress returned, ready to act.

Much of their readiness came from the fact that congressmen, like the president, lived literally in the midst of war. Soldiers streamed to the capital, first to save it from threats that came from Maryland and Virginia, then because the city became a collection point for the Army of the Potomac and other eastern armies. Trains arrived with soldiers each week, at least, coming late at night as well as during the day, awakening sleeping citizens, catching their ears as they worked. Military bands serenaded troops at night, woke them up for reveille in the morning, and between times helped teach precision drill. The streets saw constant parades and the even more frequent lounging about of soldiers off duty. Hotel lobbies and bars brought soldiers and legislators together to drink and talk. The lower levels of the capitol building itself served as a billet for some troops in the first days of the conflict, the smoke from an army bakery below wafting up into the Senate chamber. More profoundly meaningful was the fact that many of these soldiers were not strangers; they were the sons and nephews and brothers of congressmen. Thus there were many reasons for legislators to act and to be sympathetic to the action the president had taken in their absence.[27]

Gathering Congress on the symbolic Fourth of July, Lincoln explained that "public necessity" and "popular demand" had called forth his action. In the absence of Congress and with rebellion a reality, it hardly seemed likely that the Framers would have opposed action to save the republic. He further explained that he had done "nothing beyond the constitutional competency" of Congress, and he therefore expected that the legislature would later ratify his actions. It was, as Herman Belz notes, "a new and remarkable doctrine" that the president could use powers that the Constitution gave to Congress and then expect congressmen to *later* ratify executive action.[28]

Still, Lincoln was asking Congress to validate what he had done; he did not claim authority to act arbitrarily in cases where the Constitution spoke delphically. His request for congressional endorsement offered to share authority, to involve both branches of government in meeting the crisis. Lincoln wanted a constitutional process in dialogue, not in conflict.

In instances where the Constitution clearly granted authority Lincoln grasped it boldly and to its limits. He was commander in chief of the armed forces and involved himself actively in matters of strategy. He helped establish rules for governing the army, determined the nature of restored governments in reconquered territory, and his actions against slavery had significant meaning for the soldiers as well as for the slaves. Resting his power on the oath of office and the obligation to "take care that the Laws be faithfully executed," Lincoln claimed "war power" authority to use his office to the limits and to do whatever might reasonably be implied from his oath to "preserve, protect and defend the Constitution of the United States" and the Union it established. As Attorney General Bates pointed out in justifying the suspension of the writ, the president had the means to execute the ends that the Constitution set forth, and "he is . . . thrown upon his discretion as to the manner in which he will use his means to meet the varying exigencies as they arise."[29]

The Supreme Court agreed with this general principle. In the *Prize Cases* (1863) the justices were asked to decide if Lincoln's actions, taken before Congress met and declared war, were constitutional. The specific events of these cases focused on the legality of the blockade, but the principle that the Court announced, in a five-to-four decision, had a wider application. Although the president could not initiate a war, when it was thrust upon him he had the duty to respond without waiting for Congress to act: "Whether the President in fulfilling his duties, as Commander in Chief, in suppressing an insurrection, has met with such armed hostile resistance, and a civil war . . . is a question to be decided by him. . . . This court must be governed by the decisions and acts of the Political Department of the government." Throughout the war the Court supported Lincoln's warmaking.[30]

But certain aspects of the conflict required congressional action, and legislators reclaimed authority that Lincoln had temporarily assumed. Congress ratified most of the president's acts taken between 15 April and 4 July. On 3 July, the third day of the special session, the Senate began discussing a joint resolution that recited Lincoln's actions—calling the militia, blockading Southern ports, calling for volunteers, increasing the army and navy, suspending the writ—and declared them lawful.

Almost all Republicans supported this resolution in principle, but they had different views on validation, especially on the matter of the habeas corpus writ and the blockade. Action on those issues was set aside for the moment. Unwilling to divide themselves over the means of responding to the rebellion when the response itself was what mattered, Congress debated and passed laws that raised up to 500,000 three-year troops, gave Lincoln power to close ports by proclamation, authorized the increase in men and ships for the navy, endorsed the issuance of hundreds of millions in federal bonds, levied a direct tax on the states and territories of $20 million, increased the tariff, and passed an income tax. Finally on 5 August, the day before adjournment, they returned to the authorization issue. With only five Democrats voting no, Congress declared that "all the acts, proclamations and orders of the President . . . [after 4 March 1861] respecting the army and navy of the United States, and calling out or relating to the militia or volunteers from the States, are hereby approved and in all respects legalized and made valid . . . as if they had been issued and done under the previous express authority and direction of the Congress of the United States."[31]

With one omission Congress had endorsed Lincoln's emergency actions. It did so in the greatest crisis in this nation's history—a war on American soil, directly threatening the electoral process, the constitutional system, and the loss of almost half the nation's territory with its resources and the major entry ports of the entire Middle West. It is hardly surprising that Congress said yes; that body has said yes with far less provocation.

The one omission concerned the suspension of the writ of habeas corpus. Here was an act that clearly reflected the difference in the nation's experience with foreign and domestic war. Congress had agreed to Lincoln's warmaking—his marshaling of the men and materials of war, his power to kill the nation's enemies. Yet they refused to endorse his authority to jail those enemies. Accounting for the irony was the contrast between the clear dangers of Confederate soldiers shooting at Union officials and the ambiguous and more covert dangers of civilian opponents attacking with words and less obvious weapons. Still, Congress did nothing to stop Lincoln from carrying out his plan. Politics was important here: Americans were sensitive about their liberties; better to stay quiet on the subject and let Lincoln take the heat. Most important, however, their inaction showed that congressmen agreed with Lincoln. They were willing to let him do whatever it was that the Constitution allowed him to do.

Constitutional limitations still concerned them, largely because those limits had strategic importance. Crucial border states, especially Kentucky, held conservative views on the reach of national power. So did much of the Middle West below the fortieth parallel, settled as it was from the upper South. Racist, proslavery, and states'-rights opinions cohabited easily there, and Kentucky was the fulcrum for Union strength in these early days of war. The Bluegrass State was the third most populous slave state, home to thousands of potential soldiers. It was a strategic linchpin, with two major rivers pointing deep into the South and its east-west span potentially shielding almost half the Confederacy. Moreover, the state's leaders were divided over secession. "To lose Kentucky is nearly the same as to lose the whole game. Kentucky gone, we can not hold Missouri, nor . . . Maryland," Lincoln observed. To reassure this delicate region, Congress on 19 July welcomed a resolution from two border-state lawmakers, Tennessee's Andrew Johnson and Kentucky's John J. Crittenden, that "this war is not waged, upon our part, in any spirit of oppression, nor for any purpose of conquest or subjugation, nor purpose of overthrowing or interfering with the rights or established institutions of these States."[32] Then the legislators left to watch the great spectacle unfolding near Bull Run.

Preparations that both sides had been making culminated there in the greatest battle in the nation's history to that time. On 21 July while congressmen and their wives and journalists from several countries watched on nearby hillsides Confederate and Union armies met. Both sides had predicted victory, and at various times in the battle both sides might have claimed it. But ultimately rebel troops gained the day at a cost of over 2,900 Union and over 1,750 Confederate casualties.

As Union soldiers staggered back toward Washington, congressmen, appalled by the defeat, felt even more certain that it was time to close ranks and secure southern flanks. Within three days both houses passed the Crittenden-Johnson resolution by overwhelming majorities. Conservative fears that war meant social revolution could be relieved and increased efforts toward victory planned.

Even as they reassured conservatives, congressmen set in motion potential changes in the society they were trying to save. Some measures were seemingly neutral. Congress provided money for the army and the navy by authorizing Secretary of the Treasury Chase to sell $250 million in treasury notes at interest rates of 7 percent. It passed a direct tax of $20 million on states and territories, increased tariff duties, and, almost as an afterthought, passed the first national income tax in the nation's history. These laws increased the power of the national government by providing resources necessary to save the Union. Indirectly, quietly but inexorably, Washington was gaining power.

But transformations sounded less neutral when slavery was mentioned, and congressmen knew it. As with so many issues during the war, the battlefield initiated changes that lawmakers sought to organize.

Slavery, so clearly and profoundly the issue dividing the nation before Sumter, was an abstraction to most Northerners—its impact enormous but at most secondhand; few Northern civilians had ever seen a slave. Soldiers moving into the South saw them everywhere, however, and knew that slavery was a source of enemy strength. How to weaken the rebellion and still respect a Constitution and a Union that recognized slavery was a major conundrum until Gen. Ben Butler offered an answer: Slaves were "contraband of war" and could be confiscated according to the laws of war. The administration let Butler's answer stand, and by July almost one thousand "contrabands" were within the lines at Fortress Monroe in Virginia. Meanwhile, Butler pushed his superiors in the War Department for more clarification and also sent his letter to the newspapers. Pressures against slavery were mounting.

Congressional Republicans saw Butler's logic. They offered a bill in the emergency session that freed any slaves used directly by their masters to help the rebellion. The bill clung to legal traditions by requiring a judicial hearing on whether the master's "property" had been so used. But this respect for precedents did not comfort Democrats or a few border Republicans. They had supported the other wartime measures, but now they turned away, cracking the early bipartisan consensus, revealing divisions in the polity at large, divisions that would continue throughout the conflict as war changed federal-state relations. But by majorities of 24 to 11 in the Senate and 61 to 48 in the House the First Confiscation Act passed, and Lincoln signed it. Then, its emergency session over, Congress adjourned on 6 August 1861 and turned the government and the war over to the president for another four months, until 2 December.[33]

There were many tasks to keep him busy, the major one being to reorganize the army. Great expectations of Union victory at Bull Run had turned to great dejection. The panic of some units on the battlefield was matched with panic in the administration. The day after the battle Lincoln replaced Irwin McDowell, who had said his troops were not ready to fight (General Scott had agreed), with a man who could presumably bring the expected success. The president also asked for 500,000 more men for the new leader to command.

The most obvious candidate for leadership was George McClellan, a brilliantly prepared young general of the Department of the Ohio who had won some battles in West Virginia and then advertised his victories. Judging by his prewar career he seemed eminently qualified to lead. He had graduated second in his class at West Point in 1846 and served ably in the Mexican War, gained further respect in military circles after his report on military tactics in the Crimean War, and then had resigned his commission to take over as president of the Mississippi and Ohio Railroad. He thus combined military training with experience in administering the central element in the economy of a burgeoning modern nation. Gen. William Sherman called him "a naturally superior man," and George McClellan was inclined to agree with that. When Lincoln asked him if he was ready to assume the great task of commanding the Union armies as well as directing the Army of the Potomac (the name he had chosen for his new command), the thirty-four-year-old general said, "I can do it all."

He was almost right. He was an excellent choice to mobilize the resources that had begun to pour into the army. He was equally competent when it came to organizing and energizing an army that would have to fight a war vastly larger than any it had ever seen. Even more impressive, McClellan took over the army with his duties undefined; the job of general in chief would be what he made it. His ideal envisioned Cameron's War Department providing the men, supplies, and transportation while he made the military decisions.[34]

Decisions needed to be made to ready the army for the rapidly expanding war. The existing structure gave power to the heads of the army's seven bureaus, which reported directly to the secretary of war and not to the general in chief. McClellan was careful to nurture his relationship with these men. Though the lines on the chart still showed them reporting to the civilian chief, McClellan put himself in the loop of information and discussion. Most important, he began to gather data from commanders in the field, ordering them to "report at least once each day by telegram, & by letter" information about their troop numbers, condition, and position and the strength of any enemy they faced. He appointed Henry Halleck and Don Carlos Buell, men whom he knew to be careful and well-organized, to important commands in the West where reports of confusion and graft were beginning to appear. McClellan was pulling the reins into his hands, moving around civilian control, by-passing Cameron, who was so busy that he did not object.

Meanwhile, in two other places events were mastering the men charged with controlling them. First, in the War Department corruption and general chaos ruled. Faced with a task of stunning proportions—organizing and equipping hundreds of thousands of soldiers in a few months, if not weeks, Cameron showed the dangers inherent in appointing war secretaries for their political connections. He did nothing to bring under control the hundreds of private recruiting efforts that were competing with state efforts. He let huge contracts for military supplies to men of little experience and dubious honesty. His contacts with commanders of the army's several departments were irregular and unsatisfactory. Cameron was trying to do a job that would have tested anyone's best efforts, but he let the task master him, guided by past procedures and institutions and abetted by his personal experience as a spoilsman, not as an administrator. His incompetence in this most crucial of wartime offices suggests how little Lincoln was thinking of war during the secession winter.[35]

Second, General Fremont was out of control in the Department of the West. Conditions in Missouri were far from stable, with divided loyalties and a tradition of guerrilla fighting stemming from the Kansas-Nebraska days. The state was a sea of raids and counterraids, reprisals, robberies, murders, skirmishes, and brutality that would continue throughout the war and into Reconstruction.[36]

Adding to Fremont's difficulties was the administration's focus on the eastern theater, where the majority of supplies were being sent, thereby starving western commands. Lincoln had reportedly told Fremont that he had carte blanche but the president gave him little else. Surrounded by the chaos of Missouri and unable to get the resources he needed, Fremont grabbed frantically for any hold he could find. He let contracts for supplies to friends and incompetents who overcharged the government and provided guns that would not fire, horses that could not be ridden, clothing that fell apart, and boats that sank. A subsequent congressional report found "the most stupendous contracts, involving an almost unprecedented waste of public money, were given out by [Fremont] in person to favorites, over the heads of the competent and honest officials appointed by law." Furthermore, Fremont lived in a mansion that the government paid $6,000 a year for, surrounded himself with aides who often kept important eastern visitors from seeing him, and topped off his mismanagement by throwing Frank Blair, the brother of the postmaster general, in jail for insubordination. Fremont reminded Lincoln of "Jim Jett's brother," the president later told Hay: "Jim used to say that his brother was the damndest scoundrel that ever lived, but in the infinite mercy of Providence he was also the damndest fool."[37]

The military situation pushed Fremont toward disaster. A spirited battle at Wilson's Creek in southwest Missouri on 10 August 1861 had resulted in a Union defeat, the death of Union Brig. Gen. Nathaniel Lyon, and charges that Fremont had been derelict in reinforcing Lyon. In the aftermath of that battle Fremont determined to be a leader in making the rules of war at a time when Lincoln was carefully setting a course that kept to conservative pathways. The general declared martial law in St. Louis, two weeks later proclaimed martial law throughout the state, and then announced that unauthorized men caught with guns in their hands in places under Union control would be tried by military court and shot "if found guilty" (of what was not clear). Most crucially Fremont declared that the property of rebels was "confiscated to the public use and their slaves . . . are hereby declared freemen." Here was carte blanche with a vengeance.[38]

Kentucky teetered toward the South. The careful, ongoing ballet in which Union and Confederate generals and civilian leaders tried to pull Kentucky into their ranks threatened to end. The Confederate Congress had set up recruiting offices in Kentucky and voted $1 million to help its inhabitants "in repelling any invasion or occupation of their soil." At the same time Kentucky Union recruits had a camp within thirty miles of Lexington. The state legislature, composed mostly of Unionists, still preferred neutrality but would tip in favor of whichever side promised the most autonomy; its members were watching.[39]

Fremont's proclamation was a bombshell. Lincoln quickly contacted Fremont and with astonishing restraint *asked* him to change that part of his proclamation relating to slavery to conform to the First Confiscation Act—slaves could be confiscated only when it could be proven that they were used directly to help the rebellion. And he ordered Fremont to "allow no man to be shot, under the proclamation, without first having my approbation or consent."[40]

Fremont obeyed the order but rejected the request. If Lincoln wanted Fremont's proclamation about slavery changed, the president would have to change it. The president thus ordered the proclamation changed to fit the law and began considering the removal of Fremont from his command in the West. Sending Cameron and other observers to Missouri to look the situation over, Lincoln received information persuading him that Fremont was not up to the command. The president did wait to see if the general could successfully engage the enemy, but that too was beyond him. On 2 November Lincoln placed David Hunter in command and sent Fremont to West Virginia.[41]

The clash with Fremont revealed the importance Lincoln attached to maintaining executive control over the slavery question. Keeping the larger picture in mind, Lincoln had to orchestrate changes in the nation on this most explosive issue. Although equal justice under law was the moral high ground and the purpose behind much Union warmaking, the president had to think about both ends and means, ideal and immediate necessity. The strategic position of, and the delicate balance in, Kentucky restrained antislavery action this time. But Lincoln was a master of longer-ranged visions, of a time when means and ends entwined.

Passions in wartime encouraged many people to forget that integration, the need to balance the politically and legally possible with the moral imperative. Abolitionists were outraged when Lincoln revised Fremont's proclamation. Ignoring the fact that the revision did not reject lawful emancipations, men such as Garrison, Frederick Douglass, Moncure Conway, James Russell Lowell, and Sen. Ben Wade proclaimed their disgust: "How many times are we to save Kentucky and lose our self respect?" "There is no president of the United States—only a President of Kentucky." "Such ethics could only come of one born of 'poor white trash' and educated in a slave state."[42]

The abolitionists' outrage over Lincoln's revocation ended their early honeymoon with the president. Their newspapers began a barrage of criticism that condemned Lincoln for his lack of moral sentiments, his willingness to compromise with evil. Yet that criticism pushed the nation toward a stronger antislavery stand. Protest grew against military policy such as Halleck's General Orders No. 2 of early November that kept fugitive slaves from escaping into his lines. Halleck's policy was debated in the House, and legislators nearly censured him. When other Union commanders allowed loyal slaveowners to seek their slaves in camp, their policy increasingly came under searching and sometimes scorching attack. A more popular approach that followed Butler's "contraband of war" idea gained favor. Halleck's order had helped to crystallize public opinion against giving slaves back to their masters. That view added power to the forces for equality that Lincoln had to integrate with the imperatives of politics and the constitutional system. Such growing antislavery sentiment at least brought the pressures of politics more into line with the Declaration's promises. It would be up to the president to keep opinion going in that direction and thus to unravel the contradictions between liberty and order that had helped bring on the crisis.[43]

Domestic war, the great Civil War to hold the Union together, dominated the attention of the administration. The fact that Secretary of State Seward handled domestic security suggests how compelling events at home were. There were foreign affairs to handle, of course, but Lincoln's focus emphasized events at home, the example that the United States provided for other nations and peoples throughout the world. And that example depended upon the preservation of republican government. Lincoln had little interest in foreign affairs in part because he had so little time for them. Another major reason was that he had little passion for expanding the nation's borders—the major foreign policy concern of American presidents and administrations from the first presidency to the sixteenth. Indeed he had joined the Whig party protests against Polk's expansionist policies into Mexican Territory and gained some minor stature for his "Spot Resolutions," which denied that Mexico had begun the war.

Lincoln believed that America had a mission in the world but that this mission would be carried out within its own borders, not by invasion or coercion or even by expansion. He spoke of this idea as a young man of twenty-nine, describing the establishment of the nation as a product of the Founders' "ambition . . . to display before an admiring world . . . the capability of a people to govern themselves." The mature president reaffirmed the idea in his 1861 Fourth of July address, describing the war as presenting "to the whole family of man, the question whether a constitutional republic, or a democracy—a government of the people, by the same people—can or cannot, maintain its territorial integrity against its own domestic foes." By the time of the Gettysburg Address he put this idea more succinctly: "Government of the people, by the people and for the people, shall not perish from the earth." This was the role of the nation in the world; relations with foreign nations were secondary to this end. Nevertheless the survival of that government depended largely on the course that other nations would take.[44]

Lincoln usually left foreign affairs in Seward's hands. The secretary had been in Europe last in 1859. A tour of the Continent, where royalty and statesmen had competed with each other to fete the antislavery leader and, of course, the next president of the United States, had given him some experience in international affairs. But his first efforts consisted more of saber-rattling than of negotiating; in effect, Seward waved the sword as a diplomatic threat.

As the largest naval power in the world, the nation most dependent on Southern cotton, and the master of an empire that included Canada, Britain had several stakes in the expanding war. If Queen Victoria's government supported the Confederacy, gave the nascent nation the protection of British ships and recognition to permit rebel diplomats to tap the resources of the world's great empire, then the rebellion would succeed. Such support would secure cotton but at a high cost, for there were rumors that the United States might want to compensate for Southern secession by looking North. Could Britain afford making such a powerful enemy?

Yet Britain had to act because both North and South compelled it to. Three days after Sumter fell, Jefferson Davis issued letters of marque and reprisal that called for ships and sailors to prey on Union shipping; the new government also sent representatives across the Atlantic to ask for recognition. On the Northern side, Lincoln and Seward had declared a blockade of Southern ports—the ports from which cotton left for England. In reply to both actions the British government announced recognition of the Confederacy as a belligerent and of the Northern blockade.[45]

Seward was furious, and Lincoln was angry as well. "God damn them!" exclaimed the secretary of state. Furthermore, Britain not only had acted the same day that U.S. minister Charles Francis Adams had arrived but had added the insult of Foreign Secretary John Russell having had two "unofficial" meetings with Confederate representatives. Giving these actions an even more ominous cast, Britain's response had taken place even before there had been a battle to determine whether the Confederacy was sound or fury. It looked as though the Confederacy might get the support it craved.

Seward and Lincoln themselves had in part brought on the crisis. Under international law a blockade conveyed recognition; that seemed to concede to the rebels the most fundamental question—whether they were a nation or not. Seward had assumed that calling the action a "blockade" would provide a clearly defined legal context in which foreign nations might react. But when England defined the term in ways that kept rebellion alive instead of simply making the situation easier for lawyers, Seward and Lincoln were naturally upset. Unionists shared their reaction, accusing Britain of selling its soul for cotton and of seeking the death of republican government and the elevation of monarchy. New York Brahmin George Templeton Strong was outraged "that England, after all her professions of philanthropy and civilization and humanity and liberation, should turn upon us in our struggle for national life against this foul conspiracy of nigger-breeding, woman flogging oligarchs, whose sole pretext for rebellion is that they are forbidden to make slavery national and extend its area."[46]

Seward's policy joined personal pique with Machiavellian calculation. Adopting a stance that Peter Parish has called "controlled truculence," the secretary of state wrote a dispatch to Adams containing the warning that future meetings of the British government with Confederate agents would force Adams to break off discussion. Full recognition of the Confederacy would turn the United States from a friend into an enemy, and if that meant war, then Britain would have started it. The dispatch bristled with righteousness: Britain stood ready to commit a "great crime"; the president was "surprised and grieved"; Britain's actions were "wrongful," at odds with "the laws of nature"; "no one of [Britain's actions helpful to the Confederacy] will be borne by the United States." Adams was to hand the dispatch to Russell.

Before the dispatch was sent, Seward showed it to Lincoln. The president thought that his secretary of state had gone too far. Although he recognized the need for some truculence, Lincoln saw the importance of control. The dispatch left too few chances for maneuver, for diplomats and nations to reason themselves out of the crisis. Lincoln told Seward to modify his language and even the process by which the dispatch would be used. Take out the reference to "enemies," the president said; use "regrets" rather than "surprised and grieved"; Britain's actions were "hurtful," not "wrongful"; "the laws of nature" were not at stake; "the laws of nations and our own laws" were; to write that Britain's actions would "not pass unquestioned" was better than to say that the United States would not bear them. As for process, instead of handing Russell the dispatch, let Adams use it for guidance in face-to-face discussions.[47]

Lincoln's changes retained strength, letting Britain know of the nation's displeasure, but they did something else. They revealed, perhaps better than any other measure, the basic instincts of the lawyer-politician: his desire to continue the process and allow room for negotiations and his faith that reasoning together would be more likely to bring results than simply proclaiming one's righteousness.

Seward accepted the president's changes and achieved the hoped-for results. His new approach slowed the apparent march toward recognition of the rebel state. Britain backed away from the Confederacy, promising not to meet with its representatives again, even unofficially. Equally important, Lincoln had shown that the Union government could at once assert its position and still give other nations room for maneuver. Diplomacy was once defined as giving the other person your way; Lincoln had made this tactic more possible in a dangerous time.

Just how dangerous became clear in mid-November. Confederate diplomats James Mason and John Slidell were on their way to England to continue the South's struggle for international recognition, sailing on the *Trent*, a British packet. They were prepared for a long stay, for Slidell had his family with him. They sailed with some optimism because the Bull Run victory had been followed by another on 21 October at Ball's Bluff, and the Confederacy seemed to be taking another step toward independence. The Union navy, aware that the diplomats were headed toward England, had dispatched ships throughout the Atlantic to keep the two men from getting there. On 8 November Capt. Charles Wilkes made the catch, boarding the *Trent* and taking Mason and Slidell with him back to Boston; the *Trent* was allowed to go on to England.

Starved for some sort of victory the Northern populace initially was ecstatic over Wilkes's deed. The secretary of the navy called the captain a hero, and the House of Representatives voted him a gold medal. Then came news of British reaction: Across the sea popular outrage matched American celebration. The British government began to ready troops for Canada, and the prime minister prepared a note for Lord Lyons, ambassador to the United States, which sounded much like an ultimatum. In an atmosphere still echoing with Seward's bombast, these events were ominous.

Forces for peace began to surface, however. The prince consort, Albert, suggested that the prime minister's note be moderated, pointing to an escape hatch for Americans. The revised note included an expression of belief by the British that Wilkes had not acted according to orders. The queen's cabinet took up this theme and further moderated the note to mention long-standing good relations between the two countries. Privately, Russell instructed Lyons to "abstain from anything like menace" when he gave the note to Seward. Although Britain insisted on the return of Mason and Slidell, its government clearly hoped that the Union would find the path to resolution. Lincoln signaled American willingness to calm the situation by not mentioning the incident in his annual message on 3 December.

Seward was ready to step back from the brink. Great Britain, now angry and dangerous, provided resources, especially saltpeter, that the Union needed. Furthermore, there were signs that France would support Britain. The United States did not need more enemies. Having told the British that Wilkes had acted on his own, Seward was ready to deliver the rebel diplomats to England. Despite these circumstances, Lincoln dragged his feet; he was no more interested in a second war than Seward was, but he wanted somehow to avoid the embarrassment implicit in yielding directly to Britain. When Senator Sumner, whose important friends in England were sending warnings of impending war, suggested arbitration by a third nation, Lincoln jumped at the idea. The president also wanted to talk personally with Lord Lyons, believing that "I could show him in five minutes that I am heartily for peace." Lincoln kept his diplomatic distance from Lyons, but he drafted a proposal to the British suggesting arbitration.[48]

Lincoln was again trying to keep a conversation going in the hope that reason would prevail even while saving American face and appeasing popular opinion. Warned by the British to act quickly, however, Seward recognized that more discussions in this heated atmosphere kept the crisis boiling. When Lincoln called the cabinet together on Christmas Day 1861 the secretary of state had gathered reinforcements. Sumner, invited to the meeting, read dispatches from the British about the dangers of the situation. Blair, Chase, Bates, and gradually the others chimed in, urging that delay exacerbated tensions and that Slidell and Mason had to be handed over immediately. Seward met the president's implicit demands to provide an argument to persuade the voters that the Union was right, even as it was reasonable. First, he presented his justifications of why Wilkes had been right in stopping and boarding the *Trent*. Second, he pointed out that the captain was wrong in that he had acted as the British had always acted—he had asserted power without taking the ship to a prize court. Here Wilkes had acted outside his orders. In giving up the diplomats the United States was therefore adhering to principles held by Madison and Jefferson and Monroe. It was an argument that the voters would buy, whatever international lawyers might make of it. Lincoln kept quiet about arbitration although the press had heard of it and was debating its merits. After two days of discussion in the cabinet, Lincoln was persuaded. Action, not more talk, was the right policy: Mason and Slidell were given up to the British.[49]

This resolution served Anglo-American relations well; the war fever rising in both societies subsided. Even before the final release of the prisoners, the two great powers were sobered by the forecast cost of war. When Slidell and Mason were returned, passions cooled quickly. There was "no longer any excitement here upon the question of America," Lord Russell wrote from London to Lyons in Washington. And Americans in both North and South believed that the Union had benefited from the trip to the edge of war. Adams wrote Seward, "The affair of the Trent . . . was opportune," and Seward agreed; it was "fortunate that the . . . affair occurred." Edward Pollard, editor of Richmond's most popular paper, sadly concurred. The rapprochement between the North and Great Britain "gave a sharp check to the long cherished imagination of the interference of England in the war."[50]

There would be other foreign crises, and both nations were still a bit tender from the barks and bites of the *Trent* affair. But Seward had backed away from truculence and thus gained admiration from Lyons and the British government. Lincoln had erred on the side of even greater deliberation, but faced with the unanimous advice of his cabinet and the knowledgeable counsel of Sumner, the president supported conciliating British power. International politics was not replaced by war, for both sides had wanted the forum of discussion to endure. Future crises would find them again in that forum. They had learned from the crisis in other ways. John Stuart Mill, inspired by the *Trent* affair, explained to the British public the reasons that the United States made a better ally than the Confederacy, an argument that helped turn Britain toward the North. Mill also helped the Union in a time of need, assuring it that it had friends overseas. And the expanding Union strength encouraged the British elite to hear Mill's arguments with some respect.[51]

The year had seen the outlines of power being drawn. Lincoln had established the authority to be commander in chief while judges withdrew into smaller spheres. Congress had legitimized Lincoln's acts and thus amplified his power. Legislators were also beginning to send toward the battlefield resources that Union armies could use. Lawmakers were on the verge of reshaping an economy for a modern world even as war expanded into the lives of citizens. The Lincoln administration and its party were learning how to face the greatest war in the nation's history, how to build sufficient strength to save the republic and still respect the Constitution that was its foundation. But did the Union have time to use those lessons before the Confederacy won the war?

1862

★ ★ ★ ★ ★

Bellows and I called on the President yesterday to make the modest proposition that if any bill passed giving him power to appoint [the Sanitary Commission], (doing away with the fatal principle of seniority), he would hear us before making any appointments. It was a cool thing. Lincoln looked rather puzzled and confounded by our impudence, but finally said, "Well, gentlemen, I guess there's nothing wrong in promising that anybody shall be heered before anything's done." We had the unusual good fortune to catch our Chief Executive disengaged, just after a Cabinet council, and enjoyed an hour's free and easy talk with him. We were not boring him, for we made several demonstrations toward our exit, which he retarded severally by a little incident he had "heered" in Illinois. He is a barbarian, Scythian, yahoo, or gorilla, in respect of outside polish . . . but a most sensible, straightforward, honest old codger. The best president we have had since old Jackson's time, at least, as I believe. . . . His evident integrity and simplicity of purpose would compensate for worse grammar than his, and for even more intense provincialism and rusticity.

—George Templeton Strong, *Diary,* 1862

5

★ ★ ★ ★ ★

FORGING THE
RESOURCES OF WAR:
JANUARY TO FEBRUARY 1862

Discontent was growing. Just returned from visiting their constituents, legislators were feeling the need to strike boldly somewhere, to take up a role in winning the victory that Lincoln and his generals had been unable to produce. They were still bitter over the Union defeat at Ball's Bluff on 21 October 1861. One of their own, and Lincoln's close friend, Edward Baker (the president's second son was named for him), a military officer and senator from Oregon, had been killed in the battle. Baker had thrilled the Senate in August with a passionate speech against equivocating on secession. His death had sanctified his militance and fed the anger and eagerness of his colleagues to strike back.[1]

The target of their anger was General McClellan, whose great promise had set expectations so high that disappointment was practically inevitable. The general was doing his part by repeatedly drilling the army around Washington, watching parades, and rushing through the city's streets with his staff in tow but not setting forth to crush the rebellion. Half a year had passed since his appointment, clear bright months, perfect for campaigning, and the "Young Napoleon" (he actually liked the name) was still getting ready to begin.

Important legislators had had enough. Zachariah Chandler, Michigan's outspoken and radical senior senator, remembered Lincoln's comments in July about the loyalty of enlisted men but more memorably that "large numbers of those in the Army and Navy who have been favored with offices have proved false to the hand that pampered them," a judgment that sounded more true than ever now, Chandler thought.

97

He gave a speech declaring that West Point had recently hatched more traitors than in all of history since the time of Judas Iscariot, and he did not mean just the officers who had gone South. Sen. John Sherman, whose brother had graduated from the academy, offered similar, if less vivid thoughts. He doubted that "a military education at West Point has infused into the Army the right spirit to carry on this war." Further, lawmakers were frustrated with the president. Newspapers were after him, the leader of their party; the *Chicago Tribune* had decided that Lincoln was "reactionary and feeble." Sen. Ben Wade confronted the president: "Mr. President you are murdering your country by inches in consequence of the inactivity of the military and the want of a distinct policy in regard to slavery." Congress was going to act.[2]

On 5 December Chandler proposed a Senate committee to look into the causes of the defeats at Bull Run and Ball's Bluff. Iowa senator James Grimes approved but wanted to make a wider investigation and to include the House in the process. He proposed a joint congressional committee that would "inquire into the causes of the disasters that have attended public arms." Senator Sherman pushed the proposal a bit further: "To confine this inquiry to the disasters of the war would be to cripple and limit the proposed committee in all directions . . . this ought to be the committee of inquiry into the general conduct of the war." Senator Wilson supported the idea; it would "teach men in civil and in military authority that the people expect that they will not make mistakes, and that we shall not be easy with their errors." By wide margins lawmakers voted for the new committee and made Ohio senator Wade, known for his impatience, chairman.[3]

The major thrust of the committee was to investigate and question commanders about their plans, their battlefield successes and failures, and the extent to which they were ready to attack slavery as well as to destroy rebel armies. The congressmen were on the alert for generals who promised the most extreme measures, who would, as many of them put it, "take the gloves off" the war, and that meant confiscating property, people as well as possessions.

These feelings reflected the frustrations of that winter but some were long-standing. Americans who remembered Jackson's era had doubts about the elitism of a professional military. Efforts had been made to close West Point, and legislators recalled Lincoln's remarks about disloyal officers. Another suspicion grew from concerns that professionals lacked moral commitment, were simply "hired guns" or perhaps were evil geniuses like Napoleon who would take over the government. McClellan's known antiemancipation feelings caused some individuals to worry about his moral principles. Many professional soldiers in turn believed that civilians were enemies, that politicians were threats. McClellan was encouraged by his old friend and West Point colleague Ambrose Burnside: "Hold on old fellow, and don't let the politicians drive you." Nonetheless, politicians and their constituents worried about what soldiers insensitive to the people might do. Talk around McClellan's camp and in his army about dictatorship—the general liked to report such rumors to his wife, denying he was interested, of course—also made some observers nervous and gave ammunition to his enemies. Radical congressmen began to speak of "dictator," "treason," and "cowardice."[4]

This language was too violent for Lincoln, who often was annoyed at the readiness of the committee and the sentiment it represented to push quickly to extreme measures. He met with members when they wished and listened to their protests and suggestions, but he kept a distance. In January Chairman Wade proposed "Joint Rule 22," which allowed any congressman to call for an immediate executive session if he could show that the president wanted swift action on a war-related measure. Members of the committee would clearly be in the best position to transmit Lincoln's wishes. Thus a kind of combined executive-legislative "war cabinet" impended. But the president never asked lawmakers to call such a session.[5]

Lincoln shared the dark mood of the winter. He knew that the past months had seen vital and indispensable steps taken to set the foundations for a successful war effort. Britain kept at bay, the definition and recognition of the president's war powers, Kentucky held within the Union even as Congress began to stab tentatively at slavery, improved and growing organization of the army—these achievements would have long-term consequences. But at the end of 1861 the only incident that the administration could point to as a dramatic accomplishment was the *Trent* affair. Even that had produced accusations of American "cowardice" among its critics; admirers could applaud only a well-considered retreat. On the battlefield there was almost nothing to cheer. The navy and the army had established outposts on the edge of the Confederacy, with Union forces occupying the Sea Islands between Savannah and Charleston and with the navy battering the Hatteras forts off North Carolina, but these seemed minor accomplishments. The two major battles in the East were Confederate victories; in the West a battle at Wilson's Creek was another Union loss.

McClellan was shaping a formidable-looking army, but Lincoln was beginning to doubt his aggressiveness. The new lieutenants he had appointed in the West, Halleck and Buell, were both known for their administrative abilities, talents that earned little admiration from a nation starved for military victory. "If it were determined to make a forward movement of the Army of the Potomac, without awaiting further increase of numbers, or better drill and discipline," he hinted to the general, "how *long* would it require to actually get in motion?" Meanwhile, McClellan was ill, unable to explain his plans or to defend them, whatever they were. Military needs were draining the treasury so fast that Chase was in despair; in Congress men were predicting that "we will be out of the means to pay the daily expenses in about thirty days." The *Trent* affair, despite its benefits to diplomacy, had scared people so much that they hoarded gold. Banks suspended specie payment for government and for private debts, the major government debt being money owed to the 576,000-man army. Taking stock of the military inertia and economic paralysis, on 10 January 1862 Lincoln asked Quartermaster General Montgomery Meigs, "General, what shall I do? The people are impatient. Chase has no money; . . . the General of the Army has typhoid fever. The bottom is out of the tub. What shall I do?"[6]

There were plenty of specific causes for Lincoln's pain, but a deeper reason underlay his outcry: He was beginning to feel personally the weight of command. Although the Constitution names the president the commander in chief of the army and navy, no president since Zachary Taylor had had military experience in leadership. The growing professionalism of the army bespoke more complex knowledge about warmaking and hence more reason for amateurs to defer to experts. On the other hand Lincoln did not like war, even the bit of it he had experienced in an almost bloodless campaign fighting the Black Hawks in 1832. He had once condemned Polk for starting an unjust war with Mexico, and even though he had supported military heroes as Whig presidential candidates, he mocked "military glory" as "that attractive rainbow, that rises in showers of blood—that serpent's eye, that charms to destroy." He was suspicious of warmaking though by necessity deferential to warriors.[7]

Yet Lincoln now had before him Civil War. The task of conducting it would stay in his hands in the most compelling and terrible sense—the war would go on as long as he wanted it to go on; it would stop when he said it had stopped. And every day as the casualties mounted and the boys died and the families agonized, he would decide to continue or to end it. This was his war. He kept close watch on the warmaking that he was asking Union generals to direct.

McClellan seemed at first to be the almost perfect man for the job. In the first months of his command, in addition to his coordinating activities in the War Department bureaus, he gathered and organized a growing army of nearly 190,000 on the Potomac alone. He brought discipline to every element of the army, from ambulance drivers and stretcher-bearers to riflemen. He prompted Congress to pass a law setting up military review boards to examine the qualifications of officers, resulting in the resignation of nearly 170 officers who had failed to take proper care of their men or who had shown a lack of knowledge or discipline. Public displays of the powerful army built the expectation that soon there would be an advance into the South that would bring the Confederates to their senses. Those observers who witnessed the general's fifteen-hour days in his office and his afternoon sorties to inspect and inspire the troops respected McClellan's efforts and his belief that he was the leader the nation needed.

Despite such feelings, a growing sense prevailed that something was wrong: The army did not move South. Sentiment was strong for action, yet people were willing to give McClellan some time to undo the chaos in the defeated Bull Run army. But as time passed and nothing happened, patience faded. The public expected its army, the army made up of its sons, husbands, brothers, to move forward to a victory that would bring those young men back home again, soon. The congressmen who at first had admired and supported McClellan began to read their mail and to feel their own impatience growing. Lincoln, responsible for maintaining public support for the conflict, began to lecture the general on the president's area of expertise, politics.

McClellan, facing daily reminders of how little civilian life had prepared Americans for war, resented civilian demands and pressures. When he took over he commanded, in his words, a force "not worthy to be called an army." He also knew the murderousness of combat—Crimean experience had taught him that. He was the expert, the professional, and civilians at all levels were either men to be whipped into shape or meddlers to be avoided. There was much to do, and only experts knew how to do it. He told friendly newspaper editors to try to keep public criticism from interfering with the creation of his army; McClellan thought it was his war.

That belief was part of the problem. In devoting so much time to his task, in working to build rapport with the soldiers, it was becoming easier to forget that the army was, more fundamentally, the army of the United States and that the war was, as Lincoln called it, "a people's contest." Exacerbating the situation, McClellan distrusted Lincoln, who was "nothing more than a well meaning baboon," he told his wife, and the general had similar disdain for the cabinet. He kept his plans from many of his subordinates, from congressmen, and even from the president himself. His approach was the ultimate in separation of the civilian and the military.[8]

Much of McClellan's suspicion was understandable. Cameron's War Department hardly inspired admiration. Civilians seldom understood the growing complexity of warfare; they were likely to think of heroic charges up hillsides or across open fields, and many congressmen shared these feelings. Professional soldiers knew of rifles that killed at a quarter of a mile. They thought in terms of securing communications, establishing access to supplies and animals to haul them, determining how many horses and mules and forage for them were needed to supply a given number of soldiers with the ammunition and ambulances the battlefield would require. Assembling and training complex armies for such horrific duties took time. Yet newspapers shouted "On to Richmond!" and congressmen and the president, sharing their impatience, kept pushing McClellan to act.[9]

The general's response was to say as little as possible when among civilian leaders and to change his workplace to get away from "browsing presidents." On two occasions he simply snubbed the president when Lincoln called at the general's home. Perhaps the most telling incident took place at a 13 January 1862 meeting between Lincoln and McClellan at the White House. Three cabinet members, Chase, Seward, and Blair (a West Point graduate), and three generals, McDowell, Franklin, and Meigs, also attended. When the president asked the commander about his plans McClellan made some remarks about action in Kentucky and then refused to divulge his strategy unless ordered directly to do so. "No General fit to command an army will ever submit his plans to the judgment of such an assembly," McClellan said; "there are many here entirely incompetent to pass judgment on them . . . no plan made known to so many persons can be kept secret an hour." Lincoln allowed the general to remain silent on this occasion, but frustration mounted.[10]

The general's greatest troubles did not come from Lincoln initially. The president protected McClellan at first, promising to supply the army to the fullest extent possible and to support the general. He even went so far as to sustain McClellan's campaign to get Scott to retire and to appoint the general to replace him. At the same time Lincoln tried to alert McClellan to political forces by telling him to talk to the Committee on the Conduct of the War at "the earliest moment your health will permit—today if possible." Only gradually, as the time passed without an offensive, did Lincoln grow more testy. Still, when Senator Wade said that anyone was better than McClellan, the president answered that "anyone is fine for you, but I must have someone." And he stuck with McClellan. Yet the correspondence between the two men became increasingly ill-humored as Lincoln's frustration mounted.[11]

Still, with one major exception, from the end of 1861 and into early 1862 Lincoln supported McClellan with troops and supplies. The general's real problems were with Congress. Most lawmakers had welcomed him as a savior, but as the months passed and McClellan did not march south their feelings changed. This shift resulted partly because of McClellan's inaction but it also indicated emerging feelings in the society that linked his inaction with new visions of handling slavery.

Abolitionists had insisted from the first days of the conflict that the war threatened slavery. Charles Sumner, as soon as he heard that Sumter had been fired on, went directly to the White House and told the president "that under the war power the right had come to him to emancipate the slaves." "God be praised," was Frederick Douglass's reaction when he heard the news. War would surely kill slavery. "Success in the War, without Emancipation," the *Antislavery Standard* proclaimed, "is a military impossibility."[12]

Soldiers' experiences as they moved into the South helped to confirm such views. Clearly slavery fed and clothed Southern armies. Enslaved black men and women raising Southern crops left white men free to come North and shoot Union soldiers. When Butler freed contraband and when some generals let escaping slaves stay within their lines, growing numbers of soldiers cheered and wrote home about their feelings. More people were pleased when Fremont attacked Missouri slave owners. By late November Secretary of War Cameron was persuaded that black troops were needed to strengthen the Union army and sent out his annual report recommending their use before the president had seen a copy. There was applause for such advanced steps as well as outrage in many quarters when Lincoln recalled the report and had Cameron delete the offending section.[13]

Concerns over the loyal border regions and an abiding ambiguity about interpreting the Constitution limited Lincoln's options, but sentiment was growing to strike at slavery. McClellan, however, was adamantly against making the war an antislavery crusade. "Help me dodge the nigger," he wrote a publisher friend, "*I* am fighting to preserve the integrity of the Union . . . to gain that end we cannot afford to mix up the negro question." He feared that turning the war into an attack on slavery would transform the fight from a military conflict into a revolution. Possibly his affection for Napoleon made him sensitive to the uncontrollable power of a levée en masse; as a Democrat, he was also aware of the racism of much of his party's constituency. Introducing emancipation as a goal, he told Lincoln, would "rapidly disintegrate our present armies."[14]

But Congress had joined the fray, and legislators wanted action: not just attacking the South but taking the gloves off the war—freeing runaways who reached Union lines, emancipating slaves, using blacks as soldiers. These policies, part of the more radical Republican agenda, began to be transformed into tests of military leadership, signs of passion for the cause, of devotion to winning the war. As war psychology infused the population, such demands would increase, and the longer the wait for action the more intense the outcry for a more revolutionary war. McClellan was thus his own worst enemy. He might have noticed the overwhelming Republican majorities and understood that voters had chosen the party most hostile to slavery. The war would be more than just saving the Union; an enemy distinguished by its espousal and defense of slavery was not going to be fought only as a Union breaker. When Confederate soldiers killed Union soldiers the dead were not only victims of battle; they were victims of a society, a way of life. McClellan made no concessions to that sentiment, avoiding chances even to negotiate with its spokesmen. At the same time he continued advising Democratic newspapers on particular arguments to advance and thereby kept alive the suspicion that he might be too interested in politics to be a trustworthy soldier.

By January 1862 the Committee on the Conduct of the War was fed up with McClellan, but they took out their frustration on one of his subordinates, Gen. Charles Stone, for failures at Ball's Bluff. Stone had clashed with Senator Sumner on the fugitive slave issue; like McClellan he believed in returning them if their masters were loyal to the Union. During the argument Stone had written a public letter accusing the senator of being "a well known coward." Legislators rallied around their colleague and accused Stone of disloyalty, refused him access to the rumormongers who had testified against him, and persuaded the new secretary of war Edwin Stanton, to put him in jail for over six months, much of that in solitary confinement. The prosecution-persecution was recognized as a prod to other generals, usually West Pointers, to be more aggressive, not only in battle but also in subverting slavery. The committee kept up its watchdog role throughout the war. McDowell and Buell and Fitz John Porter—Democrats—felt the pressure of congressional inquiry, aided by the secretary of war. Attorney General Bates recalled the French Revolutionary Committee on Public Safety when he observed the Committee on the Conduct of the War.[15]

Secretary of War Stanton, however, found the committee useful in motivating generals—especially those who neglected to be successful on the battlefield. Lincoln did nothing to protect McClellan's colleagues as the committee went after them. The president may not have used the committee as his instrument for energizing officers, but he did not hinder its operations. Indeed he lacked official authority to interfere directly with congressional investigations, but he certainly could have pulled Stanton's reins when the secretary cooperated with the committee. He did not. Lincoln may have agreed with the war secretary's opinion that generals involved in politics, as he believed McClellan and Stone were, "risk being gored. They cannot, having exposed themselves, claim the procedural protections and immunities of the military profession."[16]

Except for its watchdog committee, Congress left most decisions on the fighting to the generals, the secretary of war, and the president. As 1862 began Cameron clearly would not do as secretary. He held the War office only because his reputation made it impossible for him to serve as secretary of treasury and because his political connections decreed that he be in the cabinet. But when war began Cameron demonstrated none of the organizational abilities that the post demanded. He could not handle the immense task of gathering and organizing the hundreds of thousands of men and the supplies necessary to put them into battle and keep them there. Cameron stirred up trouble himself with his report in 1861 advocating the use of black troops without telling Lincoln. Most important, the largest and most vital war in the nation's history was under way, and Cameron's floundering put lives and country at risk. Concern also grew because corruption and profligacy continued in letting of government contracts for the supplies of war. States competed with each other and with the national government in bidding for scarce supplies, and often profiteers were ready to sell useless, defective, materials for exorbitant prices. Fremont's involvement in such dealings was only one part of a national scandal. By mid-January almost every Republican senator was eager for Cameron to resign; Cameron himself was looking for an escape route.[17]

Thus when the ministry to Russia opened, Lincoln quickly accepted Cameron's resignation and appointed him ambassador. The president put into the War Department another Pennsylvanian in February 1862 but a different man indeed. Edwin Stanton carried a reputation for incorruptibility and for fierce unionism. He had been appointed to Buchanan's cabinet in the secession winter and had played an important role in convincing Lincoln's predecessor to resist Southern threats. Stanton, a Democrat, had been a strong critic of Lincoln's "imbecility" as he had put it, but he had been careful to maintain connections with important Republicans in both wings of the party, especially Chase and Seward. He had had some experience with War Department matters, having advised Cameron on the legality of purchasing contracts and militia enlistments and earning the secretary's trust. Stanton had also established a friendship with fellow-Democrat McClellan, giving him authority with the military professionals.

But Stanton had other, less attractive qualities. He had been instrumental in getting Cameron ousted. When Cameron asked him for advice about his annual report, Stanton had urged an even stronger endorsement of black troops than the war secretary himself had initially proposed. Meanwhile, Stanton was assuring McClellan and other Democratic associates that he agreed with them in wanting to keep racial issues off the war agenda.

At first, the new secretary balanced both Republican and Democratic views, but that lasted for only a short time. He quickly understood that he needed cooperation from congressional radicals, and he began to identify with their cause and to share their growing frustration over McClellan's inaction. Two weeks after taking the job Stanton had told a friend, "We have had no war; we have not even been playing war." McClellan was unlikely to please a man with that viewpoint.

Radical congressmen were delighted to work with someone who shared their views so precisely; Stanton benefited too. Congressional investigations gave him information that he needed to carry on his duties, and of course legislators controlled the purse strings for the necessities, small and large, of war. Stanton became a frequent participant in the meetings of the Committee on the Conduct of the War, helping its members when he could in political ways. When Senator Wade's reelection was in doubt Stanton reminded Ohio legislators that both the War Department and the president would see Wade's defeat as "a great national calamity." Wade reciprocated by telling his friends that Stanton "has the confidence of Congress and the whole country and he will never disappoint them."[18]

Stanton ran the most vital of government departments with a brisk and decisive energy. He took back the de facto authority that Cameron had allowed McClellan to exercise over the bureau chiefs in the department. Organizing them into the War Board, he gathered their advice and then issued orders about contracts and supplies, commissions, and civil liberties. Stanton brooked little opposition, defying Lincoln when he thought he could get away with it; the president let him do so much of the time. Lincoln came to admire Stanton's administrative skills. He also knew the value of having a subordinate who could take the heat for actions that the president desired but did not wish to be blamed for. Stanton could be so stern that Lincoln's secretary John Hay remarked that he would rather "make a tour of a smallpox hospital" than ask any special favors from him. Stanton on at least two occasions scolded Mary Lincoln for trying to use her position to secure favors. Indeed he had to be ordered by Lincoln to appoint his own nephew to a lieutenancy after Stanton denied the appointment, fearing charges of nepotism. Four-teen-hour days could account for Stanton's temperament, but it also re-sulted from the immense responsibilities of the job.[19]

Regardless of his motives, Stanton quickly focused the lines of power on his office. He moved the telegraph office that McClellan had put near his headquarters next door to the War Department rooms Stan-ton occupied. He revoked all previous contracts to buy supplies abroad if the products could be purchased in the United States. He standard-ized contracts between the department and suppliers and set up a com-mission to audit those contracts. When he found defective goods Stan-ton would send them back to the suppliers when possible, refuse payment, and threaten criminal prosecution. He won power over the railroads in a more subtle way. He prepared a bill which Wade pushed through Congress authorizing the president to take control of railroads. But he understood that private expertise would best serve the Union's needs. So he and the president and Quartermaster General Meigs met with railroad executives and urged them to keep rates lower and to standardize gauges, signals, and other operations. Remarking on his preference for private control, he also chatted about executive authority. The railroaders got the point; they kept control of operations but imple-mented Stanton's suggestions.[20]

Despite his own organizational talents and his professionalism in running the War Department, Stanton, when he first took office, had little respect for professional military views on making war. McClellan's recognition that battle required careful organization and maneuvering to offset the killing range of rifles and that forcing the enemy to attack by threatening his rear and communications would produce long-range victory did not impress the secretary. His visions featured "the spirit of the Lord that moved our soldiers to rush into battle and filled the hearts of our enemies with dismay." Patriotic spirit, he wrote, "with resolute courage in officers and men is a military combination that never failed."[21]

Stanton's martial images reflected public sentiment, and Lincoln had to be sensitive to it. The president understood and respected Mc-Clellan's strategic ideas—a regard that deceived the general into believ-ing that Lincoln was uniformly on his side. But the president thought of the war away from the battlefield also—within Northern society itself where the will to fight, to continue the war, was the foundation for vic-tory. Without that will, the brilliant, complex, and knowledgeable strat-egy meant nothing. Therefore, short of sending the entire population to

West Point, heroic visions of warfare, however blind to military realities, would have to be acknowledged.

Thus in late January 1862—slightly over half a year after McClellan was appointed—Lincoln ordered the young general to move his army into the South, attacking an entrenched Confederate army southwest of Washington. This order finally extracted from McClellan a full description of his larger strategy of flanking the rebel armies by attacking the peninsula between the York and the James rivers. With McClellan at last inspired to act, Lincoln wanted him to move immediately and directly into Virginia. But the general persuaded the president that his alternate plan was preferable. It would, of course, take more time to implement, but in the long run it would be more successful, McClellan promised. Lincoln agreed, and the nation waited until the middle of March for the great move to the peninsula to begin.[22]

Meanwhile, after having done its best to energize McClellan, Congress was beginning to organize and direct other forces of war. Lincoln was responsible for military leadership and could be assisted by congressional watchdogs on the periphery, but roles reversed when it came to bringing forth economic weapons. The Constitution gave the president no power to raise taxes, to pay debts, to borrow money, or to coin it. He could not even raise and support an army or a navy; legislators would have to pass the laws for that. They wanted military victory, but to win it they would have to mobilize more than an army; they would have to unleash and organize an economy as well. And Congress wanted immediate results. It was difficult for them to accept that their powerful nation could not swiftly crush rebellion, having yet to learn how enormous the war would be. Inspired by their frustration and assisted by the president, Congress went back to work.

The July-August emergency session had been limited to the immediate military crisis, but it was time to address the problems and needs of a society at war. Congress worked in harness with Lincoln. He did not publicly advocate most of the economic legislation they passed, but he did lobby Republicans to remember the platform that together they had supported in 1860. He consulted with Chase to create the banking laws for the wartime and postwar Union and mentioned similar laws in his annual messages. His mark was also on the new economic laws that Congress passed, but he had enough to do in other realms of government. Legislators led the way.[23]

The war demanded a huge outpouring of legislation, meaning that Congress would have to organize and discipline itself. The Thirty-seventh Congress, meeting from December 1861 to 1863, produced the largest number of federal laws passed to that time—428 public acts, not to mention private bills for specific constituents. The Thirty-eighth Congress in its two-year tenure produced 411 such bills. Each wartime Congress more than doubled the previous record of 201 bills, set in the Twenty-seventh Congress of 1841–43. Clearly war was creating a national government whose power reached throughout the life of the country. Congress also learned organization—the powers of the Speaker expanded, and a strong committee structure developed to manage the increasingly complex legislative agenda. The executive branch would work with and use the growing power of congressional investigative committees to gather information and especially to prod the army. Occasionally congressmen would turn that tool on the executive branch.

Although Congress was expanding its activities and influence, its major focus was paying for a war.[24] The first need was money: to pay the troops and the munitions makers and the clothing manufacturers, to buy the wagons, the boats, the mules and the horses, the tents, the guns, and countless other supplies. There was a problem, however. When war began the national government did not have a currency of its own. The circulating medium was state bank notes—from approximately 1600 state banks. The government paid its debts in gold and silver, thus limiting its purchasing power to the amount of specie available.

In the first year of the war federal expenses jumped by 700 percent, and that was just the beginning. The urgency of that beginning became clear on 30 December 1861 when the government ran out of money. Financial anxiety provoked by fears that Britain would intervene and by Chase's report of a treasury deficit caused gold to be hoarded even as military expenses reached $1 million per day. Meanwhile, Chase was demanding that bankers pay for bonds that Congress had authorized in July and August in gold delivered into Treasury Department hands. The situation spiraled toward disaster. Government contractors were not paid, and more ominously, neither was the 576,000-man military. "The treasury is nearly empty," Chase warned Congress.[25]

Most financial experts had argued that economic stability rested on the firm value of silver and gold. Democrats made specie their creed; some Republicans agreed. Yet faced with the war, the nation took a momentous step. On 25 February 1862 Congress passed the Legal Tender Act, providing $150 million in "greenbacks" that would be backed by government promises, not specie, and that would be legal tender for all but two types of debt: Import duties to the nation and interest on bonds would be paid in gold. The vast majority of the economic transactions in the country now could be made in paper on which was printed "The United States of America." Thus began the printing of federal money.

State bank notes still circulated; national outreach did not paralyze state or private energy. But citizens now carried in their pockets a reminder of national government promises, and they gained another reason to be devoted to the survival of that government. By the end of the war Congress would put another $300 million greenbacks into circulation.

The $450 million in greenbacks was one major innovation increasing the economic influence of the national government—linking Americans with ever stronger economic sinews. Greenbacks paid for a small part of the conflict, however, compared to government borrowing, which accumulated to about $2.8 billion by 1866. Through the sale of a wide array of notes and bonds the government raised money for the struggle from small and large investors, from people who would earn a penny a day on a $50 note to people who could invest in amounts of $5,000 and more and earn dollars a day on that investment. Most of the bonds sold well, demonstrating the commitment of the people to the cause. Some bonds were redeemable in twenty years—and these sold as well as others. People believed that there would be a United States of America two decades hence.

Bond sales involved people from almost every social class. Chase hired Philadelphia banker Jay Cooke—one of his political supporters—to market government bonds. Cooke brought financial experience that Chase severely lacked; the banker had sold $3 million in Pennsylvania state bonds and now welcomed the chance to expand his enterprise. He believed that he was enlisting "those capitalists who are disposed to dabble in loans . . . of the government" in the cause of saving the Union. He earned a healthy commission for his work, but he declared that he would have done it "pay or no pay."

Cooke clearly was enthusiastic about the project, and he saw the value in tapping all classes and ethnic groups. Advertising in religious and foreign language journals as well as in the regular press, keeping sales offices open at night so that day-laborers could buy bonds, encouraging ministers and editors as well as bankers to promote sales, he linked loaning the government money to patriotism. He also brought additional signs of national outreach to the wallets, purses, and portfolios of Northerners in the form of the most popular bonds, the "5–20 sixes" (6 percent bonds payable in from five to twenty years), as well as the other denominations of federal financial promises. The national debt grew from $65 million or $2.06 per capita in 1860 to $2.8 billion or $75.42 by 1866 (about half the annual gross national product). Hamilton had called a national debt a "national blessing"; the "blessing" of this debt was a united nation, an enhanced interconnection between nation and people interested in prosperity and survival.[26]

Increased taxes also linked government and citizen. The innovation of the first national income tax laid the foundation for a modern revenue system that drew money from all facets of the economy—bringing to government use the wealth derived from the nation's resources. Still, the government in the mid-nineteenth century also used its established sources—customs duties and land sales—to bring in millions of dollars. But war needs required that congressmen consider every resource of a diverse economy. The income tax emerged as an option when legislators considered the growing diversity of the Northern economy. They worried that burgeoning nonagricultural wealth would escape taxation. For fairness' sake as well as for necessity's they innovated, and the innovation was popular—as popular as taxes can be. Patriotism made taxation easier to bear. The graduated nature of the tax meant that those people who had benefited most from the nation's prosperity paid the most taxes. The first tax rate was 3 percent on all incomes over $800, and then it changed to incomes over $600 per year. Thus some people paid nothing, for the average income of urban workers was near the $600 figure. This remission compensated in some small measure for the inequities of a draft system that later would allow rich men to escape by paying a commutation fee or by buying substitutes.

But if the lower classes escaped the income tax it was a minor escape. That tax was not a major source of revenue; it raised less than 8 percent of the funds needed for the wartime North between 1863 and 1865. The major source was an excise tax passed 1 July 1862 that hit every facet of the economy. The manufacturers, distributors, and sellers of nearly every commodity made in the nation paid their toll. Farmers, miners, processors of everything from hogs to stone, makers of luxury goods such as carriages and yachts, all professions except the ministry, dealers in stocks and theater tickets, even peddlers and street jugglers— the list rolled on and on for over twenty thousand words until it was the largest single bill introduced in Congress in its prewar history. Everyone paid in some way, and the middle class and poor paid more than did the rich. But in the struggle to save the Union such inequity was usually accepted—even in an economy where inflation raised prices so quickly that real wages declined. Workers who saw the price of bread almost double and the price of potatoes go from $1.50 a bushel to $2.25 from 1861 to 1863 while their wage increases were limited to about 50 to 60 percent still accepted increased taxes, regardless of their other grievances.[27]

Other measures that Congress passed to mobilize the economy benefited the comfortable and well-established more obviously; the national banking act of 1863 provided a clear example. Chase's early rec-

111

ommendations for borrowing money had included a call for a law that established a system of national banks. State bank lobbyists and old Jacksonian fears of national banks had stifled the December 1861 suggestion, but by 1862, with the Union still needing resources, Congress was more receptive. Still it took a long, hard struggle, with active lobbying by the president, a well-orchestrated newspaper campaign by Jay Cooke and his brother Henry, and energetic speechmaking and politicking by thirty-five-year-old Sen. John Sherman, but a national bank bill was produced in mid-February 1863.

The measure set up a national system that could be joined by any group of five or more who could put up at least $30,000 in federal bonds as security. Subsequently they might issue national bank notes in an amount equal to 90 percent of their federal bonds, but they would also have to keep 25 percent of their reserves to pay the notes. Chase hoped that people would be drawn to the more uniform currency, backed by the stability of federal bonds. New national notes would take over from state issues. He also wanted to stimulate the purchase of those bonds by men who wished to join the system.

Opposition to the law came from powerful state bank interests, especially in New York City. Since the law did not wipe out state bank notes, they still circulated, now mixed with national notes and greenbacks. The system favored eastern bankers who could gather deposits from other state banks by paying interest to them. This network brought more money into the East, further increasing the possible profits of banks there. New York financiers thus stayed outside the system and even threatened not to accept national bank notes.

Their support was finally purchased by the national government in a compromise that cut the reserve requirements of national banks and that also dropped an earlier provision that had spread the $300 million in bank notes among the states based on their population. Now the notes would follow streams that led to eastern hands. Support was also purchased by an amendment that guaranteed full value redemption of national notes only at the national banks in Boston, Philadelphia, and New York. More capital flowed to the East, concentrating economic power there even further. Eastern bankers agreed to eliminate state bank notes. In March 1865 Congress placed a 10 percent tax on these notes, and they gradually ceased to circulate. A national monetary system oiling the operation of a unified economy and controlled by its most powerful operatives was established.[28]

The bank law, like the excise tax, favored those individuals with economic power, but the concentration of power was central to the war. Congress needed to gather the economic forces of the North and direct them to defeat the South. It had to enlist those people who had wealth and who managed the economic institutions and then pay careful attention to the advice of these experts. Both state and national governments lacked the expertise to challenge their claims. Government leaders saw the results that men such as Jay Cooke in banking and Herman Haupt, David McCallum, and Thomas Scott in railroading had achieved. The leaders thus called them into government service, benefited by their experience, admired their accomplishments, and simultaneously supported their enterprise and that of their colleagues in the private economy.[29]

Congress was responsible not only for paying for the war and for creating a new infrastructure for the postwar economy. It also created other institutions that would play major roles in that postwar world. Fighting the war energized and justified these new endeavors.

Prewar sectionalism had a potent socioeconomic component. North and South fought over social visions as well as over politics and law. Republicans had promised not only to restrict the expansion of slavery but to enact an economic program. The 1860 platform promised tariff rates that would "encourage the development of the industrial interests . . . secure to the working men liberal wages, to agriculture remunerating prices, to mechanics and manufacturers an adequate reward for their skill, labor and enterprise, and to the nation commercial prosperity and independence." Republicans also endorsed a homestead law, improvements to rivers and harbors, and "a Railroad to the Pacific Ocean." Implicit in these promises was a belief that government ought to assist the growth of the economy—a vision anathema to Southern Democrats and to many of their Northern allies.[30]

The war eliminated from Congress effective Southern challenges to Republican economics. The Thirty-seventh Congress had 105 Republicans and 43 Democrats in the House, 31 Republican and 10 Democratic senators. Moreover, the conflict generated an undoubted need for government energy and enterprise. Democratic laissez faire in war was unthinkable, and few Democrats were around to think it.

Congress thus easily implemented Republican campaign promises. Perhaps the most compelling was a protective tariff that had built support in the prewar years as Republicans gained legislative seats. Several Republican constituencies had united to promote protection and to increase government revenue. Most notable were the iron processors of Pennsylvania, a crucial state in the 1860 election. Other developing industries, such as woolen manufacturers, also favored protection. Many labor leaders, hoping to protect workers from foreign competition and to enrich their industries, supported it. There was even support from those farmers who believed that a prosperous manufacturing sector meant better prices and greater demand for farm products. The Republican party consistently proclaimed that the interests of all classes in the North were one. Arguing for a protective tariff, Henry Carey, chief economic theorist of the party, announced the "perfect harmony" of interest between capital and labor. Linked with the motif of free labor versus slave labor this argument provided another theme to strengthen unity in Republican philosophy. There still remained a section of the party that endorsed free trade, but they were not radical and the needs of war muffled even that dissent.

Two wartime arguments endorsed protection. First, the government needed money, and tariff duties went into government coffers. Second, as the tax system went into effect manufacturers asked for protection to help them pay the new taxes. Thus without much protest Congress passed in July 1862 increases in the February 1861 Morrill Tariff Act, enacted after Southern delegates had withdrawn. That policy of increasing protection continued with minor exceptions throughout most of the nineteenth century. By 1869 the average duty was 47 percent. The advantage was clear for manufacturers starting new industries. The war thus added momentum to the former Whig portion of the Republican party that had favored protection in opposition to former Democratic free traders. In the decades after the war Lincoln's party became more and more the party of big business. Giving abiding influence to that party was the sense that the war had sanctified an economic policy by wrapping it in a vision—a vision of a nation united not only in politics but also in a free labor struggle against a slave labor enemy. That vision, supported by influential writers such as Horace Greeley and Francis Walker, sustained Republican support among workers for many years.[31]

The wartime Congress enacted the other economic promises of its 1860 platform with similar ease. These measures demonstrated government support for economic growth in all sectors of the economy, not just those benefiting industrial business. The Republican amalgam of former Whigs and former Democrats united on 20 May 1862 in supporting the Homestead Act, which gave 160 acres to farmers over twenty-one who invested five years of labor breaking the soil and building a home on government land. As a result, by 1870 tens of thousands of new farms were settled, thus expanding the numbers of apparently independent farmers and validating further the Republican vision of the nation. But there were costs: to the Native Americans whose lands were taken and to those white farmers who did not gain immediate benefits. Some of the land was poorly watered, and some of it fell into the hands of speculators. Nor did the act reduce the numbers of tenant and farm laborers. Still, the wartime Congress had fulfilled a party pledge that symbolized the free labor image they advocated and had expanded the wealth and the promise of the nation in the midst of war. For better *and* for worse, they had defined the meaning of victory for decades to come.[32]

Republicans in the Thirty-seventh Congress looked to a more diverse economy by establishing with the July 1862 Morrill Act the basis for funding "agricultural and mechanical" colleges in every loyal state, colleges that would grow into universities of worldwide reputation. The universities of Illinois, Wisconsin, Minnesota, and California were born of or sustained by this law, and schools such as Cornell, Rutgers, and Brown gained further resources. Those resources became available when Congress set aside 30,000 acres of land for each senator and representative from a given state; that land was presented to the state for sale, with the proceeds going to the colleges that the states might designate. Ultimately sixty-nine land-grant colleges were established.

The law underwrote training in agronomy—training that taught American farmers how to increase yields, breed healthier livestock, and improve crop quality. It also trained workers in other skills, what the bill called "mechanic arts," as well as in "military tactics," "in order to promote the liberal and practical education of the industrial classes in the several pursuits and professions in life."[33] At times the scenes in state capitol buildings where legislators bribed and bargained to win the new colleges for their hometowns were often sordid, but the result advanced goals that Republicans and many Northern Democrats had sought for years. The measure laid the foundation for a broad and democratic training in the knowledge that was shaping a more modern nation.

Interestingly enough, the president apparently paid little attention to this bill. He did not mention it in his annual message to Congress in 1863, which did refer to the homestead and banking bills. There was some ambiguity about formal education in a man who had had little of it himself. He described his training as a lawyer with the proud remark that "he studied with nobody," and he noted that his idol Henry Clay had also educated himself, proving that "in this country, one can scarcely be so poor, but that, if he *will*, he *can* acquire sufficient education to get through the world respectably." Yet Lincoln extolled the virtues of an agricultural life that combined cultivation of the soil with reading in botany, chemistry, and "the mechanical branches of Natural Philosophy." Lincoln clearly believed, however, that one of the contrasts between free labor and slave labor was that free laborers were thinking people whose labor was improved by their inventiveness and whose thought was sharpened and enlivened by their labor. The Morrill Land Grant Act exemplified that image.[34]

Homesteads that spread prosperous farms across the West, colleges that applied new and established knowledge to the problems and the hopes of farmers and mechanics, these advances illustrated the free soil Republicanism that spotlighted the free, self-sufficient individual of the nation's Founding. There was almost a Jeffersonian quality: Expanding prosperity opened up opportunities that in turn increased independent workers.

Yet the instruments of prosperity had changed from Jefferson's day; indeed, direct government involvement in the economy reflected Hamilton's vision. The creation of a Department of Agriculture in May 1862, which distributed seeds and a monthly bulletin filled with information about weather, prices, and innovations, was the clearest example of that involvement. Most notably, the Republican party, despite its traditional "republicanism," sought to subsume and incorporate the railroads and other internal improvements into its visions. The Pacific Railroad Act of 1 July 1862 was part of a package of laws that had included the Homestead Act, the Internal Revenue Act, and the Morrill Land Grant Act.

Proponents of the Pacific Railroad Act benefited greatly from wartime visions. In a struggle to preserve a more perfect Union, it was expedient to bind East and West. Lincoln had long been interested in railroads. He had been a lobbyist and then counsel for the Illinois Central, having earned his largest single fee of $5,000 representing them. The president was eager to sign the measure, which passed by huge majorities in Congress. It gave millions of acres of public land and millions of dollars in loans to the railroads in return for track being built between Omaha and Sacramento. When the initial grant was alleged to be too small to cover the expenses of track building, Lincoln and Congress agreed to increase it and to offer other inducements to the companies. Railroads ultimately received almost $500 million dollars from the land and gained control over huge sections of the West and its development.[35]

This legislation opened up the West and helped shape the region that would unite the nation in the postwar era even as it had helped to divide it before the war. One might indeed see the Republican party as the western party, born of the conflict over the West and its development, led by two men of the West (first the "Pathfinder," Fremont, and then the "Railsplitter," Lincoln), represented by a platform that appealed to the West's economic development needs—rivers and harbors, homesteads, railroads, and universities to teach the arts necessary to master a new environment. Fremont and Lincoln simply continued in the tradition of Whig westerners who had run for president, beginning with Henry Clay. The profound faith that Republicans had in the role of the West as a safety valve for the potential class conflicts of the East further suggests that even eastern Republicans were shaped by western visions. Horace Greeley of the *New York Tribune* had told "young men" to "go West." Republicans envisioned themselves in terms of developing unsettled territory, forging both character (from the hard work of building "civilization out of wilderness") and prosperity out of the conquest of new lands.[36]

Republican western policy provoked inevitable conflict with Native Americans and continued a policy of removing and concentrating them on western reservations. The most notable clash took place in Minnesota in August 1862 when a Sioux uprising occurred. Rumors flashed across the country of "hundreds" of dead whites, "thousands" of white refugees, and a whole frontier in anarchy, with possible Confederate provocation behind it. Lincoln initially ordered a counterattack in which "necessity knows no law" but soon reconsidered his response. By October when a military commission recommended execution of 303 Sioux warriors captured by the army the president intervened. He reduced the death sentences to thirty-eight and imprisoned the others. Soon after, the Sioux—and the Winnebago, who had played no part in the uprising—were removed from Minnesota; and the Department of Interior, first under Caleb Smith and then under John P. Usher, continued the policy of "concentration" of Native Americans onto reservations. In his December 1862 message Lincoln recommended a reform of the entire Indian affairs system, which he believed was marbled with corruption that inspired uprisings. The Sand Creek massacre of 150 helpless Cheyenne, mostly women and children, in November 1864 produced more calls for reform. But the immense pressures of the Civil War soon overcame all such "distractions"; reform would wait until Grant became president.[37]

Republicans could ignore the need to reform Indian affairs because the wartime legislation that had an impact on Native Americans so clearly carried out party promises and platforms. During the war these laws signified Northern strength and growing nationhood, the shaping of a society stronger than that in the South and burgeoning with vigorous enterprise. After the war, darker consequences would emerge. The foundations for the Gilded Age were established, a world where concentrations of wealth resulted in large social costs to unskilled workers, where fortune served selfish purposes, where westward expansion would nearly exterminate western Indian nations (the reforms of the Grant era hardly helped) and would dislocate many small farmers of the region, and where rapaciousness first developed and then destroyed much of the environment Americans were so eager to master.[38]

But Civil War America had little interest in clouds on distant horizons. A few individuals protested the growing contrast between the children of poverty and the affluence of wartime millionaires. An occasional labor spokesman decried "selfish, haughty, proud, insolent" capitalists who were feeding off "the poverty, wretchedness and utter ruin of their helpless victims" or protested the hypocrisy of "those who in words most magnify labor" but wanted labor that "crouches to their cupidity." Declines in real wages for many urban workers, the consequent increased labor unrest, and the growing numbers of poor women in jail and children as workers pointed to economic inequities, but war's imperatives outshouted every other claim. Americans kept their eyes on battlefields where their resources would arm and protect their sons and advance the Union cause. Years after Appomattox Oliver Wendell Holmes, Jr., would treasure the war as a time when the nation had seen "the snowy heights of honor . . . above the goldfields." War's immediate imperatives emphasized the uses of such wealth in helping the Union forward to victory.[39]

Congress was doing its part, pushing generals to greater efforts and gathering the resources of the Northern economy. Lincoln was endorsing their endeavors by acquiescing in the former and by signing laws that would carry out the latter, meanwhile encouraging the work of vigorous cabinet officers. McClellan had been sent off to war with the largest and most well-supplied army in the nation's history. Still, these measures promised only future success, and the North was increasingly impatient for that future to begin.

6

★★★★★

NORTHERN POWER EMERGES:
MARCH TO JUNE 1862

"I distinctly remember that a feeling of discouragement came over me as I drew near the city of Washington," Julia Ward Howe wrote. She thought of the women whose sons were at risk, who were themselves nursing in hospitals, and of women who were helping the newly created Sanitary Commission with its work of supplying soldiers with necessities from home. But "something seemed to say to me, 'You would be glad to serve, but you cannot help anyone, you have nothing to give and there is nothing for you to do.'" Yet as she traveled around the city, seeing soldiers coming from and going to the battlefields, an idea came to her. She had heard soldiers singing, "John Brown's body lies smoldering in the ground / His soul goes marching on," but other words seemed needed, words that perhaps might inspire men to fight, that could direct their spirits on a crusade to save and transform the land. Rising early one morning she picked up an old pen and wrote, "Mine eyes have seen the glory of the coming of the Lord; / He is trampling out the vintage where the grapes of wrath are stored; / He hath loosed the fateful lightning of his terrible swift sword: / His truth is marching on." The *Atlantic* published "The Battle Hymn of the Republic" in February, just as new signs began to appear that Union power could wield that sword on both land and sea and that dying "to make men free" was, somehow, an inescapable duty.[1]

While the Union waited for McClellan to fulfill his promises in the East, the momentum of war accelerated in the West and began to unleash changes that reached beyond battlefields. Command of the West

119

was in the hands of Henry Halleck, known for his mastery of military literature and for his administrative talents. But Ulysses Grant was the figure who emerged as the fighting general of the West—as the man who fought and won battles, fighting instead of explaining.

Grant's first victories opened vital arteries into the South. Forts Henry and Donelson protected the Tennessee and Cumberland rivers; control of these rivers would provide control of transportation of armies and supplies that could advance through central Tennessee and as far as northern Alabama. Nashville was within reach as were three railroad lines that extended deep into the Confederacy. Also accessible were iron works and gunpowder factories. Employing his own foot soldiers and shallow-draft river gunboats commanded by Andrew Foote, Grant took Fort Henry on 6 February and immediately telegraphed his intention to attack again—at Fort Donelson on the eighth. There was no talk about the enemy outnumbering his troops, no demand for more soldiers, no mention of the unreadiness of the men he had. He would attack. Bad weather delayed him for about a week, but Grant soon took Donelson with a flourish that sounded throughout the North. When Confederate general Simon Bolivar Buckner asked for terms of surrender Grant replied, "No terms except an unconditional and immediate surrender can be accepted. I propose to move immediately upon your works." Buckner called the terms "unchivalrous and ungenerous" but gave in and surrendered nearly 13,000 men to the new Union hero. Lincoln promoted Grant to major general—in the West only Halleck outranked this man generally known for his drinking and his prewar failures. Now the whole North knew of an alternative to McClellan and his style of warfare.[2]

The consequences of Grant's success were not yet fully clear; at this stage it set the entire North celebrating as hopes for victory soared again. The *New York Tribune* announced even before Donelson fell, "It now requires no very far-reaching prophet to predict the end of the struggle." Such feelings grew after Donelson was followed by a Union victory at Pea Ridge in Arkansas on 7 March.

March also witnessed an event that forecast Union victory in another element. An arms race had been under way between North and South over who would control the sea. Early in the war Confederate Secretary of the Navy Stephen Mallory had commissioned an ironclad ship—impervious to the guns of anything afloat. Such a ship would allow the Confederacy to weaken and perhaps destroy the blockade that Union naval superiority was inexorably expanding. Northern leaders, especially Stanton, feared that this new monster could sail up the Potomac and into New York and Boston harbors and bombard the cities, meanwhile destroying anything set against it. The test of this ship, the *Virginia*, began on 8 March at Hampton Roads at the mouth of Chesapeake Bay. The 264-foot "floating barn roof" attacked and destroyed two ships of the line, killing at least 240 sailors, and as the sun set, was ready to sink three other helpless Union vessels, two of which had run aground in their panic. The *Virginia* sustained minor damage, and in the glow of burning ships in the harbor awaited any response that the Yankees might offer.[3]

Northern industrial inventiveness and resources were ready. Union spies had discovered the *Virginia* early in its making and in a Brooklyn navy yard had created a 172-foot "cheesebox on a raft." This ship, the *Monitor*, also was an ironclad and equally impervious. Despite the Confederates' three-month head start, the Union inventor, Swedish-born John Ericsson, subcontracted part of the craft to New York shipmakers and completed his ship in a mere one hundred days, two weeks before the *Virginia* was launched. The strengths of Northern industrial society, its openness to immigrant labor, the diversity of its manufacturing base, and the availability of skill and resources to create the ship, all were ominous for the growing war. The South had to stretch its resources to build one ironclad, but the North could produce almost as many as it needed.[4]

But the *Virginia* seemed almost enough until the *Monitor* appeared. On 9 March 1862 the two ships engaged at Hampton Roads; a new age of naval war had begun. Neither ship could disable the other even though they fired their cannon at point blank range. At the end of the day both the *Virginia* and the *Monitor* withdrew, but the threat to Northern shipping and the blockade was for all intents and purposes over. The North had checkmated Confederate plans, overcoming an advantage that had lasted about twenty-four hours.

The clash at Hampton Roads made the headlines, but underlying this Union success was the work of Gideon Welles and his subordinates. Lincoln supported his secretary of the navy and was interested in advances in maritime technology. In the July 1861 session the president had persuaded Congress to provide $1.5 million to build one or more ironclads. An initial request by the Navy Department for $50,000 to test iron plates had been turned down, but Lincoln ordered the money spent anyway; Congress then provided the larger amount to build the *Monitor*. The decision may have won the war: Although the *Virginia* could hardly have destroyed Northern cities, it endangered the blockade, and without the blockade Northern victory would have been precarious.[5]

Gideon Welles took over the Navy Department with slightly more experience than Cameron or even Stanton had. But he surrounded himself with able and energetic men experienced in naval matters. He also recruited businessmen who oversaw the formidable tasks of blockading over 3,500 miles of coastline and of patrolling the thousands of miles of rivers supporting the army, opening up the Mississippi, and capturing major Confederate ports. There were approximately fifty ships available to perform these duties. Welles used the talents of Gustavus Fox to coordinate the military operations, William Faxon to handle the budgeting, contracts, and routine administration, and George Morgan to oversee major purchasing at the nation's biggest harbor in New York. By midsummer the secretary was building the navy the nation needed for its seas and for its rivers in the West.[6]

The blockade began slowly—almost a paper blockade, existing more as declaration than as reality. The policy posed a problem, however, because international law required that a blockade be effective to be respected by foreign powers. Yet it was commonly recognized that a blockade would have to gain force gradually; therefore foreign powers, especially Great Britain, were willing to allow a time for the blockade to take hold. It soon grew in strength until by midwar it had cut Southern trade to one-third its prewar size so that merchants and consumers experienced shortages in dry goods, salt, and groceries. Further, inflation grew rapidly to reflect the chasing of few goods by many dollars. The blockade apparently did not keep rebel armies from gathering the weapons they needed, but it played a major role in teaching rebel civilians the price of war, in generating a desire for peace, and in undercutting the will to fight on.[7]

Lincoln let Welles alone most of the time; he left most secretaries free to run their own shops. He had more crucial things to do than to try to run the affairs of departments he did not understand. Still, he backed Welles fully on construction of the *Monitor* and on the expansion of the ironclad navy. He may have learned to trust Welles on the day that the cabinet met to discuss the rebel ironclad. Stanton had panicked upon hearing of the *Virginia*'s early victory: As Welles observed, quietly smirking, the secretary of war "ran from room to room, sat down and jumped up . . . scolded and raved." The president was also agitated, rising up to look at the Potomac in concern over the *Virginia*'s next port of call. But Welles remained calm and explained the ship's limitations as well as its strengths. When Stanton suggested sinking sixty canal boats at the mouth of the Potomac to stop the *Virginia*, Lincoln allowed the boats to be gathered but told Stanton to wait until the *Virginia* was sighted near Washington. When the imagined threat quickly vanished Lincoln joked about "Stanton's navy . . . as useless as the paps of man to a suckling child." "Neptune was right," he added; and "Father Neptune," as the president called Welles, was given a free reign in his domain.[8]

As war accelerated the president was developing his management style, a style reflected in his relationship with Welles. He gave cabinet officers a free hand in most of the operations of their departments. He told Chase, "You understand these things, I do not," when asked for an opinion on the complexities of trade regulations. He let the treasury secretary control almost all of the day-to-day activities. In foreign affairs Lincoln left so much to Seward that after the war former minister Charles Francis Adams eulogized Seward as the real brains behind the administration. Cabinet officers were responsible for dealing with Congress on matters that related to their domain. Stanton, for example, was largely responsible for conscription laws, Chase for bonds and money. "The Administration is merely departmental," Chase told Welles, who agreed.[9]

The lines of authority were initially vague. When Cameron's incompetence left a vacuum, Seward rushed to fill it from one side and Chase stepped in from the other. Once Stanton took over at the War Department the lines were well-defined and Seward and Chase stepped back into their own territories. For the first six weeks of the administration there were no regular cabinet meetings, and only after Chase and Bates complained were Tuesdays and Fridays set aside as regular meeting days. Seward objected, but that was because he liked an environment where he could cross departmental lines and meet with the president without having to answer arguments by other members of the cabinet. Seward and Stanton often met individually with Lincoln, however, generating resentments within the cabinet that lasted throughout the war. Meanwhile, each department was run without the benefit of the opinions of other cabinet members, a situation that Welles, especially, deplored.[10]

Despite the administrative isolation and occasional conflict, Lincoln may have benefited from his lack of administrative experience. He did not try to master the details of the army, of the treasury, of the navy, of foreign affairs. He was free to consider matters that he understood better—larger matters of grand strategy, recognizing the interconnections between politics and military operations. He found men he could trust with ongoing operations and let them do their jobs. Leaving other men to work out the details, Lincoln bent his energies to the "*great* task" remaining before the nation.[11]

A major part of that task involved responding to changing public opinion as the war continued. Changes were at work as spring 1862 advanced; proemancipation opinion in particular was growing. Once a despised minority, abolitionists delighted in their newfound popularity as lecturers who spoke in the House of Representatives, in Cooper Union, in most of the respectable halls of the nation. In December 1861 abolitionist William Goodell wrote, "Never has there been a time when Abolitionists were as much respected as at present. . . . Announce the presence of a competent abolition lecturer and the house is crammed." Wendell Phillips was introduced by Charles Sumner on the Senate floor, and the vice-president left his seat to come and shake the radical's hand. The public mood was shifting toward the goals of abolition.[12]

But how far and how fast? Even abolitionists differed over supporting an immediate or a more deliberate policy. Faced with the alternative of having an implacably racist Democrat replace the slow-moving Lincoln in the White House, many abolitionists went along with the president while grinding their teeth over his pace. Garrison, the outspoken advocate of immediatism, wheeled into line with the president. Earlier he had attacked both the Union and the Constitution as symbols that paralyzed abolition; he had proclaimed the Philadelphia charter a "covenant with Death . . . an agreement with hell." By late 1861 Garrison was telling large crowds, "I am now with the government to enable it to constitutionally stop the further ravages of death, and to extinguish the flames of hell forever." Other antislavery leaders, noting that the administration still allowed soldiers to return the fugitive slaves of loyal masters even as it attacked the power of disloyal slaveholders, lashed out at such mixed morality. "There has never been an Administration so thoroughly devoted to slavery as the present," Stephen S. Foster asserted in January 1862; "no other ever returned so many fugitive slaves, nor did so much to propitiate the Slave Power." And Garrison did keep agitating to push Lincoln toward the promised land.[13]

But as events moved forward, the issue became not when but how slavery might die. Victories in the West and on the sea brought emancipation within sight, and the serious responsibilities of forming a policy instead of agitating for truth led some men to pause. James Russell Lowell, once a member of the abolitionist band, began to wonder about the meaning of the freedom that might be gained. Writing in the common dialect he adopted in poetry, Lowell anguished over the alternatives:

> I want's to have all we gain stick,
> An' not to start Millennium too quick:
> We hain't to punish only, but to keep,
> An' the cure's gut to go a cent'ry deep.

Then in behalf of immediate action came the retort:

> It's Slavery that's the fangs an' thinkin' head,
> An' ef you want selvation, cresh it dead,
> An' cresh it suddin' or you'll learn by waitin
> Thet Chance wun't stop to listen to debatin'.
> God hates your sneakin' creturs thet believe
> He'll settle things they run away an' leave.[14]

Lincoln was seeking a solution to the slavery problem that would stick. He was trying to achieve as many of his and the nation's goals as he could, weaving emancipation into the fabric of existing values and institutions. Abolitionists had the luxury of agitating in behalf of their single cause; Lincoln had to satisfy the potentially contradictory range of goals that Americans sought: respecting the Constitution, ending the rebellion, destroying the power of slavery to threaten national goals, preserving the ideas of consent of the governed and equal liberty (however vaguely that might be defined).

These wide-ranging factors contended for dominance as the president, after the western victories, shaped his policies. When Donelson fell not only was Tennessee open to Union dominance, but more important, Kentucky was safe. Thus emancipation was at least for a time no longer hostage to the strategic importance of the border states.

Kentucky had always been strategically vital. Its geographic position and the large number of potential soldiers it housed meant that it was indispensable to the Union. But Kentucky and the other border states mattered to Lincoln for additional reasons. He had been born and raised there, and when he moved first to Indiana and then to Illinois he was still surrounded by much of its culture. Tens of thousands of Kentuckians had moved to the southern part of these states, and central Illinois in 1858 was referred to as "old Kentucky." His wife and his best friend were both from the Blue Grass State; personal ties were strong. Politically, he most admired a Kentuckian, Henry Clay, and especially Clay's handling of the deepest crisis of the age, slavery.[15]

Critics accused him of being the "president of Kentucky" when he revoked Fremont's proclamation in order to keep the state in the Union, but a larger issue was at stake. Lincoln focused on Kentucky, and on the border states it exemplified and led, not just because "to lose Kentucky is to lose the whole game" but because in 1862, at least, he believed that to win Kentucky would mean to win the game. And it would be won by voluntarily ending slavery. Military control of the state was crucial but even more vital was to convert the border states from slavery to freedom.

In the interval after Grant's army took Donelson, Lincoln moved quickly to destroy slavery in the border states. Speed was essential because he understood the power of slavery. He knew of course that slavery controlled the lives of black people. Yet impressing him more deeply was the power of slavery to control the destiny of the best government in the world—the world's "last best hope." Slavery had threatened the basic values of the nation; it caused people to deny the truths of the Declaration of Independence. It thus simultaneously distorted the Constitution and corrupted the concept of free labor—that a man had the right to keep what he had earned by his own sweat. Most ominously, slavery had produced the disunion of the country and challenged the processes of popular constitutional government.

Though slavery divided the nation, it united the South. It created a potential sodality willing to sacrifice everything to protect it—secession had already proven that. Yet, why had the border states not joined the Confederacy? Because Union armies had supplemented the efforts of loyal people and thus undercut the power of proslavery people who wanted to take Kentucky and the other border states out of the Union.

Still, the force of slavery there was only slightly limited; at any moment it might be resurrected. Lincoln had seen how dramatic the reaction to Fremont's emancipation proposal had been. He knew that within the population of the border region—including those Northerners with border-state roots—lurked feelings that might be responsive to the rhetoric of slavery and racism. If ever the tide flowed against Union arms that powerful proslavery feeling might reemerge and the border states would slip back to their baser instincts. The Confederates knew that too, enmeshed so powerfully in proslavery experience; they knew that white people did not escape slavery as easily as fugitive slaves did.

Lincoln sought another option: The border-state people had to break their own chains—to show that slavery did not have the power to drive them to mad and evil acts. The liberation of the South could follow. If the border slave states turned themselves into border free states, then the prophecies that slavery was on the course to ultimate extinction would have been proven true; even the South would see it.

"The leaders of the existing insurrection," he told Congress, "entertain the hope that this government will ultimately be forced to acknowledge the independence of some part of the disaffected region and that all the slave states North of such part will then say 'the Union, for which we have struggled, being already gone, we now choose to go with the southern section.' To deprive them of this hope, substantially ends the rebellion." Deep South states would know that their rebellion would never expand, and, as he repeated later, the act that would "substantially end the rebellion" would be for the border states to surrender slavery.[16]

If border states could be persuaded to abolish slavery, a mortal blow might be delivered against the rebel states. The Confederacy's major hope, Lincoln thought, was that the power of the slave system would ultimately bring loyal slave states to the rebel side; and as the Confederacy itself was thus expanded, Union hopes would be dashed. Lincoln wanted to reverse that possibility in the most effective way.

On 6 March 1862 Lincoln asked Congress to pass its first official act against slavery out of the context of the battlefield: He requested "pecuniary aid" to any state "which may adopt gradual abolishment of slavery." Congress was then debating a bill to end slavery in the District of Columbia. It had passed the First Confiscation Act to take the slaves of rebels who used them directly to assist rebellion, but this proposal included loyal and rebel states, states not then in battle, and every existing slave state in the nation. If Congress enacted the measure and states accepted it, especially the symbolically and strategically vital border states, then slavery in the United States would be dead.

War thus fostered revolution, but constitutional and political realities restrained it. Lincoln emphasized that he preferred gradual emancipation, within the existing constitutional framework. He noted that "the general government, sets up no claim of a right, by federal authority to interfere with slavery within state limits." He wanted the states to begin a step-by-step process that would result one day in a freedom that would endure, and he believed that "gradual and not sudden emancipation is better for all." Lincoln wanted emancipation to be a process more than an event. He believed that a freedom chosen by former masters and implemented by them was more likely to be enduring than one brought by the sword. Hope still endured in Lincoln's mind in early 1862 that the war would end before it became a revolution.[17]

Lincoln's suggestion revealed an insider's instinct for implementing changes with the least possible damage to existing institutions and assumptions, but it had its flaws. Fundamentally it was far more sensitive in its appeal to whites to accept the process than it was in foreseeing the consequences for blacks. Had states and the existing white leadership of 1862 retained control over emancipation, the prospect of civil and political rights would surely have been limited. Implemented before blacks proved their capacities and earned national obligation by their service in the war, state-controlled emancipation would have done little to change the ideas about the rights blacks could exercise, or the benefits the nation might gain from allowing them those rights. Emancipation controlled by states meant that no national power could checkmate local oppression, that no Fourteenth or Fifteenth Amendments could come to be. When at the end of the war Southern states were forced to implement a system for freed blacks before Congress imposed its ideas, the defeated Southern whites produced the black codes. These state laws mandated an ignorant peasantry confined to the land, exercising no voting rights and few important civil rights. The two amendments at least provided potential national authority to expand black freedom. No such option would have existed if Lincoln's state-run, compensated emancipation scheme had been accepted.

Although emphasizing the benefits to slave states of acting within a prewar framework, Lincoln also painted a future in which continued war might lead to more dramatic events. He would use all means that "may seem indispensable, or may obviously promise great efficiency towards end in the struggle." And he continued the war even as Congress passed the measure on 2 April, the president meanwhile providing editors and legislators with specific calculations proving that paying to free slaves cost less than fighting the war.

People most interested in new directions had mixed reactions. Some abolitionists welcomed the plan, but others damned its limitations and many were troubled that Lincoln might stop with this unlikely "will of the wisp," as Garrison called it. Yet Phillips noted that "if the president has not yet entered Canaan, he has turned his face Zionward."[18]

The momentum of Union success was pleasing radicals as well as conservatives, at least among members of the Republican party and its allies. Indeed optimism about the progress of the war was so advanced that Stanton blundered. On 3 April he called a halt to federal recruiting, closed recruiting offices, and told personnel to sell their office furniture and return to regular duties with their field units. Prevailing hopes for early victory explained part of this decision, and the confusions and complexities of recruiting itself helped inspire it. The national government called for the troops and assigned quotas, but twenty-three separate states actually gathered the troops. Governors from different parties and with different state agendas carried out the process, from organization of community rallies to the appointment of officers up to the rank of colonel; they also oversaw the initial organization of the units. Moreover private individuals added to the confusion by enlisting and organizing their own regiments and presenting themselves for service. In December McClellan had tried to streamline the process by having the War Department appoint federal recruiting supervisors in each state and by telling the governors to accept no more troops without a direct requisition from Washington. Stanton added his own flourishes to the reform, telling congressmen that he wanted to suspend recruiting for two months. He was still so new to his job that he did not expect the resulting criticism from many soldiers in the field, who were beginning to feel the need for reinforcements. He did not know what was about to happen near Shiloh Church or on the peninsula.[19]

For two days, 6 and 7 April, beside the Tennessee River Union and Confederate armies attacked and defended courageously on both sides. First, the Confederates surprised Grant's army, pushing it back toward the river. Then during the night Buell joined Grant, ferrying 20,000 reinforcements into the lines as the rain fell and federal gunboats fired into rebel lines and the thousands of wounded men lay moaning or in quiet agony. On the second day Union soldiers attacked; Confederates grudgingly retreated, and the young soldiers fell in such numbers that, as Grant reported later, he could walk across the battlefield on their bodies. Almost 11,000 rebels, over 13,000 Unionists were casualties that day—a carnage that eclipsed any other battle in the Western hemisphere to that time, that exceeded the combined casualties of the five major battles that had preceded these bloody two days. More Americans died at Shiloh than in the Revolutionary War, the War of 1812, and the Mexican War combined. The slaughter was so enormous that it overshadowed a major victory at Island no.10, which opened up the Mississippi for Union traffic.[20]

The carnage awakened the Union to a new understanding of war. Grant reported that he now abandoned visions of limited war. "I gave up all hope of saving the union except by complete conquest," he wrote. By late summer he was receiving orders to "live upon the country . . . handle rebels within our lines without gloves." Meanwhile, John Pope was taking over in the East near Washington, giving orders to shoot captured rebel guerrillas, expel civilians who refused to take loyalty oaths, and seize rebel property without paying for it. In tune with the escalating trend Stanton resumed recruiting early in June. The war on the battlefield was losing its early restraint, and there were signs that these sentiments were shaping decisions behind the lines as well.[21]

Abolitionists' long-standing beliefs that war would mean the death of slavery were endorsed by growing radicalism on the battlefield, and their criticism of Lincoln's gradual emancipation plan increased. To ask slave owners to consent to free their slaves—to pay them to stop treating human beings as things—seemed to concede the premises of slavery: that states should control the destinies of blacks and that this principle was more important than justice and more vital than bold measures that promised immediate blows against the rebellion. Wendell Phillips was struck by the contrast and saw the inexorability of emancipation: "Abraham Lincoln may not wish it; he cannot prevent it; the nation may not will it; the nation can never prevent it. . . . I do not care what men may want or wish; the negro is the pebble in the cog wheel, and the machine cannot go until you get him out. . . . Abraham Lincoln simply rules; John C. Fremont governs."[22]

But as Phillips was proclaiming these words Fremont, removed from Missouri, governed only the newly created Mountain Department, where he was unsuccessfully trying to cope with Stonewall Jackson. Lincoln's rule encompassed the entire nation, and he was trying to find a way to unite it and to end slavery. Crucial to his determination was his intention to control the complexities of the emancipation issue. Thus when on 9 May 1862 Gen. David Hunter, commander of Union forces in Georgia, Florida, and South Carolina, declared the slaves there "forever free," Lincoln revoked the order just as he had undone Fremont's emancipation declaration. Despite urging from Chase that Hunter's proclamation be respected, the president declared curtly, "No commanding general shall do such a thing, upon *my* responsibility, without consulting me." He could not allow generals to make final decisions on perhaps the most important question of the war. They might see it as a question of military policy, but Lincoln's view was grander. He was endeavoring to find in the war environment a lasting means to end slavery. He was seeking a solution as complex and comprehensive as the problem of slavery in the constitutional union itself; given the scope of the effort, it was possible that no perfect solution would emerge.

Using the revocation of Hunter's proclamation as a forum, Lincoln again asked the border states to provide an enduring solution, begging them to open their eyes to the direction the war was taking. "I do not argue. I beseech you to make the arguments for yourselves. You cannot, if you would, be blind to the signs of the times. I beg you a calm and enlarged consideration of them, ranging it may be, far above personal and partisan politics." Gradual, compensated emancipation would produce a change that "would come gently as the dews of heaven, not rending or wrecking anything. Will you not embrace it? So much good has not been done, by one effort in all past time, as, in the providence of God, it is now your high privilege to do. May the vast future not have to lament that you have neglected it."[23]

Lincoln's hoped-for resolution also included colonization of freed blacks. For years before the war he had identified himself with the colonization movement, taking a leading role in the Illinois Colonization Society in the 1850s, advocating colonization in debating Douglas. During the conflict he discussed the subject with cabinet members, congress-men, diplomats, and private entrepreneurs who wanted to colonize blacks in South America in return for the profits they might get. In De-cember 1862 Lincoln proposed a constitutional amendment that would pay for colonizing any blacks who wished to emigrate. "I cannot make it better known than it already is, that I strongly favor colonization," he asserted.[24]

Underlying his advocacy was a clear recognition of the power of racism in the nation and the impact it had on blacks. Speaking in Au-gust 1862 Lincoln had noted to a delegation of Negroes from the District of Columbia, "We have between us a broader difference than exists be-tween almost any other two races. Whether it is right or wrong I need not discuss, but this physical difference is a great disadvantage to us both, as I think your race suffers very greatly, many of them by living among us, while ours suffer from your presence. In a word we suffer on each side. If this is admitted, it affords a reason at least why we should be separated." Pointing out that slavery had caused the war and, there-fore, without the presence of blacks there would be no conflict, observ-ing that "on this broad continent not a single man of your race is made the equal of a single man of ours," Lincoln saw further reasons why "it is better for us both, therefore, to be separated." He urged them to ac-cept the temporary inconveniences of moving to another country so that their race might benefit by building for themselves a future free from white oppression.[25]

Yet colonization was indeed a doubtful solution to the problem. Blacks rejected it, abolitionists had condemned it, Southerners were suspicious of it, foreign governments opposed it. In operational terms it was also suspect. The ships necessary to send 4.25 million blacks out of the country did not exist. Lincoln had doubted in 1859 that Kansas could afford to send to Liberia even the small numbers of slaves that po-tentially would enter its borders; he noted that there probably was "not surplus money in the world" adequate to pay for sending America's blacks abroad. In the discussions of colonization Lincoln never carefully considered the operation of such a large effort. He supported two small expeditions into the Caribbean and had funds from Congress to support more but spent only a little more than one-twentieth of those funds. The discrepancy between the rhetoric on the subject and the reality is striking. One historian has suggested that Lincoln needed to avoid ex-tensive inquiry into the subject for psychological reasons, blocking out available information in order to believe that there was a resolution to the problem of freeing the slaves.[26]

Certainly he was susceptible to tricks of the mind. Lincoln may have needed an unexamined dream to sustain him—that is what dreams are for. But another explanation also makes sense: He knew the limitations of colonization. Conceived as a vast project for freeing the nation of blacks, its failings were apparent. Colonization, however, could be seen in a more limited sense, as an idea with two purposes— relieving white apprehensions and helping blacks gain greater acceptance in the white world.

White fear of migrating blacks was strong. Republicans had promised since their party's birth that excluding slavery from the territories also would keep blacks out. Northern whites feared that emancipation would attract blacks into their communities, thus bringing crime, immorality, and economic dependence. Colonization provided a placebo. And Lincoln seems to have made most of his public comments about colonization even as he was moving toward emancipating the slaves, advancing toward freedom while calming white fears. Lincoln surely knew of this appeasing potential in colonization rhetoric. An associate in the late 1850s had observed that colonization helped "ward off attacks made upon us about Negro equality." Less elegantly, one Ohio politician said, "It is a damned humbug. But it will take with the people."[27]

Yet colonization also might be a practical answer to the problem of freed blacks. Too often historians have fallen on the scheme as though it were the single resolution that Lincoln held and clung to until events made it impractical. But colonization did not have to be a panacea to be effective. As *the* solution to the emancipation question it was full of holes; as *a* solution it had merit on several scores. First, it would help those blacks who wanted to escape a world where white prejudice oppressed them. Many people believed that in the past, black nations had been the places where black genius had flowered; they might be again. Second, if a separate black nation or colony could succeed, it might demonstrate to whites the capacity of the allegedly inferior black race to work with self-discipline and dedication. One of the most attractive elements in sending colonists to a virgin territory would be that it allowed blacks to repeat the archetypical Republican success story—man conquering frontier and self,. forging prosperity and character. Urging blacks to colonize in August 1862, Lincoln emphasized the need to sacrifice and the frontier nature of the enterprise and he urged the power of the example: "Now, if you could give a start to white people," he pleaded, "you would open a wide door for many to be made free." Colonization offered an effective illustration of the success blacks might accomplish once they gained their freedom.[28] At the same time it remained a potent means to deflect racist challenges to emancipation. Lincoln was not ignorant of both of its qualities.

These early proposals for ending slavery failed. The border-state representatives to whom Lincoln had pleaded turned him down. In Missouri and especially in Delaware measures urging acceptance of Lincoln's ideas came close but did not pass. State sovereignty arguments, fears of social upheaval, bickering over how much money Congress would actually provide, and beliefs that the Confederacy would react to the measures with implacable resolve doomed the plan. In July 1862 Lincoln made a last appeal to the border-state delegation in Congress to accept his compensated emancipation plan, but by a vote of twenty to nine they turned him down. Despite Lincoln's wish to interweave freedom gradually into the fabric of tradition and society there was no chance to do so in the loyal free states. The border states had made gradual change impossible; they had also made radical change inevitable.[29]

That change was compounding with increasing force throughout the North. Not only was Lincoln pushing it deliberately on border states, but Congress also was writing an increasingly liberating record. Many congressmen shared Lincoln's conservative feelings; still, as legislators turned to the problems of making laws about slavery and the Negro, ideas that were more advanced than those in the White House surfaced. Cooperating with Lincoln when they could, prodding him when possible, taking the lead and quarreling with him when necessary, congressmen moved toward liberty by walking a path that respected legal limitations as they journeyed toward unchartered ground. They simply walked a little faster than the president.

When the Thirty-seventh Congress ended, lawmakers had passed twenty-six measures attacking slavery. The body worked with the president in ratifying an 1862 treaty between the United States and Britain that secured the ultimate destruction of the slave trade. The United States proved its commitment to ending the trade in February 1862 when the captain of a slaver, Nathaniel Gordon, became the first American to be executed for that crime. The law had been in disuse for so long that people were insisting that "they dare not hang him." Lincoln granted a stay of execution only to permit Gordon to make "the necessary preparation for the awful charge which awaits him." Lawmakers also approved the recognition of two black-led republics, Liberia and Haiti. Southern opposition had stopped this move before the war; the idea of entertaining and negotiating with black diplomats in the nation's capital threatened white prejudice. But now the black men joined Washington's diplomatic corps, at least America's diplomacy had become color blind.

Acting independently Congress wrote an antislavery record. The conflicting policy over soldiers' treatment of fugitive slaves was finally settled by a March 1862 article of war that forbade military personnel from returning fugitives. Opponents had protested that the Constitution, for which the Union forces were allegedly fighting, still contained its fugitive rendition clause. But proponents of the measure argued that the highest obligation was to save the Union, and giving laborers back to the enemy was not good policy. Yet constitutional commitment stayed firm; the federal government would still return fugitives until June 1864, when Congress killed the fugitive slave law.[30]

The irony of this two-pronged policy could be seen outside the capitol building itself. Even though Congress freed the slaves in the District of Columbia in mid-April 1862 the measure did not affect the status of escaping slaves who sought refuge in the District. Hundreds of such fugitives ran away from Maryland owners and thus precipitated clashes between proponents of freedom and supporters of the laws. The head of the police in Washington, Ward Lamon, a personal friend of Lincoln, insisted that his men would return escapees to loyal masters. But soldiers stationed in the city frequently disagreed and took runaways under their wing. Several clashes between the two groups ensued, with soldiers rescuing fugitives from the police, police sneaking up on soldiers and recapturing the alleged slaves, police being placed in army jails, and soldiers being locked up in city jails. The scenes often suggested comic opera, but they showed the complexities of preserving a constitutional Union that protected slavery and yet was threatened by it.[31]

Fugitive slaves may have posed constitutional difficulties, but no such security existed for slavery itself in the nation's capital. Congress exercised its plenary power in the District as early as 16 April 1862, emancipating all slaves there. Following Lincoln's suggestions that compensation be available for loyal slave owners, Congress provided $300 for each slave freed. The president's views were also reflected in a provision to provide $100,000 for colonization for the freedmen. District slaveholders protested vehemently, and the board of aldermen urged Congress to avoid turning their city into "an asylum for free negroes." Some people forecast "a hell on earth for the white men," but Congress acted. The opportunity to be free of constitutional restrictions and immune from electoral reprisals was too strong. When a member of the House insisted that no emancipation take place in the District without the consent of residents, Thaddeus Stevens stopped him. Emancipation was right and no popular vote should stand in its way; to act otherwise would be like allowing the damned in hell to be punished only if they consented to it. Emancipation in the District took place in an orderly manner: The "damned" were compensated and the freedmen gained their liberty; "hell" remained at some unmeasured distance.[32]

Similarly, Congress acted forcefully in the territories where the disreputable *Dred Scott* decision stood in the way. The large Republican majorities in both houses made that decision only a paper barrier. Democrats might plead that the rule of law demanded respect for the Court, but Republicans were not willing to respect a decision that they had despised since party infancy. Congress killed slavery in the territories. With fewer than forth-six slaves in the territories, the actual freedom provided was minor, but the vindication of the long-treasured principle was sweet. On 19 June 1862 Lincoln signed the bill. "Thus closed forever," Massachusetts senator Henry Wilson wrote, "the long contest between freedom and slavery for the vast Territories . . . of the United States."[33]

By mid-1862 Congress, reflecting the mood of voters, was moving against slavery, hitting it boldly in places clearly in the public eye, facilitating the war effort, punishing rebels, and advancing the skirmish line of freedom. Lincoln also was active, working within the established constitutional system, asking states to control the escalating change and to make for themselves societies and communities at last freed from slavery. He was increasingly sensitive to pressures from abolitionists and soldiers alike to strike at slavery, sap rebel strength, and redeem the nation from its greatest sin. God and the battalions were joining forces and seemingly were on the march; at least in parts of the army and the society the linkage was being made. Yet a major obstacle to this combined operation remained. On the peninsula in Virginia George McClellan, commanding the greatest number of those battalions in a slow advance, saw the voices against slavery as enemies and not as allies.

7

★★★★★

LEAVING OLD MOORINGS—
McCLELLAN AND EMANCIPATION:
JUNE TO DECEMBER 1862

"I am tired of the sickening sight of the battlefield, with its mangled corpses and poor suffering wounded!" General McClellan wrote. "Victory has no charms for me when purchased at such cost." The real fighting was just beginning, and yet the North's leading general was dismayed. Saddened by the dead and suffering young men, he was disturbed that forces in Washington were in motion that would undermine the great effort he had under way. "I am as anxious as any human being to finish this war," he asserted. "Yet when I see such insane folly behind me I feel that the final salvation of the country demands the utmost prudence on my part, and that I must not run the slightest risk of disaster, for if anything happened to this army our cause would be lost." Distressed by the blood of the battlefield, fearful of the criticism of a growing band of enemies, the young general was on the peninsula, but not in a bold frame of mind.[1]

Part of the blame for McClellan's hesitancy could be laid at Lincoln's feet. Although the president had accepted McClellan's Virginia strategy and given him added time to set it in motion, he had hedged his bets. He and Stanton worried about the capital. McClellan's peninsula offensive would take the soldiers who stood between Washington and the rebel armies one hundred miles away. If Union troops were gone Confederates might capture the nation's capital—with catastrophic effect on Northern morale. McClellan's insistence that his presence near Richmond would keep the enemy away from Washington did not persuade the civilian leaders. Therefore, while sending him to the peninsula with

100,000 men, they kept 35,000 south of Washington. They also removed him from the position of general in chief, making him commander of the Army of the Potomac. He approved the demotion for he wanted to concentrate on the peninsula, but it did undercut his public image. And McClellan was angry, then apprehensive about the reduction in his invasion force. Those 35,000 men were to be the vanguard of his movement toward Richmond. Cautious and careful near any battlefield, he slowed down even more in his first advances. He thus increased the demands that he be more aggressive, demands that intensified when his month-long siege of Yorktown proved to be almost foolish. When his army broke into the town they found defenses so weak that the rebels could have been defeated swiftly and decisively. "No one but McClellan," a Southern commander observed, "would have hesitated to attack."[2]

Still McClellan's huge army moved slowly up the peninsula, closer to Richmond. Optimism soared in the North as Confederates were pushed toward their capital. Then the South struck back. First Joseph Johnston and then Robert E. Lee attacked the Union army in late June and early July. The bloody Seven Days campaign pushed McClellan away from Richmond and forced him into a series of brilliant logistical maneuvers that in his mind showed his mastery of warfare. He was not entirely wrong. This retreat inflicted over 20,000 casualties on the Confederacy, while absorbing 16,000 of his own. Nevertheless, by the end of the seven days the Army of the Potomac was only fifteen miles from Richmond and was over 100,000 men strong. McClellan exulted that he had saved the Union and the army. He also continued bitterly to criticize the secretary of war for not supplying him with the increased troops and supplies that he constantly asked for. In the midst of the campaign he wrote, "I have seen too many dead and wounded comrades to feel otherwise than that the government has not sustained this army. If you do not do so now the game is lost. If I save this army now, I tell you plainly I owe no thanks to you or to any other persons in Washington. You have done your best to sacrifice this army." Stanton did not see those last two sentences; a telegraph officer in Washington deleted them. But McClellan's mood revealed a lack of self-discipline that combined strangely with his public image of decisive expertise.[3]

McClellan suffered from a perfectionist's flaw—he wanted to be, needed to be, the master of any domain he touched. This quality made him an excellent administrator whose attention to detail was legendary, but when he faced a situation he could not control his sense of powerlessness grew. He multiplied the extent of his problems, most notably by believing that Confederate armies always were larger than his own.

During the Seven Days battles the general told his superiors and his own troops that they fought outnumbered, "attacked by vastly superior forces." Lee had 200,000 men, McClellan reported. In fact, Lee had a number closer to 90,000—Montgomery Meigs, reading Confederate newspapers in Washington, had figured that out. But the Union commander needed more soldiers—at least 100,000, he told Stanton—or his army and the Union and George McClellan would fail.

Meanwhile, the general insisted that he had won the Seven Days campaign, and there was an argument for that opinion. In terms of comparative casualties he had; twenty thousand to sixteen thousand was an impressive ratio in the Union's favor. The smaller Southern population could hardly sustain such imbalances for long. And perhaps in terms of military strategy McClellan was right, too, since his huge army still menaced Richmond and Virginia as a whole and hence the Confederacy.

The general public had a less sophisticated vision. They knew that Lee had pushed McClellan away from Richmond, and they saw retreat, regardless of any talk of strategic superiority. And they became increasingly suspicious about the value of strategic superiority when McClellan did nothing to menace the rebels. He did not take the offensive against Lee; he did not threaten the railroad nerve center at Petersburg, only twenty-two miles south of Richmond. He simply sat and complained about lack of support. Although most of the army and many newspapers—most of them Democratic—continued to support him, some of McClellan's own soldiers, once so proud of "our general," now were writing about the humiliation of retreating. "I think officers and men are disgusted with & have lost confidence in McClellan," one wrote. Another agreed: "McClellan issues flaming addresses though everyone in the Army knows he was outwitted." He may have won a campaign on a battlefield, but in the larger fight for the minds and hearts of the people, even among some of his own soldiers, he was losing ground. And congressmen were not impressed. The Committee on the Conduct of the War opened hearings on the Peninsula campaign while its chairman ridiculed McClellan: "Place him before an enemy and he will burrow like a wood duck."[4]

But McClellan was not completely inert. He justified his sitzkreig so persuasively that Lincoln did not demand movement immediately. He did tell the general that "if, at any time, you feel able to take the offensive, you are not restrained from doing so."[5] Four days later Lincoln decided to travel to headquarters at Harrison's Landing to see the situation for himself. McClellan meanwhile was preparing a letter on the military and the political situation that he planned to give to the president.

The Harrison's Landing letter was McClellan's counterattack on growing radical sentiment. The general may have hoped that once Lincoln was away from Washington and face to face with his most important general, the president would adopt his views. "He was always much influenced by me when we were together," McClellan later recalled. Sitting in his tent, surrounded by the great army that he had shaped, he would show Lincoln what war meant and how it could be fought and for what ends. He had much to say about the interconnections between domestic politics and the making of war. Certainly the great cause "must never be abandoned; it is the cause of free institutions and self government." Lincoln would like that. And the general's letter reminded Lincoln how important the presidential office was; Lincoln had the constitutional authority to shape both civil and military policy directed toward ending the rebellion. That was a little obvious, but might be sufficiently flattering, and it did link the two commanders as comrades in arms. General McClellan was hoping to inspire "General" Lincoln: two commanders across the table from each other. As one commander to another, he wanted Lincoln to take that authority "or our cause will be lost."

The question, of course, was the meaning of "our cause." McClellan mapped it out by describing a world that Democrats still clung to but that Lincoln was moving away from. Restraint was needed in fighting this war, the general said. The war should not be seen as subjugating a people but as defeating the rebel army and government. Property should not be confiscated, states should maintain their governmental institutions. Above all, the general told the president, forcible emancipation must not happen. Such a policy would turn the war into a revolution, making recruiting "almost hopeless." McClellan believed that escaping slaves could be taken as contraband of war, and he conceded that compensated emancipation might be necessary. Yet "a declaration of radical views, especially upon slavery, will rapidly disintegrate our present armies."[6]

McClellan has been criticized for the political tone of this letter, but that was a minor flaw. Politics and military decisions were entwined throughout the nation. In Congress the Committee on the Conduct of the War was certainly using its authority to intimidate Democratic, not Republican, generals. Congressmen generally tested military devotion by the position that generals took on slavery, and few Democratic generals were hostile to it. Since generals were often appointed by Lincoln because of their politics as well as for their soldierly qualities, such testing was inescapable. Furthermore, soldiers themselves were passionately interested in politics, voting when possible in camp or at home on election day and discussing politics constantly around campfires. Citizen soldiers wore military uniforms but they did not forget they were citizens. As one correspondent observed, "A volunteer army, accustomed to voting at home, on going to camp, yet remain citizens." Perhaps most important, in the army slavery met Northern policy. Whether soldiers or congressmen made decisions about slavery, they would be felt first in the army. In such a situation McClellan's desire to shape the goals of war as well as to make war was not surprising.[7]

Two factors, however, made the letter unfortunate: its timing and its substance. McClellan does not seem to have understood that Lincoln had already lost much of his faith in the general's judgment. The president was in the process of appointing Henry Halleck to McClellan's former post as general in chief. Halleck was urging Lincoln to try another strategy for the eastern theater, uniting McClellan's forces with General Pope's in northern Virginia. When Lincoln visited McClellan the president brought with him a series of questions for other generals in the army about their commander's military strategy and was especially interested in their thoughts about abandoning McClellan's grand peninsular campaign. McClellan was unlikely to influence Lincoln, even outside the capital city; Lincoln did not give him the chance. Instead of using the letter as the occasion for a review of strategy between leaders, Lincoln thanked the general, pocketed the letter and took it back to Washington to read.[8]

The letter was at best perhaps half right. McClellan, being a committed Democrat, had heard what he wanted to hear or at least what those subordinates who agreed with their commander would say to him. A highly politicized society certainly contained its share of Democrats who were strongly conservative on the slavery question and unenthusiastic about freeing slaves. McClellan was probably right in saying that freeing Southern slaves would enflame the fears and determination of a culture that saw slavery as race control. A reasonable response, however, would have been to ask, "How much more passionate can you get than seceding from the government and going to war?" Unionist Southerners had so far been powerless in the face of that passion; why should their feelings be considered now, especially with Kentucky secure? In short, McClellan's advice to Lincoln was too little and too late. Moreover, for anyone to give Lincoln advice on politics, especially someone who had never been elected to office, was superfluous at best.

Lincoln did not take McClellan's advice to disconnect saving the Union from emancipation. Such a position had always been against his basic ideals, and by midsummer 1862 public opinion was moving toward Lincoln's views. McClellan was crying out against a surging emancipation tide. Ironically that tide was being governed by the very military necessities of which McClellan claimed to be master.

Public frustration and anxiety boiled in summer 1862. The grand hopes for early victory spawned by western successes at Forts Henry and Donelson and at Shiloh and by the fall of New Orleans to Adm. David Farragut in late April had vanished. Although Grant wanted to invade quickly, Halleck felt the need to secure supply lines and to resupply the soldiers. The cost of Shiloh had been brutal, and even though Grant's victory was celebrated rumors circulated that he had been surprised by the rebels. Halleck, hoping to avoid future surprises, geared down the western war almost to a crawl. The eastern story was worse. With high hopes McClellan had taken the apparently unstoppable juggernaut of the Army of the Potomac to the peninsula in Virginia. By 2 July he had been turned back from Richmond and stood at Harrison's Landing, pleading for more troops and scolding the administration for its lack of support. Ominously while leaders demanded action, recruiting of soldiers slowed down. The early enthusiasm for war was waning. Northern governors began to ask for increased bounties to spur enlistments; some even urged a draft.[9]

Increasingly, Lincoln recognized the need for more troops but worried that calling directly for them in this climate would suggest desperation. "I would publicly appeal for this new force," Lincoln told Seward, "were it not that I fear a general panic and stampede would follow, so hard it is to have a thing understood as it really is." Seward devised a strategy whereby he would contact Northern governors who then would ask that Washington call for more men. Thus it would appear as if public enthusiasm was ahead of, not behind, federal needs. The governors were persuaded to make the call and Lincoln requested 300,000 more men, but the need for the scheme showed the administration's concern that things were coming apart. Overseas the British government was considering the possibility of recognizing the Confederacy or at least of proposing mediation in the Civil War—an act that would have the same result. The administration knew that such intervention would make reunion practically impossible.[10]

Frustration over McClellan's apparent inertia began to consolidate a group of Republican lawmakers that historians, and people at the time, have termed "radical Republicans." Before the war they had been close associates of abolitionists, but in Congress they had to work within the law while abolitionists were free to make the purest morality their standard. Characterized by their vocal demands for a more aggressive war, these men were distinguished by their wish to expand the liberty, and later to promote the equality, of freed slaves. Charles Sumner, Zachariah

Chandler, Benjamin Wade in the Senate, and Thaddeus Stevens, Owen Lovejoy, James Ashley, Henry Winter Davis in the House were the most notable of the group, but other legislators joined or ignored them, depending on the issue. Radicals divided on economic issues, some favoring and some opposing higher tariffs, greenback currency, and the national banking system, but they agreed on advancing the rights of blacks. Marching ahead of their moderate Republican colleagues, they were the first to insist on emancipation, then on black troops, then on civil rights, then on black suffrage.[11]

The most extreme of this radical group would push for confiscation of the lands that slave labor had made prosperous. To achieve their goals they would try to turn Southern states into territories, giving Congress power to make an entirely new legal code for states in rebellion. The most extreme measures did not pass: Congress never territorialized the rebel states nor did it confiscate rebel land. But on the questions of first freeing, then arming, and then granting rights to blacks, growing numbers of Republicans joined more radical men who had advocated such measures early.

Lincoln was frequently the target of radicals. He moved too slowly to satisfy them in his attempts to appeal to conservative constituencies as well as to more egalitarian ones. Still, the president stayed on good terms personally with men such as Charles Sumner, Owen Lovejoy, and James Lane. Speaking of the radicals in Missouri (though the comment applied to others as well), Lincoln said they were "the unhandiest devils in the world to deal with" but added that "after all their faces are set Zionwards." He told Sumner that radicals in Congress were about six weeks ahead of him in expanding black liberty.[12]

The major issue that would divide the president from these more radical men would be reconstruction. They would argue for months about it, but after a clash in early 1864 they worked toward a compromise. There is strong reason to believe that Lincoln was moving toward them in the last weeks before he died. Lincoln's most ardent adversaries were hardly the radical Republicans, however. That dubious honor goes to the Democrats of the age who fought almost every step that Lincoln took toward a more egalitarian, free nation. Radical Republicans and the president would have an occasionally stormy, frequently contentious, relationship. Yet as the war would demonstrate, the relationship survived and would prove challenging and often enlightening to both parties.

At this early stage in the war Lincoln and the radicals had not yet clearly defined their differences, but they were beginning to agree that McClellan was not the aggressive leader they had hoped for. Though

Lincoln kept his doubts to himself, Congress grew increasingly militant, insisting that the war be prosecuted with the gloves off. At first they had defined bare-knuckle battle in terms of freeing escaping slaves or even a more general emancipation; then new visions appeared. Images of grateful freedmen were overlaid with pictures of armed men, perhaps with scores to settle. Proposals emerged that went beyond freeing the slaves and taking rebel property. By summer 1862 the idea of using black troops began to take its place as a serious option for the Union. With thousands of white soldiers already dead or wounded, with the war so clearly becoming a war over slavery as well as against its masters, the use of black soldiers, at least as laborers, seemed obvious. Reflecting these sentiments, Michigan's radical senator Zachariah Chandler wrote to his wife, "McClelland [*sic*]) is an imbecile if not a traitor. He has virtually lost the Army of the Potomac and should in my estimation *Suffer* the *Extreme penalty of the Law*. I will neither relax or let up in my position. . . . Michigan has lost 4000 men in the Army of the East, 2500 of them *by the Spade*. McClellan will not make Negroes to dig ditches, cut down timber & do hard work, but will force my brave boys to do this menial work & die in doing it rather than take Negro Slaves belonging to rebels & who only ask freedom in return. 40,000 brave men have been sacrificed in this Negrophoby & I will no longer keep quiet. It is wicked."[13]

A growing religious sentiment also demanded increased militance against slavery. Northern Protestants had long looked for signs indicating God's goal for the nation and the Union, and they saw in the stalemated war a signal of his intentions. As early as November 1861 members of the First Congregational Church of Sandwich, Massachusetts, were told, "It is preposterous for us to suppose that we can keep us long before a civilized world, and nourish the very cause of all our disasters. The venom of slavery is in the fang of treason; let us extract the poison, and the teeth of rebellion will be drawn." The failures of summer 1862 persuaded Protestants throughout the North that the time to reenlist God on the Northern side had come.[14]

The numbers of people calling for action increased daily. Unmistakable signs emerged that Lincoln or Congress would have to expand their offensive against slavery. Abolitionists kept up their pressures, and the public increasingly listened. The most influential Northern preacher, Henry Ward Beecher, and its most influential editor, Horace Greeley, were both demanding emancipation. Women long active in the abolition movement increased their efforts at ringing doorbells, circulating petitions, and giving speeches; growing numbers in the North responded. Susan B. Anthony toured Upstate New York, preaching emancipation to large crowds. Angelina Grimke Weld published a petition that declared war on slavery and carried it through the streets of solidly Democratic Perth Amboy, New Jersey: Hundreds of people signed it. Senator Sherman wrote his brother, "You can form no conception of the change of opinion here as to the Negro question. . . . I am prepared for one to meet the broad issue of universal emancipation." Even the conservative *Boston Advertiser* could declare, "the great phenomenon of the year is the terrible intensity which this emancipation resolution has acquired. A year ago men might have faltered at the thought of proceeding to this extremity in any event. The majority do not now seek it, but, we say advisedly, they are in great measure prepared for it."[15]

As the days grew longer Congress increased its strikes against slavery. The Second Confiscation Act of 17 July was sparked by the radical's desire to punish rebels by confiscating their property. Thaddeus Stevens saw in this possibility a chance to transform the South: "I would seize every foot of land, and every dollar of their property as our armies go along," he said, "and put it to the uses of the war and to the payment of our debts. . . . I would sell their lands to the soldiers of independence: I would send those soldiers there with arms in their hands to occupy the heritage of traitors, and build up there a land of free men and of freedom, which fifty years hence would swarm with its hundreds of millions without a slave on its soil." The revolutionary potential was obvious, and the vision of turning the South into the Northern society idealized by Republicans was clear. But conservative imperatives challenged radical dreams.

Confiscation provoked as much discussion as any other issue in the entire war. Legislators believed they had something to say that either their colleagues or their constituents needed to hear. The issue generated powerful feelings within the Republican party, dividing radical from moderate, to say nothing of the outrage that emerged from Democrats. Lawmakers debated the issue of presidential versus congressional power, the constitutionality of slavery itself, the meaning of treason, the applicability of due process of law to the taking of the property of men who were attacking the government, discusions showing their constitutional concerns. But passions flowed, too; accusations of tyranny were countered with charges of self-righteousness. Men who accused others of trampling on the Constitution were told to go meditate over the graves of fallen soldiers. With property rights and constitutional limitations matched against antislavery feeling and passion for saving the Union, a profound struggle among the elected representatives of the people was unavoidable. The Second Confiscation Act as it emerged from Congress revealed the incomplete resolution they reached.[16]

The act provided that the slaves of rebels could be made free if they came under the control of the army. At first glance here was emancipation for all the slaves that victory by Union forces could guarantee: Wherever the army advanced slaves might find freedom. The goal was revolutionary, but the means to reach it were not. The only way that actual freedom could be gained was on a case-by-case basis before a federal court, which would have to find that the owner of the slave was in fact a rebel. If individual slaves from the estimated 350,000 slave owners in the South were to seek freedom under this act there would have to be one case for every owner; the courts would have been able to do nothing else for years. It is little wonder that Lincoln could say as late as 13 September 1862, "I cannot learn that that law has caused a single slave to come over to us."[17]

Yet the force of military necessity was undercutting slavery just as it had been since Union soldiers first met escaping slaves. Increasing numbers of self-freed men and women gathered around advancing Union armies, and the need for troops made Chandler's anger over "Negrophoby" more persuasive. Within the Confiscation Act was a provision that authorized the president to "receive into the service of the United States, for the purpose of constructing entrenchments or performing camp service, or for any other labor or any military or naval service for which they may be found competent, persons of African descent." The law even provided pay for that service. Lincoln told Congress on the day the measure passed that he was ready to let military commanders "employ, as laborers, as many persons of African de-[s]cent, as can be used to advantage." Five days later he had Stanton order the military to "employ as laborers . . . so many persons of African descent, as can advantageously be used."[18]

Congress ensured that some form of black military service would take place. On the same day that the Second Confiscation Act passed, lawmakers sent to Lincoln the Militia Act. The president was empowered to call 300,000 nine-month militiamen, ages eighteen to forty-five, from the states, based on their population. If the states did not supply the men, Lincoln could make the necessary regulations to fill the quota. Recruitment and surreptitious conscription were the main elements of this measure, but it also expedited the evolution of black military service since the law allowed blacks to be accepted as soldiers to fill the state quotas. In addition Lincoln could emancipate any slaves who enlisted, and their families, if the masters were rebels. Thus even before slaves were emancipated by open proclamation military policy promised to strike off the chains of some fighting blacks and their families.[19]

Congress was doing its best to attack slavery and in so doing was helping Lincoln arrive at a decision on emancipation. He had his doubts about confiscation measures passed by Congress. He worried that the provisions of the act might violate the Constitution by working a forfeiture that would include descendants of the rebel, thereby punishing people whose only crime was to be related to an alleged traitor. He required Congress to provide a resolution declaring that confiscation would not extend beyond the life of a rebel. To make doubly sure that the measure was so understood Lincoln sent the veto message he had prepared in case Congress refused along with the signed bill. Lawmakers gave him the resolution.[20]

Lincoln was grasping constitutional limitations with one hand and reaching for revolution with the other. With Congress pushing, with popular sentiment growing for emancipation, with the war seemingly stalemated, with concern growing over foreign recognition of the Confederacy, with the border states turning down gradual, compensated emancipation for the third time just two days before Congress passed the Confiscation Act, and with the battlefield constantly on his mind, the president was shaping a bold stroke. Sometime in late June, as McClellan had bogged down on the peninsula, Lincoln, in one of his countless visits to the telegraph office in the War Department to learn of the military situation, began to write a proclamation of emancipation. By mid-July the writing was done; he was ready to raise the standard of emancipation as the leading principle in the struggle for the Union. He was also beginning to formulate an attack on slavery that eroded and challenged it from every constitutional direction.

On 21 July, the day after border-state lawmakers rejected his compensated emancipation plan for the third and last time, Lincoln rode in a carriage with Seward and Welles on a sad journey. Secretary of War Stanton's baby son had died, and the three men were attending the funeral. (Five months before Lincoln had buried his own boy, Willie.) The president had decided to free the slaves, he told the men, for slavery was clearly "the heart of the rebellion." Emancipation had military benefits; it would weaken the Confederates by drawing slaves to Union lines. Southerners who had begun the rebellion would have to face the consequences of their acts; it was too late for them to hope for constitutional protection for their peculiar institution.[21]

The full cabinet got the news the next day. Lincoln read to them a proclamation stating that on 1 January 1863 the slaves in all states still in rebellion would be free. But Lincoln did more than just announce the declaration that would become the Proclamation of Emancipation. He placed his executive action in the context of a wide range of options, all of which would in one way or another challenge and undermine slavery. The proclamation he read warned rebels to return to loyalty or face the confiscations promised under the Second Confiscation Act—that was one avenue by which slaves might gain freedom (no one yet knew how ineffective the law would be). He also announced that he would recommend to the next Congress another measure for loyal states to adopt compensated, gradual emancipation—that would provide freedom for slaves in loyal states. And then he promised to free all slaves in places still in rebellion as of 1 January 1863—that would reinforce Congress' confiscation policy. The Second Confiscation Act covered rebels as of 17 July 1862; the proclamation would cover those still in rebellion six and one-half months from mid-July. Finally, he would ask for a constitutional amendment to bring freedom to loyal slave states. Almost every inch of slave territory and every slave in the nation was covered by one of these measures. In the meantime generals in the field would be employing blacks in military duties and thus probably freeing them. As of mid-July 1862 slavery was under attack from every conceivable quarter.[22]

Lincoln had been careful not to make a firm public decision on employing black troops, in contrast to his public opposition when Fremont and Hunter freed slaves. Generals in the field were left to make their own policy, just as they had on the question of returning fugitive slaves, until in March 1862 Congress passed a law proclaiming that officers who helped masters capture runaway slaves would be dismissed from the service. Lincoln had kept quiet on that point, too; he was allowing events to take their course. The president was not ready to arm blacks. He speculated publicly that they might give up their weapons, and he told his cabinet that he was not going to give them arms. But he was permitting other people to enlist blacks to help the armies and navy advance.[23]

One criticism of the Emancipation Proclamation would be that Lincoln freed the slaves where he could not touch them. Yet few critics and historians have understood that although Lincoln may not have been "touching" slavery in the South, his generals were roughing it up rather dramatically while the president was carefully maintaining "no policy."

The proclamation surprised the cabinet. Even Chase, the most radical on emancipation, was impressed at how far Lincoln had reached. Chase suggested a quieter approach—let the generals in the field organize and arm the slaves as they encountered them and proclaim emancipation on a piecemeal basis. He feared too loud a trumpet would arouse the political opposition to militant counterattack. The secretary of the treasury especially worried that general emancipation would be so shocking as to undermine government credit. He may also have worried that Lincoln was taking his own place in the party as spokesman for advanced antislavery views. The rest of the cabinet was more supportive, but Seward raised a telling objection. The very environment of stalemate that had provoked Lincoln to act might give the wrong meaning to emancipation; it would sound as if it were "our last shriek on the retreat." Far better to await a victory and let the proclamation of freedom be accompanied with "fife and drum and public spirit." Lincoln accepted Seward's argument. He would wait for a military victory.[24]

Meanwhile, the president was not inactive. He pushed McClellan forward even as events pushed his administration in the same direction. But McClellan would not advance, and he told such exaggerated stories of his predicament that people began to doubt his other claims, his overall strategy. Stonewall Jackson had helped challenge these claims with a campaign through the Shenandoah Valley that threatened Washington while McClellan inched up the peninsula, convincing Lincoln that keeping part of the Army of the Potomac to protect the city had been a good idea. Halleck, appointed on 11 July 1862 to general in chief, was now saying that the McClellan "does not understand strategy and should never plan a campaign." Stanton had also given up on McClellan.[25]

On 2 August Halleck and Lincoln decided to pull McClellan's army off the peninsula, given his apparently unshakable reluctance to fight, his seemingly inexhaustible ability to find excuses not to risk the army he believed he had created. Strategic considerations also influenced the decision. Lee was sending Jackson north toward Washington. Even though Pope was there to meet him, Union leaders, perhaps influenced by McClellan's constant messages about the size of Lee's army, decided that McClellan should move north to help Pope counter Lee. But McClellan delayed his withdrawal, and Lee defeated Pope at the second battle of Bull Run, 28–29 August. Rumors spread that McClellan had delayed on purpose, declaring that "Pope [should] be allowed to get out of his own scrape his own way." The president told his young secretary, John Hay, "Unquestionably [McClellan] has acted badly toward Pope. He wanted him to fail."[26]

Yet Pope's failure left the Army of the Potomac in such disarray that Lincoln replaced him with McClellan. Whatever his failings Young Napoleon knew how to organize an army. And he was needed, for Lee was reportedly heading north and someone had to stop him; otherwise, the

Union would be in grave danger and hope for ending slavery would die.

Meanwhile, even as McClellan was withdrawing from the peninsula and as Pope faced Lee, Lincoln prepared the public for the proclamation that would come if only McClellan—or someone—would give the Union a victory. Horace Greeley provided the first opportunity to lobby the North. Twenty million Northerners, the editor proclaimed, were praying that Lincoln would vigorously enforce the Confiscation Act and thus free the slaves; only such a policy would save the Union. To attempt to "put down" the rebellion and at the same time uphold its inciting causes was "preposterous and futile." "Timid fossil politicians hailing from the Border States" were unduly influencing the president; "your Generals . . . habitually disregard" the laws that required freedom for slaves who escaped into Union hands. These generals were not reprimanded, yet Fremont and Hunter, who freed slaves, were. "What an immense majority of the Loyal Millions of your countrymen require of you is a frank, declared, unqualified, ungrudging execution of the laws of the land."[27]

Lincoln's reply stressed his agreement with Greeley. He avoided controverting any factual errors or trying to refute false inferences. He even waived the "impatient and dictatorial tone . . . in deference to an old friend, whose heart I have always supposed to be right." He wanted to make clear that his "paramount object in this struggle *is* to save the Union, and is not either to save or to destroy slavery." He would save the Union by freeing some of the slaves, none of the slaves, or all of the slaves. "What I do about slavery, and the colored race, I do because I believe it helps to save the Union; and what I forbear, I forbear because I do not believe it would help to save the Union." Here were words that based any action he took on the firmest possible foundation, one that Democrats and Republicans could rally around. Lincoln even quoted the Democratic phrase "the Union as it was" in insisting that a quick saving of the Union would preserve conservative goals.[28]

But the president knew that the time for keeping that old Union was rapidly passing. Private letters he wrote in late July about events in Louisiana stressed the breaking of eggs that could not be unbroken. He told correspondents that the state could save itself from having slavery touched only by returning to the Union quickly, and he allowed Gen. John Phelps's policy of welcoming fugitives into Union lines and using them as soldiers to proceed. To Democratic financier August Belmont the president was more direct and a bit angry: "This government cannot much longer play a game in which it stakes all, and its enemies stake nothing. . . . They cannot experiment for ten years trying to destroy the government and, if they fail, come back into the Union unhurt." And he told Sen. Reverdy Johnson, "I shall not surrender this game leaving any available card unplayed."[29]

In this context Lincoln's closing remarks to Greeley suggested that the "Union as it was" might very well be a part of the past, not the future. He told the editor and his hundreds of thousands of readers that he would try to correct any errors that he might have made in the past and that "I shall adopt new views so fast as they shall appear to be true views." He also wanted to remind everyone that it remained always his "personal wish that all men everywhere could be free."[30]

On the one hand telling Greeley and his readers to remember the Union in all the government's dealing with slavery, Lincoln on the other hand showed an understanding of racial fears about emancipation. His comments to the District of Columbia's delegation of blacks occurred even as the Emancipation Proclamation lay in his desk, awaiting announcement. In his comments urging colonization, Lincoln reminded his audience and everyone who would read about this meeting that he understood the extent of prejudice in the North and was seeking in colonization some response to it.

Less than ten days before he would issue the proclamation, the president was still preparing the public mind for the inevitable. When a meeting in Chicago of "Christians of All Denominations" passed a resolution in favor of emancipation, a delegation presented him with a memorial of their resolution, and Lincoln replied at length. He recited the various objections to emancipation that had been proposed and noted how difficult the issue was. Congress, with a majority of antislavery men, had not been able to come up with a general emancipation measure. He knew that religious people believed that God's will was clear, but he pointed out that religious people also spoke for the other side. He even teased them a bit by remarking that "if it is probable that God would reveal his will to others on a point so connected with my duty, it might be supposed he would reveal it directly to me." Despite his earnestly seeking to know the right thing to do, no revelation had been forthcoming.

He wondered whether anything he could say would make a difference on emancipation. "Would my words free the slaves, when I cannot even enforce the Constitution in the rebel states?" Even if blacks should rush to the Union lines upon hearing of emancipation there was the problem of caring for them. Furthermore, where slaves were freed because the Union army accepted them, when the army moved away blacks were often made slaves again. Lincoln asked his audience for their answer to these concerns. Perhaps he was trying to find out where the temper of the public stood, what they would allow, what they would support, how strong the feeling for emancipation was.

The delegation was ready for those questions. The right, which must be served, clearly favored liberty; the rebellion was a punishment for slavery. The difficulty of enforcing the Constitution was no reason to avoid doing the right thing. The existing peril to the Union would escalate pressures on Congress to support emancipation. Foreign nations would support a Union fighting for freedom. Lincoln agreed. He knew emancipation would be supported in Europe, and would draw off laborers from the South. He certainly recognized slavery as "the root of the rebellion, or at least its sine qua non." He did worry about the opposition in the North and was concerned that weapons in the hands of blacks would be lost to the enemy. The major concern, however, was the "fifty thousand bayonets in the Union armies from the Border States." But here he provided his own rebuttal: Every day that passed increased pro-Union feelings in the border states; continued conflict aroused their desire to beat the rebels. Still, he pointed out to his audience that "constitutional government is at stake," is "a fundamental idea, going down about as deep as anything."

The delegation gave him the answer he wanted. They had been among the people and were ready to sustain emancipation. A war for "Liberty and Union" would "rouse the people and rally them to his support beyond anything yet witnessed." Underlying their response was the assertion that "the people know that *nothing else has put constitutional government in danger but slavery*; that the toleration of that aristocratic and despotic element among our free institutions was the inconsistency that had nearly wrought our ruin and caused free government to appear a failure before the world, and therefore the people demand emancipation to preserve and perpetuate constitutional government. Our idea would thus be found to go down deeper than this, and to be armed with corresponding power." At this point Lincoln interrupted to say, "Yes, that is the true ground of our difficulties."[31]

Thus assured of the strong public demand for freeing the slaves and for a recognition of the connections between liberty and Union, Lincoln prepared to act whenever the army gave him a victory. In the meantime battlefield emancipation continued unchecked and moved toward its most extreme manifestation—black men carrying not only shovels and hoes, but guns.

As early as 3 April 1862 General Hunter wrote to Stanton requesting 50,000 muskets and 50,000 pairs of scarlet pantaloons with an eye to "arm such loyal men as I can find in the country." This request was quickly followed by Hunter's emancipation of slaves in his area of command—the Sea Islands of South Carolina. Lincoln countermanded this proclamation, but that did not stop Hunter from looking for black soldiers and organizing the "First South Carolina Colored Regiment." Newspapers found out and began debating the wisdom of using black soldiers. By early June this unofficial recruiting came to the attention of nervous proslavery Unionists. Congressman Charles Wycliffe of Kentucky persuaded his colleagues to pass a resolution asking the secretary of war for information about the alleged arming of fugitive slaves. Stanton dodged. He denied that he had authorized Hunter's actions and sent the resolution to the general for an explanation. Hunter replied in early July, just as Lincoln was deciding on an emancipation policy, that there were no fugitive slaves in his department, only a regiment of loyal men whose late masters were "fugitive rebels." There was no "fugitive master law," Hunter lamented, but the deserted slaves were going to rely on the treason law that gave them the right to "pursue, capture and bring back those persons of whose protection they have been thus suddenly bereft." Hunter's reply sent the House into an uproar of laughter that surely was heard in the White House. The army kept on gathering black soldiers.[32]

In early August Gen. Benjamin Butler, pushed by the initiatives of General Phelps, changed a policy of not accepting black enlistments when he took over the command in New Orleans. Some of the black enlistees had been forced into service by white soldiers, but others were willingly taking oaths and receiving uniforms. At the same time in Leavenworth, Kansas, Jim Lane opened a recruiting office that accepted blacks and whites. When Lane told Stanton, the war secretary took his time in disapproving and then replied that only the president could legalize black enlistments. Lane ignored Stanton's letter; Stanton probably was glad. He had been pushing quietly for black soldiers for months, turning his head when necessary but calling no halts except when forced to. He also gathered reports from a leading authority on the law of war, Columbia professor Francis Lieber, and from the judge advocate general, Joseph Holt, both of whom supported using Negro troops. Their reports were available in August and early September.[33]

On 25 August 1862, almost a month before Lincoln announced the preliminary Emancipation Proclamation and even as the president was explaining to Greeley and to delegations of ministers why he was not emancipating slaves, Secretary of War Stanton authorized the first official recruiting of blacks. In the Sea Islands of South Carolina General Hunter had been replaced by Rufus Saxton, and he inherited the manpower shortage. His request to Stanton to meet this need resulted in an order that, for the first time in history, authorized directly the arming, as well as the clothing and equipping, of black soldiers. Stanton authorized a regiment of only 5,000 troops, but the order made official the quiet revolution that had been under way for months.[34]

Meanwhile, a much more thundering transition was announced with cannon. For two months Lincoln had been waiting for the military tide to turn so that emancipation would be wrapped in victory, not tainted with desperation. On 17 September 1862, at Antietam Creek in Maryland, McClellan's Army of the Potomac provided that victory. Its cost was staggering: nearly 6,000 dead, 17,000 wounded, thousands missing—the largest number of American casualties of any single day in the nation's history. Twice as many died as in the War of 1812, the Mexican War, and the Spanish American War combined. There were four times the casualties of D-Day 1944. In the entire country only thirty-five cities had as many people as were casualties on 17 September 1862. The battle allowed Lincoln to announce a new birth of freedom, but it was a bloody birth indeed.[35]

McClellan telegraphed the president that he had won a great victory. He believed himself savior of the Union, believed that now he would be rid of his critics, that he could force Lincoln to oust Stanton and Halleck and restore him to the post of general in chief. He may even have hoped that his Harrison's Landing proposals would become national policy.

Lincoln's response showed how out of touch McClellan was. The president made no changes in command and celebrated only for a moment. And he took the step that McClellan had most feared. Five days after Antietam he issued the preliminary Emancipation Proclamation. The measure housed its proclamation of freedom within conservative goals, proposed means for moderating the effect of liberation, and linked its presidential action with existing congressional regulations. Moreover, it offered the South a means to avoid freeing any slaves at all. Lincoln carefully showed the conservative context in which he was operating, clearly indicating that he wanted to harmonize the devotion to the Union and its institutions with the liberty he was proposing. The goal of the war remained, he said, that of "practically restoring the constitutional relation between the United States and the rebel states." Any state that was in the Union as of 1 January might hope for compensation if owners would voluntarily emancipate their own slaves, either gradually or immediately. He would put this proposal before Congress. Certainly he would respect the measures already passed by Congress that forbade soldiers and sailors from returning fugitive slaves and that freed the slaves of rebels, but those measures still permitted loyal slave owners to keep their slaves by application to civilian authorities. Furthermore, Lincoln promised to continue efforts to colonize blacks who wished to leave the country.

Within this conservative context, however, the goal of liberty was born: If the rebellion continued after 1 January 1863, all slaves within rebel borders would be freed. More than 2.9 million slaves would be "forever free"—over 82 percent of the slaves in the Confederacy. That was 74 percent of all the slaves in the United States.[36]

After that date no judicial process would be required to challenge in individual cases the right to hold people in bondage. No allegedly loyal Southerner could recapture his runaways if he resided in rebel territory on the first day of 1863. The loyal slave owners of the South were given one hundred days to bring any or all of the states of the Confederacy back into the Union if they wanted to keep holding slaves; if they failed, no one would own slaves there.[37]

The proclamation was silent on a major point: Lincoln did not sound the reveille for black soldiers. Primarily, the fall proclamation was designed to lure Confederate states into the Union; it would hardly have made sense to threaten them with their worst nightmare. They did not have to be warned of a specter that they could see around them as generals like Butler and Lane and Saxton continued recruiting even though Lincoln had preempted their emancipating.

The September proclamation drew mixed reviews. Comparing the measure to the Great Reform Bill of 1832, the Declaration of Independence, and British emancipation measures in the West Indies, the *Atlantic Monthly* wrote, "These are acts of great scope, working on a long future and on permanent interests, and honoring alike those who initiate and those who receive them. These measures provoke noisy joy, but are received into a sympathy so deep as to apprise us that mankind are greater and better than we know. At such times it appears as if a new public were created to greet the new event." Most abolitionists were exultant. Frederick Douglass declared, "We shout for joy that we live to record this righteous decree." "I am half crazy with enthusiasm," Theodore Tilton wrote Garrison. "I would like to have seen whether *you* laughed or cried on reading it: *I* did *both*." Privately, Garrison was concerned for the qualifications he saw in it but publicly spoke of "an important step in the right direction . . . an act of immense historic consequence." Gov. John A. Andrew in Massachusetts split the difference between the conservative context and the radical goal: "It is a poor document, but a mighty act."[38]

Representatives of the centrists in the Republican party also were pleased. Eleven loyal governors meeting in Altoona, Pennsylvania, sent their enthusiastic endorsement. Henry Ward Beecher, speaking on behalf of the New York Congregational Churches, announced the unanimous approval of his associates. Greeley was staggered when he learned that the prayers he had spoken of to Lincoln had been answered. On the day that he heard the news he could write only, "It is the beginning of the end of the rebellion; the beginning of the new life of the nation. God Bless Abraham Lincoln." The next day Greeley was more effusive. In a long editorial he proclaimed that the nation had passed from "the semi barbarism of a medieval age to the light and civilization of the Nineteenth Christian Century. . . . There has been no act of one man or of one people so sublime as this emancipation of a race." Other major Republican papers agreed.[39]

Some people saw in the act a new birth of freedom, a larger sense of union that could now be brought forth once the nation proclaimed, as it had not since independence, that it was opposed to slavery. Thoughtful writers suggested the worth to a society and to a nation of asserting its best values, of affirming its hopes, not pandering to its fears. Greeley envisioned a new and nobler nationalism than ever before. The powerful force of unity that so long had restrained hatred of bondage could now flower unequivocally with freedom nurturing it. The end of slavery would mark the end of hatred, bitterness, division, and "Our Union will be one of the bodies, not merely, but the souls."

A vision of the meaning of equality found echo in Walt Whitman's midwar poetry; brotherhood might now emerge from the bloodshed once the cause of strife was gone. "Over the Carnage Rose Prophetic a Voice" expressed his hope that "affection shall solve the problems of freedom yet." Men from all parts of the nation would join together as comrades, and "It shall be customary in the houses and streets to see manly affection / The most dauntless and rude shall touch face to face light / The dependence of Liberty shall be lovers. The continuance of Equality shall be comrades. / These shall tie you and band you stronger than hoops of iron. . . . (Were you looking to be held together by lawyers? / Or by an agreement on a paper? or by arms? / Nay, nor the world, nor any living thing, will so cohere.)[40]

Emerson also saw that the nation had turned toward its ideals and now called upon the best from its citizens. "The aim of the war on our part is indicated by the aim of the President's proclamation, namely to break up the false combination of Southern society, to destroy the piratic feature in which it makes our enemy only as it is the enemy of the human race, and so allow its reconstruction on a just and healthful basis. Then new affinities will act, the old repulsions will cease, and the cause of war be removed. Nature and trade may be trusted to establish a lasting peace." This hope for a new, uncorrupted unity helped Emerson to believe that the "government has assured itself of the best constituency in the world: every spark of intellect, every virtuous feeling, every religious heart, every man of honor, every poet, every philosopher, the generosity of the cities, the health of the country, the strong arms of the mechanic, the endurance of the farmers, the passionate conscience of women, the sympathy of distant nations—all rally to its support."[41]

These assessments of the consequences of emancipation were overly optimistic, at least in 1862. Opposition was formidable, including almost every Democratic newspaper in the land. The politics of fear retained its power; race baiting increased in volume. When Lincoln suspended the writ of habeas corpus two days after this preliminary Emancipation Proclamation, the Democrats stepped out boldly as the party of civil liberty and racial purity. The drums were beat again against the Yankee Puritan with his meddling ways. Lincoln was said to be in the hands of abolitionists and hence ready to thrust opponents into jails and blacks into the arms of whites. Furthermore, emancipation meant that the South would never give in. On the eve of the 1862 election the most vocal organ of Democratic opinion in the North, the *New York World*, consolidated the arguments against emancipation in cataloging reasons to vote for the party of Jefferson and Jackson: "This election . . . decides whether a swarthy inundation of negro laborers and paupers shall flood the North, accumulating new burdens on taxpayers, cheapening white labor by black competition, . . . and raising dangerous questions of political and social equality."[42]

Democrats carried the elections in the Midwest impressively: Ohio, Illinois, and Indiana fell to the party; Democratic state legislatures would make policy in those states. In Michigan, Wisconsin, and Minnesota, Republicans also lost ground. New York and New Jersey elected Democratic governors, and the highest electoral office at stake in Pennsylvania went to the Democrats, too. Democrats also had taken thirty-five Republican congressional seats and raised their vote total over 5 percent in the major corridor of states from Connecticut to Illinois, states that contained ten more electoral votes than were needed to claim the presidency in 1864.

Lincoln had worried about the effect of the proclamation on the fall elections, and his concern had been justified. Republicans did not lose only because of emancipation, but no other cause was so capable of inspiring Democratic voters. When Republican leaders John Sherman and Thomas Ewing in Ohio and Orville Browning in Illinois explained their losses, emancipation was listed first.[43]

Despite the political consequences the proclamation stood as people anxiously awaited the new year and watched the battlefields.

The conservative elements in the document made some people fear and others hope that the proclamation was a threat only, or that something less than full freedom was intended. Others feared that the South would respond and then keep slavery. Several conservative writers, hoping to interdict emancipation, published extensive arguments claiming that Lincoln had violated the Constitution. Former Supreme Court justice Benjamin Curtis and the professor of constitutional law at Harvard, Joel Parker, headed this list. But Lincoln held firm. He told a delegation from Kentucky in late November that he would rather die than take back a word of the proclamation. He consulted his own constitutional authorities to reaffirm what he had always believed: that as commander in chief he had the right to take extraordinary measures to put down the rebellion.[44]

Even as he marshaled constitutional supporters and kept his eyes carefully on the elections, Lincoln was trying to get McClellan to move again. The president believed that Antietam should be the beginning of an offensive. Victory in his eyes meant the destruction of the Confederate army, not merely the repulse of Lee's move northward. He insisted that McClellan chase Lee down and crush him. Perhaps the president saw political advantage in keeping McClellan in command. The part of the electorate that admired McClellan's conservatism might still find Republicans appealing; keeping the general in the fold might counteract the powerful reaction to the preliminary proclamation. While he continually pushed McClellan to act and even explained basic military strategy to him, Lincoln's letters conveyed no warning that the general's command was in danger or even a hint that almost the entire cabinet had agreed, especially after second Bull Run, that McClellan should be ousted. Chase, in fact, was suggesting he should be hanged. Still, less than a week before the president fired McClellan he wrote to the general, "I am much pleased with the movement of the army."[45]

But Lincoln was profoundly frustrated at the military situation in fall 1862. The Union armies in the West had won victories at Iuka, Corinth, and Perryville and in the East at Antietam. But none of these had been followed up with offensives against the Confederates. Buell insisted that, despite Bragg's retreat from Perryville, he lacked the supplies necessary to give chase. Even Grant was explaining to Halleck and hence to the president that he was not ready to advance. And McClellan, after the bloodiest and greatest battle of all, added his explanations and excuses.[46]

By late October and early November Lincoln's frustration peaked. He began compiling lists of the size of the Union army, almost as though the numbers themselves would overwhelm the South. And something like a late fall "massacre" took place as the president began to replace his generals. On 20 October he ordered John McClernand to organize troops to assault Vicksburg. McClernand had no military qualifications; he was an Illinois politician who had acquired a general's star. He was being assigned to a region that already had a general organizing a campaign: Grant. Perhaps the president, along with his enthusiasm for a plan McClernand had proposed for attacking Vicksburg, was sending Grant a message; messages were in the air. On 24 October Lincoln removed Buell from his command. He prepared to replace Ben Butler in Louisiana with Nathaniel Banks, a preliminary move to beginning a campaign up the Red River. Signals were flashing that change was in the air, and McClellan's signal flashed most brightly.[47]

McClellan had to go, for he had been *the* general of the North. When he failed his failure was as great in the public mind as his opportunities had been. If Lincoln wanted to revitalize the military situation, removing McClellan was inescapable. There clearly were strategic reasons to be rid of McClellan. He would not move; he explained and explained again why he could not: tired horses, exhausted men, ignorance of the terrain, depth of the Potomac, inadequate wagons, broken cannon, the potential superiority of Confederate numbers, lack of boots and blankets (many of Lee's troops were barefoot), the list went on and on. Only the immense loss of life was persuasive, and even that might be balanced against the fact that Lee had lost almost as many men. McClellan was not hurting Lee, and he was damaging public morale. As the president's frequent statements about how "the nation" or "the people" would respond to military success or failure demonstrate, Lincoln wanted to remedy both situations.[48]

For six, seven weeks Lincoln had pushed McClellan to act. Each time the general replied with reasons why he would not, could not do so. Finally Lincoln's patience gave way, no longer restrained by the political advantages of keeping him around. The day after the elections were over the president replaced him. McClellan felt betrayed, and Democrats were dismayed, having seen in the general "the representative of Conservative principles in the army," as New York party leaders told Lord Lyons. But politically and militarily, McClellan's time had passed. Even though the electorate still harbored strong conservative ideas, their relevance was fading; and the army, the spearpoint for emancipation, had little need for a general guided by the spirit of Harrison's Landing. On the battlefield the correctness of Lincoln's ousting of McClellan was clearer: "I hate to see McClellan go," Robert E. Lee wrote to his wife. "He and I had grown to understand each other so well."[49]

McClellan was officially relieved on 7 November and after his emotional farewell to the army three days later, Ambrose Burnside took over. The thirty-eight-year-old general looked like a bold and dashing soldier—he dressed the part to add to the image, but he doubted his own abilities and tried to reject the command. Yet Lincoln insisted, and Burnside accepted, determined not to make McClellan's mistakes. He would be bold and attack. He moved the massive army of 120,000 south and headed toward Fredericksburg, fifty miles directly north of Richmond. Lincoln visited the army, talked to Burnside about strategy, and suggested attacking from three points at once; but Burnside insisted on a direct assault across the Rappahannock, through the city, and up Marye's Heights behind it. Lincoln returned to Washington to prepare his second annual message as Burnside assembled his forces.

Eighteen sixty-two had baptized the nation in blood: Donelson, Shiloh, Seven Days, Antietam. And now as armies gathered at Fredericksburg no one could doubt the gruesome toil this war demanded. With the blood had come transformations in race relations in the nation. Slavery, for over two centuries the keystone of half the nation, so influential throughout the rest, was deeply in danger. Congress had passed laws outlawing slavery in the territories and in the District of Columbia. It had set up mechanisms to confiscate the slaves of all who persisted in rebellion. Experiments were in process along the western border, in Louisiana, and along the Atlantic Coast in using blacks as soldiers. The clock was ticking on the September proclamation; about one month remained for those Southern regions still in rebellion to give up, or they would lose their slaves. They gave absolutely no signs that they were even thinking about doing so.

If the antislavery storm was gathering, counterforces were at work to restrain it. The voices of Northern conservatives sounded loudly as 1862 ended. Voting totals revealed that a substantial number of people clung to the prejudices of a lifetime, still respected the world that Jackson and Taney and Douglas had helped create. They held on to the past for bad reasons, the racism that for decades had flowed powerfully through the "Democracy" and had swept along some Republicans as well. They clung to the past also for more respectable reasons—because the constitutional-political system they ultimately ruled had given them prosperity, active involvement in the institutions that shaped their lives. Lincoln needed to address these feelings and to speak of a world where states controlled their destinies, where complex problems might be unraveled through time, where deep-seated and long-formed racial feelings could slowly be reconciled, where the growing prosperity of a great nation would somehow solve problems that the raging and bloody war was now trying to settle. Conservatives as well as radicals made up the nation he led, and fundamentally he was one with them.

Lincoln was influenced also by other imperatives that counseled caution. He was beginning to shape a strategy for reconstruction that required accommodation to familiar ideas. As Union armies moved south and then captured New Orleans, Louisiana and other states were taking the first undefined and vague steps toward returning to the Union. The process was difficult in the midst of war because no Southern state in this process fully belonged to Unionists; rebels still controlled parts of Louisiana, Arkansas, and Tennessee. The president wanted to assist and encourage Unionists; and to attract neutrals in the South. Throughout October and November he initiated, pushed, questioned the process of restoring the states of Arkansas, Tennessee, and especially Louisiana to the Union. He wrote to generals Butler and Shepley in Louisiana, to generals Steele and Phelps in Arkansas, to General Grant and Gov. Andrew Johnson in Tennessee with one message: Do as much as you possibly can to help Unionists set up loyal governments in these states. Use the threat of emancipation to inspire support. "Follow forms of law as far as convenient, but at all events get the expression of the largest number of the people possible. All see how such action will connect with, and affect the proclamation of September 22nd." The people should be reminded that if they returned they would "avoid the unsatisfactory prospect before them, and . . . have peace again upon the old terms under the Constitution of the United States." Lincoln hoped war-weary Confederates would join Unionists if they believed that their future could be familiar and livable.[50]

As Lincoln wrestled with the problems of reconstruction in Louisiana, Arkansas, and Tennessee, he had before him the parallel but anomalous situation of West Virginia. Here was a place where Unionists had acted to stay within the Union, insisting on their loyalty, defying the pressure of secession and slavery. West Virginia was unique because it was the only state that had carried the logic of secession to the next step of seceding from seceders.

West Virginia may have been a model in Lincoln's mind for his 2 December proposals, for there a loyal government opposing secession had been set in motion quickly. The rebel Virginia legislature passed its ordinance of secession on 17 April 1861 and sent it out for popular ratification. Within five days a mass meeting in Clarksburg called for a convention to meet in Wheeling the next month. On May 13 that group gathered and called for another convention in June should the people of the state ratify the secession ordinance. When they did, the convention met on 11 June, claiming to be the lawful government of Virginia. It organized a government that chose two senators to replace the two from the seceded state, and these senators were seated by Congress in December 1861. Meanwhile, the movement to create a new state was under way. In October 1861 an election was held; western Unionists voted 18,408 to 781 in favor of the new state. February 1862 saw the writing of a new constitution for West Virginia, and by April voters had endorsed it by an equally huge margin. The next month the existing Unionist government of Virginia gave its constitutionally required assent to the making of the new state. The situation was filled with constitutional ambiguities: Was the Unionist government of Virginia, which represented much less than half of the state's people, legitimate? Could part of a state "secede" from another part? But the United States Senate, unimpeded by these concerns, acted on 14 July 1863 to admit West Virginia to the Union. The Senate's sole requirement was that the state accept gradual emancipation of its few slaves. The House did not have time to act on the bill, and it was held over for the new session beginning in December. Even as Lincoln prepared his December message the House was debating West Virginia statehood. Here was a state where Unionists had quickly launched a loyal government, one which would gradually emancipate its slaves. It could be done.[51]

Yet with change advancing inexorably, Lincoln's December 1862 message to Congress was a curious and revealing document. It combined a response to conservative voters, attention to the incipient onset of reconstruction, and above all a final effort by Lincoln to sustain the past in the midst of transformations. It looked backward, at least as much as the swift flow of events allowed. It spoke of a heritage that abided, even as change accelerated. It hinted at vast change, yet its tone was traditional, sounding as though Lincoln, having now removed his more conservative generals and having announced potential racial revolution, was looking over his shoulder wistfully at a world he was leaving or perhaps lingering over the memory of a road he knew just before being propelled onto a new path. The message reveals not only where Lincoln stood after more than a year-and-a-half of war but also outlines a legacy that was being lost as the nation advanced across its diverse battlefields.

He began with perfunctory comments about foreign affairs (only a quick glance toward colonization suggested the major part of the address to come). Then came talk about developing the resources of the West, the need for attention to raising revenues for the nation, a report on income and debts of the government, a short comment on the Indian uprising in Minnesota. But these topics were almost pro forma—a reporting in a quick survey to Congress as the Constitution demanded.[52]

The heart of the message began with a memory—and a definition of a nation as permanent as the land it occupied. Generations passed, "but the earth abideth forever." The president resurrected his words of almost twenty-one months before to bind the moment to that earlier day. In March 1861 he had noted that "the only substantial dispute" was over the question of the rightness and wrongness of slavery and its consequent extension. Specific disputes over issues such as fugitive slaves were being settled grudgingly but about as well as they could be settled where such differences existed. But Lincoln's fundamental point had been, and was now, twenty-one months later, that "physically speaking we cannot separate." Even if the sections continued to fight they would still remain side by side.

Again and again Lincoln spoke of how the land and its shape united the nation. Rivers did not divide regions; they were highways easily crossed and drawing people to them for the trade that swept both banks. Other borders were "merely surveyors lines over which people walk back and forth." At the heart of the nation was the "great interior region," from the Alleghenies to the Rockies, over one-third of the nation's land, with a population of 10 million and predictably 50 millions— "the great body of the republic" and so rich in potential resources as to make it one of the most important places in the world. This great region was linked to those lands it touched East, West, and South so that no natural boundary was comprehensible. "Our national strife springs not from our permanent part; not from the land we inhabit; not from our national homestead." The "strife pertains to ourselves—to the passing generations of men; and it can without convulsion, be hushed forever with the passage of one generation."

Slavery, however, endangered the nation; no one doubted that. Lincoln then presented his vision for disentangling the nation from its corrosive foe. The most sweeping measure he offered almost in passing. He declared that slaves freed by war would remain "forever free." Those two words covered every slave in Alabama, Florida, Georgia, Mississippi, North Carolina, and South Carolina, states with no known organized Unionist action, as well as slaves in states such as Virginia, Louisiana, Arkansas, and Tennessee where there was such action. If Unionists were not successful in those states, slaves would still be free. Here was a revolution of staggering proportion.

Yet Lincoln, characteristically, wrapped change in conservative cloth. He proposed a constitutional amendment for Congress to consider and then pass along for ratification by three-fourths of the state legislatures or conventions. Given how far war had already eroded slavery Lincoln's proposal was startlingly respectful of constitutional and social traditions. Indeed, it echoed his 22 July statement to the cabinet, when emancipation was first announced. He wanted Congress to provide bonds to pay slave states to abolish slavery at any time and in any manner it saw fit over the next thirty-seven years; the states would receive the bonds at the time or over the time that they emancipated their slaves. Should a state choose to reinstitute slavery it would have to return the bonds and the interest paid on them. At a time when national authority was being asserted by nearly one million soldiers, when national influence was expanding throughout the economy, when nationalism was being trumpeted in every newspaper, certainly every Republican newspaper and not a few Democratic ones, and from pulpits in thousands of churches and in religious newspapers circulated to millions, Lincoln was suggesting that states control how and when and whether slavery would die—and that they might even change their minds.

How did this proposal fit with the impending emancipation proclamation? Lincoln said his proposal was "recommended as a means, not in exclusion of, but in addition to, all others for restoring and preserving the national authority." The amendment would have to be ratified, he noted, by seven of the slave states. Yet that qualification clarified very little. Since he had already said that slaves freed by war were "forever free," did he mean that Mississippi, for example, might somehow reverse Lincoln's emancipation and then gradually emancipate with compensation? If he meant the amendment to apply only to the border states, then why would at least three of the seven slave states still at war with the Union ratify it?

Such questions were unanswered. One senses that Lincoln remained so committed to preserving an abiding constitutional process, even as he and the war changed, that his heart for a rare moment trumped his mind. The most satisfactory rational explanation of Lincoln's plan is that it spoke to many audiences and thus was intentionally vague, perhaps even intentionally confusing. In its details it could apply to border states that might claim compensation if they would free their slaves, as yet unaffected by wartime emancipation measures. These states, always so important to Lincoln for their influence on the whole South, might thus show the seceded states that social transformation was acceptable. Moreover, the plan for compensated, gradual emancipation might serve as a last-minute bribe to the Deep South: come back quickly into the Union and face emancipation, but at a much slower pace and with compensation for losses. Clearly the plan was supposed to appeal to Southern Unionists and to potential fellow travelers by its appeal to tradition.

Lincoln's personal conservatism was also alive in his proposal, along with his recognition of the power of racism to shape white attitudes. He acknowledged the traditional racial feelings of Americans by including in his proposed constitutional amendment the colonizing of "free colored persons, at any place or places" outside the United States. He may have had hopes that these racial attitudes could change, but he recognized the power of prejudice enough to provide for separation of the races. Still, he did try to persuade whites not to be threatened by blacks. Blacks would probably stay in the South when freed, he argued; even if they did come North they were too few to threaten the jobs or the social fabric of whites. He was firm on the point that none would be colonized who did not wish to be.

The length of time for emancipation was a feature Lincoln liked. During that period the states would somehow save the slaves "from the vagrant destitution which must largely attend immediate emancipation in localities where their numbers are very great." The time span also gave whites an opportunity to accommodate themselves to emancipation. And the length of time had an economic advantage: Since population and wealth would be increasing, the cost to individual Americans of paying the compensation would be less each passing year. This point was important enough that Lincoln used seven paragraphs with two charts to prove it.

Recent historians have downplayed Lincoln's proposal, emphasizing that it was, as James McPherson says, "a peace measure to *abolish the institution* everywhere by constitutional means." Lawanda Cox calls Lincoln's arguments about the economic benefits of his plan "unpersuasive" and focuses on the part of the measure that sustained wartime emancipation. Like McPherson she points to Lincoln's peroration as a declaration of the fervency of his desire to end slavery. Peter Parish, on the other hand, calls the message "a piece of propaganda, a public relations exercise."[53]

Yet Lincoln's peroration was no triumphant egalitarian call. It followed his extended argument for state-controlled, gradual, compensated emancipation with colonization and showed his abiding commitment to an orderly, gradual process of change. He spoke so passionately for the idea that one senses a last-minute desire to control the whirlwind. There remained the hope that the war would not overwhelm the best option Lincoln could think of: peaceful, gradual, compensated emancipation. Somehow war would not do what it seemed clearly to be doing: closing down options for gradual change, pushing the nation toward racial revolution. He believed that respecting order would "shorten the war, and thus lessen its expenditure of money and blood" and "restore the national authority and national prosperity and perpetuate both indefinitely." And he believed that if both he and Congress appealed to the people, his proposal could be adopted. He knew that there were other proposals possible but wondered if they would work better than his. He spoke passionately, eloquently on this plan to save the Union: it gave freedom to the slave, and when that was done, "we *assure* freedom to the free . . . honorable alike in that we give and what we preserve. We shall nobly save, or meanly lose, the last best hope of earth. Other means may succeed; this could not fail." He had spoken with similar emotion when he had asked the border states months before to accept this plan for themselves. He cared deeply for it.[54]

And yet this measure could not pass, did not pass. Congress ignored it even though it had approved Lincoln's earlier suggestion for border-state compensated emancipation. Its support for such a measure was still on the record, but events and history were moving too fast. Lincoln himself knew that even though he applied his knowledge, strangely, to argue for the amendment. "The dogmas of the quiet past, are inadequate to the stormy present. The occasion is piled high with difficulty, and we must rise with the occasion. As our case is new, so we must think anew and act anew." Ironically, Lincoln's proposal spoke to a world and for conditions that the "fiery trial, through which we pass," was altering momentously. Poised on the brink of entering that new and terrible world, Lincoln paused, gathering together the strongest argument he could make for transforming society within the old federal system, respecting local prejudice and state practice. He offered a fantastic option for emancipation as in his heart of hearts he wished it could be—a gradual process evolving within the constitutional institutions he admired and understood so profoundly. Then, after 1 January 1863, he never seriously mentioned it again. He and the nation turned toward a transforming and enigmatic future. Much more than before he began to speak of events controlling him.[55]

8

★ ★ ★ ★ ★

CABINET CRISIS:
DECEMBER 1862

Confederate Gen. Edward Porter Alexander had placed his artillery at Fredericksburg to cover every inch of any potential Union attack—on Maryes Heights behind the town, on Prospect Hill to the south. "A chicken could not live on the field when we open on it," he promised Gen. James Longstreet. Burnside sent his men across the river and then up the heights again and again, six, seven times in rushes that Longstreet would later call the noblest thing done in the war, in charges that even had the Confederates cheering the bluecoats before slaughtering them. "We might as well have tried to take Hell," one Yankee later said.[1]

Burnside had wanted to try it one more time, leading the charge himself, but his generals told him no. And so the Army of the Potomac gathered its dead and wounded and turned the supply wagons away from Fredericksburg as the death notices went out to over one thousand homes, letters describing wounds came to over nine thousand families, and over two thousand households agonized over those men listed as missing in action. Making it harder to bear, the rebels' total losses were less than one-third as high.

It was a stunning defeat after the hopes of Antietam, and it was not the only event eroding Northern hopes. The loss built upon political reverses for Republicans in the elections of 1862, and frustration mounted. The North, like the South, had been whipsawed between optimism and despair for months: victory at Donelson, then slaughter at Shiloh, then greater carnage in the Seven Days, then despair at Second Bull Run, then the horrors of Antietam, which again intertwined victory and loss, not only of thousands of young men but of the chance to end the war by crushing Lee. The unmitigated anguish of Fredericksburg left the nation in a state of exhaustion and anger, a reaction that translated into political anxiety among Republicans, for the losses in the fall elections also spoke of no easy victories. Emancipation measures were blamed for most of the Democratic gains, but Illinois' Trumbull explained the result as a protest by "hundreds of republicans who believed that their sons and relatives were being sacrificed to the incompetency, indisposition or treason of proslavery generals." Staggered by the losses, Republicans were blaming almost everything.[2]

The same tendencies were growing within the cabinet. Some problems grew because of the personalities involved. Lincoln liked Seward—his humor, his passion for politics, his urbane charm (which appealed to Lincoln's backwoods heritage and his ambition to escape it).[3] He appreciated Stanton and Welles for their abilities to handle the main tasks of warmaking. He had less to do with Smith and Blair, whose duties were merely background to the war. Bates also did his important job adequately but could be a bit of a bore. Lincoln respected Chase's ability, knew that he needed the Ohioan in the cabinet to represent radical voices, but simply did not like the man. As Welles put it, "He is fond of Seward who is affable. He respects Chase, who is clumsy. Seward comforts him. Chase he deems a necessity."[4]

Lincoln relied on the older, more experienced Seward for advice on simple matters of protocol and on more complex matters of presidential speeches. He soon developed the habit of dropping by Seward's in the evening; the two men also got together for Sunday outings. Seward cultivated Lincoln in small ways, too. He gave the Lincolns a pair of kittens when they moved into the White House and, in part because he loved children, Seward played with Lincoln's sons as often as he could. None of this impressed Mary Lincoln, who did not like the secretary, but it pleased the president very much.[5]

Seward enjoyed Lincoln's friendship, but, experienced politician that he was, he also understood the value of being known as the president's confidant. He knew that public perception increased his reputation as a manipulator with great persuasive powers. Adding to the image was the gossip that during the Sumter crisis Seward had offered to take charge and generally conducted himself as though he were party leader. Lincoln's quiet leadership style further encouraged people to believe that Seward was very influential. Seward liked the role.

Cabinet members, almost every time they met, could observe his performance. Welles recalled that Seward ("the Premier as he liked to be called") essentially treated the cabinet meetings as his personal arena. He announced to the others when the president wanted a meeting and arrived "some little time before the Cabinet assembled." Since there were no assigned seats for the meeting, the secretary of state "from his former position as the chief executive of the largest State in the Union, as well as his recent place as a senator, and from his admitted experience and familiarity with affairs, assumed, as was allowed, as was proper, to take the lead in consultations and also to give tone and direction to the manner and mode of proceedings." Seward also "was not slow in taking upon himself to prescribe action and doing most of the talking, without much regard to the modest chief, but often to the disgust of his associates."[6]

Yet even when there were few cabinet meetings and matters were decided by cabinet members individually, Seward usually knew what was going on. "Seward is inquisitive and learns early what is doing by each of his associates," Welles added, "frequently before we meet in council, while the other cabinet officers limit themselves to their provided duties and are sometimes wholly unadvised of his." Cabinet members often found out what the administration was up to by reading the newspapers—for example, when Lincoln suspended habeas corpus throughout the North. In short, Seward monopolized Lincoln's attention and time, and Lincoln let him do so. Welles admitted that Lincoln summarized discussions in the meetings and at times made decisions at odds with Seward's views, but the day-to-day experience of cabinet members was that Seward overinfluenced most policy decisions.[7]

There was certainly personal pique here and not a little jealousy, especially on Chase's part. The feeling was rooted in the belief that the cabinet ought to perform the political functions that had governed its creation—that all voices in the new party had something important to say and needed to be heard, not just represented. In addition, decisions that affected cabinet members and their departments were being made without their input. Lincoln's policy of having no policy might have left him flexible and open to change, but it generated frustration in his cabinet and a feeling in Congress that the administration was rudderless— or more precisely that the hand on the tiller was not that of the man elected to sail the boat. Most infuriating to legislators was that the helmsman, despite the preliminary Emancipation Proclamation, still clung to the conservative ideas that they had rejected months earlier, the most recent sign being the Second Annual Address.

As the rush of events reduced the number of cabinet meetings, moderates Caleb Smith and Welles and the more radical Chase began to feel that they were losing touch with vital decisions, decisions they believed the president and the secretary of state were making informally.

Even Stanton, who saw Lincoln frequently on war matters, grew increasingly frustrated at the ineffective nature of the cabinet. Since every cabinet member was in frequent contact with legislators, proposing or advising on legislation, their irritation became known through the general gossip of Capitol Hill. Welles and most of the others simply resented this state of affairs, but Chase saw the situation through the lens of his own presidential ambitions and principles. He began to complain to his friends in Congress, especially to Sen. William Fessenden, chairman of the Senate Finance Committee, about the declining influence of the views he represented. This move was more than political ambition on Chase's part; legislators and much of the public considered him to be the representative of the party's antislavery wing. Apart from Chase's intentions, there were reasons to wonder if antislavery views were being smothered by political intrigues and compromises that before the war had frequently imperiled ideas of equal liberty.[8]

By early December 1862 Lincoln's fluctuating course on emancipation fed the concerns of more radical men. Chase could look back on Lincoln's revocation of General Hunter's order to emancipate slaves throughout Georgia, Florida, and South Carolina in mid-May; he could remember the president's intolerable patience with McClellan, whom Chase as well as friends in Congress had opposed months before Lincoln finally replaced him. It seemed to Chase that Congress was far ahead of Lincoln in attacking slavery. Even though he knew of the president's intention to issue the Emancipation Proclamation in July, Chase, and even Seward, thought that a quicker way to achieve that result was through the day-to-day actions of Union generals in freeing slaves as the armies advanced into the South. This policy promised to put blacks into fighting units sooner than Lincoln's more gradual policy that emphasized using them in auxiliary units. And Chase was troubled by the inclusion of a commitment to colonization and compensation, even in the 22 September proclamation. Finally, the delay of one hundred days seemed to signal some possible reversal or diminishment of the promise. "How much better," Chase said, "would be a manly protest against prejudice, against color, and a wise effort to give freed men homes in America."[9]

Seward meanwhile was making other important enemies, chiefly because of his lack of passion for emancipation. His most formidable adversary was an old friend. Charles Sumner had once enjoyed Seward's fellowship in the prewar antislavery cause, but by December Sumner despaired that Seward had become a mere politician, no longer dedicated to the cause of human freedom. Seward's political cohort Thurlow Weed had worked against Sumner's reelection bid in 1860, and

Seward himself virtually sat on the sidelines in the 1862 governor's race in New York, letting democrat Horatio Seymour win. Most vexing was a dispatch to minister Charles Francis Adams from Seward on 5 July linking Southern proslavery fanatics with abolitionists as trying to "precipitate a servile war." Seward himself had edited these dispatches, published just as Congress began its December meeting.[10] Seward had included in this diplomatic correspondence not only the equation between secessionists and radicals but also a letter written on 10 April 1861 in which he claimed that Lincoln accepted the idea that "the Federal government could not reduce the seceding States to obedience. . . . Only an imperial or despotic government could subjugate thoroughly disaffected or insurrectionary members of the state."[11]

It was highly unlikely that Lincoln held such views in April 1861, but their publication after the war had gone on for twenty months pushed Seward's stock even lower in Congress. Moreover, it was widely believed that Seward had been McClellan's earliest and most steadfast supporter even as the general was being targeted as everything from an amoral traitor to an overtrained incompetent. Joseph Medill, editor of the *Chicago Tribune*, echoed a growing opinion that "McClellan in the field and Seward in the cabinet have brought our grand cause to the very brink of death. Seward . . . is Lincoln's evil genius. He has been President de facto and has kept a sponge saturated with chloroform to Uncle Abe's nose all the while, except for one or two brief spells."[12]

By December Seward had established two certainties in the minds of important senators—he was influential with Lincoln and he opposed most of their advanced views. In the gloom after Fredericksburg and the fall elections, the frustration crystallized around an effort to remake the cabinet.[13]

In two caucuses of Republican senators on 16 and 17 December, thirty-one of the party's thirty-two senators agreed on the need to meet with Lincoln to explain why Seward had to go. They worried about his influence and disagreed with his policies. They also believed that the executive branch was not operating according to important constitutional principles. Jacob Collamer, venerable moderate from Vermont, argued that "the theory and practice of our government recognized a Cabinet council." But Lincoln did not consult his cabinet "as a body, upon important matters." Collamer had heard that the president "expressed the opinion that it was best to have no policy, and let each member of the Cabinet attend to the duties of his own department."[14]

The next day Collamer elaborated: "The theory of our government, and the early and uniform political construction thereof is, that the President should be aided by a Cabinet council, agreeing with him in political principles and general policy, and that all important public measures and appointments should be the result of their combined wisdom and deliberation." Senators also believed in an even larger constitutional forum. When they presented their resolutions to Lincoln they noted that the senators were "his constitutional advisors," empowered "to tender him friendly counsel when, in their judgment, it was rendered necessary by an emergency."

It was a predictable theory to justify the action that the Republican senators were taking, and it had some merit. Given the importance of party balance within the cabinet it was vital that a range of options be heard and discussed. Lincoln's apparent susceptibility to Seward's conservative influence naturally brought forth a demand that more radical voices be heard. It seemed to the senators that other cabinet members could not effectively argue these more radical positions because of Seward, positions made even more important because of the virtual unanimity of Republican senators against most of Seward's domestic policies. Lincoln appeared to be losing contact with the reform elements, the egalitarian idealists of the party, who increasingly were the men demanding a commitment to total war. By December that group included almost every Republican senator.

Lincoln was troubled. When word leaked of the gathering storm, the secretary of state offered his resignation. Lincoln told a colleague, "Since I heard last night of the proceedings of the caucus I have been more distressed than by any event in my life." He took the caucus personally: "They wish to get rid of me and I am sometimes half disposed to gratify them."[15]

Yet Lincoln was also politically savvy enough to know that he had to listen, to seek a solution, not a justification or a vindication. He recognized the seriousness of the crisis. Seward conducted foreign affairs ably and was politically and personally important to Lincoln. Although the radical voices were in the ascendant in Congress, the president could read the election returns as well as anyone, and he knew the power of conservative strength. Furthermore, as his annual message had shown, a large part of him longed for conservative ways.

Still, the president knew that he needed to be sensitive to more radical options and that after the conservative sentiments of the December 1862 message his bridges to Congress might need repair. He asked a delegation of senators to come to the White House to give him their protest in person. He met with them for almost three hours the night of 18 December and heard their demands: The command of the armies should be in the hands of vigorous and unrelenting leaders; too many Democrats still had influence while Lincoln did not support more radical men such as Hunter and Fremont—even McClellan was accusing the administration of not supporting the war effort adequately. Seward was the special target. He had "entirely lost the confidence of their constituents," James Grimes of Iowa and Jacob Howard of Michigan said. Fessenden asserted that Seward was "not in accord with the majority of the Cabinet and exerted an injurious influence upon the conduct of the war." Sumner joined in to complain that Seward was ridiculing Congress to foreign diplomats and was equating Congress with the Confederates in terms of radicalism; it was the same equation that the Copperheads were fond of making.

Lincoln listened without much interruption. He did show them a bundle of papers and letters demonstrating that McClellan "had been sustained by the government of the utmost of its power." The president read aloud several of the letters to McClellan to prove his point. He also defended Seward tangentially by noting that the secretary of state often read to Lincoln dispatches that he sent before they went out. The cabinet was not involved in this process, Lincoln noted, and he said he did not remember the dispatch that had made Sumner angry. After three hours the senators left. Lincoln promised to consider their views carefully and told them he was satisfied "with the tone and temper of the committee." Fessenden thought that the president was "apparently in cheerful spirits, and so far as we could judge, pleased with the interview."[16]

But Lincoln was clearly troubled, whatever face he presented to the senators. Calling a special cabinet meeting the next day (Seward did not come), Lincoln told them what had happened; perhaps to reassure them he reported that he had told the committee how "shocked and grieved" he was at this movement, that despite past party divergence and occasional differences, the cabinet members were cooperative. And "he had been sustained and consoled by the good feeling and the mutual and unselfish confidence and zeal that pervaded the Cabinet," as Welles put it. In sum, Lincoln tried to create cabinet unity, perhaps to raise sympathy for Seward, and to ensure that no one in the cabinet would stir up further conflict on his own. He was in charge, but he wanted their help. He asked that they join him in a meeting that evening with the senators.

They responded initially with different opinions. Chase and Bates were opposed, Chase pleading ignorance of the whole situation. Bates first delivered a lecture on the differences between the British system of cabinet ministry, drawn from the legislature, and the United States' separation of powers, then argued that "no good would come from a [joint] interview." Welles and Blair thought that a joint meeting was a good idea, Welles emphasizing that if Lincoln wanted them, then it was their duty. They finally agreed to the meeting.[17]

The meeting was set for 7:30 P.M., and Lincoln managed the preliminaries skillfully. Apparently the cabinet kept quiet about their earlier meeting with Lincoln, including the fact that they were going to be at the White House when the senators arrived. Both groups waited in the anteroom, legislators presumably surprised at not being there alone. Then the senators were ushered into Lincoln's office, and the president told them he wanted a friendly and frank discussion of the situation and asked their permission to include the cabinet members—whom they knew were waiting just outside the door. "Having no opportunity for consultation," Fessenden recalled, "the committee made no objection, and the Cabinet, excepting Mr. Seward came in."

Lincoln set the agenda, summarizing the purpose of the meeting and then launching into a statement about the unity of the cabinet. He admitted that under the pressures of time the cabinet had not met regularly. Still, he thought that most questions of importance had been adequately discussed and that after decisions were made all members acquiesced in them, despite some understandable disagreements that would come from any group of able men. He spoke especially of Seward's being energetic in prosecuting the war; indeed the secretary of state had "sometimes consulted with Mr. Chase."

Then Lincoln turned to the cabinet members for confirmation. Chase spoke up quickly, first to say that he would not have come had he known he was to be "arraigned before a committee of the Senate." Fessenden interrupted to note that it was the president, not the committee, who had called cabinet members into the room (implying that if someone wanted Chase arraigned it was not legislators). Chase was on the defensive now. Caught between men who had heard his complaints about the cabinet and a president who was challenging the secretary to call him a liar in public, Chase tried to have it both ways. The president was generally right in saying that the cabinet discussed important issues and acquiesced in final decisions, Chase said. Still, he did think that more thorough discussion might have been needed on some issues even though he conceded that there was unity in the cabinet to the extent that members did not oppose policies once they were decided upon.[18]

To Chase's credit, he confessed his reservations. Every other member but Seward had complained about how the cabinet was run. Both Smith and Stanton later told Fessenden that complaints about the cabinet were valid; Welles and Blair and even Bates had grumbled to lawmakers about their concerns. But that night Welles and Smith and Stanton "did not say a word during our interview with the President," Fessenden remembered caustically.

Lincoln had won the endorsement of his cabinet and taught a lesson to Chase. Yet more was at stake: Different visions of the presidency were also in combat. The senators' vision required consultation before important decisions were made—an assembling of the factions of the party and the expertise of cabinet officers to debate and determine the direction of the nation. No one minister and hence no one factional viewpoint would triumph by bypassing this sharing of views and balancing of party power. Jacob Collamer argued that the president's advisers "should be consulted on the great questions which affected the national welfare, and . . . the ear of the Executive should be open to all and . . . he should have the minds of all." Fessenden offered a confused concurrence—the president should consult often. John Quincy Adams had allowed himself to be overruled by the majority vote of his cabinet, and though Lincoln did not have to go that far it was an instructive model.

An increasingly independent presidency was emerging, however, and the circumstances of war were validating it. A former Whig and a former Democrat, Bates and Blair, said that the president could ask for as many opinions or as few as he wished; he need not consult with them unless he wanted to. The president himself was accountable for his administration and by implication the only point at which congressmen could challenge a cabinet member was at confirmation hearings. There could be no such thing as a "plural executive," in Welles's words.

At the conclusion of the meeting Lincoln asked the senators whether they still wanted Seward removed and how their constituents would react to such a move. Four senators, Grimes of Iowa, Trumbull of Illinois, Sumner of Massachusetts, and Pomeroy of Kansas, urged removal. Harris said that in his state of New York Seward had so much influence that his removal would hurt the party and the government. Howard, Collamer, and Fessenden declined to say, but the latter was noncommittal for an important reason: He wanted to know if Lincoln would accept the advice of a caucus of the Republican senators. Personally, he thought it best if Seward were out of the cabinet (indeed he complained that Lincoln should have consulted with the Senate in 1860–61 when he appointed the cabinet). Would Lincoln "follow the wishes of the Republican senators when ascertained?" "Do you wish us to advise with our fellow-senators?" Fessenden asked. "I think not," Lincoln answered. Lincoln wanted Republican legislators' opinions, but he was going to keep the executive authority fully in his own hands.[19]

Although the president, the cabinet, and the senators had aired the issues and in the process challenged the accusations about a divided cabinet, the crisis was not over. Four senators still wanted Seward out; another three let their silence speak; only one openly thought Seward should remain. Seward still had his resignation registered, and should he resign, as Lincoln explained later, it would have meant that "the thing would have slumped over one way and we should have been left with a scant handful of supporters."[20]

Lincoln needed a way to establish a balance, to keep the support of conservatives and radicals. He could not solve the problem simply by keeping the status quo—because the Republican members of the Senate would assume that he was deaf to their opinions. Radicals had to have something, too, something more than just keeping Chase in the cabinet. Lincoln needed to offer a gesture to radicals without alienating Seward and his supporters—but the radicals wanted Seward's head.

Lincoln would not give them that, but neither would he ask for Chase's resignation. If Seward and Chase left, both wings of the party would be inflamed. Only one way seemed clear: to gratify Seward and his people by rejecting Seward's resignation—thus showing conservatives that Seward's views mattered in the cabinet. At the same time Lincoln needed to appease the radicals by showing that Chase would also be heard. Since Seward was out on a limb, Lincoln needed some way to get Chase out there also to permit a balanced settlement. Ironically, Chase, who had precipitated the crisis, would give Lincoln the opportunity he needed to make the gesture that would please the radicals.

Lincoln first had to settle the problem over Seward. The morning after the joint meeting, Lincoln eagerly accepted Welles's offer to assure Seward that the president did not want his resignation. Chase was the next problem; Lincoln needed his resignation without demanding it. He called him in, and in the presence of Welles and Stanton, told Chase that "I sent for you because this matter is giving me great trouble." Chase knew what the president was talking about. He immediately explained that the meeting the previous evening had been a total surprise to him and it had affected him a great deal. He had decided that he would submit his resignation. Lincoln asked, "Where is it?" "I brought it with me," Chase replied, delaying things. "I wrote it this morning." "Let me have it," Lincoln said and held out his hand. Chase looked reluctant, wanting to say something else, but Lincoln was not watching. He took the letter and quickly opened it. Then he turned to Welles, and "with a triumphal laugh," as Welles later recalled, Lincoln said, "This cuts the Gordian knot. . . . I can dispose of this subject now without difficulty. I see my way clear."[21]

Lincoln had triumphed for a more subtle reason than the one usually offered by historians. The point was not that he had shown radicals that if Seward resigned, Chase also would be lost. The president could have obtained Chase's resignation any time he wanted it but to do so would have alienated senators and much of the radical wing of the party. Only the loss of Seward would have placated them but that would have destroyed conservative support. Crucial to Lincoln's solution was to get Chase to offer to resign so that Lincoln could reject the offer. Thus the president could send similar messages to both wings of the party: I need and will listen to both viewpoints. Chase in particular understood the situation. He wrote to Lincoln, "Something you said or looked when I handed you my resignation this morning made on my mind the impression that having received the resignations of both Governor Seward and myself you felt you could relieve yourself from trouble by declining to accept either, and that this feeling was one of gratification." Chase tried to leverage things a bit by arguing that neither he nor Seward was really necessary to the success of the administration, but Lincoln was not persuaded and neither was Chase. When Lincoln wrote notes addressed to both men asking them to stay they both agreed though Chase waited until he saw Seward's answer to reply. [22]

Lincoln's strategy worked, and it also taught lessons to the principals. Both factions believed that their side had won a victory and would now be more influential than before. Ironically, however, Seward himself discovered his vulnerability. Lincoln had not instinctively taken up the sword to defend him. For almost three days the secretary of state had twisted slowly in the wind while Lincoln listened to his most vocal critics and weighed the options. Welles recalled that during the crisis Seward had told him that "he thought the subject should be disposed of one way or the other at once. He is disappointed, I see, that the President did not promptly refuse to consider his resignation, and dismiss, or refuse to parley with, the committee." Seward also discovered how profoundly unpopular he was within his party and learned to focus on doing his job in the State Department, instead of acting like the premier. And he grew closer to Lincoln, recognizing that ultimately Lincoln had protected him. [23]

Chase's lesson contained similar ironies. Many of his supporters outside Washington believed that the crisis had produced a triumph for his radicalism, but Chase had lost face with important senators. They now believed he had lied about the extent of difficulties in the cabinet and been exposed. They also had been able to compare Chase with Lincoln in a delicate situation; Chase had not gained from the comparison. He would have to work overtime to regain the support he hoped for in his drive toward the presidency in 1864. Lincoln would be the clear beneficiary of Chase's weakness.

Although Lincoln was the overall victor, he too learned something. Senators and factions of the party still thought that consultation was important, that they needed to be heard in any important decision. Thus the president made a point of relying on extensive consultation with the cabinet in the aftermath of the crisis on two major questions of late 1862, West Virginia statehood and the final Emancipation Proclamation.

West Virginia's statehood posed interesting constitutional issues, and because the president insisted that he was defending the Constitution and the laws, it was important that he receive the fullest constitutional argument available. Representing a range of views across the party spectrum, the cabinet provided an excellent forum for obtaining that justification. Could these forty-eight western counties create a new state? Did the loyal government of Virginia have the legal standing to agree to its division into Virginia and West Virginia? Lincoln asked for written opinions from every cabinet member on the legality of the extraordinary events that made the new state.

The cabinet divided. On one side were the conservatives, Welles, Blair, and Bates, arguing that the so-called loyal government of Virginia, which had agreed to its own division, was a sham that represented a tiny proportion of the people within Virginia's borders. Almost no votes had been cast for the new government outside Unionist counties; the only people who voted were supporters of the new state. It was similar to allowing the rebel South to call itself the United States government and then having it agree to divide the country and thus recognize the new Confederate government. Although the Unionists in Virginia could be recognized in some instances, they lacked the authority to agree to so momentous an act.

Chase, Seward, and Stanton disagreed. The assertion by rebels in Virginia that they were the true state did not make it so. Indeed such claims supported the secessionist argument; the loyal citizens of the region were the source of legitimate authority. It would be outrageous to deny loyal citizens the right to establish their own government while accepting the claims of the disloyal.

Lincoln sided with his more radical advisers, accepting the distinction between recognizing a loyal government and a disloyal one. He added his own flourish by noting that "it is a universal practice in the popular elections of all these States to give no legal consideration whatever to those who do not choose to vote as against the effect of the votes of those who do choose to vote." The opponents of the new state chose not to vote and made that choice while in open rebellion. "Can this Government stand, if it indulges constitutional constructions by which men in open rebellion are to be accounted man for man, the equals of those who maintain their loyalty to it?"

Underlying Lincoln's argument was the question of saving the Union and undermining slavery, the source of disunion. "Is the admission into the Union of West Virginia expedient?" he asked, and answered, "We can scarcely dispense with the aid of West Virginia. . . . Her brave and good men regard her admission into the Union as a matter of life and death." The Union cause gained since the new state increased the opponents of slavery. "The admission of the new State turns that much slave soil to free; and thus, is a certain and irrevocable encroachment upon the cause of the rebellion." The president had some doubts about the constitutional precedent of allowing such division. "But," he argued, "a measure made expedient by war is no precedent for times of peace." Wasn't this secession "tolerated only because it is our secession?" "If we call it by that name there is still difference enough between secession against the Constitution and secession in favor of the Constitution." Since Lincoln opposed Southern secession and slavery because of their challenge to the constitutional process, it is not surprising that he found the difference persuasive. On 31 December 1862 he signed into law the "Act for the Admission of the State of West Virginia into the Union."[24]

The Emancipation Proclamation posed a different problem. In Lincoln's mind the legal issue was clear. He had authority under his war powers to free slaves in places where war was being made. Moreover, the president had consulted fully with individual cabinet members during the summer before issuing the preliminary proclamation, and he took full responsibility for it. He told them then, "I do not wish your advice about the main matter—for that I have determined for myself." The December discussions were thus about matters of style more than substance. Only Chase's objection to excluding any portions of the affected states was significant, and Lincoln was firm on that point. He would free slaves only where his constitutional authority was clear, where his war powers reached. As he explained to Chase later, to act only because he thought emancipation was "politically expedient and morally right" would "give up all footing upon constitution or law." He accepted modifications of language, but the act of freeing the slaves was Lincoln's—President Lincoln's.[25]

These meetings reaffirmed the importance of the cabinet in the public eye and showed congressmen that Lincoln had learned the need for broader discussions. But the meetings may have been more for display than for substance because after this late 1862 flurry cabinet involvement in major decisions did not increase. Lincoln continued to consult individual ministers on matters within departments, and some cabinet members, especially Seward and Stanton, preferred to operate on that basis. Stanton did not attend half the cabinet meetings, and Seward avoided bringing things to the cabinet for discussion. Chase reported that "there is almost never any consultation on matters of importance. . . . What are called Cabinet Meetings have fallen pretty much into disuse." Welles continued to complain that "there should be free and constant intercourse and exchange of views, and a combined effort." But he believed at times that cabinet discussions were called "to make it appear that all were consulted." Lincoln used the meetings as a sounding board to discuss the timing or the language of statements or for actions he was about to take or messages he was about to issue. The real business of government occurred when the cabinet members worked in their own domains and when Lincoln consulted with them one-on-one and then acted. Since the major business was fighting the war, the president made policy predominantly with Stanton and with his generals or alone. Cabinet government remained an illusion.[26]

By midwar that system had its benefits. It kept intraparty quarreling from seriously affecting the day-to-day duties of carrying on the great war. Clearly, the potential for disruption was present. Blair was said to hate Chase, who returned the feeling. Blair also told Welles that Stanton and Seward were "unprincipled hypocrites." Bates believed that Blair was a conniving, self-serving politician. Chase still thought that Seward stifled Lincoln's reforming instincts. When a friend asked Seward why he did not keep a diary, the secretary of state answered that it would be filled with stories of quarrels within the cabinet and such information was best not set down where gossipmongers might get their hands on it. As the Battle of Gettysburg approached Welles complained that the president called off a cabinet meeting in order to closet himself with Stanton and Halleck. "This is wrong, but I know no remedy. . . . The Government should not be carried on in the War or State Departments exclusively." But primarily it was.[27]

Yet within their departments the cabinet members performed well. They cooperated when they had to and kept their subordinates hard at work, so hard, in fact, that some suffered from exhaustion and almost broke down. Stanton especially was a brutal taskmaster. Subordinates complained of spending night after night in their offices, month after month, seldom having time even to change their clothes. Stanton had to order sentries at the War Department not to admit one subordinate who had broken down, "flat," as he reported. Stanton himself complained of not seeing his wife, Ellen, for days at a time, and one day in his office he collapsed and had to be taken home in an ambulance. Twelve-to-fifteen-hour days took their toll but were imperative in organizing the vast war effort. Similar situations could be found in the other departments of government, including the presidency.[28]

The executive branch had established its ultimate autonomy, and Lincoln had clearly shown himself master of it. He, not Congress, would determine who his advisers would be. He would listen to their advice, but he did not require their consent. His cabinet would continue to work with legislators but would report to him. Congress would be placated by knowing that there were cabinet meetings in which major events were discussed by men from all party wings, but the president would decide what to do or even if those discussions mattered. The demands of war would determine such questions, and the huge war demanded so much attention, so much energy, that the cabinet officers were generally consumed by their duties. Their role as voices for party opinions was being overwhelmed by the need for armies and ships to advance and to bring to life Lincoln's promises and the other goals of the conflict.

1863

★ ★ ★ ★ ★

I shall never forget my first interview with this great man. I was accompanied to the executive mansion and introduced to President Lincoln by Senator Pomeroy. The room in which he received visitors was the one now used by the President's secretaries. I entered it with a moderate estimate of my own consequence, and yet there I was to talk with, and even to advise, the head man of a great nation. Happily for me, there was no vain pomp and ceremony about him. I was never more quickly or more completely put at ease in the presence of a great man than in that of Abraham Lincoln. He was seated, when I entered, in a low armchair with his feet extended on the floor, surrounded by a large number of documents and several busy secretaries. The room bore the marks of business, and the persons in it, the President included, appeared to be much overworked and tired. Long lines of care were already deeply written on Mr. Lincoln's brow, and his strong face, full of earnestness, lighted up as soon as my name was mentioned. As I approached and was introduced to him he arose and extended his hand and bade me welcome. . . . Proceeding to tell him who I was and what I was doing, he promptly, but kindly, stopped me, saying: "I know who you are Mr. Douglass; Mr. Seward has told me all about you. Sit down, I am glad to see you."

—Frederick Douglass, *The Life and Times of Frederick Douglass*, 1863

9
★ ★ ★ ★ ★

EMANCIPATION AND THE LIMITS OF DISSENT: JANUARY TO JUNE 1863

As 1863 began the hundred days had run out. Lincoln had threatened and promised emancipation on the first day of the new year. Millions of antislavery men and women, their numbers growing every day, anticipated the beginning of a new age for the nation; their opponents forecast the end of the republic they had known. Both groups waited to see the act of emancipation, the most important and individual of Lincoln's policies, come to life. But 1862 ended with doubts on the battlefield, and those doubts cast heavy shadows on the moment. Lincoln might proclaim emancipation but warmaking would give the act life. A war measure, and only a war measure—legitimated by executive war power, directed against and applicable only to the Confederate enemy, meaningful only if Union armies advanced to protect promised freedom—the Emancipation Proclamation would mirror "the Pope's bull against the comet" unless the army and navy produced victory.

Memories of Fredericksburg still resounded, and in other theaters there was not much to inspire hope. Since October Grant had been moving south toward Vicksburg; by early December he was near Oxford, Mississippi. By the middle of that month he and Sherman were advancing on Vicksburg, but on 20 December rebel raider John Morgan had flanked Grant and cut his supply line even as Nathan Forrest was successfully raiding further north of Grant's army, tearing up rails, destroying telegraph lines. Sherman was also in trouble by 29 December when an assault on the bluffs near Chickasaw Bayou, a few miles north of Vicksburg, was repulsed with heavy losses.

Further north and east in Tennessee, Gen. William Rosecrans was now the commander of the Army of the Cumberland, and he too seemed unable to handle rebel cavalry. Even as Sherman's army fell back from Chickasaw Bayou another young and daring cavalryman, twenty-six-year-old Joseph Wheeler, rode all the way around Rosecrans's army near Murfreesboro, destroying wagons and supplies and capturing ammunition. But Rosecrans managed to advance until by 30 December his 42,000-man army bedded down within earshot of Braxton Bragg's 34,000 Confederates, preparing for the carnage to come. A strange, frightening, yet sadly comic bravado struck the bandsmen of the two armies that night. Yankee musicians began to play "Yankee Doodle" as loudly as they could; rebels answered with "Dixie." Union bands countered with "Hail Columbia" and were answered with "The Bonnie Blue Flag." Then one of them, knowing what the morning would bring, began to play "Home Sweet Home," and the musical conflict faded under the sound of thousands of young armed men singing, "Be it ever so humble, there's no place like home."

By the time that the battle was over indelible scenes had been chiseled in soldiers' minds: Rosecrans riding along with an aide, suddenly the man's head gone and Rosecrans's uniform splattered with the gore; an attack into a forest and the noise so ear-shattering that soldiers pulled cotton from the bolls around them and stuffed it in their ears; the cries of wounded men sounding in the night; the next day another charge that cost the rebels 1,500 men in an hour; finally on 3 January, 1863 the gray-clad soldiers quickly grabbing knapsacks, guns, lifting wounded who could be taken away, and retreating into the night; the dead and wounded soldiers who could not leave strewn in sleep-disturbing memory across the landscape. The Union army took 31 percent casualties—nearly 13,000 men; the rebel army lost nearly 12,000, one-third of its young men. With the average age being twenty-five for all Civil War soldiers, the dead were almost always the young men.[1]

As the soldiers lay dying in the field at Murfreesboro, people throughout the North waited in anxiety and expectation. The one hundred days had passed; no part of the Confederacy had abandoned the rebellion. Fredericksburg especially and then this bloody battle showed how powerfully white Southerners clung to their desire for an independent slave-based republic. The bargain promised in September by Lincoln—end rebellion and preserve slavery—had been rejected irrevocably. It was time to take the next step.

Though clocks throughout the nation were gearing up to strike the emancipation hour, some friends of freedom could not be fully hopeful. The president's speech of early December had seemed such a step backward. "We cannot refrain from expressing our astonishment at the folly and infatuation evinced in his plan of buying up Southern treason 'in lots to suit purchasers,'" William Lloyd Garrison said. Conservative newspapers such as the *New York Herald* and the *New York World* happily proclaimed that the message revealed that the president had changed his mind about emancipation. Charles Sumner came to the White House quickly and had a long talk with Lincoln. He left reassured and told his friends that "the Presdt. is firm. He says that he would not stop the Procltn if he could, & he culd not if he would."[2]

Although Sumner's reassurances were not fully convincing, crowds gathered throughout the North on 1 January 1863, waiting for the promised proclamation. The most influential abolitionists met together in the Music Hall in Boston to celebrate if and when the document appeared. Most people were optimistic as the meeting began late in the afternoon. A symphony orchestra from Philadelphia played Beethoven's Fifth Symphony and a chorus sang Mendelssohn's "Hymn of Praise." Emerson read a poem he had composed for the occasion. When an announcement was made that the proclamation had been signed, the crowd erupted in cheers as people stood and waved hats and handkerchiefs and cheered three times for Lincoln, again and again.

But the announcement was premature. Boston's establishment may have been satisfied that all was well, but for others disappointment had followed hope too many times. Another large crowd of three thousand had gathered at Tremont Temple in the early evening, uncertain that the proclamation actually had been signed. Frederick Douglass recalled that eight, then nine, then ten o'clock passed and "a visible shadow seemed [to be] falling." But just when "suspense was becoming agony, a man with a face fairly illumined with the news he bore, exclaimed in tones that thrilled all hearts, 'It is coming! It is on the wires!'" Finally they celebrated everywhere, in Boston and throughout the North for days, proclaiming a new era, a revolution. Indeed the step that Lincoln had taken changed fundamentally the nature of much of the nation.[3]

The words of the final proclamation were hardly moving, having "all the moral grandeur of a bill of lading," as Richard Hofstadter described them. The listing of the counties in various states that were exempt from emancipation also muted the trumpet of freedom. Blacks who gathered in Washington to hear the proclamation listened carefully to see if the counties in Virginia that they had escaped from were now free soil. "I am free!" some could shout, but others could not as easily proclaim their freedom. Karl Marx, correspondent for a London newspaper, spoke of how lacking in eloquence the proclamation was. Lincoln's "most formidable decrees which he hurls at the enemy and which will never lose their historic significance, resemble—as their author intends them to—ordinary summons, sent by one lawyer to another."[4]

Yet such critics forget several important point about the proclamation, and their oversight obscures the meaning of the act and the nature of the war and of the presidency. Lincoln did not, as some charged, free the slaves only in places where he could not reach them; he freed the slaves in the only place that he could legally reach them—in places that he ruled under presidential war powers. The language of the great deed had to be a lawyer's language because Lincoln was taking legal action. He was placing the great ideal of freedom within the constitutional fabric—the only place that it could have life in a constitutional republic.

Indeed Congress, where much more radical sentiment prevailed on emancipation, also acted only where its clear constitutional authority reached. Legislative action in behalf of freedom also lacked "moral grandeur"; it merely had legal power. Congress freed slaves in the District of Columbia under its Article 1, section 8, clause 17, grant to "exercise exclusive Legislation in all cases whatsoever" over the District. It eliminated slavery from the territories under its clear power "to make all needful rules for the territories." It permitted confiscation of the slaves of rebels under its authority to set the penalty for treason, and under its right to establish law to govern the armed forces, it had stopped soldiers from returning fugitive slaves. When Lincoln objected to confiscation that worked a forfeiture beyond the life of the individual, Congress pulled back within constitutional guidelines by explaining that confiscation affected only one generation. Most congressional action on emancipation used the conservative instrument of the courts to determine who had lost their property for rebelling against national authority. Lincoln's actions on emancipation were limited by similar restraints.[5]

Lincoln was lawyer enough to know the difference between a statement of law and the flourishes of dicta, however enlightened, in a legal document. The January proclamation was not without its flourish: "Upon this act, sincerely believed to be an act of justice, warranted by the Constitution, upon military necessity, I invoke the considerate judgment of mankind, and the gracious favor of Almighty God," it concluded, just before the formalities of seal and date. Lincoln had not originally thought of those words, however; Chase had suggested them. Chase had the luxury of rhetorical flourish; he was not making law. The president was. Lincoln could outflourish Chase when the occasion required, but when he assumed his role as enforcer of the laws Lincoln spoke as a lawyer. There would be seasons for inspiring rhetoric, times to unshackle minds as well as bodies.[6]

Yet the proclamation, so formal and stilted in its legal rhetoric, still housed revolutionary realities. Potentially it freed over 3 million slaves, every slave in the remaining Confederacy. It also exemplified new forces steadily pushing emancipation, even as the White House fashioned the words giving legal recognition to a million private decisions that had been made by generals and privates and black men and women throughout the South. The meaning of freedom expanded as the army moved further south; more and more blacks were freed of shackles, no longer grasping hoes, axes, and the reins of supply wagons. In increasing numbers they were taking up guns, for Lincoln proclaimed not just freedom but the arming of black freedom fighters.

Unlike the September proclamation, this document did not mention colonization or compensated emancipation. Lincoln had asked for both in his December annual message, but the January proclamation included different visions. Here was a call to the freedmen to stay, to fight to sustain the Union and their freedom. That summons portended rights beyond mere freedom. Since citizenship was widely recognized as linked to military service, the offer of such service meant a promise of equal citizenship. Wendell Phillips noted the difference between the two proclamations: "Will you go away if I venture to free you?" said the president on the twenty-second day of September; "May I colonize you among the sickly deserts or the vast jungles of South America?" On the first day of January, he said to the same four million, "Let me colonize you in the forts of the Union, and put rifles in your hands! Give us your hand to defend the perpetuity of the Union."[7]

The January proclamation was an immense step forward, an effort that marked a determination not just to restore the Union as it was but to create the Union that would be. Yet the nation did not go gentle into that new day; the proclamation unleashed an impassioned debate between proponents of past and future. Even as antislavery became abolition and abolition evolved into some form of equal liberty, the voices of conservatism grew louder. As growing numbers of black soldiers joined the Union army the portent of revolution became inescapable. Debate became increasingly heated as reactionary forces, especially in the Middle West and in eastern cities, lashed out at a changing nation. Lincoln remained sensitive to those feelings.

He pushed changes but enfolded them within conservative contexts. His main task, among many, was to ensure that conservatism was not represented by racism. A debate had been under way since the prewar days when he had tried to save the Constitution from the proslavery and racist visions of Taney and Douglas. Still, the same question abided: Was the constitutional system the one envisioned by the Founders in their hopes, or would dark Jacksonian visions triumph? Would racism corrupt democracy and the Constitution become a covenant with death? By January 1863 more optimistic answers to those questions were possible.

Yet no answer was possible without winning the war, and that meant more troops had to be raised. The disaster at Fredericksburg and the carnage at Murfreesboro discouraged enlistment. Foreign-born workers, in New York particularly but in other places as well, were especially embittered. Irish American soldiers had shown unparalleled bravery at Fredericksburg, and their communities felt their losses profoundly; some people believed that generals risked Irish lives carelessly. The Emancipation Proclamation had alienated large numbers of potential recruits who hardly needed excuses not to join such a bloody and ongoing war. Especially in the regions of the Middle West settled from the South and in cities where job competition existed between the races, people resented the idea of fighting in order to free blacks.

Even in solidly Republican New England enlistments slacked off. New Hampshire had to double its state recruiting bounty from ten to twenty dollars, then raise it to fifty and finally to one hundred dollars. Some communities paid even more as they competed for volunteers. Meanwhile, in the army, sickness, casualties, and desertion thinned the ranks. One estimate was that over 100,000 men of the nearly 900,000 Union soldiers were absent without leave in late 1862. Smaller groups told a similar story. Cpl. Edwin Weller from Havana, New York, had enlisted in August 1862. On 17 January 1863 he wrote his father, "There was four men belonging to our company Deserted last night. This makes 12 in all that has Deserted our company. We have Twenty Six in Hospitals. This leaves our Co. with but 49 enlisted men now. When we left Elmira we had 98 Enlisted men and three commissioned officers."[8]

Such sentiments from the battlefield were ominous echoes of antiwar politics at home. Democratic state officials elected during the conservative reaction of fall 1862 had taken their places in state governments. Most articulate was New York's Horatio Seymour, whose elevation to governor of the most powerful state in the Union instantly marked him as a presidential candidate in 1864. Seymour presented a governor's message on 7 January 1863 that wrapped its antiadministration challenges in the rhetoric of civil liberties, denouncing civilian arrests and the habeas corpus suspensions and proclaiming the virtues of local self-government. Democratic newspapers reprinted Seymour's message throughout the North. The anti-Lincoln majority in the Indiana legislature passed a joint resolution of praise for Seymour and prepared to deny their Republican governor funds to fight the war. One New York supporter rejoiced that the governor's message had unleashed a just criticism of Lincoln's policies: "Men whose lips had been sealed for months (except in their family circles) upon the great questions agitating the country, and dared not express their honest convictions in public for fear of arrest felt that the fetters had dropped from their limbs—and their tongues were loosed." Pamphlets written by men whom the administration had arrested began to appear protesting their imprisonment and describing Lincoln's administration as enslaving the guiltless who had merely opposed national tyranny.[9]

Congressional debate fueled public discussion about the outreach of national power. In 1863 legislators were beginning their debates over a conscription bill and also over a bill to legalize suspension of the writ of habeas corpus. The threat that archconservative state judges would use the writ to discharge suspected rebels or reluctant soldiers from army custody remained. Congressional Republicans had avoided debate on the writ during the first years of the war, letting the president take the lead and the heat, but now they sought the legal boundaries of this national power.

The Habeas Corpus Act authorized the president to suspend the privilege of the writ whenever "in his judgment the public safety may require it." That settled the question of legislative versus executive authority to suspend—the *Merryman* argument. Congress had legalized executive authority. Ultimate authority was still a bit ambiguous, but clearly Lincoln had the authority to suspend, regardless of its origin. Yet the authority was hardly arbitrary. The secretaries of war and state were required to furnish lists of "political prisoners" to federal judges, and the prisoners would be released upon taking a loyalty oath if a grand jury met in their district and failed to indict them. And if lists were not forthcoming by 23 March the prisoners could be released. Not surprisingly Democrats emphasized the power given Lincoln, Republicans the limits on that power.

Conscription was clearly in their minds as lawmakers wrote the habeas corpus law. The Militia Act of 17 July 1862 had been followed quickly by an executive proclamation that suspended the writ to allow the arrest of anyone running from, or interfering with, the draft provisions of that law. Conservative state judges had been accepting suits to protect men from such suspensions and from confiscation of property as the Union army moved south. These suits often charged federal officials with violations of state trespass, false arrest or libel laws.[10]

The Habeas Corpus Act gave immunity to federal officials acting under presidential suspensions and allowed cases to be removed from state to federal courts when defendant soldiers faced state accusations. It was an important provision for the future. At the conclusion of the war thousands of suits would be launched in the defeated Southern states suing Union soldiers and officials for allegedly unlawful seizures, destruction of property, or deprivation of liberty. This law would protect the victorious Unionists from rebel vengeance. During the war Northern Democrats damned the act as justifying even the most egregious and excessive use of federal authority. They argued that it, like the draft law, gave the administration monarchical powers.

As the Habeas Corpus Act neared completion, leading Democrats met at Delmonico's in New York City to form the "Society for the Diffusion of Political Knowledge," organized "to promote a sound political education of the public mind; to the end that usurpations may be prevented, that arbitrary and unconstitutional measures may be checked." Thirty-seven Democrats in the House filed a protest that federal officials were free to trample even more violently on the rights of honest citizens.[11]

But the habeas corpus issues, impassioned as they were, were overcome by an even greater outreach of power when the national government acted to meet the seemingly unrelenting need for soldiers. The older system was inadequate; that doddering scheme consisted of state-based efforts whereby governors were responsible for recruiting regiments, which were then mustered into federal service. This system had two disadvantages, one in terms of the kinds of units it gathered, the other in that it was incapable of gathering the numbers of men needed.

First, instead of sending new recruits into existing experienced units, Union recruiting allowed established units to wither away by attrition. They were then replaced by new, inexperienced units. This older system built the camaraderie of neighbors enlisting, training, and fighting together and thus strengthened and reflected the powerful traditions of local self-government and attachment to communities. But it sent these unseasoned friends and neighbors to meet Confederate regiments made up of new troops who had joined battle-hardened veterans. Jefferson Davis, who had a conscription system established nearly a year before the Union had one, described the result of many of these encounters: "Our many memorable successes are with justice ascribed in large measure to the reorganization and reinforcement of our armies under the operation of conscription."[12]

Second, the more substantial Union difficulty arose from the breakdown of local and state efforts; more troops were needed than these enlistment systems could produce. The 2 July 1862 subterfuge in which Seward had quietly persuaded Northern governors to ask for 300,000 volunteers to serve for three years did bring in men, but, with desertions and the general poor health of many recruits, these were not enough. Congress had tried to raise more troops on 17 July 1862 when it gave Lincoln the authority to use state machinery to call up 300,000 militia. Built into the act was the possibility of conscription, but the cumbersome use of state devices and the lack of enthusiasm among potential recruits raised only one-quarter of the 300,000 men Lincoln asked for, and these were nine-month recruits. The president, however, did not resort to the draft power he had been given.[13]

Clearly, a draft had to be instituted. The ninety-day militiamen called up in early August were nearing their discharge day. The 300 regiments called in early 1861 would serve for another year, but more and more people understood that victory in a year was unlikely. The provost marshal general reported that desertion was becoming "a formidable and widespread evil." And generals in the field, counting their depleted regiments after Fredericksburg and Murfreesboro, looked to Washington to see if there was stomach to carry on with the bloody task. Horace Porter, an aide to Rosecrans, whose army was still licking its wounds after the new year's ordeal, wrote, "We are all anxiously awaiting for the conscription to fill up our old regiments, which are dwindling rapidly. I hope it will clear the street corners of those idlers who ought to be here putting their shoulders to the wheel!"[14]

The new law of 3 March 1863 established a national conscription system to supplement the state-based operations. It gave to the provost marshal general the responsibility of enrolling, with a few minor exemptions, all men between the ages of twenty and forty-five who would thereby become eligible to be drafted. The president could set quotas for every district in the Union based on population and the number of men already in service. National enrollment officials ventured into every neighborhood in the North to ensure enforcement. As often as possible they were appointed from the region in which they would work, and in keeping with the patronage system of the age, most of them were Republicans who needed work and who shared party doubts about Democratic loyalty, a practice that would lead to charges of corruption and favoritism.

Some methods existed to avoid being conscripted, however. Medical exemptions were possible. Men who were sons of dependent older parents or were in other ways the sole support of families could be exempted. Most objectionable to critics, however, were escape hatches based on wealth. Men could pay substitutes to serve in their places or could pay the government commutation money. The price in either case was $300 (the average worker made about $600 a year).[15]

Although the national authority now set goals and standards for drafting an army, there was still room for local action. The draft would begin only if and when state- and community-based recruiting failed to meet quotas. Public servants and town councils in most frequent contact with the people still played major roles in calling the young men to war through appeals to local and state pride and to national ideals. Communities depended upon local resources to pay bounties to attract recruits to fill their quotas as before. Ironically, in casting their lures so broadly, communities often changed the local nature of the regiments they organized; men from distant towns and places enlisted in their units, but these were still considered as local, as "our" regiments.[16]

The process of enrollment took some time as officers compiled lists of eligible men, compared the lists with past volunteers, and checked on exemptions. The delay was designed to allow and to encourage districts to gather volunteers, a feature that worked to the benefit of potential soldiers. In order to reduce their quota of draftees, county and city governments raised enlistment bounties for service. In some places a combination of national, state, and county bounties could reach from $600 to $1000. This system led to bounty jumping, a scheme enabling the dishonest to earn even more.

The draft law provoked an outcry ranging from technical to constitutional objections. Several Republican governors objected to the quotas their states were assigned; Democratic governors accused Provost Marshal General James Fry of imposing higher quotas on Democratic districts. There was some truth to both objections since quotas were established according to previous numbers of volunteers. Democratic districts, less enamored of "Mr. Lincoln's War," had sent fewer troops. Republican disputes arose from questions over how many men had already been sent.[17]

The constitutional objections came from surprising as well as from predictable quarters. Horace Greeley wrote to Stanton claiming that a draft was "an anomaly in a free State; it oppresses the masses. Like imprisonment for debt . . . it must and will be reformed out of our system of political economy." Democratic opposition shocked no one. Eighty-eight percent of the party's congressmen voted against it, and Democratic governors such as New York's Horatio Seymour protested the breadth of federal power over citizens of states. Seymour asked that Lincoln at least await the judgment of the Supreme Court before acting. Chief Justice Taney prepared an opinion striking down the draft as an unconstitutional exercise of national authority over the state governments, but it stayed in his desk. The Supreme Court never took a case on conscription during the war; indeed it would not do so until 1918 when a unanimous Court upheld it.[18]

Lincoln had no doubts that the draft was lawful, and he was not about to wait on the Supreme Court to validate it. The demands of war came too quickly and the issue was too important. The Confederate draft was proceeding, unimpeded, he believed, and it was creating armies that might gain victories and perhaps ultimately rebel independence while the Union government debated alternatives or awaited the final voice of the high court. He wanted to act constitutionally, he told Seymour, but he was also going to be "practical in performing the important duty . . . of maintaining the unity and the free principles of our common country." Yet practicality alone apparently did not satisfy him. His own respect for constitutional tradition and his knowledge that many Americans were deeply suspicious of being compelled to fight for their country led Lincoln to write and keep in reserve an extended argument on the necessity and the constitutionality of the draft. Emphasizing the clear and unlimited constitutional authority of Congress to raise and support armies, the precedent established during the War of 1812, the need for troops, the extended congressional debate over the bill, and the need to accept a complex procedure that might require adjustment to ensure fairness in determining quotas, Lincoln asked if people would "shrink from the necessary means to maintain our free government. . . . Are we degenerate? Has the manhood of our race run out?" Regardless of the state of the national character, however, the president asserted that "it is my purpose to see the draft law faithfully executed."[19]

Lincoln was also concerned about fairness in the operation of conscription. When Seymour protested the bias of his state's quotas and documented some disproportionate calls on Democratic districts, the president set up a commission of inquiry that endorsed Seymour's claims. Lincoln quietly changed the quotas and corresponded extensively with the governor, seeking to win rather than to compel his support.[20]

The Draft Act of March 1863 accomplished its purpose; it helped end the manpower crisis. Union armies grew as Confederate ranks declined. The major source of the growing numbers was still volunteer enlistments, brought to the army by ever-richer bounties and by an abiding patriotism that continuing Union victories fed. Tens of thousands demonstrated their commitment to the cause by reenlisting, but corruption permeated the conscription process as substitute brokers and bounty jumpers made millions of dollars. Unfairness was implicit in a system that put poorer men at greater risk than richer ones, no matter how many of those men might somehow get the $300 that would protect them. Political favoritism was also likely when Republican provost marshals decided if Democrats should be soldiers. But prodded by the threat of a draft, state governors called for and got the army that was needed. Lincoln was wise enough to give play to the force of state energy and to allow state and city officials to make decisions that would produce Union-saving ends by their own means.

The law was executed. Despite murders of a few enrollment officers, threats of death to many others, and actual riots, the government put the draft law into effect. The enrollment process began in May, and some names were drawn as early as June. There were high hopes that hundreds of thousands of men would now replenish the diminished federal regiments.

Many historians have claimed that the draft itself was a failure. It is true that only 50,000 draftees ultimately donned uniforms, only 7 percent of the men who served in the military. But a better count would include not only draftees but also the substitutes who went into the service. Though the law did not produce soldiers in the numbers expected, it did bring in a respectable number. The War Department made four draft calls, the first in July and three later in 1864. Out of the 776,000 men who were called, 161,000 simply ran away, despite laws that punished such men as deserters and denied them the protection of civilian courts. About 315,000 found ways to persuade doctors that they were medically unfit or proved that they were the sole support for widows, motherless children, poor parents, or orphans. Eighty-seven thousand paid commutation even though it protected a man for only one draft call at a time; this money was used to pay for the recruiting process. The number of actual draftees who entered the army was about 50,000, and around 120,000 furnished substitutes. Thus the draft directly produced 170,000 soldiers, about 21 percent of those called and about 43 percent whose health or family situation did not exempt them or who did not have the $300 commutation fee. About 17 percent of all the Union soldiers as of January 1865 had been provided under the 3 March law.[21]

The fundamental purpose of the law was not to draft people, but to raise an army: to encourage, inspire, intimidate, frighten, cajole men into enlisting and communities into recruiting the soldiers needed to preserve the Union. It worked. About one million volunteers signed up during the same period that the draft law operated. Generally they joined members of their communities in units bearing state names, thus preserving that aspect of the federal republic. Combined with the draftees they gave Lincoln and Grant an army that almost daily grew in size and strength and potentially provided a civilian reserve force that almost could have doubled even that vast assembly. The North had about 3.5 million men of service age in 1860; about 2 million of these served in the army at one time or another. They infused the nation with a soldiering citizenry that demonstrated unforgettably the meaning of a government of the people. The draft played a crucial part in shaping that demonstration.[22]

But the draft signified more than flags and banners. Though it brought forth an army, it also inspired sordid behaviors. The increasing amount of the bounties inspired some men to enlist and desert and enlist again. The substitution provision engendered a brokerage business in which some men were tricked out of their money and others connived in cheating the government of their services. Substitution and commutation generated the slogan "a rich man's war and a poor man's fight," suggesting that the rich could buy their way out of defending the country. Yet both practices had precedent in earlier wars, and the $300 figure was set comparatively low so that, as Lincoln explained, the price of substitutes would not be bid so high that only the rich could afford them.[23]

Recent studies suggest that poor as well as rich districts of the North could afford substitutes, refuting or at least challenging the notion of the "poor man's fight." But during the war, the slogan ran through the North and helped energize widespread opposition to the draft, especially in the poorer regions. Large numbers of poorer men "skedaddled to Canada," despite state and federal laws punishing evasion of enrollment.[24]

As the enrollment of soldiers began and the argument about national power intensified, a new commander of the Army of the Potomac grasped the reins—"Fighting Joe" Hooker had come in after Burnside's humiliation at Fredericksburg. Hooker had connived and carped behind Burnside's back, angling for the command, believing that he was the man who could rebuild "the finest army on the planet" and give the Union the victory it deserved. He had also publicly suggested that the administration was "imbecilic" and that the Union would never win until a dictator took over.

Lincoln turned to Hooker to lead his largest army; the general's self-confidence impressed the president, especially in the face of Burnside's lack of it. Hooker also had important backing among congressional radicals—a factor worth considering given Lincoln's recent clash over the cabinet. As a corps commander under Burnside, Hooker had experience and knew the army he was asked to lead. He was also popular with the men and became even more so after taking command. He improved their rations, granted more liberal furloughs, found six months back pay for his men, established identifying badges for divisions to build unit pride. Rumors about his drinking and his interest in prostitutes, soon called "hookers," were counterbalanced by well-documented good points that reinforced Lincoln's decision. Writing to the new commander, Lincoln was honest and direct: "I believe you to be a brave and skillful soldier. . . . you do not mix politics with your profession. . . . you have confidence in yourself . . . a valuable, if not indispensable quality." Lincoln also told the general, "There are some things in regard to which, I am not quite satisfied with you." Hooker had wronged Burnside and thereby the country in thwarting his commander's plans; there was also that talk about dictators: "It was not *for* this, but in spite of it, that I have given you command. Only those generals who gain successes, can set up dictators. What I now ask of you is military success, and I will risk the dictatorship."[25]

Hooker's leadership worked at first. Morale soared, desertions and requests for sick leave declined, and the general's early execution of a plan to pit his 130,000 men against Robert E. Lee's 60,000 went well. Lee was confused about Hooker's strategy and feared the worst. Yet when the day of battle came Hooker failed. Lee's audacious tactics of dividing his smaller forces to attack two major wings of the Union army undid Hooker's plans. He had boasted before the battle that he had Lee where he wanted him, that God should have mercy on Lee for he would have none, but by the end of the four-day battle at Chancellorsville (1–4 May) Hooker was retreating, trying to account for his 17,000 casualties against the 13,000 Lee had lost. Although the Confederate victory was stunning, there were positive aspects for the Union: Lee could not afford to lose 21 percent of his soldiers; Hooker and the North could replace the 15 percent he had lost; Lee could never replace Stonewall Jackson, who was mistakenly shot by his own men and died eight days later.[26]

The Union loss had its predictable impact on public opinion in the North. Democrats insisted that Chancellorsville showed the folly of continuing an unwinnable war that took the lives and fortunes of Northerners, concentrated unwarranted power in national government hands, threatened a revolution in Northern race relations, and might unleash race war in the South. Republicans asked for increased resolve. Lincoln did not panic; he offered advice and aid to Hooker, suggesting another advance but leaving matters in the general's hands. The war would go on, but it was time to tighten loose ends on the homefront. This was imperative because Lee and President Jefferson Davis had decided to send Lee's army north, where signs were strong of anti-Lincoln feeling that might be played upon to end the war, especially with an election in view.

Even as Hooker headed his troops toward Lee's army, Burnside, now commander of Union forces behind the lines in Illinois, Indiana,

Ohio, Michigan, and eastern Kentucky and still frustrated at his battle-field failures, issued General Order no. 38: "Treason, expressed or implied, will not be tolerated in this department. . . . The habit of declaring sympathy for the enemy" would be punished, and the punishment might be death if persons were convicted in a military commission trial of committing "acts for the benefit of the enemies of our country."[27]

On the very day that the battle of Chancellorsville began, Clement Vallandigham, former congressman from Ohio and the most notorious Copperhead of the age, threw the civil liberties gauntlet in Burnside's face. Speaking to a large crowd in Mt. Vernon, Ohio, Vallandigham warned of federal oppression that would send "military marshals" into every Northern community to plunder it of its civil liberties. Vallandigham was after his party's nomination for governor of Ohio and believed that there was a large audience for such attacks on "King Lincoln." Burnside responded quickly. Within three days Vallandigham was arrested at night in his home; three days later a military commission sentenced him to prison for the duration of the war. Lincoln changed the sentence to banishment behind Confederate lines, trying to dilute the power of Vallandigham's martyrdom.

It worked only partially. Most of Lincoln's supporters were pleased at the idea of putting the Copperhead among his alleged friends, but vocal Republicans such as Greeley thought that the government had gone too far. The editor of the powerful *Harper's Weekly* proclaimed that "the mistake of the government lies in not trusting the people sufficiently." They could "understand any amount of seditious nonsense, be it uttered so glibly." And Ohio Democrats were so delighted with Vallandigham's arrest that on 10 June 1863 they nominated him for governor; the campaign there, as well as throughout the North, was fueled with charges of executive tyranny and laced with the usual Democratic doses of negrophobia.[28]

As Ohio Democrats were choosing Vallandigham, more ominous opposition to Lincoln was headed north. Robert E. Lee was advancing, expecting support from that same sentiment that had propelled Vallandigham. Both Lee and President Davis believed it was profitable to prospect among Copperheads. Rebel general P. G. T. Beauregard proposed that some Confederate general should "get into Ohio and call upon the friends of Vallandigham to rise for his support." This was overly optimistic, but hopes existed that the Confederacy at least might nurture and enliven arguments that the war was unwinnable. Meanwhile, Northern Democrats filled the air with challenges to Lincoln's policy on civil liberty. New York Democrats led by Congressman Erastus Corning met just after Vallandigham's conviction to denounce "a fatal blow at the supremacy of law"; they sent their protest to the president.[29]

Lincoln had ignored the Corning letter in May, but in early June with Lee advancing and dissent growing, the president decided that the time had come for a statement that would show some steel and recapture support for his policies. Lincoln spent many hours on his response, seeing it as public persuasion, not mere communication or argument with Corning and friends. He knew he was fighting for the minds and the hearts of Northern citizens, and he probably also knew that Confederates would read it for signs of his determination and his ability to build Northern resolve.[30]

Lincoln's reply to Corning was reassuring and threatening at the same time. It demonstrated a serious concern for constitutional justifications and an ominous definition of how far his hand might reach. It was an argument to chill dissent as well as to let Confederates know that Lincoln's arsenal was not empty; he could find ways to handle potential rebel supporters.[31]

Lincoln first thanked the Democrats for declaring that they would sustain the government "in every constitutional and lawful measure to suppress the rebellion" but then attacked them from every angle. Did they announce themselves Democrats? "I would have preferred to meet you upon a level one step higher than any party platform." Did they lecture him on his violation of the treason clause of the Constitution? They were reading the wrong part of the Constitution, Lincoln parried; the arrest of people such as Vallandigham was not carried out under that clause. His authority was lawful, however, for the Constitution clearly and directly justified suspending the writ "when in cases of rebellion or invasion the public safety may require it."

So far Lincoln was scoring with jabs, but then came a series of haymakers that justified a broad sweep for executive power. First he asserted that enemies of the government had long used constitutional limitations to hinder efforts to save the Union. This point linked Corning and his friends with potential disloyalty. Then Lincoln defined a startling and bold threat to the Union: "The man who stands by and says nothing when the peril of his Government is discussed, cannot be misunderstood. If not hindered, he is sure to help the enemy; much more, if he talks ambiguously—talks for his country with 'buts' and 'ifs' and 'ands.'" Thus even silence might be punishable, but where? Near the battlefield? No. Wherever words or action occurred that would interfere with raising and supplying arms. The threat might be as overt as a Vallandigham speech, but it could also be as subtle as writing to a soldier that his cause was bad or the administration too weak to punish desertion. "Must I shoot a simple-minded soldier-boy who deserts, while I must not touch a hair of the wiley agitator who induces him to desert?" Lincoln asked, using one of those compelling images that trumped paragraphs of reasoning.

Lincoln scored even while retreating. Personally, he was not sure that he would have arrested Vallandigham as Burnside had, although he was responsible for the arrest. He would certainly act differently in less crucial times, he assured them. But the Constitution itself distinguished between peace and cases of rebellion or invasion when greater force could be exercised. This condition was temporary, and he could no more believe that the people would lose their liberty in peace because of wartime imperatives "than I am able to believe that a man could contract so strong an appetite for emetics during temporary illness as to persist in feeding upon them during the remainder of his healthful life."[32]

When Ohio Democrats in convention challenged the president on civil liberties and Vallandigham's arrest Lincoln again took the time to prepare an extensive letter defending the constitutionality of his actions. He argued that the law favored his course, that he was the legitimate authority to suspend the writ, that the Constitution acknowledged the need for different rules in war and in peace, that it allowed men like Vallandigham to be stopped from interfering with actions imperative to saving the Union. He thus reached out to persuade a Constitution-respecting public whose opinion was very much a factor in the outcome of Lee's invasion. But Lincoln knew that his audience responded to less sophisticated appeals. Loyalty did not rest only on respect for the law but also consisted of heartfelt patriotism and support for soldiers in the field. Clearly Vallandigham knew that there was armed resistance to the draft and to enrollment and that "quite a number of assassinations have occurred" as officers tried to enforce the law. Whether Vallandigham specifically advocated desertion and discouraged enlistment or resisting the draft, he knew the environment in which he spoke, and "I solemnly declare my belief that this hinderance, of the military, including maiming and murder, is due to the course in which Mr. V. has been engaged, in greater degree than to any other cause."

Furthermore, Lincoln continued, the Ohio Democratic convention was having the same effect. They did not state their thoughts on the constitutionality of using the military to save the Union or even that they knew there was a rebellion to destroy the Union. But they knew that Vallandigham opposed the use of the military, and they were defending him. "Your own attitude . . . encourages desertion, resistance to the draft" because it showed potential resisters that Ohio Democrats would defend them. The Democrats might not intend this result, but "both friends and enemies of the Union look on it in this light."

The convention could dispel such ideas by a simple act. Lincoln was sending them a copy of his letter: they could sign it and thereby endorse the fact that there was a rebellion in process to destroy the Union and that the army and navy were lawful means to suppress it. They would also promise that they would not do anything to "lessen the efficiency of the army or navy" and would do all they could to ensure that the troops were "paid, fed, clad, and otherwise well provided and supported." If they would sign the letter he would publish it and would thereby revoke Vallandigham's banishment. Their support for the war effort would bolster and sustain the army and counterbalance any harm that Vallandigham might do. They declined to sign. Lee continued his march north.

Over two years of war were now behind Lincoln and the administration. They had learned to work together, divisions within now sidetracked or subsumed in the great task of organizing a victory. Lincoln was enlisting logic, patriotism, and fundamental ideals with an occasional hint of repression to fight his domestic foes. Congress and the executive were working in harness, both focused on defeating the rebellion by every constitutional means and with broad definitions of those means. Increasingly, emancipation was enlisting black soldiers and conscription promised to add more men. The Union was gathering and concentrating its awesome power. Yet unless Lee was stopped these accomplishments meant only more war, not foreseeable victory.[33]

10

★ ★ ★ ★ ★

UNION POWER AFFIRMED:
MAY TO JULY 1863

The newspapers broadcast the invasion: "Rebel forces in Maryland and Pennsylvania. Their Advance to Hagerstown . . . and Greencastle and Chambersburg. . . . Harrisburg in Imminent Danger. . . . Pittsburgh to be Invaded, Sacked and Burned. . . . Main Body of the Enemy in the Shenandoah Valley." The situation was not desperate, yet, and no one had anything to say about the little town of Gettysburg but Lee's movement was spreading panic and selling newspapers in the North.[1]

Meanwhile, Union leaders were debating how and when to stop Lee. The president and the general in chief were hopeful that Lee was marching his way into a disaster—cutting himself off from supplies and retreat. Lincoln and Halleck wanted General Hooker to strike Lee's army as it was spread along the line of march. Hooker let that opportunity slip away and then began to show McClellan-like symptoms. He was outnumbered, he insisted at the time when the Army of the Potomac outnumbered the rebels by almost 25,000 men. He wanted all the soldiers in the East placed under his command; then he wanted to attack Richmond while Lee was heading in the opposite direction. Lincoln stymied that idea and told him that "*Lee's* army and not *Richmond* is your true objective point. If he comes toward the Upper Potomac, follow on his flank, and on the inside track, shortening your lines, whilst he lengthens his. Fight him when oppertunity [sic] offers. If he stays where he is, fret him, and fret him."[2]

Generals within Hooker's command had suspicions about their

commander. They complained to Lincoln about his morals and his leadership and had done so since Chancellorsville. The president initially upheld Hooker, even after that disaster. Lincoln tried to improve his man, and the president's efforts reveal the weaknesses of his virtues. Lincoln knew that Hooker was sensitive and volatile, but he saw qualities in the general that he thought could be developed into successful leadership. Hooker felt that he had a special relationship with Lincoln as well. After reading the letter that explained so eloquently the reasons for his appointment, Hooker reportedly said, "He talks to me like a father." Lincoln encouraged Hooker to believe in his special status by allowing the general to report directly to him and by sending suggestions and orders to Hooker, often bypassing Halleck. When Hooker visited Washington he went straight to Lincoln, ignoring not only Halleck but also Secretary of War Stanton. Stanton placed the resulting Hooker-Halleck resentment at Lincoln's feet.[3]

With Lincoln thus inflating Hooker's self-importance, a ploy that may have been necessary to inspire his efforts, Halleck, having had prewar clashes with Hooker, also fretted, annoyed at being bypassed. He alleged at times that he did not know where the Army of the Potomac might be, and he was displeased at presidential interference. Meanwhile, Hooker complained that Halleck was his enemy, that Halleck would not agree to proposals that Hooker felt were imperative to success. Such resentments echoed McClellan's earlier jibes at Stanton even as Hooker seemed to be reciting McClellan's former litany. Generals in Hooker's army continued to complain, and rumors of Hooker's riotous drinking habits circulated within the cabinet. The pot was simmering. Halleck and Hooker were clearly not communicating as they should. Hooker wired Lincoln that he lacked the confidence of the general in chief and that such an attitude would undermine current and future operations. All the while Lee's army was moving north.

Finally understanding that his efforts to guide Hooker were costing more in confusion and resentment than they were gaining in strengthening Hooker's will, Lincoln took charge: "To remove all misunderstanding, I now place you in the strict military relation to Gen. Halleck, of a commander of one of the armies, to the General in Chief of all of the armies. I have not intended differently; but as it seems to be differently understood, I shall direct him to give you orders, and you to obey them." The president cushioned this order with a personal letter reassuring Hooker that Halleck at times agreed with him rather than with the president and urging that both men be as frank with one another as he was with both of them. "I need and must have the professional skill of [you] both."

But Hooker could not let the matter rest; he seemed more interested in a showdown with Halleck than with Lee. As reports came to him from Lincoln and others of the operations of Lee's army he shied away from engaging the man and the army that had routed him at Chancellorsville. More troops were needed, he insisted, complaining that he was being asked to protect too many fronts. Although promising to cut off Lee's retreat and to protect Washington he sent an aide to Lincoln to demand reinforcements. Lincoln turned to Halleck. Halleck said no; there were positions to defend other than those Hooker was dealing with. Hooker responded by asking permission to pull troops from another command to meet his needs. Again, Halleck said no, and Lincoln backed him up. Meanwhile the president had told Navy Secretary Welles, "Hooker may commit the same fault as McClellan and lose his chance. We shall soon see." He hoped for a victory, thought that it could be won, but this looked sadly familiar.[4]

The president was cutting loose from his Hooker project. Halleck and Stanton were clearly in charge, and Lincoln found he wanted it that way. When Hooker, smarting over two rejections of his military requests, asked to be relieved (Lee now was in Pennsylvania), Halleck went to Stanton and the two took Hooker's request to the president. "Accept his resignation," Lincoln said. On 27 June 1863 a corps commander of the Army of the Potomac, George Meade, was awakened from his sleep with the news that he was Hooker's replacement. He began to gather the reports on where Lee's whereabouts and turned toward Gettysburg.[5]

It was the largest battle ever fought in the New World. For three days over 160,000 young men, average age twenty-four years, and their officers, averaging forty-one years for Union generals and forty-four for Confederates, killed and mutilated each other with rifles, cannon, swords and bayonet until by the evening of 3 July there were 43,000 casualties. One-quarter of the Union army, one-third of the Confederate, were gone.

The day after the battle Union survivor Lt. Frank Haskell described what had been done there: "The whole neighborhood in rear of the field became one vast hospital of miles in extent. Some could walk to the hospitals; such as could not were taken upon stretchers from the places where they fell to selected points and thence the ambulances bore them . . . to their destination." Some died as they were carried and were buried around the hospitals—Union and Confederate soldiers together. "At every house, and barn, and shed the wounded were; by many a cooling brook, or many a shady slope or grassy glade . . . they gathered, in numbers a great army, a mutilated, bruised mass of humanity." Men of all ages were there and rebels lay along side Union waiting attention. "Every conceivable wound that iron and lead can make, blunt or sharp, bullet, ball, and shell, piercing, bruising, tearing, was there." Some men were cheerfully talking about the victory and the battle they had fought. But others were "downcast, their faces distorted with pain. Some have undergone the surgeon's work; some, like men at a ticket office, await impatiently their turn to have an arm or a leg cut off." And in the operating tents, as the insects swarmed about, the surgeons were busy "with coats off and sleeves rolled up, and the hospital attendants with green bands upon their caps, are about their work; and their faces and cloths are spattered with blood; and though they look weary and tired, their work goes systematically and steadily on." You could tell how long they had been working by the piles of "legs, arms, feet, hands, and fingers" that steadily grew in size. The mounds "were not there day before yesterday. They will become more numerous every day."[6]

Haskell rode through the cemetery that gave Cemetery Ridge its name and wondered "how these quiet sleepers must have been astounded in their graves when the twenty pound Parrott guns thundered above them and the solid shot crushed their gravestones." The flowers that families and friends had planted in remembrance were now "trampled upon the ground and black with the cannon's soot." Two marble monuments, one a white lamb over the grave of a child, the other a white shaft pointing to the sky, now stood next to a broken gun carriage and a dead horse.[7]

As Haskell reviewed the carnage of Gettysburg Lincoln first rejoiced and then grew increasingly frustrated over the meaning of the battle. There was the victory, joined with the news of the final surrender at Vicksburg, that pointed to perhaps a coming end of the war. Yet despite his urgings, Meade did not follow up as Lee retreated and then escaped with his army intact, back into the South to rebuild and to prepare to fight again. When Meade heard from Halleck of Lincoln's displeasure he replied within an hour: "Having performed my duty conscientiously and to the best of my ability, the censure of the President conveyed in your dispatch . . . is, in my judgment, so undeserved that I feel compelled most respectfully to ask to be immediately relieved from command of this army." Halleck denied Meade's request, but Lincoln was almost despondent. His secretary John Hay remembered the president saying, "We had them within our grasp. . . . We had only to stretch forth our hands & they were ours. And nothing I could say or do could make the army move." It was "a dreadful reminiscence of McClellan." Meade seemed delighted that he had driven Lee south "away from our soil." "Will our Generals never get that idea out of their heads?" Lincoln wondered. "The whole country is our soil."[8]

Despite Lincoln's criticism, Meade had reason not to pursue Lee. He had polled his generals about attacking Lee's retreating army, and they were almost unanimously against it. The rebel general had established powerful defensive positions to cover his retreat. Union officers had just witnessed the cost of a frontal attack on strong defenses. Lincoln's focus on the overall strategic advantage of annihilating Lee's forces clouded his ability to see the realities his generals understood quite well—attacking large entrenched armies with rifles that killed at one-quarter of a mile was a dangerous, deadly game.[9]

Although Lincoln's tactical understanding remained flawed, his larger strategic ideas were sound. Pressure on the Confederacy across the vast front would ultimately lead to the collapse of the rebellion. As early as January 1862 the president had told Don Carlos Buell and Henry Halleck, "I state my general idea of this war to be that we have the *greater* numbers and the enemy has the *greater* facility of concentrating forces upon points of collision; that we must fail, unless we can find some way of making *our* advantage an overmatch for *his*; and that this can only be done by menacing him with superior forces at *different* points, at the *same* time." That strategy was finally taking shape on the field. Even as Lee retreated from Gettysburg the Union had won another major victory, this time in the West.[10]

Throughout late winter and early spring 1863 the Union's western armies had been gathering resources to take Vicksburg. Overlooking the Mississippi from an almost impregnable position, it controlled the "father of waters" as it drained the huge valley from Ohio to Missouri. The entire Northwest looked down the river to ship its products from New Orleans to eastern cities and on to international marketplaces. Lincoln, like thousands of other midwestern boys and men, had taken goods down that river and knew personally how vital it was to midwestern futures. Crucially, now that war had broken out, the Mississippi divided the eastern from the western Confederacy. The men and materials from Texas and Arkansas would be prevented from joining the rebellion if the river floated blue and not gray gunboats. Furthermore, fertile bottom lands lined the river, bringing forth riches in cotton and in thousands of slaves that would fall into Union hands. Those slaves (now that emancipation made them soldiers and not emigrants) might add to already overwhelming Northern superiority in manpower.

Lincoln was deeply interested in the Mississippi. He reportedly told a friend that the capture of Vicksburg would be worth twenty takings of Richmond. General Halleck, who multiplied the figure to be "forty" such takings, believed that Lincoln wanted all available troops in the West placed in service of the move to the South. Lincoln's passion for the project was so intense that in October 1862, as part of his general shake-up of the army, he commissioned a political professional but a military amateur, John McClernand, to raise 60,000 troops and the necessary number of gunboats from the Midwest to help take the river. He did this despite the fact that one army, led by experienced professionals, was already in the field focused on the same target; its general, Grant, thought that "two commanders on the same field are always one too many" and that McClernand, whom Grant believed incompetent, was especially problematic.[11]

Feeding Grant's pique, the president had neglected to tell him of the plan; even Halleck complained that Lincoln's "fingers itch to be into everything going on." But Lincoln had the political as well as the military picture in view. McClernand was a popular Democrat from the Midwest who influenced the Unionists of his party even while dissenters proclaimed defeat, called Lincoln "tyrant," and urged reconciliation. Although Lincoln later placed McClernand under Grant, the president made sure that Illinois Democrats would be involved in the movement on the Mississippi.[12]

For months that offensive failed. Attacks from the north and the west of Vicksburg were stymied, huge efforts to divert the river to provide drier ground proved useless, maneuvers to chop through bayou vines and trees gave one naval commander a nervous breakdown and ultimately little more. Two months of backbreaking, heartbreaking, mindbreaking labor, and Vicksburg was still in rebel hands.

Rumors revived that Grant drank too much and that his drinking explained Union failures at Vicksburg; McClernand was among the rumormongers. Yet Lincoln had faith in his most successful general, and perhaps he understood that Grant's military failures still served a political purpose. Grant later claimed that he himself had doubts about the military advantages of his army's efforts, but he knew that any retreat from the fortress would further damage Northern morale. Here was a sensitivity that the president could appreciate. Lincoln kept Grant's critics at bay and then let Stanton send Charles A. Dana, an assistant secretary of war, west, ostensibly to check out payroll snafus but really to watch Grant. If Grant was collapsing the Vicksburg expedition would be in jeopardy.

Fortunately for the Union Grant befriended Dana and let the former journalist watch and report freely. Dana repaid the confidence with stories to Stanton and Lincoln of a general beloved by his troops, clearheaded and intelligent, and determined to move forward. Lincoln's faith in Grant endured; the expedition toward Vicksburg continued.[13]

By late March 1863, even as Hooker was organizing the Army of the Potomac in the East, Grant moved down the west side of the Mississippi looking for a place to cross and to take Vicksburg from the south—if the river navy could break through from above Vicksburg and cover his crossing. On 16 April eleven of Adm. David Porter's twelve vessels made it, and the campaign against Vicksburg had a firm base. In a series of quick maneuvers Grant sent a raid led by Benjamin Grierson deep into Mississippi to divert attention from his main enterprise. Then Grant struck quickly against two rebel armies, defeated them both, and by 18 May had begun the siege of Vicksburg. The people of the city held out as long as they could, cutting from one-half to one-quarter rations, then eating mules and even rats as the Union gunboats in the river hurled shells that dug holes seventeen feet deep. Finally Vicksburg could withstand no more: On 4 July, Gen. John Pemberton surrendered the city and over 2,000 officers and 27,000 enlisted men.[14]

Gettysburg and Vicksburg—two huge victories almost on the same day. Despite Lincoln's frustration over Meade's failure to destroy Lee's retreating forces there was much to celebrate. The Union was proving its strength on the battlefield, and its victories endorsed the burgeoning power of the Northern economy. The fall of Vicksburg, Grant wrote, "with the victory at Gettysburg . . . lifted a great load of anxiety from the minds of the President, his Cabinet and the loyal people all over the North. The fate of the Confederacy was sealed when Vicksburg fell. Much hard fighting was to be done afterwards and many precious lives were to be sacrificed; but the *morale* was with the supporters of the Union ever after." From the ranks Capt. Will Lusk wrote home with the ecstatic present on his mind: "The dawn has broken . . . the collapsed confederacy has no place where it can hide its head. Bells are ringing wildly all over the city. Citizens grin at each other with fairly idiotic delight. One is on the top of his house frantically swinging a dinner bell, contributing . . . his share . . . to the general ding-dong. . . . All hysterical nonsense is pardonable now. . . . Just dance through the house for me, and kiss everyone you meet."[15]

Now, at midwar (who knew then it was midwar?) Northern advantages, marshaled by the Lincoln administration, were gathering organized momentum. Black troops began to further swell Union armies—nearly 100,000 by December 1863, almost 180,000 by the end of the war—the Confederacy could not match these armed brigades. Union material resources increased, too. At the beginning of the war Union buyers had swarmed to Europe to acquire guns and ammunition. By late 1862 they stopped buying overseas as Northern factories were able to meet a need many times that of 1861. By midwar the North had increased by ten times its store of field artillery and stood ready to issue twice as many more new cannon as had been available in 1861; it had over fifty times as many cartridges and was ready to issue over 150 million more. An estimated 1.25 million men in service were waiting to receive this bounty. Lincoln could write to one of his generals that the effort to supply armies with every conceivable piece of equipment, "this expanding, and piling up of *impedimenta*, has been, so far, almost our ruin." He was echoing Halleck, who complained that the failure to follow up after Union victories was partly due to the belief by Union armies that they needed much more equipment than was in fact necessary. By the end of 1863 the president boasted that "no considerable body of troops . . . were ever more amply provided, and more liberally and punctually paid; and it may be added that by no people were the burdens incident to a great war ever more cheerfully borne."[16]

Halleck as general in chief infused order and discipline and built the efficiency of the Union armies in tangible ways, down to the detail that subordinate commanders were punished when their men failed to carry adequate ammunition—the one hundred rounds that Halleck required. Company commanders and physicians had orders to inspect each meal served in the field. Trained West Point officers at the top, such as Quartermaster General Montgomery Meigs and Maj. Gen. Philip H. Sheridan, supervised the minutia of war: good food, good roads, proper entrenchments, plentiful mules, horses, and wagons, adequate uniforms and boots, rifles, cannon, and ammunition. Union forces almost always had these supplies as the North increased its wealth while the Confederacy increased its needs.

The Union was prospering even as the Confederacy suffered from the blockade and from the occupation by blue-coated soldiers of Southern granaries and factories. One estimate stated that as of December 1863 the Confederacy had lost more than two-thirds of its territory and three-fifths of its population. Slaves first served Union forces as laborers and then as arms-bearing soldiers. And huge and almost prodigally supplied Union armies were facing into Dixie.[17]

Behind the armies and ready to supply every military need stood a generally booming economy. In the midst of the war, opportunities to make money abounded. Profits rose in almost every aspect of business. Responding to government orders for clothing, shoes, wagons, weapons, iron, blankets, tents, meat, condensed milk, locomotives, and railroad cars set producers on the road to prosperity. The influx of green-back currency provided money to pay for these goods. Greenbacks and the war-stimulated demand for goods sent inflation upward, but that allowed old debts to be paid more cheaply than when they had been contracted. Debtors, in the words of Cyrus McCormick, now "pursued [creditors] in triumph and paid them without mercy." Railroads especially built up large cash reserves that they could use to pay enormous dividends and interest on bonds and to engage in the vast rail-laying of the postwar years. Thousands of small-scale businesses also leaped into the melee and prospered—places such as a Philadelphia textile factory that was "known for the superiority of its mourning goods"; makers of coffins as well as weavers of silk and crafters of delicacies profited from the wartime boom that gave the rich the chance to buy. Across the whole economy wealth grew so enormously that, despite the loss of the Confederate states, the Gross National Product (GNP) grew from $3.804 billion in 1860 to $4.019 billion by 1864.[18]

Such prosperity gave Northerners powerful reasons to continue the fight and concurrently limited dissent. It was hard to believe in anything but the vitality and burgeoning strength of the Union as midwar publications exclaimed: "It may well surprise ourselves and all other nations . . . during a year of the greatest civil war on record, our country in her productive and commercial interests has been wonderfully prosperous"; and "The magnitude of the contest can scarcely be realized by us in the North, . . . the peculiar horrors of war have never reached our homes and firesides. . . . Our northern cities are full of life and activity . . . all our material interests appear to be thriving." Congressmen and the president broadcast more of this good news. Sen. John Sherman wrote of the "wonderful prosperity of all classes . . . [that] has a tendency to secure acquiescence in all measures demanded to carry on the war." He saw "increased production, new manufacturing establishments, new railroads, houses and other gains. . . . Every branch of business is active and hopeful." Lincoln affirmed the same vision in October 1863. War had strengthened and enriched the Union: "Needful diversions of wealth and of strength from the fields of peaceful industry to the national defense, have not arrested the plough, the shuttle or the ship; the axe has enlarged the borders of our settlements, and the mines, as well as of the precious metals, have yielded even more abundantly than before." Gov. Richard Yates of Illinois in December 1863 stated proved that state-based observers saw the same boom: "In the three departments of industrial progress—agriculture, manufacturers, and commerce—there has been a most remarkable development . . . not withstanding the war [that] has diverted so large a proportion of the

211

most effective and most skilled labor of the country from its ordinary fields of usefulness."[19]

Although there was a wartime boom, not everyone shared the prosperity or even admired it. Editorials protested an age of the shoddy and of venality in which the rich dressed their children "in silks and jewels" and "homeless children of the city" lacked even a decent place to sleep. Inflation, averaging about 80 percent, gobbled up wage increases; real wages fell by an estimated 20 percent. The price of staples went up dramatically: bread prices doubled in a two-year period, potatoes and eggs went up as fast, and so did rents and fuel. The *New York Tribune* estimated in mid-1864 that it cost $16 a week for a family of six to live in the city, not counting clothing, medicine, and transportation; and wages were exactly $16. The next month the paper put the weekly cost at $18.50; wages did not keep pace.

Frustration over economic hardship fed, and was fed by, Democratic allegiance. Already suspicious of the nativist origins of many Republicans, immigrant workers in large cities opposed Republican-made laws that made life harder for them. The huge number of excise taxes fell most heavily on wage earners. Increased immigration, supported by Lincoln and his party, increased job competition; the leader of the iron workers union called the idea "infamous." Even more of an outrage was the use by employers of black workers, sometimes to break strikes, other times simply to work for lower wages. Traditional Democratic racism had much to work on here. Higher tariffs also hurt some workers, though others favored them. The exemptions from the draft let men with $300 go free, but those for whom $300 was almost half their yearly wages had to scramble to raise the money if they could do so at all. Even where town, city, or county councils helped raise funds the legislation clearly favored the people with money, money that increased in wartime boom. "We are coming Father Abraham, three hundred dollars more," Democrats taunted; "since poverty has been our crime, we bow to the decree; We are the poor who have no wealth to purchase liberty."[20]

Lincoln had a reputation as a friend of labor, despite his work as a well-paid attorney. He had said before the war that labor was the source of economic value and that "workingmen are the basis of all governments." Apparently supporting the Lynn strike of 1860 he said that he was glad to live in a nation where men could strike and believed that in most cases worker grievances were justified. Party philosophy hid class divisions. As the "free labor" party Republicans recited their rags-to-riches stories, exemplified in Lincoln's rise, persuading many workers that Republicans stood against the oligarchical slave owners and fought for the rights of workingmen. In several cities of the North workers voted in 1864 for Lincoln, not McClellan; even Lynn with its recent history of labor troubles voted overwhelmingly Republican that year.[21]

These factors undercut class divisions. But they did not eliminate them. And the draft sparked these divisions into violence as its outreach into the daily lives of working-men energized protests throughout the North. Pennsylvania Irish coal miners, Vermont Irish stonecutters, laborers in Chicago, Albany, Milwaukee, Boston, Troy, Portsmouth, St. Paul rioted against the draft. So did farm workers throughout the Midwest, men who tended to be poor and often foreign-born Democrats.[22]

Then from 13 to 17 July 1863 New York City exploded. For five days mobs of workers and their families, variously representing different parts of the city's working classes, attacked soldiers and civilians connected with the draft process, policemen and firemen sent to protect lives and property. The mobs then turned savagely on any black person they could find, murdering and mutilating, burning buildings and people until finally their fury was brought under control by troops that rushed from the Gettysburg campaign and subdued the rioters.

The attention of the nation was riveted on events in the city, on the vast homefront violence—it was the most murderous urban riot in the nation's history. And it raised a vitally important question: How dedicated was the administration to upholding the draft law, or the rule of law itself? The New York City Republican elite demanded a draconian response. Members of the Union League Club urged Lincoln to declare martial law and to send regiments to control the city—preferably headed by Ben "Beast" Butler—and to hang or shoot not only rioters but conservative Democratic politicians and journalists. They saw Confederate influence behind the outbreak, a fifth column continuing by more insidious means Lee's recently repelled invasion. A Pennsylvania Republican spoke for observers in the rest of the nation when he told Lincoln, "Depend on it, sir, the draft cannot be enforced in this county if the Administration compromises with the rebels in New York. The loyal men here will not sustain the draft unless it is enforced in New York." Another correspondent wrote, "The whole country is observing with interest the course of the Administration in dealing with the New York Conscription." Within the cabinet at least Welles believed that the riots were part of a Confederate plot and feared that "if the mob . . . controls the action of the government lawful authority has come to an end." The pressure to strike with an iron fist was intense.[23]

Despite his sweeping rhetoric of June when he had warned of "the man who stands by and says nothing when the peril of his government is discussed," Lincoln rejected the pressure to react with mere iron. He did not declare martial law or suspend the writ. Rather than sending in "the Beast" he appointed John A. Dix to the city command. Dix was a Democrat with strong ties to party leaders and links with Tammany Hall, which had cautioned calm and opposed the rioters even while protesting the draft. Dix used soldiers discreetly, letting local leaders such as Archbishop John Hughes subdue passions by appeals to decency mixed with empathy, and politicians began to raise money for commutation and substitutes so that city workers could avoid compulsory service. Troops were available when rioters became violent, but they were used to preserve and restore calm, not to provoke protest.

This federal restraint allowed New York City to work out its own compromises with the pressures of war. The city council voted almost $2 million to shield the city's workers from further military duties; it also used the fund to protect its firemen and policemen. Public officials chosen by Tammany Hall began trials to prosecute the most egregious of the rioters, bowing to the demands that the anarchy of mid-July be punished. Few people were punished, but the forces of order had flexed some muscle. Meanwhile, Republican leaders and conservative Democrats, appalled at the violence, began to take back the public spaces that mobs had once controlled. They joined in publicly supporting the draft even though Democrats promised to challenge its legality. When Dix resumed the draft on 19 August city leaders had prepared the way. Troops were stationed unobtrusively throughout the town, but people knew they were there. Tammany leaders stood nearby as names were drawn, implicitly endorsing the process. The proceedings went "quietly and orderly as a New England Sabbath," one soldier observed. Meanwhile the Union League Club began recruiting a regiment of black soldiers, and on 5 March 1864 1,000 armed and uniformed black men assembled in Union Square before a crowd of nearly 100,000. The wives, mothers, and sisters of Union League leaders came forward to give the troops their colors and to promise that they would minister to them and glory in their achievements. "But yesterday they were hunted down like rats," one observer noted; now they stood in arms receiving the admiration of the city's most prestigious patriots.[24]

The administration continued the draft despite protests and violence, but it also used discretion when necessary. For example, when Pennsylvania governor Andrew Curtin pointed to the intense and widespread violence in the state's coal mines and asked for a way to meet the state's quota without sending troops into the region, Lincoln gave him a choice: Either enforce the law or make it appear that the law had been enforced. Curtin chose the latter way, backing away from coercion. The government was persuaded to count previous enlistees who had once lived in the district.

The Union could afford these bargains as its power increased to meet most of the emergencies of war. The organizational talents that had marked Northern industrialization were being employed at all levels of the military, from the gathering of clothing, equipment, and arms by purchasing agents to their distribution by supply sergeants and quartermasters. The Union army had the best-fed, -clothed, -housed, and -armed troops in the world. Its strategy and supply were directed by men who knew how to play their roles effectively. Stanton directed the equipping of the army through the able talents of Montgomery Meigs. Former railroad executives now in military service, Thomas Scott, Herman Haupt, and David McCallum, reported to Stanton and built, controlled, and supplied over 2,000 miles of rails on which the armies moved. The secretary of war also was in charge of recruiting and helping to train the soldiers. At the controls stood the president, setting the overall strategy in conference with Halleck and other leading generals, cajoling, praising, urging the field commanders forward as he had always done.

The organization of military effort grew from Lincoln's prewar economic vision—an outlook that prepared him to fight the war. His Whig philosophy emphasized government support for economic enterprise. Since the 1840s he had, in Gabor Boritt's words, "demanded from Congress a centralized and co-ordinated American system of economic improvements." Now he was coordinating the resources of the North under government control to save the Union in wartime. He was urging congressional support for economic growth that would enrich the domestic economy and add strength for war, knowing that those resources would overwhelm the South. As he boasted in his last annual message, "We have more men now than we had when the war began; . . . we are not exhausted . . . we are gaining strength, and may, if need be, maintain the contest indefinitely. . . . Material resources are now more complete and abundant than ever. The national resources . . . are unexhausted and, as we believe, inexhaustible."[25]

In yet another sense Lincoln's economic vision helped win the war. He had argued throughout his life that the Northern economy rested on equal opportunity for all in the struggle for life. In that struggle some men would rise to the top by their efforts; implicitly, others would fail. As Lincoln looked for a general he pushed ahead the younger and often obscure commanders who proved their abilities to win battles. He replaced quickly (some critics have argued too quickly) men who could not perform. By the end of the war the North could say, as Jefferson Davis could not, that its generals had emerged and won the struggle for their place at the top of the military ladder. Davis's generals had been in place since 1861. Here was another sign of how Lincoln and his nation's visions had been employed and organized to win the war.[26]

Union resources were falling into place. Two great victories on the eastern and western fronts portended ultimate Northern victory. If Lincoln's nation kept the will to fight it clearly had the means to win. Its economic and military power were burgeoning and each reinforced the other. Farm revenues jumped by $200 million between 1862 and 1863 (providing taxes for military needs); 800,000 new immigrants (most of them young men and hence potential soldiers) were pouring into the country; four thousand miles of new railroad track had been laid (most of it transporting men and arms to the front); 2.659 million new acres of grain had been cultivated (feeding soldiers and bringing in foreign capital to pay for war); nearly $400,000 in military pay went home each month to supplement homefront incomes—these were only a few examples of a Union attaining colossal strength.[27]

There was much pain in this growth—the huge and horrible losses in only three days at Gettysburg, the smaller number but day-to-day agonies that persisted on other battlegrounds. Behind the lines many lower-class workers felt victimized, their riots joining the outcries of the battlefield as sounds of protest—birth cries of the emerging nation. But momentum was on the Union side. Sometimes reaching out, sometimes stepping back, Lincoln was learning to find and to employ the resources of the nation that would produce victory in the field, thus freeing him to apply his talents in the ongoing political battles of the day. He would help to operate the partisan process even as he defined the most enduring qualities of the political-constitutional system.

11

★ ★ ★ ★ ★

THE MEANING OF WAR:
JULY TO DECEMBER 1863

Lincoln was learning by mid-1863 whom he could rely on and what that reliance would consist of. The president began a process after Hooker's failure that turned the day-to-day command of the armies essentially over to Halleck and to Stanton, the professional military man and the powerfully efficient bureaucrat, "Old Brains" and "Mars" as Lincoln called them. He still offered strategic advice and communicated with generals, sending them his thanks or suggestions, but the organized war was now in place. The North's great physical strengths, its wealth in population, and its materials were matched with the expertise and organizational capacity that living through the modernizing prewar years had called forth. Lincoln still played a significant role as commander in chief and kept a general strategic vision in mind: the greater resources of the North should be employed to attack the South on several fronts at once. The goal was to hold Lee's forces in Virginia while western armies increasingly took away Southern warmaking resources and eroded rebel morale.[1]

But at midwar he was loosening his hand, withdrawing his natural instinct to take control of fighting and winning the war, no longer reading books of strategy and firing off letters asking generals where they were and what they were going to do. His project of molding generals to meet his needs, his "Hooker Project," had failed, just as his McClellan project had. His efforts to push Meade, when the post-victory enthusiasm of Gettysburg and Vicksburg was high, had also been unsuccessful. The president's frustration had reached the boiling point when

Meade did not follow and crush the retreating Lee. Yet Lincoln may have learned from his inability to control this vast and complex contest: Events could indeed control him, but the war had its own momentum and complexity that experts such as Halleck and Grant and Sherman and Thomas and even Meade understood. Lincoln would still direct overall strategy, but he withdrew from reaching into day-to-day details.

The president increasingly told the generals, "You are master" of the details in the field. He worked through Halleck, who passed on Lincoln's ideas, translating them into more particular military language. Occasionally when the other generals moved too slowly Lincoln pushed them himself, but usually Halleck gave the orders. This system had two advantages: The generals received their instructions in the military language and detail that professionals understood, and Halleck took the criticism for unpopular decisions.[2]

More efficient organization of the military administration was paralleled by the effective settlement of foreign problems. The greatest potential foreign threat to the Union success was Britain, where the blockade of Southern ports had a huge impact, wiping out almost one-quarter of a million jobs, placing nearly one-half million people on relief. Politicians in that country wanted an end to the war in order to improve economic conditions and to stabilize international trade. But Lincoln and Seward feared that the British might prize peace enough to accept disunion. William Gladstone, chancellor of the exchequer, twice suggested as much and provoked American anger. In October 1862 Gladstone spoke of the South as having "made a nation"; the next summer he announced that reunion between the sections was impossible. Both times Seward fired off a protest, and Union victories at Antietam and Gettysburg defused the force of Gladstone's remarks.[3]

But there were other reasons to keep a close eye on Britain, and these intensified in late summer 1863. British yards had been building ships that the Confederates turned into seagoing raiders. Led by the most notorious of them, the *Alabama*, these rebel raiders destroyed in the course of the war 250 Northern ships, valued at almost $15.5 million. British law forbade making warships for the rebels but was ambiguous about ostensibly peaceful ships, which the *Alabama* had been before the Confederates rerigged and armed it. The Foreign Office promised a careful watch. Then word leaked out that Laird Brothers of Liverpool was building two rams that would put to sea and threaten Union shipping. When Minister to Great Britain Charles Francis Adams heard the news he warned the British that if the ships went to sea, "this is war." British foreign affairs minister Lord Russell had already decided to interdict the rams, partly because Adams had been protesting throughout the summer. He told Adams that the rams would not leave the yards. This settlement of the Laird Rams dispute effectively soothed Anglo-American relations, a calmness made more permanent by the sinking of the *Alabama* in June 1864.[4]

With Britain quieted the diplomatic front was basically in order. French emperor Napoleon III wanted to intervene between North and South, but without Britain's support he was powerless. He did intervene in Mexico to put his nephew Maximilian on a shaky throne, but Seward was so sure about Union power and French weakness in the Western hemisphere that he raised only a minor protest. The visit of the Russian fleet to New York in September 1863 tended to counterbalance Napoleon III's escapade in Mexico, for it was seen as a sign of Russian support for the Union cause. When the war was over General Sheridan was sent to the Mexican border to intimidate Maximilian's government, and Seward used the goodwill still echoing from the Russian visit to buy Alaska from Czar Alexander II. The stability of foreign relations meant that the Civil War could claim almost full attention.

Despite the victories at Gettysburg and Vicksburg there was still much fighting to do. The increasingly effective Union military command was promising, but Southern armies remained in the field and Southern resolve continued. Even as the celebrations echoed over the midsummer victories there was reason to be cautious. Near Chattanooga, Tennessee, on 17–19 September Gen. Braxton Bragg, reinforced by James Longstreet's 12,000 troops and two divisions from Mississippi, mauled William Rosecrans's army in a bloody battle at Chickamauga Creek. Only a dogged holding action by Gen. George Thomas and his men kept the Union forces from being swept from the field and pushed north. Rosecrans retreated into Chattanooga, and Bragg had dreams of Vicksburg: He would lay siege to the town, envelop a Union army, and force a surrender that would show the Yankees they could never prevail.

Bragg's hopes might have been fulfilled had the Union forces been as cut off from support as Pemberton had been at Vicksburg. But the ability of Union leaders to gather and dispatch the increasing resources of the North was extraordinary. The image of an agrarian South facing an urban North has never been true. Fewer than 25 percent of Northerners lived in towns larger than 2,500; Lincoln's Union was preponderantly a Union of farmers. But it was developing sinews of industrial power with an emerging infrastructure of rails and organizational talents that bound its distant parts, not only tying New York to Illinois but, ominously for the Confederates, linking Virginia to Tennessee and the Army of the Potomac to Rosecrans's Army of the Cumberland.

Stanton had figured it out. If the tracks between Meade's army and

Rosecrans's forces could be cleared of all other traffic, 30,000 soldiers could get to Chattanooga in five days. The secretary of war called a meeting in his office after midnight on 24 September to push his idea, helped by Rosecrans's telegraphed call for quick reinforcements. The president was there along with Halleck, Seward, Chase, and McCallum, the organizing genius of military railroads, and one of Stanton's assistants. Lincoln doubted that in five days that many men could get out of Washington. Stanton answered that if 30,000 bales of cotton could move that fast, that far, then so could men. They argued about it, Halleck and Lincoln dubious, worried that Lee might attack Meade if the Army of the Potomac lost that many men. But Chase and Seward supported Stanton, and Lincoln gave in. At 2:30 A.M. Halleck told Meade to get ready to move in twenty-four hours.

Stanton meanwhile called the leaders of the railroads together. By noon the next day they were planning the route, ordering bridges built, gauges changed, freight trains sidetracked. The troops began to flow from Culpepper, Virginia to Washington, from there to Baltimore, then across the Appalachians and over the Ohio River to Benwood, Ohio, to Columbus, to Indianapolis, to Jeffersonville, Indiana, across the Ohio again to Louisville, to Nashville, and finally to Bridgeport, Alabama. A twenty-six-mile march took them to Chattanooga. By 3 October 20,000 men, provisioned with ammunition, artillery, and horses, joined Rosecrans's army. "You may justly claim the merit of having saved Chattanooga for us," came a telegram to Stanton. The secretary of war may have been a bit upset; he had been wrong by five days.[5]

Chattanooga was "saved," at least for a while, but a battle was impending for the reinforced army and its new commander, Ulysses S. Grant. Grant's presence meant action, but observers could only predict a victory, not celebrate one. Gettysburg and Vicksburg had inspired hope, as had Donelson and Shiloh, and Antietam, but the Seven Days and Fredericksburg and Chancellorsville were reminders of the dangers of hoping too much.

Meanwhile, another election faced the Union, and despite the war campaigning had been ongoing. Local and state elections occurred throughout the year, and every state and town seemed to be choosing someone to some office almost every day. Voters were advised repeatedly to make the "right" choice. At one level the electoral process validated the ideals that Lincoln said underlay the war: Ballots, not bullets, elections, not secessions, would determine who governed. By conducting elections and ensuring that soldiers and civilians participated, both parties endorsed almost daily the ideals of popular government.[6]

But parties wanted to win, not just glory in the game. Every election was a referendum on Republican policy. Since opinions changed dramatically when battles were lost or won and transformations in race relations and new economic laws were part of the equation, each election cast a different set of dice.

The elections of 1863 asked voters how they felt about entering their future so quickly. The war had gone on for over two years and had entered a more revolutionary phase than most people could have imagined when it broke out. The Crittenden-Johnson resolutions denying the war was fought to change the Union lay in a distant past. Large segments of the Union had now accepted the challenge brought on when the crisis began—removing slavery from the complex web of constitutional thought, political necessity and cultural prejudice that enfolded it.

The constitutional foundations eroded first. When slave states became enemies to the Union, arguments that states' rights preserved slavery put its proponents on the defensive. Political supports weakened when secession took away the need for a national party to appease huge slave state constituencies. The Democratic party could thus be the party of Stephen Douglas's ideals, not Breckenridge's or Buchanan's.

Yet the cultural traditions that had built the party abided, and none was so potent as racism. Most white people disliked blacks as a group, as a race that was inferior and corrosive of ideals they cherished. They did not want blacks to live, shop, play, learn, celebrate, worship, or even be buried anywhere near them. Entwined with these feelings was a general sense of loss of control—the nation was changing and Democrats could not control that change. Since the war was unleashing such vast change, Democrats kept up their litany that the war could not be won, that it would bankrupt the country, that civil liberties were threatened, and that blacks would swarm into white communities and take jobs, increase crime, and endanger morals.

Democrats continued especially to target the March draft law and its $300 commutation provision. "Three Hundred Dollars or Your Life!" was a common Democratic headline, and the theme played well in foreign-born and lower-class neighborhoods. Blaming "the Meddling Party" for unleashing forces that undermined security, Democrats called themselves the "Let Alone Party" and promised somehow to restore a simpler, more stable America, where races knew their place and the old older prevailed. "The Constitution as it is; the Union as it was, and the Negroes where they are" captured Democratic visions.[7]

Yet the war made the Constitution Hamiltonian, not Jeffersonian. War justified the expansion of government power instead of proclaiming weak government's benefits. The Union "as it was" rested on protecting slavery and hence on nurturing the seeds of self-destruction. The Negroes in blue uniforms undermined Democratic dogma: Northern whites increasingly recognized the benefits gained when "the sable arm" was raised to defend a Union that whites (and blacks) cherished. Gen. John Logan expressed their crudest feelings in appealing to midwestern constituencies: "I had rather six niggers . . . be killed than one of [my] brave boys."[8]

Lincoln, still conscious of white prejudice, spoke to better angels. Illinois Republicans in late summer 1863 feared Democratic power and thought a visit from their president would checkmate conservative strength. He considered it but determined that he could not leave Washington. Still, recognizing the need to do something, Lincoln decided, "I shall send them a letter instead; and it will be a rather good letter." He made it good because he knew it was important. He cared about how the letter sounded, telling his friend James Conkling, who was to preside over a major rally, "You are one of the best public readers. I have but one suggestion. Read it very slowly." He cared about how the letter looked in print and was "mortified" when he found it "botched up, in the Eastern papers, telegraphed from Chicago." Shaping public opinion continued to be perhaps his most vital duty.[9]

He thanked his supporters and offered "the nation's gratitude" to those people "whom no partizan malice, or partizan hope, can make false to the nation's life." He assured his readers that he had received no offer of peace from anyone in authority in the rebel government. The war had to continue. Then he came to the main point, speaking to his primary audience, his opponents (and beyond them to voters in the upcoming election): "You are dissatisfied with me about the negro." Clearly there was a basic difference in philosophy: "I . . . wish that all men could be free, while I suppose you do not." Yet he had never done anything for the blacks that contradicted support for the Union, an institution loyal Democrats claimed devotion to. He insisted that the Emancipation Proclamation was constitutional, that it was imperative for military success. "You say you will not fight to free negroes. Some of them seem willing to fight for you; but no matter. Fight you then, exclusively to save the Union. I issued the proclamation on purpose to aid you in saving the Union." Some of the Union's most successful commanders "believe the emancipation policy, and the use of colored troops, constitute the heaviest blow yet dealt to the rebellion." To get those troops to risk their lives, blacks, who, "like other people, act upon motives . . must be prompted by the strongest motives—even the promise of freedom. And the promise being made, must be kept."

Lincoln continued: "The signs look better. The Father of Waters again goes unvexed to the sea." Soldiers and sailors from all over the nation had gained this triumph, and soon peace would come "and come to stay; and so come as to be worth the keeping in all future time." Such a triumph would demonstrate that "among free men, there can be no successful appeal from the ballot to the bullet." When peace came, "there will be some black men who can remember that, with silent tongue, and clenched teeth, and steady eye and well poised bayonet, they have helped mankind on to this great consummation; while I fear, there will be some white ones, unable to forget that, with malignant heart, and deceitful speech, they have strove to hinder it."[10]

The letter had an immediate impact. It was reprinted throughout the country by enthusiastic editors. Senator Sumner called the letter "a historical document . . . all but the wicked must confess its force. It cannot be answered." "It will be on the lips and hearts of hundreds of thousands this day," Henry Wilson wrote. Ninety-one-year-old Josiah Quincy was inspired to thank the president for his "happy, timely, conclusive and effective" letter. In New York City George Strong called it "very good; a straightforward, simple, honest, forcible expression . . . likely to be a conspicuous document in the history of our times . . . a brilliant and successful move. The squirmings of the [Democratic newspapers] the *World* and *Express* are painful to behold."[11]

Potent as it was, Lincoln's message guaranteed only that the Republicans would have the best of the debate in the 1863 contest; it could not guarantee the result. White Americans needed more than reason to change their attitudes toward blacks. Clearly victories at Gettysburg and Vicksburg had anointed the Republican party with glory and endorsed the party's candidates and ideals. But two other events in mid-July specifically had already undercut the power of Democratic racism. In the first, blacks were helpless victims, in the second, brave martyrs.

The New York draft riot had featured such horrible antiblack brutality that racist appeals were sullied by association. Backlash against the mutilations, burnings, and murders eroded the power of Democratic hatemongering. Two days after the riots ended, black heroes further challenged Democratic negrophobia. On 18 July 1863 the Fifty-fourth Massachusetts led an attack on Fort Wagner. This regiment was the most well known of the black regiments organized after 1 January 1863. Frederick Douglass had two sons in the ranks, some of the most notable Massachusetts families were represented among its white officers, and it was led by Robert Gould Shaw—admired among the Boston elite and hand-picked by state governor John Andrew for the colonelcy. The attack failed, but the soldiers fought courageously and Shaw died leading his men. Newspapers all over the North heralded the story that blacks would fight and die for the Union and for their liberty. When the North discovered that Confederates had tossed Shaw's body into the pit dug for dead blacks and had told the Yankees, "We have buried him with his niggers!" resentment and outrage joined admiration to challenge Democratic racist politicking.[12]

Republican organization played its crucial role in the elections of 1863, with the president quietly using his influence to implement both the dark and the brighter forces of Republican party campaigning. The party's major instrument was the Union League. Organized in the early days of the war and then in the border states by 1862 to defend the administration and the Union cause, these leagues had grown lethargic in the aftermath of the electoral successes by Democrats. But early in 1863 they were reviving again because of the energetic efforts of Lincoln's supporters and friends. The governor of Illinois, Richard Yates, was especially encouraging, faced as he was with a Democratic majority in the state legislature by January 1863. He put the authority and resources of the governor's office and of the Republican party behind the league and helped to send agents to other midwestern states. Lincoln's old friends and associates began to appear in local leagues; the Springfield branch gained membership and influence when Lincoln's friend James Conkling became president. Midwestern Republican governors started using the league to checkmate Democratic opposition. In Indiana Oliver Morton launched his state's league with a large "gift" from a banker friend to organize and recruit new league members, and state locals began to emerge. Michigan and Iowa also saw league popularity grow, but Illinois still led the way. Over 140,000 members had joined as 1863 ended.[13]

The big cities saw similar growth. Boston, Philadelphia, and especially New York City had active Republican elites who gave money and time to the revitalized coalition. They organized Union Leagues, subsidized public meetings and fairs, and began publishing pamphlets and broadsides that damned the Democrats and endorsed administration policies. By the time of Appomattox over 1 million copies of nearly 200 pamphlets had been distributed throughout the North by state branches of the league.[14]

These pamphlets set a high standard of election rhetoric. Throughout the 1863 and 1864 elections Union Leagues explained and argued constitutional questions, debated financial options, described the experiences in war of other nations, and presented the views of thoughtful writers from overseas justifying the Union cause. Women like Emma Willard, Mary Abigail Dodge, and Anna Carroll contributed to the debate. Lawyers, historians, and religious leaders joined politicians to promote the Northern cause with passion, logic, and history among their weapons.

At the state and local level, and occasionally at the national, however, the political propaganda could be dishonest, unchecked by standards of fairness or reason. State political organizations attacked with charges of treason and conspiracy, asserting that opposition to the president equaled disloyalty and was probably spawned in Richmond or some other Confederate locale. Almost any charge was legitimate, and conspiracy theories were staples of the campaigns. The president could not directly control or shape the arguments that the leagues used to defeat the Democrats in the election, but their speeches and actions were not beyond his knowledge or his influence. A word of disapproval from him and tactics would have been moderated, rhetoric restrained. Yet with so much on the line and with war critics challenging his party, he did not interfere when Republicans charged Democrats with organizing secret "Dark Lantern" societies—treasonous groups with plans to help the Confederacy by seizing the Indianapolis arsenal, massacring Union League supporters, and importing fifty thousand voters from other states to elect Vallandigham in Ohio. In other midwestern states stories were circulated about the purported strength of the Knights of the Golden Circle and their plots. Lincoln looked the other way.[15]

The capital had its branch of the Union League too, engaged in similar pamphleteering and organizing. Not surprisingly, Lincoln's ties to it are obscure but probable. James Edmunds, an old friend of the president's from Illinois, was the leader, and he organized a national council and began to issue charters to leagues organized by neighboring states. Edmunds contacted the midwestern group, and they planned a national convention that met in Cleveland in mid-May 1863. Men with close administration ties dominated the meeting. The postmaster general gave the major address; Chase sent some treasury workers; Stanton also had a representative. John Forney, a close political adviser of Lincoln's, was prominent in the convention's activities, and his two newspapers gave the meeting publicity. William O. Stoddard, one of the president's personal secretaries, became corresponding secretary. The organization designated the District of Columbia as headquarters and chose its nine officers from the District. There were autonomous state councils, but they reported to Washington, through Stoddard, whose office was in the White House. This national league was practically a wing of the Republican party but one that shared the president's perspective overwhelmingly. In 1864 it held its convention the day before the Republican National Convention in the same city, Baltimore, and in the same hall.

When a few members, led by Missouri and Kansas radicals, tried to get a more extreme candidate than Lincoln nominated for the presidency they were beaten badly; the league endorsed Lincoln. The next day two thirds of the members of that convention showed up in the National Union Convention—the name the Republicans chose to run under in 1864. This convention also nominated Lincoln.[16]

Before Lincoln could be renominated, however, the elections of 1863 had to be won. In Pennsylvania and Ohio Democrats placed the question of war or peace, innovation or reaction, in the starkest terms. Over the objections of more flexible associates, they ran two men well known for their opposition to the war. Clement Vallandigham had achieved notoriety when Burnside's military tribunal found him guilty of disloyalty and Lincoln had sent him into exile in the South. Ohio Democrats, boiling with anger and seeing a chance to exploit public attention, nominated him for governor. In Pennsylvania the party ran Judge George Woodyard, who had recently declared the draft law of 1863 and the Legal Tender Act unconstitutional. In their campaigns both men challenged every change that the war was bringing. They proclaimed that the habeas corpus law expanded executive tyranny, that the draft rushed poor men to their deaths, that emancipation would unleash race war in the South and erode the social fabric in the North. Because they so clearly pitted the conservative against the liberal issues of the war these state contests grabbed national attention. The Ohio vote was especially significant since Democrats throughout the North used Vallandigham's arrest as the symbol of Republican oppression and scorn for traditional liberties. "The importance of the . . . contest in Ohio cannot be exaggerated," a pro-Lincoln Democrat wrote. "The triumph of the National Government . . . will be of no less (possibly of greater) consequence, than the repulse of the armed enemy at Gettysburg and the capitulation of Vicksburg."

Lincoln watched the two states carefully and began to arrange events so that Union men would have the best chance. He gave government workers a two-week furlough to return home to Ohio to campaign. The party assessed workers on government payrolls 1 percent of their pay to help the campaign. Cabinet members enlisted in the fight: Chase went home to Ohio for the first time since the war had begun and campaigned hard; Stanton authorized furloughs for Pennsylvania regiments. Efforts were organized to get government arsenal workers and other employees and voters to the polls. Ohio soldiers could vote in the field, and campaigning among the soldiers was vigorous.[17]

The results on election days dismayed Democrats. Their 1862 advances had signified to them a war-weariness that could only increase as the body count, the tax burden, and the draft quotas mounted and as innovations in race relations accumulated. Yet they lost every statewide race that they contested in New England, California, Wisconsin, Minnesota, Pennsylvania, New York, and Ohio.[18]

In Ohio they suffered their soundest and most publicized whipping. Vallandigham's race increased voter turnout by over 113,000, but the Democrats won only about 3,000 of these votes. Republican margins climbed over 110,000 from the year before. The North's best-known conservative Democrat received less than 40 percent of the vote in the state. Ohio Republican candidates won even in Richmond, Virginia's Libby prison where 163 Buckeye soldiers were being held. Committed to the electoral process even behind prison walls, on election day, 13 October 1863, they chose and then swore in election officials and cast their votes. The results: John Brough, Republican, 162; Clement Vallandigham, Democrat, 0. The other vote was cast for the 1861 Democratic candidate for governor.[19]

The elections of 1863 were a major and crucial victory for the administration, marking what Peter Parish has called a "political watershed." They provided a powerful public endorsement of Lincoln and his party for their efforts to end slavery and thus to purge the Union of its most corrupting influence. The year before, the president recalled, "The tone of public feeling and opinion was not satisfactory. With other signs the popular elections . . . indicated uneasiness among ourselves." The basic source of concern was that "the policy of emancipation, and of employing black soldiers, gave the future a new aspect, about which hope and fear, and doubt contended in uncertain conflict." Lincoln had hoped that he would not have to disturb the constitutional system and attack slavery where it existed. Yet he knew that it might be necessary to emancipate to win the war and that "the crisis of the contest would then be presented." Nevertheless, a year after emancipation the crisis had passed. Slavery had been changed from a problem within the constitutional system to a recognized evil that threatened it. Parts of the Confederacy now in Union hands witnessed slave owners "declar[ing] openly for emancipation in their . . . states." Maryland and Missouri, not covered by the proclamation, were discussing "the best way to end it within their limits." Blacks were proving to be good soldiers and were helping to win the war. These issues had been "fully discussed, supported, criticized and denounced," yet when the people spoke they supported the changes the administration had brought about. "Thus we have the new reckoning. The crisis which threatened to divide the friends of the Union is past."[20]

In 1862 the people had run away from emancipation, frightened by

Democratic race baiting, not yet reassured that they would gain when black freedom came, apprehensive that war's changes would erode the securities of their world. But the force of Union military victories, of black soldiers' courage, of general prosperity for most of the North, and of skillful political persuasion ranging from reasoned realism to demagoguery combined to provide the "new reckoning." It endorsed what war and Lincoln had done. When Democrats offered the old world in 1863, large majorities responded that they were ready to accept a new day.

But winning the political victory did not mean understanding its larger meaning. In a narrow but important sense the North understood that in winning the war they would end slavery and save the Union; that was administration policy, and large majorities had affirmed it as theirs. But Lincoln had more to say, and the people would hear it on 19 November at the dedication of a cemetery in Gettysburg, Pennsylvania.

It was not enough to list the goals of war and to observe that the people had endorsed them. A larger possibility, perhaps a duty, remained. Those goals must be endowed with the quality of enduring ideals, ideals made ultimately more significant to the nation through their interconnectedness to each other and to matters of ultimate concern. Lincoln had made known their interconnectedness before; he managed no "sleight of hand," no "revolution in thought" at Gettysburg. Those 272 words at the cemetery drew their indelible power from their linkage with the tens of thousands of dead young men and from Lincoln's recognition that the immediate events of the war were entwined with larger meanings that emerged from their sacrifices.[21]

Lincoln lived with death. He lived with it as an omnipresent public reality, commanding a nation that was in the process of killing more American soldiers than would be killed in all American wars from the Revolution to the Korean War combined. He lived with death as a personal burden. He still ached with memories of Willie, the favorite son, dead only a year-and-a-half. Young men close to him had died, Elmer Elsworth, Eddie Baker, Ben Helm, his brother-in-law. The president had wept. He comforted young Fanny McCulloch upon the death of her father, spoke of her grief and said, "I have had experience enough to know what I say." He dreamed of his own death, read to friends poems and passages from plays that spoke of human mortality. And, of course, he could never escape knowing that his orders ended the lives of thousands of young men.[22]

Such knowledge perhaps caused him, as he began the address, to link the deaths to a larger cause, one with the religious authority that came from a founding act by "our fathers" and that would be "nobly advanced" because these men had given "the last full measure of devotion." In these sentiments the president set forth a frame of heart and mind that united his audience in a common grief, a common history, and a shared hope that prepared them for reconciliations to come.

In a cemetery dedication such words and ideas were appropriate but perhaps also predictable. What is surprising for the occasion, though not for the man, is that Lincoln used religious ideas to give meaning to politics. Strikingly, Lincoln moved from religion to the polity, from faith to government, entwining the two and setting the stage for integrating the ideals of the nation with each other and with the shared community of the nation's grief-nurtured faith. The rhetorical device allowing this move was a history that united the nation. The forefathers' nation, "conceived in liberty and dedicated to the proposition that all men are created equal" was still at issue, the war was testing whether such a nation "can long endure." The soldiers had left the task of preserving that nation unfinished, and the living must take it up—they were joined in the enterprise of bringing history to its fruition, part of the historical process themselves. They were linked to a mission that transcended their present divisions. Death, faith, and history were the fabrics that united the people in purposes beyond the immediate. The smaller stories of partisan politics, the greater but still temporary story of division between North and South were subsumed in a larger story that the people of the Union were living if they could only understand it.[23]

These three unities, death, faith, and history, thus pervade and inform the other messages of the address. They provide the foundation for Lincoln's integration of the three political ideals that also are basic to the address—democracy, equality, and government. It was a significant and imperative integration, unifying American political-constitutional thought that had been divided in the prewar nation. Before the war democracy, manifested as Douglas's popular sovereignty, and equality, exemplified in Lincoln's insistence on the primacy of the self-evident truths in the Declaration of Independence, were two sides of a debate. Lincoln insisted that the clause "all men are created equal" included blacks as well as whites, and Douglas claimed that popular democracy allowed a form of government that denied blacks equality. But at Gettysburg Lincoln reconciled democracy with equality by avowing that equality was the Founding ideal of this people's government, an ideal that the honored dead had given their lives to defend.[24]

The address provided a second reconciliation. Before the war abolitionists had called the law of the land and its government a "covenant with death." They insisted that equality and the constitutional system were at war. Defenders of that system had been on the defensive, for constitutional obligations compelled protection for slavery. At Gettysburg Lincoln harmonized government and equality by proclaiming that the government of the Founders was dedicated to the proposition of equality. Implicit here also was the idea that since equality was a "proposition" the endurance of this government would allow the people the last best hope for proving that proposition true. They had always been fighting for that government, most explicitly for the right of changing governments by the ballot, not by secession or gunfire. It was through that electoral process that popular government chose values, carried out ideals, demonstrated and discovered the unfolding meaning of the propositions it was founded to defend. There was a "great task" remaining before them: to give freedom a new birth, a goal that was possible only if the government of the people, resting on the ideal of equality, was fought for and preserved, as the young men all around them, lying in marked and unmarked graves, had died to preserve it. At Gettysburg Lincoln had shown Americans how to think of their government and themselves in a way that affirmed their finest possibilities.[25]

But something else was at stake here. Lincoln spoke in the midst of a transformation in the understanding of liberty and government. National armies were growing in strength, reaching into the rebel states and protecting and freeing hundreds of thousands, soon millions, of slaves; economic prosperity spawned by war was fostered by government action; a draft law brought the federal power to everyman's doorstep; military officers watched and occasionally arrested protesting citizens; federal taxes pulled dollars from pockets around the country—a new vision of liberty and government was emerging in the crucible of war. An older idea of liberty from government was being transformed into a vision of liberty because of government. The government's new responsibility was to assist, to enable, to provide an environment for liberty.[26]

The justification for a new expansion of government in behalf of liberty was manifold. Fighting against the hypocrisy of a society that demanded the liberty to enslave 4 million people revealed the potential moral poverty of the rhetoric of negative liberty. The United States was clearly using its power to free those slaves. Furthermore, secession was not an exercise of liberty in Northern eyes; secession was, as Lincoln called it, "the essence of anarchy" and as such was as much a threat to liberty as any tyrant. Indeed Americans had for years warned that anarchy produced tyrants. Thus the act of secession created a crisis in law and order that demanded national power to counteract it. Washington was using its power to preserve its constitutional institutions, institutions that most Americans deemed imperative for ordered liberty.[27]

The extent of the change is nowhere more evident than in the amendments to the Constitution in the prewar and post–Civil War nation. The first ten amendments limited national authority. After the Civil War six of the next seven amendments empowered national lawmakers to act: "Congress shall have power to" end slavery, protect civil rights, end race discrimination in voting, collect a federal income tax, prohibit the manufacture and distribution of alcohol, protect women's right to vote. Power had become the guarantor, not the nemesis, of liberty. These actions exemplified the birth of new freedoms, secured and enlarged by being linked to the power of the government of, by, and for the people, dedicated to, and more crucially, willing to fight for the proposition that all men are created equal. These amendments lay in the future but a not-too-distant one, and the path to them had been charted and defined at Gettysburg in a two-minute speech.[28]

Moving to that future required continuing the war. It meant realizing and demonstrating the meaning of government of the people, and it also meant discovering the extent to which that government would fulfill the proposition that all men are created equal. The election of 1864 and the profound and complex problem of reconstruction would show how well the words at Gettysburg had been understood by the audience—and by Lincoln himself.

12

★★★★★

RECONSTRUCTION BEGINNINGS:
MAY 1862 TO DECEMBER 1863

It was early May 1862 and New Orleans was surrounded by Union gunboats. Its Confederate defenders had escaped, and Admiral Farragut was listening to the mayor of the town. The admiral had ordered that Confederate flags on public buildings be replaced by flags of the Union. The mayor, one John T. Monroe, was telling him what he thought about that: "The city is yours by the power of brutal force," the mayor said. "As to the hoisting of any other flag than the one of our own adoption, the man lives not in our midst whose hand and heart would not be palsied at the mere thought of such an act." You have, he continued "a gallant people to administer; a people sensitive to all that can in the least affect its dignity and self respect. Do not allow them to be insulted by the interference of such as have rendered themselves odious and contemptible by their dastardly desertion of the mighty struggle in which we are engaged, nor of such as might remind them too painfully that they are the conquered and you the conqueror." Things were not beginning well for New Orleans' reconstruction.[1]

Reconstruction had been under discussion from the day the war began. First visions, as early as the Crittenden-Johnson resolutions of 1861, forecast little change. A defeated South would be quickly restored to the Union, its institutions intact, its bondsmen still controlled by masters. Only secession would have been lost, and slavery would vanish gradually. Outlawed in the territories by Republican dominance it would weaken, and masters would gradually have to remove it from their states. As the war continued, however, visions of reconstruction changed, and the death of slavery had a new timetable, challenged by growing national authority and linked with the enterprise of saving the Union. The official process began in February 1862 when Lincoln appointed Andrew Johnson military governor of Tennessee. Arkansas also received a Northern commander early in the year, but the most important reconstruction state was Louisiana.

The story there began when Benjamin Butler entered New Orleans on 1 May 1862. Admiral Farragut's squadron had destroyed the defending coastal defenses the week before, and Butler's 15,000 Massachusetts Volunteers marched into a city shocked by the suddenness of the surrender and bitter that Yankees were marching through their streets. A few Unionists made their appearance: poorer workers eager for food and shelter, jobless because of the effect of the Union blockade; merchants and lawyers who had quietly accepted rebel dominance and now promised loyalty. But most of the populace treated Butler and his men with as much disdain and contempt as possible. When Butler wanted a meal at the St. Charles Hotel the manager refused. Butler threatened to confiscate the building, and the manager changed his mind. A mob gathered outside the hotel, and Butler warned that if the police could not disperse them his artillery could. The mob went home, but the resentment remained and Butler helped feed it, first by the exercise of a conqueror's justice, second, and perhaps worse, by an outrageous insult to Southern womanhood.

Five days before Butler took over, just as Farragut was occupying the city, William Mumford, a local gambler but still a man of some standing (the traits were not incongruous in the Crescent City) tore down a Union flag that Farragut had raised over the U.S. Mint and bragged widely about it. He even ripped the flag into strips and handed them out to admirers who wore them on their lapels. When Butler heard the story he determined that such defiance might spread and that the people of the city had to learn that the army would use its power. He ordered a military commission to try Mumford for an offense against the "laws of war and his country." Mumford was convicted and ordered executed. There had not been an execution in the state for eighteen years, and many people doubted there would be one now. Respected citizens went to Butler to plead for Mumford's life; the gambler's wife and children came to beg for mercy. Butler ordered Mumford hanged. With stories of these final scenes to inflame Southern hearts, threats of reprisal came from all over the Confederacy, and the general was named "Beast." But New Orleans learned about the limits of defiance.[2]

Butler tried to maintain as many of the ongoing operations of this city of over 140,000 as he could. That effort meant balancing the need to keep the infrastructure intact, on the one hand, with the insistence that Union goals not be stifled on the other. When six newspapers in the city stepped over the line in excoriating Union rule, the general suspended them, but the army let most regular functions of the city proceed. Newspapers (once they had learned restraint), banks, local courts went about their usual business, giving a semblance of regularity to daily life.

But there were ways other than newspapers of showing how the South felt about Yankees. The women of the town ostentatiously scorned Union soldiers, drawing their broad skirts back to avoid contact, making rude comments and faces as soldiers passed, leaving rooms and public places as soldiers entered, occasionally even spitting. These women were taking advantage of their pedestals, but they underestimated Butler's ingenuity. The general decided to use the culture of chivalry to end their behavior and devised the infamous "Women's Order": "Hereafter when any female shall by word or gesture or movement insult or show contempt for any officer or soldier of the U.S. she shall be regarded and held liable as a woman of the town plying her avocation." The outrage against this order rang throughout the South, prices for Butler's head were offered, and leaders everywhere who had access to a forum decried "this license to your officers and soldiers . . . to commit outrages . . . upon defenseless women," as Mayor Monroe charged. In response Butler deposed the mayor, offered the rebuttal that decent women would hardly fall prey to the order, and appointed Gen. George Shepley as the new mayor. The "Women's Order" put a stop to the insults to soldiers. Shepley's appointment brought more ordered loyalty, but resentment still smoldered—school children learned to sing "The Bonnie Blue Flag" and were taught a course on Confederate history. The pride, the memory, and the traditions of the South remained deeply entrenched.[3]

Butler did more than use force to rekindle allegiance in Louisiana. He reached for the loyalty of the unemployed in New Orleans with a program to pay fifty cents a day to two thousand men to clean the streets and drain the canals and ditches. He distributed beef and sugar to the hungry. And he began to gather around him a group of well-off citizens to form a new and loyal government for the city and then for the state. Few people in the city were charmed. When Butler announced that public officials had to take loyalty oaths, many individuals resigned their offices. When he ordered that those people who wanted to use the court system take an oath the response was sullen. Only about one-tenth of the people in the city took the oath. By using threats of property confiscation, part of the Second Confiscation Act of Congress, he increased the number to 68,000. Still, Butler had a nucleus of men of varying degrees of loyalty on record; he could work with them. Reconstruction was under way.[4]

But it was early in the war, and military necessity shaped all policies that touched even pacified parts of the South. The nation still was recovering from the bloody victory at Shiloh and McClellan was on the peninsula moving slowly toward Richmond; there were no signs of impending surrender. In this environment debate focused on whether conservative or radical changes were necessary to forge a Union victory with abolitionists and many congressmen arguing that the ongoing conflict required emancipation. Meanwhile, General Hunter in South Carolina was preparing to announce freedom for slaves in his district.

Lincoln was leaning toward emancipation, but he moved cautiously. In August 1861 he had reversed Fremont's proclamation of emancipation in Missouri. By March of 1862 the president was prepared to be more open in challenging slavery by asking the border states if they would emancipate their slaves, suggesting that it should proceed gradually and be compensated. At the same time he noted that ending slavery would damage the Confederacy. Implicit in that recognition was the potential for more radical action.

This balanced and careful strategy illustrated the many imperatives that shaped Lincoln's decisions on reconstruction. These requirements often conflicted and interacted in ways that made policy in this area perhaps the most complex of any the president faced. First, Lincoln was trying to bring disaffected states back into the Union—that effort involved carrots as well as sticks. If he could appeal to Unionists within Confederate states the West Virginia experience might be repeated—a secession from the rebellion, territory and men shifting to Union hands, snatched from the Confederacy. Few white Southerners, however, felt any enthusiasm for transforming their race relations; thus some promise was imperative that even if change occurred, it would take place in controllable ways. Lincoln was recruiting in the South, behind enemy lines.

Second, the president paid primary attention to making war. Principally, the Union would prevail by defeating Confederate armies; if Lincoln had to support a policy that made winning easier for his generals or one which complicated their lives he would go with the first. The importance of the military was one reason that Lincoln wanted to keep reconstruction in his hands; clearly congressional interference would complicate the command structure. As commander in chief of the armed forces he could guarantee his generals that no congressional majority would let conscience rather than military strategy be their guide. Lincoln's reconstruction policies were enforced by generals or by military governors. Given the growing recognition by many soldiers that hurting slavery hurt the Confederacy, Lincoln's policy was sure to shift toward those forces in the nation who believed in protecting and expanding black rights. But he wanted questions that involved changing race relations in the South under his control as much as possible.

Third, his favoritism toward generals was not just a matter of policy; it was what the Constitution permitted. Lincoln's control of reconstruction rested almost entirely on his authority as commander in chief. Except for the authority to pardon people from offenses against the national government, any action he took could be taken only in areas still subject to military control—his policy had to be predominantly a wartime policy.

Fourth, winning the war required gathering support from Congress and the people, whose sacrifices were greatest and most necessary. With a diverse population to appease, Lincoln had to avoid extreme measures that would alienate or divide northern groups. He had to move with the growing antislavery tide but still reassure conservatives. He could not satisfy the implacable Democrats; Vallandigham would never join him. Yet if he could persuade moderates in the most Constitution-respecting nation in the world that legal traditions were important to him, he could transform them into the responsible opposition, not the enemy.

Thus reconstruction would require the balancing of Northern military strategy, political imperatives, and constitutional limitations as well as Southern racial fears and the potential loyalty of Southern Unionists. It meant keeping the support of Northern constituencies even as he attracted wavering rebels by offering terms of surrender that would diminish their ardor for rebellion. The president clearly recognized that he could not promise the Union as it had been. Slavery would have to die and the Union be reembraced; then the nation would attend to the restored and slaveless Union.[5]

In this balancing of constituencies and perspectives white men held the strongest hands. Because Lincoln had to take the political environment as he found it, he had to give most attention to those groups with the most power. He had to account for, if not respect, the prejudices of Northern conservatives, white Southern Unionists, and the rebels whom he was trying to bring back as loyal citizens of a self-governing republic. Blacks had the weakest position. Although they held a strong card because of their growing numbers fighting for emancipation and Union, the vast majority were dependent on white largess. Lincoln could give only those things that white constituencies could be persuaded to provide.

These contingencies would be worked out in Louisiana. The president was most directly involved there, newspapers gave it serious attention, and the public discussion about reconstruction usually used examples from Louisiana. The appearance of congressmen from the state seeking seats in Congress during the war further brought Louisiana to prominence. When Congress debated options for reconstruction Louisiana was the focus. Abolitionist leader Wendell Phillips called the state, "Mr. Lincoln's model of reconstruction." After May 1862 people North and South looked at the Bayou State to see a prototype of a restored Union. Careful consideration of events there provides the best picture of the effects of local Southern realities on Lincoln's policy.[6]

Louisiana's population and politics offered a considerable challenge as well as many opportunities to good policymaking. On the bottom rung of its society were the nearly 333,000 slaves, 47 percent of the state's total population. The reputation of slavery in Louisiana was grim and horror-filled; Harriet Beecher Stowe's brutal Simon Legree had murdered Uncle Tom in the most oppressive and hopeless picture of slavery she could describe, and millions of readers knew that story. Solomon Northup, a kidnapped free black, had spent most of his dozen years of bondage in Louisiana, and the thousands of readers of *Twelve Years a Slave* carried his picture of slavery's degradation sharply in their minds.

In contrast to this image of oppressed and brutalized black people stood the nation's most enlightened and accomplished black population. Included in a black community of about 25,000 in New Orleans were nearly 11,000 free men and women—the largest free black community in the South. They owned nearly $2 million in property; a few of them were slave owners and comparatively wealthy. Many free blacks owned their own businesses and conducted their own trade. They controlled skilled trades such as shoemaking, carpentry, bricklaying, and cigar making. Some of them spoke only French and sent their children to schools in Paris or to private academies in New Orleans. Most were light-skinned, descendants of early French settlers or Haitians; not surprisingly, attachments to European culture were strong. They had a record of service to the antebellum white community, having fought with Andrew Jackson at the Battle of New Orleans and even having served in a militia that guarded against slave uprisings. When war first broke out they offered to help Confederates preserve the Southern way of life, but when Butler occupied the city they became Unionists and offered their services as soldiers. At first Butler had rejected them, but by late summer 1862 he needed men so badly that he formed the Corps d'Afrique and began a recruiting process that ultimately brought nearly 25,000 black Louisianans into Union ranks.

Native Louisiana free blacks clearly had strong claims on equal citizenship as the Reconstruction process developed in the state. The claims of these men, not the emancipated slaves, became the first focal point for debate over equal rights in Louisiana. Their quality of life clearly separated them from the slaves who surrounded them so that at first they ignored their racial kinsmen, identifying with a master rather than a slave class. They wanted to have the right they had not achieved before, the vote, but only for themselves, not the slaves. As reconstruction began, they were not interested in the rights that recently emancipated black people, carrying the scars of Simon Legree's world, might want.[7]

But the legitimacy of their claims gave the Crescent City's "Creoles," or *gens de couleur* as they were often called, no power to shape their future. That power initially rested in the hands of white Unionists in the city, the unstable nucleus around which the Lincoln administration hoped to build a loyal state. The state itself had been closely divided in the election of 1860; Breckenridge had won a plurality of only 45 percent over the combined vote for Douglas and Bell. Still, when war came the number of Confederate soldiers outnumbered Union enlistees 56,000 to 5,000.

Although a cluster of four parishes in the north-central part of the state had Unionist leanings, most Union sentiment centered on New Orleans, where unionism was promising because 43 percent of the white population in the state lived in the Crescent City. Offsetting this strength was another fact of the census—the great majority of Unionists had been born outside the South—over 70 percent according to one estimate. Thus Unionism not only carried the burden of disloyalty to Confederate patriotism, it also had to counter the stigma, potent throughout the Deep South at any time, of being an outsider. Indeed, several Union leaders were of foreign birth; these men had been drawn to New Orleans where they made their living as lawyers and merchants. Their economic views and experiences made them natural allies for Republicans, who saw victory partly as a chance to modernize the South and bring it into the free-labor orbit. However, these views made the Unionists no friends among the large majority of white Louisianans inside the city and particularly not in the hinterlands beyond the range of Union guns.[8]

The vast majority of Southern whites supported the Confederacy—secession and the continuing war showed that. Loyal Unionists, however, were divided into potentially antagonistic factions. On one end of the spectrum were Unionist planters who wanted to preserve the Union but hoped to preserve slavery. Next to these white men stood the merchant businessmen and workers of New Orleans, loyal to the Union and willing to see slavery die in the war, in part because bondage gave economic and political advantages to the rural population. Most of these Unionists were hardly egalitarians. They wanted advantages for themselves; they would concede as many rights to the freedmen as were necessary to ensure their own influence.

The problem for Lincoln and for those people who sought to bring the Bayou State back into the Union was to keep this fragile coalition together. Adding to the complexity was the problem that increasing rights for blacks alienated growing numbers of whites. In an ideal world white Unionists would take Lincoln's journey—learning that expanding rights for blacks was imperative to save the Union and was legitimate on moral grounds. More expediently, they might calm their fears by recognizing that the transition from slavery to freedom would still maintain white dominance economically. And they might soon understand that giving blacks the right to vote would not undermine white dominion. But Louisiana was hardly an ideal world. Powerful, abiding prejudice and the environment of war meant that coercion would be necessary to promote education, and some would never learn.

Fear challenged change and kept before the Southern whites' vision not the sophisticated *gens de couleur* but the much more threatening and far more numerous slaves. As Union armies advanced into the countryside slaves who were close enough ran to them; others grew restive and at times hostile. The discipline of slavery began to erode. "There is an uneasy feeling among the slaves," a New York journalist reported in July 1862. "They are becoming insubordinate, . . . I cannot think that another sixty days can pass without some sort of demonstration." "For more than fifty miles up the river [slaves] are in a state of insubordination," another wrote; "the country is given to pillage and desolation." A planter told this story: "The negroes have erected a gallows in the quarters and give as an excuse for it that they are told they must drive their master off the plantation." Other slaves drove overseers away or killed them when the whites tried to beat them back to work.

From the time the Union army arrived through 1862 such stories were common in the countryside and even reached into New Orleans itself. Police began to arrest daily numbers of blacks for "insubordination, and impudence." On one occasion forty black runaways attacked police, only to be driven away by soldiers; on another, fifteen fugitives armed with canes, knives, and clubs were spotted entering the city in the early hours of the day. Such incidents fed anxieties about how close to white throats black freedom might reach. Some, probably most, reports reflected overreaction by whites who had oppressed blacks for decades. Yet there was enough disorder to merit the concern expressed by the *Daily Picayune* in August 1862: "Recent events have made many of the negroes in this city and neighborhood almost unmanageable." White fears of black revenge or at least of general disorder—in occupied and unoccupied regions of Louisiana—increased demands for discipline and control.[9]

The army that had liberated New Orleans now faced a more complex challenge. Soldiers, like native whites, wanted stability. Fighting rebel armies was difficult enough without having to respond to insurrection in occupied regions. Just as it had in the Union command as a whole, a split developed among Louisiana generals over the appropriate response to the disruption of slavery. Butler wanted to preserve the status quo; the disorder around him was threatening. "I shall treat the negro with as much tenderness as possible," he promised Salmon Chase, "but I assure you it is quite impossible to free him here and now without a San Domingo. A single whistle from me would cause every white man's throat to be cut in this city. Accumulated hate has been piled up here between master and slave, until it is fearful. . . . An insurrection is only prevented by our *Bayonets*." The general ordered his troops to return runaways to loyal masters and cooperated with planters who wanted to keep blacks at work on the sugar crop. In New Orleans city police were made responsible for rounding up fugitives and holding them for owners.[10]

Meanwhile, an alternative policy for ensuring stability emerged—one that promised liberty and order. Brig. Gen. John Phelps insisted that slavery caused the disruptions Butler feared; once the army brought the promise of liberty blacks would continue to challenge their chains. "The best way of preventing the African from becoming instrumental in a general state of anarchy," Phelps argued, was to make him a soldier. Blacks recruited into the army would learn discipline and might be educated, bringing stability. By August 1862 the two generals had reached an impasse. Phelps kept enticing blacks from plantations to make them soldiers, and although Butler did not want to order him to stop, planters in the region were complaining to the commander that Phelps was generating an uprising. Butler then provoked Phelps's resignation.[11]

Butler had no time to celebrate his victory, however. In Washington the administration had gradually overcome initial objections to blacks joining the army. Congress had passed the Second Confiscation Act and the Militia Act, the first confiscating the slaves of proven rebels and the second letting blacks help fill state militia quotas. Both Chase and Stanton wrote to advise Butler that new policies on slavery were emerging, and Lincoln was sending careful signals that new directions impended.

When Unionist planters wrote to complain that Phelps's policies would create a black insurrection, Lincoln used the occasion for a double purpose. First, he encouraged Unionists to create a loyal government; second, he recognized the inevitability of change in the South's race relations. Since these loyalists had recently left the Union because they feared such change, the president was intentionally ambiguous about the meaning of restoration. He wanted to attract as many supporters as possible to restore the Union, and he knew that fear of social revolution was a potent threat. In July 1862 Lincoln told two correspondents that the people of Louisiana could avoid "the presence of General Phelps" by organizing a loyal government that would take its "place in the Union upon the old terms." The remark was designed to inspire unionism among conservatives, but at the same time, by making "the presence of General Phelps" a condition of the bargain, the president implicitly endorsed Phelps. Butler began to believe that black liberty had a higher priority for Lincoln than black labor. Proslavery Unionists would have a difficult time sustaining a proslavery future.[12]

Still, less than a month after the preliminary Emancipation Proclamation Lincoln was still appealing to conservatives with a promise that if there were elections right away Louisiana might "avoid the unsatisfactory prospect before them and . . . have peace again upon the old terms under the constitution." Implicit in this promise was Lincoln's abiding belief that self-government was not a passive process; it inspired the involvement and hence the loyalty of participants. Yet *imposing* self-government could undermine the ideal. So far as possible, within the imperatives of winning the war, Lincoln wanted to encourage indigenous self-government. In November 1862 he told General Shepley, the military governor as of 10 June, that congressional elections that year should be "a movement of the people . . . and not a movement of our military and quasi military people there." He also gave public assurance that the candidates for office would not be Northern officeholders. Louisiana loyalists had their future in their own hands, he suggested. But it was a changing and not a stable future.

All around them were signs of slavery's collapse and of Lincoln's lack of enthusiasm for the institution. Even while assuring proslavery Louisiana Unionists, Lincoln increasingly spoke of the inexorability of antislavery momentum, telling a correspondent that "I might as well surrender this contest directly, as to make any order, the obvious purpose of which would be to return fugitive slaves." He sounded both magnanimous and ominous when he spoke of Louisiana: "I am a patient man," he told one senator, "always willing to forgive on the Christian terms of repentance; and also to give ample *time* for repentance. Still I must save this government if possible. . . . I shall not surrender this game leaving any available card unplayed." "I shall do nothing from malice," he told a Louisiana loyalist. "What I deal with is too vast for malicious dealing." And yet Lincoln warned, "I shall do *all* I can to save the government, which is my sworn duty as well as my personal inclination." "Would you drop the war where it is?" he challenged. "Or, would you prosecute it in [the] future with elder-stalk squirts charged with rose water?"[13]

The growing radicalism in Washington during midsummer 1862 was indicated by the continuing debate over using black troops. Having decided to emancipate slaves, Lincoln personally was holding back on the issue of the black soldiers. The White House was quiet, but Secretary of Treasury Chase, the most liberal man in the cabinet on black rights, kept in touch with Butler. He reminded the general that Andrew Jackson had used black troops to defend New Orleans in 1815 and spoke of "intimations from the President that it may possibly become necessary, in order to keep the river open below Memphis, to convert the heavy black population of its banks into defenders." Butler took the hint; by November black troops were marching with Union regulars, acting as guards of railroad lines and other installations but ready for other duty.[14]

Meanwhile, efforts were under way to create a loyal government that would restore Louisiana to the Union. Within a month after Butler's forces took the city the first Union meeting was held on 21 May 1862, and within a week a new organization had been formed with a constitution establishing the "Union Association of New Orleans." Supported by Butler this group became the government of the city by August and September, receiving funds from assessments on former active Confederates and administering the public works projects that Butler instituted to clean up the city. General Shepley opened the courts for civilian business. In Washington Lincoln had talked to a prominent citizen about procedures, sending him to New Orleans in October with a letter to Butler and Shepley to help organize elections for state and national offices. By December 1862 two congressmen, Michael Hahn and Benjamin Flanders, were elected from the state and traveled to Washington to see if Congress would seat them.[15]

Congressmen were troubled when Hahn and Flanders arrived, chiefly over the legality and hence the legitimate authority for forming governments in the South. As recently as May 1862 the House had been debating a bill to give Congress plenary authority over conquered parts of the South. Using the power of Congress to "make all needful rules" for the territories, legislators had wanted to territorialize the South, destroying state boundaries and the restraints of federalism, which kept control over health, safety, and morals, integral to race relations, in state hands. This argument grew from two protests: the first against Lincoln's rejection of General Hunter's proclamation freeing slaves and the second against the fact that Lincoln's appointed military governor for North Carolina, Edward Stanley, had closed a school for freedmen in New Bern because he wanted to get conservative support for unionism in eastern Carolina. Congressmen had angrily challenged executive authority, but when they calmed down they rejected territorialization and acquiesced in Lincoln's warmaking efforts.

By December most congressmen still held to their beliefs, however. As the fight over the cabinet showed, they wanted to push the president to more radical ground. At the same time they remained jealous of their own legislative prerogatives on constitutional grounds. They worried about executive lawmaking, about Lincoln imposing government by military fiat. As Congressman John Bingham noted, the Constitution clearly said that state legislatures would establish when, where, and how congressmen would be chosen, subject to revisions by Congress. It said nothing about presidential authority. Perhaps a constitutional convention should be called in Louisiana so that the new government would clearly rest on popular consent.

When conservative Democratic legislators jumped in passionately to defend the same idea, Republicans retreated. They recognized the novelty of the situation and were for a time willing to allow executive latitude. Furthermore, by January 1863 both branches of the government were pushing emancipation and the proclamation released good feelings that swept aside recent quarrels. The inclination to reconcile after the December cabinet fight was strong. When legislators were assured in an eloquent speech by Hahn that "the large majority of People in New Orleans and southern Louisiana have never voluntarily done anything that could in any way taint them with disloyalty," they agreed to seat Hahn and Flanders until the end of the session. But they did not forget their concerns about executive power and Lincoln's conservative inclinations.[16]

With the January Emancipation Proclamation Lincoln abandoned solutions that protected slavery. Blacks not only were promised freedom; they were now invited to enlist. Yet even with this leap forward Lincoln still moved under the guise of a moderate. In mid-December 1862 Nathaniel Banks replaced Ben Butler as commander of the Department of the Gulf. Butler was known for his tough talk and stern behavior, using the army quickly and decisively whenever opposed. He had followed Lincoln's policy in recruiting black troops and had established higher wages for the freedmen's labor. Yet Butler had also used white soldiers to make sure that freedmen worked. This last practice, though preserving a semblance of the economic status quo, had not erased the image of the "Beast" who desecrated sacred womanhood and hanged rebel martyrs. Belief that Butler was "violent and high handed and that the people were suppressed rather than won over," as Banks put it, required a new policy. That policy, he added, "was foreshadowed as conciliatory. Kindness after the rod is a strong card."[17]

Kindness meant finding and shaping new directions that fit into existing habits and institutions. Lincoln's instinct was to implement his policies in ways that would enlist support from as many motives as possible and political self-interest was a motive he understood well. He made friends with congressmen Hahn and Flanders and had several discussions with them while they were in Washington about possible moves to restore Louisiana. When they returned home they joined Thomas Durant, a New Orleans attorney, to mold a restoration that would produce a loyal and proemancipation government. To provide the means to do so the government gave them jobs that ensured their influence. Durant was made commissioner of registration of voters and attorney general of the state; Flanders was made an agent of the Treasury, and Hahn kept his position as congressman designate. When these three men recommended appointments for the important positions of U.S. marshal, U.S. district attorney, and judge of the U.S. District Court their choices were appointed. The legal machinery of the civilian government of Louisiana would be in the hands of Lincoln's supporters, who had personal and policy interests in the president's emerging free-state plans.[18]

But Lincoln respected the momentum of economic necessity just as he recognized the value of political patronage. When Banks replaced Butler he did not bring full economic liberty for the recently freed slaves. Shortly after taking over, the new commander issued orders ensuring that blacks would not turn their newly won freedom into economic chaos. On 29 January 1863 Banks published requirements that blacks sign year-long contracts with employers to work ten-hour days in return for wages or for part of the crop. Vagrant blacks would be arrested and placed in unpaid public-work labor. Employers had to provide shelter, clothing, and food, give up whipping, and submit to oversight by army supervisors who monitored the contracts and the treatment of freedmen. It was a step up from slavery, but it drew the fire of reformers who wanted freedom for black workers to mean the same thing as it meant for whites.

Yet military needs limited the reach of economic freedom. Banks believed that Union success in the region required the support of planters. Furthermore, the number of slaves following Union invaders was growing, becoming, as one general said, like "the oncoming of cities." Hundreds came each night, "a perfect stampede of contraband," General Rosecrans called them. Other generals were shaping policies designed to keep the huge refugee problem from overwhelming military operations. The president respected army policy. That policy, implemented first by Banks in Louisiana and then by Grant, Sherman, and Lorenzo Thomas and continued by the Freedmen's Bureau, after Lincoln's death, emphasized labor control more than labor opportunity. Banks set a tone that underlay many of the operations and policies: "The well being of these people [former slaves] requires that they should labor, and be preserved from vagrancy and idle, vicious habits." This type of thinking would inspire angry protests from many defenders of black rights and set the foundation for struggles between Lincoln and legislators.[19]

Military necessity and demands for economic stability defined the boundaries for reconstruction in Louisiana, but Lincoln was setting in motion a government that could bring profound change if it could triumph. Flanders, Hahn, and Durant tried to organize a constitutional convention that would, they hoped, bring a changed Louisiana back into the Union. But their Free State Association was competing with conservative Unionists for control of the process. The free-state forces were registering people to vote for a convention to write a new constitution for Louisiana. They believed that the old law reflected the secessionist and slavery ideals and recognized that the old constitution provided greater representation of planter interests. On the other hand, conservative Unionists still clung to the hope that their unionism would purchase the survival of slavery, perhaps in the places exempted in the Emancipation Proclamation. Their goal was the continuance of the prewar constitution. A major source of their power stemmed from the narrowness of the ground held by Union forces; as late as summer 1863 thirty-six of the forty-eight parishes in Louisiana were still outside federal control. Even within the Union enclave conservative opinion was strong. Cognizant of their influence conservatives wrote to Lincoln in June 1863 asking for an election in November under the old constitution.[20]

Lincoln did not wish to alienate them completely. He cautiously answered that he knew of other plans to organize an election to amend the state constitution and therefore did not wish to commit the government to the old constitution. He also suggested that support for the old constitution might weaken the military position. There was "abundant time" for events to take their course "without any order or proclamation from me. The people of Louisiana shall not lack an opportunity of a fair election for both Federal and State officers by want of anything within my power to give them." He left conservatives with the hope that they might still shape the emerging order.[21]

Privately, Lincoln was encouraging the liberal elements in the state. Since Chase controlled much of the patronage in Louisiana, Lincoln worked with his treasury secretary to push emancipation ideals on treasury appointees. (When conservatives heard of these efforts, Chase, not Lincoln, was scolded.) And on 8 August 1863 the president wrote to General Banks explaining his goal but stressing that the means to that end would determine whether he achieved it. "While I very well know what I would be glad for Louisiana to do, it is quite a different thing for me to assume direction of the matter," he said. Lincoln personally wanted a new constitution that would recognize emancipation under the January proclamation and that would bring that freedom to places exempted in January. He promised that he would never return anyone to slavery who had been freed either by his proclamation or by Congress. He also wanted "education for young blacks" and he hoped that Louisiana would "adopt some practical system by which the two races could gradually live themselves out of their old relation to each other, and both come out better prepared for the new." He thought perhaps that private contracts between the two races would be the simplest and most flexible way to set up the new relationships.

The president offered a goal but wanted the people of Louisiana to work out a way to achieve that goal—the abiding force of history and experience gradually would be changed so that people could "*live*" their way into a free society. Lincoln was pleased to note that a process of registering voters for a constitutional convention was under way. To encourage that process Lincoln sent a copy of his letter to General Banks to Hahn, Flanders, and Durant, who were to "observe my directions to him"; Banks replied that he would "execute your orders." Lincoln was doing a bit more than expressing his wishes; he wanted his operatives to produce a constitution that promised enduring liberty.

Although insistent on getting what he wanted, the president was committed to using existing legal-political institutions to get it. Process and ideal were intertwined. To have meaning, government of the people had to signify that citizens in a restored Union would control the processes of self-government. But Lincoln's citizenry did not yet include blacks; thus his goals made more radical men suspicious of the president's direction and of his definition of self-government.[22]

While Lincoln turned his attention elsewhere for a while events in Louisiana suggested flaws in Lincoln's apparently open policy. Conservatives, aware that they reflected the opinion of most of the state, were busy organizing a government that could return to the Union with slavery under the old constitution. The president's quiet efforts were a bit too quiet; his support for limited economic change in the region gave hope that he had strong conservative instincts. Furthermore, the president made no effort to tell conservatives in unmistakable words that slavery was dead. He worked by having others work for him, perhaps the best policy under the circumstances. Public opinion throughout Louisiana feared racial change, and even within the Union enclave conservative opinion predominated. Beyond Union pickets loyal Confederates were using guns and artillery "to keep the past upon its throne." Lincoln's flexibility had brought misunderstanding, a division among his supporters about how far he was prepared to go to guarantee freedom.

Louisiana conservative Unionists tested Lincoln's purpose shortly after Lincoln had told Banks and associates of his "wishes." In September and October 1863, while liberal Unionists were still unable to set up their election, conservatives, despite the opposition of Shepley and Banks, held one of their own. Voting predominantly outside New Orleans, they chose two men who left for Washington to await the opening of Congress in December. Louisiana liberals could only explain and rationalize their impotence to Lincoln.

On 1 October 1863 Durant wrote in reply to the president's two-month-old letter to Banks. He reported that he was not registering people to vote for a new convention because there were not enough people under Union control and that considerable time would be needed to bring about that situation. The delay did not bother Durant, who doubted that the absence from the Congress of representatives from Louisiana would hurt anyone.[23]

Lincoln had his doubts. He had discovered that the Louisiana conservatives were part of a plan by the clerk of the House, Emerson Etheridge, to place conservative congressmen on the roll of members and to leave off some Republicans who might have inadequate credentials of election. This scheme might allow Ohio Democratic congressman S. S. Cox to be elected Speaker, with considerable power to interfere with Republican lawmaking. The two recently elected congressmen from Louisiana would be added to the roll. The president acted quickly to abort the Etheridge plan by writing to leading congressmen and urging them to contact their governors to ensure that members from their states had impeccable credentials. When Congress met, the Republicans were ready for Etheridge; faced with a strong and alert opposition he backed down and the conspiracy collapsed. As John Hay recalled, the House chose Republican Schuyler Colfax as Speaker; he "made a neat speech and we went home."[24]

Lincoln on 5 November wrote to Banks to energize and support the apparently dispirited Louisiana liberals. "I . . . urge you and them [Durant and Flanders], to waste no more time." The president wanted a "tangible nucleus which the remainder of the State may rally around as fast as it can, and which I can at once recognize and sustain as the true State government." Lincoln warned Banks of an "adverse element" of "professedly loyal men" who wanted to set up a state government that would repudiate the Emancipation Proclamation and even reestablish slavery. Lincoln would never recognize such a government; he demanded that a government act "consistently with general freedom." A government that continued slavery would be "a house divided against itself." Yet the president could read the strength of conservative feeling in Louisiana from a thousand miles away. Though insisting on emancipation, he told Banks and other liberal leaders that the new government might, without his objection, "adopt a reasonable, temporary arrangement in relation to the landless and homeless freed people," sending a clear signal that freedom might be bounded by a security that would preserve much of the economic order.[25]

Lincoln's letter did energize the liberals in Louisiana. Flanders replied that there would be "commendable zeal and entire unity of action among the friends of the government." The president's letter had given the Union men "great encouragement and satisfaction," and it also "has had the desired effect upon the Military leaders; they are stimulated to action." Flanders assured Lincoln that they would create a "*free* State government for Louisiana" and asserted that "the measures taken for this great object will I think be stamped with prudence, and we hope the result will meet your expectations."[26]

Lincoln did not support the conservative Unionists in the state. In response to their abortive election Chase demoted the customs commissioner in New Orleans who had apparently advocated it. Lincoln surely knew of and approved this message, yet at the same time he was moving cautiously, sending indirect rebuffs, soothing fears of revolution with promises that men on the scene might regulate the nature of emancipation.

Perhaps elections in the North made him cautious. He worried about the power of Northern Democrats to play the race card and was sensitive to charges of dictatorship. His strongest arguments for Union and for continuing the war rested on invocations of self-government. Tennessee and Arkansas were now within Union lines and trying to determine the meaning of reconstruction. Imposing an egalitarian policy on Louisiana could offend other men in the South who, in the midst of the war, might be planning to stop the fighting and find a way back home. The more rebels who abandoned the cause, the sooner the war would end and Republican goals of Union and liberty be achieved. Lincoln was watching the entire playing field—and so vast and complex was it that he honestly and often said that he was not in control of events.

Yet by the end of 1863 he needed to take control. Louisiana foundered in ambiguity and confusion as both conservatives and liberals contested for power. Apparently a clear statement of leadership would rally supporters to the Union side and not only create a loyal and free government but also deplete the rebel supporters who still believed that the old way of life would abide. On 8 December 1863 Lincoln sent to Congress his annual message and a proclamation of amnesty. It was seen so much as a wartime measure that the *Tribune Almanac* headlined it without mentioning reconstruction, but the message contained Lincoln's first clear statement of reconstruction policy.[27]

The message was vintage Lincoln in its attention to legal grounding, its willingness to be inclusive in the making of policy, and its flexibility. It targeted every congressional faction that could be reached—and it worked. He appealed to conservatives with an emphasis on local control, to liberals by requiring compliance with emancipation and the range of laws that sustained emancipation, to men sensitive to his recruiting strategy in the South with the 10 percent requirement, to the institutional loyalties of Congress by asking for congressional input, and indeed to anyone with a plan, promising that his own plan was openended.

Lincoln at once told Congress that he had the power to begin the reconstruction process, allowed it to participate with its own plan if it chose, conceded ultimate authority to Congress as to its membership, and noted that legislators and the Supreme Court could play important roles in determining the nature of oaths that returning rebels swore. Lincoln also promised that returning states, suffering their great change—from being slave to being free—might control important parts of their destiny as they began to live in a new and free world.

Lincoln's requirement from the states was relatively simple. He would recognize and treat as "the true government of the State" any government created by 10 percent of the voters qualified in 1860 to vote, so long as these men would take an oath of future loyalty and agree to accept the laws of Congress and the proclamations of the president ending slavery. Some men need not apply, however: officers of the "so called confederate government," soldiers above the rank of colonel in the army and lieutenant in the navy, and anyone who had broken his oath of loyalty as an officer of the Union government to join the rebellion. There would be no pardon for anyone who had treated black soldiers or their white officers other than as prisoners of war (a reference to Confederate threats to execute white Union officers and to sell black soldiers into slavery). All others were eligible to form a new government that Lincoln would recognize.

There were promises to attract Southerners to his plan. First, there was vagueness concerning the restrictions they would have to conform to, other than ending slavery. They might reestablish much of the world they had lost. Lincoln told them that it was "suggested as not improper" that the restored state keep its old name, boundaries, subdivisions, code of laws, and constitution so long as they abolished slavery. They could also pass laws "which may yet be consistent, as a temporary arrangement with [the freedmen's] condition as a laboring, landless, and homeless class." Lincoln's recruiting office was still in business.[28]

He was also placating congressmen. His proclamation clearly announced that the legislators would determine whether the men sent to Congress from these states would be seated or not—thus giving the House and Senate a lever to influence reconstruction. He noted that programs other than the one he was proposing would be acceptable: "Saying that reconstruction will be accepted if presented in a specified way, it is not said it will never be accepted in any other way." Again, congressmen would have a hand in the process—this concession even before Congress had agreed on any plan at all.

Essentially Lincoln's proposal was designed to get Louisiana quickly back into the Union. He wanted to resolve a situation, he explained to Congress, "wherein the element within a State, favorable to republican government, in the Union, may be too feeble [to challenge] an opposite and hostile element, external to, or even within the State . . . precisely the cases with which we are now dealing." He hoped to make it easier for the loyal people to attract others to their number by allowing "any reasonable, temporary State arrangement for the freed people." That aspect would appeal to "the already deeply afflicted people of those States." He still retained the power to prevent any abuse, he reassured Congress. As with much else in his proposal, flexibility would permit changes. It was a plan that fit the circumstances of winter 1863–64; other plans might be needed for other seasons.

There was almost unanimous support for Lincoln in Congress as both conservatives and radicals praised the message. Henry Wilson of Massachusetts grasped the young John Hay, Lincoln's secretary, by the shoulders and said, "The President has struck another great blow. Tell him for me, 'God bless him.'" Sumner was also "beaming," and Chandler was "delighted." "At the other political pole [James] Dixon & Reverdy Johnson said it was highly satisfactory," Hay recalled. "I have never seen such an effect produced by a public document."[29]

There may have been harmony in Washington, but events in Louisiana were dividing the Unionists into two camps and Lincoln would have to choose between them. The choice would not be based so much on the degree of radicalism over black rights as on the military necessities of the time. Lincoln's enduring devotion to expanding liberty in the political arena would confront his inescapable need to preserve an environment where the army could prevail. Louisiana was providing a testing ground for the ongoing search for balance between commitment to order and expanding liberty.

In the midst of the war military necessity claimed priority. Banks led Louisiana's reconstruction because he was commander of the Department of the Gulf. Stretching from Florida to the Rio Grande, it was the largest of the Union commands. Notwithstanding his reconstruction responsibilities, Banks's major assignment was to gain control of the region. If he did not, any plans to reconstruct Louisiana or anyplace else would be, at best, in peril. Banks therefore devoted his attention to campaigning in the Red River region and into Texas. While he was away campaigning the confusing contest for control of Louisiana's reconstruction continued, and Lincoln was clearly frustrated that no resolution was in sight. This situation, among others, had prompted his proclamation and his letter in early November to Banks.

The general shared Lincoln's frustration but was especially sensitive to the president's suggestion that plans were going awry on his watch. On 6 December 1863 he gave Lincoln a picture of administrative confusion that explained why he had not taken control, claiming that "all the officers of the [Louisiana] government" had been informed that General Shepley was in charge. Both Shepley and Durant officially had told him that the "subject of an election or state organization had been exclusively committed to . . . the military Governor [Shepley]." Banks had never been given authority to control Louisiana's reconstruction and had never been recognized as being in charge. This response was slightly disingenuous because in September, when the president had written a letter outlining "what I would be glad for Louisiana to do," Banks had replied, "I shall . . . execute your orders."[30]

Still, there was sufficient confusion in the evolving situation in the state, and especially in New Orleans, that people there wondered how many helmsmen were steering. Banks wrote Lincoln on 16 December elaborating on the confusion. There were at least four different governments there, he said, and each claimed to be acting under instructions from Washington. Perhaps Lincoln wanted that, the general said, but if so he should make things clear and someone should be held responsible for the results. Banks described the disarray: civilian authorities seizing a ship Banks was planning to use for military purposes, decisions by local courts that military authorities had no power to resist civil law, those same courts taking jurisdiction over crimes committed by soldiers, police "in the hands of civil authorities & ill disposed toward the army." Added to this there was a "crazy" district attorney in office, corruption among judges, and 6,000 people on charity—with funds that were supposed to take care of them having been acquired by the Treasury Department. Nevertheless, Banks assured Lincoln that "with proper management" the situation could be handled "with as little trouble as it would take to make and execute a dog law in Massachusetts."[31]

Lincoln, persuaded that his vague policy had produced no meaningful progress, then made an unmistakable choice among the players in New Orleans. "I have all the while intended you to be *master*, as well in regard to reorganizing a State government for Louisiana as in regard to military matters in the Department," he wrote Banks. Apologizing and explaining that he had written directly to Shepley in order not to bother Banks, Lincoln declared that he had not been more explicit because it had not occurred to him that anyone but Banks was in charge. "This, in it's liability to be misconstrued, it now seems was an error in us." There would be no ambiguity this time; Lincoln used the phrase "you are master" three other times in the comparatively short letter.[32]

Putting Banks unequivocally in charge was probably inevitable. The general was responsible for an important theater of the war and had to control both civilian and military affairs. But in New Orleans Banks had to reclaim and not simply assert power. While he had been campaigning Flanders and Durant were organizing elections, holding meetings, feeling proud and accomplished in shaping the state along the lines they chose. When Banks became "master" he became a rival power to men who had invested their energies and hopes in having their way. Moreover, these men operated surrounded by the mass of white Louisianans who were profoundly opposed to any moves away from white dominion. Durant and Flanders, indeed all radical Unionists in wartime New Orleans, were, in Ted Tunnell's words, "collaborationists." "In such a situation," he continues, "no military commander (in that war or any other) intended giving independent power to such people." Durant and Flanders were unlikely to agree; a contest for power was sure to come.[33]

Banks was in charge, but what did that mean for reconstructing the state, for the antebellum free blacks and for those recently emancipated, for the white Louisianans who hoped to prevail? Banks clearly wanted the end of slavery, and he wanted to expand the privileges of voting to increased numbers of blacks; the question was how. His favored approach was to rely on a judge to do it. He wanted U.S. District Court Judge Edward Durrell to decide that any person who was at least half white had full citizenship equal to all white people. Using that ruling would have allowed about 30,000 "blacks" to vote. But the idea died. Even among Unionists the black suffrage issue remained delicate.[34]

The *gens de couleur* were obviously qualified voters; their education, wealth, and other accomplishments argued for full equality. They had been organizing and campaigning for it since Unionists had taken over the government in mid-1862. Yet not even the most liberal Unionists would support officially giving them the vote. The blacks could attend meetings that advocated full emancipation, they could listen to and join private discussions and hear an occasional speech about their rights, but the white Unionists would not publicly support their right to vote. In November 1863 the group finally petitioned General Shepley to give the vote to those Louisiana blacks who were "born free before the rebellion." "We are men," a delegation of prominent *gens de couleur* told Shepley, "treat us as such." When Shepley did not respond they sent their petition to Lincoln and to Congress early in January 1864.[35]

The failure of local Unionists to support these highly qualified black men provided continuing evidence of the volatile race relations in Louisiana. These blacks were not advocating the extremely radical position of enfranchising all blacks, slave or free, in the state; they wanted the franchise for themselves. But their white allies kept their distance. When the Free State General Committee (the umbrella group for Unionists) met in convention as the Friends of Freedom in December 1863 a delegation of black men asked to join them, and only after vigorous debate did the whites agree. There was even an argument when a black delegate was proposed to lead the opening prayer. The committee was hardly a radical organization; it clearly did not propose a society freed of color distinctions, and it said nothing about votes for any black men. In the midst of the war it was content to protest against slavery. Individual members tested the waters in behalf of suffrage for the *gens de coleur* and Durant supported limited suffrage for them, but few people went further. No one who held power advocated rights beyond emancipation for former slaves; Banks's position reflected this attitude.[36]

Both civilian reformers and the commanding general in Louisiana had decided that reform would have to respect the powerful prejudices of Louisiana's white society. They recognized that the war was still in the balance and so therefore was the viability of reform itself. It was an understanding that Lincoln shared and that reflected Northern and Southern realities. Few people doubted that Northern power would ultimately prevail, but the crucial question remained: How far would it reach to shape and change the South? That question would be at the center of a presidential election that was beginning in the North.

1864

★ ★ ★ ★ ★

A little after midnight as I was writing . . . the President came into the office laughing, with a volume of [Thomas] Hood's works in his hand, to show Nico[lay] and me the little caricature "An unfortunate Bee-ing," seemingly utterly unconscious that he with his short shirt hanging above his long legs & setting out behind like the tail feathers of an enormous ostrich was infinitely funnier than anything in the book he was laughing at. What a man it is! Occupied all day with matters of vast moment, deeply anxious about the fate of the greatest army in the world, with his own fame & future hanging on the events of the passing hour, he yet has such a wealth of simple bonhomie & good fellowship that he gets out of bed & perambulates the house in his shirt to find us that we may share with him one of poor Hood's queer little conceits.

—John Hay, *Diary*, May 1864

13

★★★★★

LINCOLN AFFIRMED:
JANUARY TO JUNE 1864

While Louisiana Unionists were trying to decide, as 1863 became 1864, what democracy meant in the South, Northern voters were about to demonstrate how it operated in the North, an enterprise remarkable in itself. In the middle of the greatest war in the nation's history, a war being fought within their own country, the people of the North were holding a national election. They were voting on the most immediate and important issues they had ever confronted—should this vast war, already claiming a quarter of a million of their sons' lives, continue? If it did, what kind of country would those deaths have purchased? At Gettysburg the president had spoken of a government of, by, and for, the people, "dedicated to the proposition that all men are created equal." That seemed a persuasive goal in late November 1863. Within a week after Lincoln's address Grant's army showed what citizen soldiers could do—charging up a quarter mile of steep mountainside to rout Confederates at Chattanooga—another victory added to Vicksburg and Gettysburg. Then in early March 1864 the new Lieutenant General Grant (no one had held that rank without brevet since George Washington) was sent east to carry on the Army of the Potomac's Gettysburg momentum, leaving behind in the West the powerful forces under General Sherman ready to advance further into the Confederacy. The future was promising and Lincoln's reelection was easily predicted.

One of the reasons for confidence was that Lincoln had at last found a general who combined organizing skills with a determination "to drive his head through a brick wall," as one observer said. Grant would fight, wanted to fight, knew that fighting rebel armies was *the* road to victory. He knew the means as well as the end. It was for this reason that Lincoln could let Grant take the reins. "You were right, and I was wrong," the president told Grant in discussing the best strategy for taking Vicksburg. That concession built on Grant's implicit recognition that Lincoln needed no advice on political strategy, and Grant offered none. He knew his army was part of the propaganda of war winning—it had to fight: to attack and to keep Lee under siege. He had no interest in telling Lincoln which political ends the victory should ensure; he faced south, not north, his attention on fighting battles, not on lobbying leaders. "General Grant," Lincoln told Ambrose Burnside, "is a copious worker and fighter but a very meager writer or telegrapher." Satisfied that the general had his eyes on the battlefield and that he would keep on fighting, Lincoln turned the military details of warmaking over to him:

> Executive Mansion Washington
> Lieutenant General Grant. April 30, 1864
> Not expecting to see you again before the Spring campaign opens, I wish to express, in this way, my entire satisfaction with what you have done up to this time, so far as I understand it. The particulars of your plans I neither know, or seek to know. You are vigilant and self reliant; and, pleased with this, I wish not to obtrude any constraints or restraints upon you. While I am very anxious that any great disaster, or the capture of our men in great numbers, shall be avoided, I know these points are less likely to escape your attention than they be mine. If there is anything wanting which is within my power to give, do not fail to let me know it.
> And now with a brave Army, and a just cause, may God sustain you. Yours very truly A. Lincoln

Grant replied that since the early days of 1864 when he had taken over as general of the armies, he had been "astonished at the readiness with which everything asked for has been yielded without even an explanation being asked." It would be his "earnest endeavor" that neither Lincoln nor the country would be disappointed. "Should my success be less than I desire, and expect, the least I can say is, the fault is not with you."[1]

After Grant took over from Halleck as general in chief, Halleck remained as liaison between Lincoln and Grant and the seventeen military department commands, including over 530,000 men who came under Grant's authority. Grant was responsible for formulating overall plans and strategy for the army. His concurrence with Lincoln's ideas and his consistent advances guaranteed that the president would give him a much freer rein than previous eastern generals had had.

When he wrote his memoirs in 1885 Grant would depict Lincoln as a relative innocent in military strategy who learned it adequately only when Grant instructed him. Lincoln, however, had held for some time the same general strategic ideas that Grant held: Union superiority in numbers meant that pressure all along the Confederate front would wear out and break down Southern resistance. When Grant offered his picture of that strategy Lincoln pithily summarized it: "Those not skinning, can hold a leg." As 1864 began Grant was turning the increasingly powerful Army of the Potomac toward the task of holding Robert E. Lee in Virginia; Sherman was sharpening the skinning knives in Georgia.[2]

Such a military outlook gave Lincoln's nomination a sense of inevitability although not everyone was delighted with the prospect. As early as November and December 1862 Salmon Chase had been complaining that Lincoln lacked the energy and focus to bring about radical goals. His complaints helped create the cabinet crisis in which almost every Republican senator challenged Lincoln to oust Seward. Chase lost that skirmish but now he had approximately 15,000 agents from his Treasury Department throughout the North and the South working earnestly to give Republicans a new nominee. Chase's high opinion of his own talents and his belief that Lincoln was not sufficiently active in expanding equality inspired his electioneering. The treasury secretary consistently told people that he personally liked Lincoln but that one term was sufficient for anyone and that "a man of different qualities from those the president has will be needed for the next four years."[3]

Perhaps inhibited by his December 1862 debacle Chase had kept a low profile politically; despite that failure, he remained influential in radical circles and decided to try again. The campaign of 1863 inspired his energies. Returning to Ohio to campaign against Vallandigham and for Governor John Brough the treasury secretary basked in the popularity of the Republican cause and predictably determined that that popularity was personal. He wrote friends to remind them how people admired him in the Midwest, even as he described to his audiences the connections between voting Republican and the successes in his Treasury Department and in the administration. He further worked to stand out in the public mind by putting his own picture on the new one dollar treasury notes that were appearing, rationalizing that he had put Lincoln's picture on higher-denomination notes. He spent off-duty hours writing letters to help a supporter prepare a campaign biography.[4]

Chase was personally ambitious, but that ambition rested on egalitarian goals. He knew that in the cabinet he represented the most advanced principles. Seward and at times Blair stood for the more conservative position, believing that public prejudice and commitment to existing institutions demanded caution. Lincoln balanced conservative and liberal ideals, seeking to use respect for institutions and even prejudices of voters to confirm the proposition that a government of the people could secure equality and preserve itself. Chase's role in the drama, in the dialogue that shaped and often was the government at its best, was to represent the more radical option—to insist on equality as the standard. It was a matter of emphasis—Chase had been within the establishment for two decades—but the emphasis was important.

Many abolitionists looked to Chase as their spokesman and hoped to see him replace Lincoln in 1864. Their feelings were further inspired by Lincoln's December 1863 reconstruction proclamation; they saw the limited protection of freedmen's rights in that document. Wendell Phillips quickly targeted the major flaw: The president had conceded too much control over freed slaves to former masters. He complimented and even honored Lincoln for freeing the slaves, but the December message left "the freedmen and the Southern States under the control of late slaveholders." The president had shown "no desire, no purpose, no thought, to lift the freed negro to a higher status, social or political, than that of a mere laborer, superintended by others." Lincoln's promise that reconstruction governments could make laws "consistent . . . with [the freedmen's] present condition as a laboring, landless, and homeless class" meant to Phillips that the "Government in its haste, is ready to sacrifice the interest and honor of the North to secure a sham peace." The proclamation left "the black man naked, homeless."[5]

Not all abolition leaders agreed. Garrison wanted to modify Phillips's charge; although he worried about leaving the freedmen unprotected he had great faith in Lincoln. The president moved slowly in the right direction, needed "spurring on to yet more decisive action," but was moving as fast as public opinion allowed. When the Massachusetts Antislavery Society met in January 1864, however, it supported Phillips's position, if narrowly. Chase was rallying the chief voices for full equality.

That support grew because he shared the belief that the president was not sensitive enough to the economic imperatives of emancipation. Impressed by Phillips's argument congressional radical Republicans recognized that land reform, enabling black workers to be economically independent by making land available to them, or at least keeping them from the economic power of former masters, was a long step toward freedom. To achieve that goal Chase, backed by supporters in Congress, had been trying since late 1863 to gain control over the freedmen in the Mississippi Valley, especially in Louisiana and in South Carolina.

Claiming that the Treasury Department was already charged with handling abandoned lands in the South under the 1863 Abandoned Property Act, the secretary proposed higher wages for freedmen's work and a plan for leasing land to freedmen. He also tried to induce landlords to sell land to former slaves and to have freedmen paid wages on a weekly or monthly basis, a far more immediate reimbursement than the yearly wages or twice-yearly wages that the army system was offering. In both the Mississippi Valley and in South Carolina Chase encouraged land sales in small lots—twenty to eighty acres; poor men could more easily afford such plots. In October 1863 he sent an agent, William Mellin, to the West to take over from the army all the land not clearly used for military purposes. In South Carolina on 31 December 1863 Chase authorized freedmen to preempt abandoned lands in small plots if they could pay 40 percent of the value.[6]

Chase was no political innocent. In the political environment of early 1864 the secretary moderated his views a bit, but he still stood for black economic independence going far beyond the measures that Thomas and Banks, with Lincoln's support, were implementing in the Mississippi Valley. Radical congressmen thought highly enough of Chase's plans that Senator Sumner tried to place the Freedmen's Bureau, an agency that Congress was creating during winter 1863–64 to assist the freedmen, under Treasury Department control.[7]

But Lincoln supported the military option. In South Carolina abandoned lands were sold in large lots and most often to white investors from the North who promised to keep blacks at work in orderly ways as they learned the discipline that free labor required and that slavery had allegedly eroded. In late February 1864 Lincoln, as part of his effort to control reconstruction in Louisiana, told General Thomas that he was to "go to the Mississippi river at once and take hold of, and be master in, the contraband and leasing business"; he was to take over the activities that Chase's agent, Mellin, had under way. The treasury secretary's proposal, the president said, was "doubtless . . . well intended," but it would be too difficult to implement. He preferred a system that would allow former plantation owners to contract with former slaves for wages and so employ "the idle and destitute people."[8]

Lincoln's policy was thus many-faceted. At times it appeared contradictory because the president did not believe in equal rights at the same time for all blacks, yet he knew the importance of persuading whites that freedmen deserved equal liberty. He wanted blacks to vote, but only those who had demonstrated the type of self-discipline that proved them ready for independent citizenship. The educated blacks of New Orleans clearly qualified and so did soldiers, the latter having earned the ballot by fighting to preserve the Union. At the same time Lincoln did not believe that all black men had equal claims. He clung to military control over blacks in the fields, to letting their contracts be enforced by soldiers and the courts. Perhaps through their labor blacks would learn the discipline necessary for full citizenship.

Most crucial for the president, however, was the problem that while the war continued the army needed to control the thousands of blacks who rushed away from slavery and asked for military protection. Moreover, white constituencies in both North and South still needed courting. Southern Unionists would be more attracted by conservative than by radical changes in race relations; once within the Union fold they might be willing to take longer steps. Northern moderates and conservatives watched attentively for signs that Lincoln and his administration were not the "amalgamationists" and "revolutionaries" that the Democrats invoked at election time. The race card had been potent in past elections; Lincoln knew the power it retained. Success in the South and in the war itself meant moving carefully in that minefield.

Congressmen had little sympathy for Lincoln's problems. Many legislators, already touchy about executive power, were hearing from constituents and from opinion shapers that the president's policies paid too little heed to destroying slavery. Persuasive abolitionists led the charge. "To free the slave, and then to abandon him . . . betwixt bondage and manhood, is not this as cruel as slavery?" one asked. The president was "giving the lambs to the nurture and admonition of wolves," another claimed. Phillips, still the most compelling speaker of the age, toured the East Coast and spoke of freeing the slave but forgetting the Negro, of serfdom replacing slavery. Phillips called for a constitutional amendment that would end racial distinctions. He wanted blacks protected in the South until they had their own land, homes, schoolhouses, and the ballot.[9]

Congressmen were equally concerned, and their attention spread across several issues connected to Lincoln's tolerance for reconstruction by white Southerners. Initially ready to welcome the December 1863 message as an outline that they could fill in with details, by February 1864 suspicions grew that their options were being closed, not invited. They were worried that state-level definitions of black freedom would not protect the freedmen and that Southern whites of dubious loyalty would too quickly acquire power over black liberty. Congress wanted several things: to impose more national control, to provide for a longer process of reconstruction, to increase the standards of loyalty for leadership and participation in government, and to provide better guarantees for black liberty. Congressmen wanted a more general plan, one subject to national influence and enforcement more directly from Washington, and if necessary, one more enduring in that it would operate under the mechanism of national laws, enforced in national courts by national officials. In contrast, any rights blacks might gain in Louisiana, where Lincoln's attention was focused, would be granted by a state authority that could easily revert to men who had allowed and perhaps condoned both slavery and rebellion.

To interdict that possibility Congress began in late 1863 and early 1864 to write its own reconstruction plan. These efforts corresponded with Chase's growing challenge to Lincoln, setting larger stakes for that political battle. Written by Ben Wade of Ohio and Henry Winter Davis of Maryland, the bill followed some of Lincoln's proposals. A provisional governor would begin the process of calling an election and would determine the loyalty of voters and officeholders. In setting up a new government legislators agreed with Lincoln that an oath of future loyalty would be enough, but Congress wanted stricter guarantees of loyalty. Delegates to a proposed constitutional convention, and the men who voted for them, would take oaths of past and future loyalty. Men of long-term loyalty, not recent rebels, would write the fundamental law of the state. There would also be a broader constituency for the new governments; 50 percent, not just 10 percent of the voting population of 1860, would need to take that original oath. Men who had held office in the Confederate government were excluded from voting; so was anyone who had "voluntarily borne arms against the United States." No one who had been a rebel government official at either state or national level could vote for, or be, legislator or governor. There was even the threat that anyone who persisted in high office under Confederate authority after the bill was passed would lose his citizenship.[10]

Of the two options, Congress' was more prescient, Lincoln's more immediately useful. A president with a vastly different perspective on reconstruction would follow Lincoln, and his standard for loyalty made no demands on egalitarianism. A quick restoration under such leadership would have left blacks without even promises of equal justice. But Lincoln faced immediate, short-range military goals that demanded resolution. He thought in terms of gaining allies to help expand Union influence in the South as quickly as possible. It is not surprising that Congress did not share his outlook. Congressmen did not receive daily dispatches from soldiers filled with demands, requests, alternatives, complaints that translated into lives lost, bodies mutilated, families destroyed. They might hear from constituents and read in newspapers of battles and lives in peril and glory, but Lincoln felt the inescapable imperative of acting and deciding quickly on measured that would serve the army and the Union immediately. He was trying to weaken the Southern will to make war. He feared that too much challenge to local prejudices would only inspire further opposition. When it was time to wage peace and not war his policy could change.[11]

The congressional plan clearly provided a greater arena of freedom than Lincoln's did. He promised men at the state level that, slavery dead, they would have almost full control over shaping their postwar world. Congress established guidelines that threatened national intervention should states try to preserve too much of their prewar past. The Wade-Davis bill prohibited state courts from recognizing any "law or usage whereby any person was heretofore held in involuntary servitude." It also gave federal courts authority to discharge anyone who was "restrained of liberty under pretense of any claim to such service or labor." And the bill promised that anyone who tried to force freedmen into involuntary labor could be punished by a fine of $1,500 and a jail term of five to twenty years. Congress was carefully limiting Lincoln's promise of December 1863. New Southern governments might control "the landless and homeless class" but not with new forms of slavery.

The bill, though it challenged Lincoln's plan, maintained conservative features. Its constitutional legitimacy rested on guaranteeing to states a "republican form of government." It thus recognized state prerogatives, keeping in operation, for example, state laws and tax systems unrelated to war until such time as state lawmakers might change them. State courts and other offices were still to operate. Most notable, given congressional commitment to protecting blacks, was the feature that both voters and jurors in the new government would be white. Lincoln's proposal was not different on this point.[12]

The central imperative of the more radical vision, black economic independence, gave voters and politicians clear options. Chase tried to build his political base on the ideals embodied in the Wade-Davis plan. He quietly encouraged the activities of a group of congressmen and other politicians to organize a national Chase for President Committee, headed by Kansas senator Samuel Pomeroy. It was a delicate business, for Chase was testing the waters, seeing if there was sufficient popular sentiment for the more liberal option. He could hardly strike boldly against the leader of his own party, an incumbent president in the middle of a war. Yet if public feeling was ready for expanding equality beyond Lincoln's limits then Chase felt that his beliefs and his experience made him the obvious choice to replace the president.

He did what he could quietly to stir up, he might have said to discover, support. He complained constantly that the administration had no central focus: "There is no unity and no system, except in so far as it is departmental. There is progress, but it is slow and involuntary; just what is coerced by the irresistible vast force of the people. How under such circumstances, can anybody announce a policy which can only be made respectable by union, wisdom and courage?"[13]

Continuing cabinet disarray gave some support to this charge. Secretary of the Navy Welles complained throughout the spring of government by departments without a unified direction—this left the president himself "less informed than he should have been." Stanton and Seward had virtually established their own cabinets, Seward disliked Blair and Chase, who, on good days, hated each other, and Welles was suspicious of most of his colleagues. "At such a time," Welles wrote, "the country should have the combined wisdom of all."[14]

The president observed this criticism and believed that Chase was behind much of it, spreading rumors among people whom Lincoln had offended and hinting that Chase would be more sympathetic. The president knew of the secretary's activities and thought Chase was able: "I hope we may never have a worse man," he remarked to Hay. Yet at times Lincoln's annoyance emerged. Chase's politicking was like "the bluebottle fly which [lays] his eggs in every rotten spot he can find." Meanwhile, the treasury secretary kept up a large correspondence that at once spoke of his devotion to the president but also of his "reluctant" willingness to lead a more reformist and vigorous administration.[15]

Lincoln handled Chase's maneuvers shrewdly, helped immensely by the public's recognition that the war was going reasonably well at the very time that the Chase forces had to organize. Abolitionists might criticize emancipation efforts that fell short of equality; Chase might quietly but constantly tell correspondents that the administration needed consolidated leadership and higher ideals; but the abiding memories of Vicksburg, Gettysburg, and Chattanooga and the promising new leadership of Grant and Sherman suggested that the administration was doing well. The president refused to provoke a cabinet crisis by challenging Chase. Letters reporting Chase's politicking went intentionally unread; White House visitors recounting anti-Lincoln organizing were listened to without comment. Lincoln was refusing to be provoked so that he would not be forced to comment on events that would become more important only if he noticed them. "I have determined," the president told John Hay, "to shut my eyes to everything of the sort."[16]

There were political benefits in ignoring Chase's activities. Within the cabinet the secretary could not overtly criticize his president without being seen as an ambitious carper, but resignation in the midst of war would make Chase look unpatriotic. Moreover, his patronage power would vanish the moment he resigned, and he had been almost obsessive in insisting on full control over patronage in his department. Thus, unless some military disaster provoked public demand for new leadership, Lincoln had Chase under control that was exercised best by denying that there was a problem between them. And of course the president profited from the success of most of Chase's work as treasury secretary.[17]

Lincoln was concerned enough, however, that his political operatives were busy checkmating Chase. Starting with Chase's birthplace, New Hampshire, state legislatures and party gatherings saw proadministration resolutions passed. New Hampshire juggled its endorsement to support Lincoln, to applaud Chase's financial talent, and then, archly, to warn the secretary to watch out for corruption in his department. Simon Cameron wrote from Pennsylvania to assure the president that "I have kept my promise" and thus to report that the entire state Republican delegation would soon ask Lincoln to run again. Lincoln himself may have signaled to Chase that his supporters were at risk. Chase's biggest patronage appointment in New York was the collector of the port, Hiram Barney, who was busy working for Chase. On 11 January 1864 the president dispatched a note to the secretary: "I am receiving letters and dispatches indicating an expectation that Mr. Barney is to leave the Custom House, at New York. Have you anything on the subject?" Chase quickly replied that the rumor was not true, that Barney represented reform in his position, and that he retained the secretary's "undiminished confidence." But Chase was on notice that Lincoln was watching and that he still controlled the patronage and the administration.[18]

Chase's supporters tried to overcome these disadvantages by quietly drumming for support at first, but response was ambiguous and they escalated their efforts. In February they went public with a pamphlet on "The Next Presidential Election." Without mentioning Chase by name the pamphlet spoke of the need for a statesman who "fully comprehends the age in which we live," specifically a man "profoundly versed in political and economic science." Since Lincoln had proven a failure in leading the nation, the people wanted and required some new leader. The public found out within a week just who it was they wanted.

On 20 February Senator Pomeroy sent out a circular naming Chase as the man but also providing a series of reasons explaining why Lincoln was not. The circular was marked for private distribution but quickly made its way into the newspapers. It was clearly propaganda designed to create and not just to report Lincoln's limitations, but it did suggest why his political opponents in his own party found reason to complain. After claiming that the premature efforts of Lincoln supporters had required a proper response, the circular recited the pro-Chase argument: Lincoln could not be reelected; his growing patronage had so consolidated his influence that the "one term principle" was necessary to protect republican government; and should Lincoln be reelected "his manifest tendencies towards compromises and temporary expedients will become stronger in the second term than it has been in the first." Consequently, "the cause of human liberty, and the dignity and honor of the nation" would suffer, and the war would drag on while the debt increased intolerably. In contrast, Chase, his popularity growing so quickly that even his admirers were astonished, "a statesman of rare ability and an administrator of the very highest order" with a private character that guaranteed "economy and purity in the management of public affairs," would ensure victory. That victory would provide "speedy restoration of the Union on the basis of universal freedom"; it would also reduce taxes, increase resources, raise the standard of public and private morality, and make the nation the model of human progress for the rest of the world.[19]

The Pomeroy circular backfired; instead of gaining allies for Chase, it rallied and multiplied his enemies. A ground swell of opposition, encouraged by Lincoln men, rose up before the treasury secretary and his supporters. Senator Sherman, whose franking privileges had been used to distribute Chase material, faced such anger from his constituents that he had to declare lamely that he had been tricked by the misrepresentations of Chase men. Worse for Chase, the circular caused state Republican organizations to organize rallies that in state after state endorsed Lincoln. Most crucially, in Chase's home state, Ohio, Republicans met just five days after the circular went public and, with the governor's enthusiastic support, declared for Lincoln. One Lincoln supporter summarized the reaction: The Pomeroy circular, he said, "don't make the Chase pudding rise."[20]

Chase had never openly joined in this boomlet. He adopted the standard posture of presidential candidates of the day and waited, publicly, for the office or nomination to find him. This fooled no one, except perhaps Chase himself, but it did give him a graceful way out of the campaign. He wrote to Lincoln just after the circular became public and, while admitting that he had allowed supporters to circulate his name as a nominee, insisted that he had no connection with the circular or other anti-Lincoln publications. Within weeks he openly announced that he was not a candidate for the nomination. Some supporters wishfully said that he was merely retreating to advance later, but indeed the Chase option had shrunk almost out of sight. The most powerfully positioned radical leader would stay on the sidelines. Movement toward equality would remain in the hands of Lincoln, not in those of reformers more sensitive to ends than to means.[21]

Lincoln was helped by the circumstance that abolitionists, increasing in popularity throughout the war, were engaged in their own civil war over the relationship between means and ends. Wendell Phillips held out for a leader whose commitment to equality was unalloyed. The limitations of Lincoln's reconstruction rankled him: "Mr. Lincoln's model of Reconstruction . . . puts all power into the hands of the unchanged white race," Phillips said. "[It] makes the freedom of the negro a sham and perpetuates Slavery under a softer name." Phillips's ideas were popular enough throughout May 1864 to earn the endorsement of three major abolition organizations, the American Anti-Slavery Society, the Church Anti-Slavery Society, and the New England Anti-Slavery Society. These groups joined forces with a movement that had been gathering momentum throughout the previous fall to nominate John C. Fremont. Anchored in the antislavery German American community and fostered among Missouri's radical Republicans, the Fremont drive began to attract disappointed Chase supporters when the secretary withdrew. With Phillips and his supporters in tow calls went out for a Fremont convention in Cleveland on 31 May so that true radicalism might anoint its champion.[22]

Yet the Fremont movement was not carrying all the radicals with it. In addition to Phillips, Elizabeth Cady Stanton and Frederick Douglass signed on, but Garrison and his friends stuck with Lincoln, giving the president powerful leverage on the Left. After the deflation of the Chase balloon congressmen stayed away from more left-wing options; Garrison's support of Lincoln sheltered them from political threats and reassured them ideologically. The most prominent congressional radical, Sen. Charles Sumner, though he did not campaign for Lincoln, stayed off the Fremont wagon, helped in part by Garrison's position. (Moreover, the Lincolns made special efforts to court Sumner socially—plying the senator with frequent invitations to dinner, operas, and the theater, an effort facilitated by Mary Lincoln's fondness for Sumner.)[23]

By 31 May the Fremont movement made interesting headlines but posed little threat. Radical agitators came to Cleveland and were gladdened by platform planks that proposed confiscating rebel property and that called for a constitutional amendment basing emancipation on the expansive principle that "all men" should be guaranteed "absolute equality before the law." Had it been passed this amendment could have provided freed people with direct federal protection against any law or private action denying their equality; it would have done much more than simply set slaves free. But other constituencies came to Cleveland, and they also had to be appeased. That required adopting planks that for all purposes contradicted the egalitarian promises that Phillips and his associates desired. Although the proposed constitutional amendment predicted strong national authority and confiscation portended economic revolution, wartime Democrats insisted on condemning federal outreach over civil liberties and on urging greater economy and integrity "in the administration of the government." How a weakened national government could expand equal liberty was a contradiction that no one there could answer.

The contradictions continued at the convention when the vice-presidential choice was made: John Cochrane of New York. Before the war Cochrane had voted for Pierce and Buchanan and Breckenridge. The contradictions compounded when both Fremont and Cochrane wrote their letters accepting the nominations. Both men rejected the plank on confiscation of rebel property, and Fremont devoted only two sentences in his twelve-paragraph letter to the amendment ending slavery; Cochrane said nothing at all about it. The originators of the Fremont movement had damned Lincoln for his political expediency, arguing that his compromising sapped the force of the struggle. It was now difficult, to say the least, to offer themselves as an option on that ground. Uniting with Democrats, they had undercut the radical alternative on what emancipation might mean. Even though Phillips and a vocal group of allies stayed faithful, the Fremont movement of May frightened few Lincoln supporters.[24]

When the Republican convention met in Baltimore within a week of Fremont's nomination Lincoln controlled most of it. His political appointees dominated the party's executive committee. They had located the convention in close proximity to Lincoln, and they ensured that the president set the ideological agenda. His version of the struggle for liberty and Union abided. Within the first five minutes of the meeting Senator Morgan, chairman of the convention, was saying that "the bones of our soldiers lie bleaching in every State of the Union, and . . . this has all been caused by slavery. The party of which you gentlemen are delegates and honored representatives, will fall short of its great mission, unless among its other resolves, it shall declare for such an amendment of the Constitution as will positively prohibit African slavery in the United States." The platform praised the army and the navy for their courage, demanded the "unconditional surrender" of the rebels, endorsed Lincoln's prosecution of the war, specifically the use of

271

black soldiers, urged "harmony . . . in National Councils," and demanded that soldiers of all colors be given "full protection of the laws of war." The platform concluded with an endorsement of foreign immigration, the Pacific Railroad, national currency, "economy and rigid responsibility in public expenditure," and (taking a shot at the French expedition into Mexico) warned "Monarchical Governments" to beware of threatening republican government in the Western hemisphere.

The platform reflected Lincoln's views as did the new party name chosen for the election. The president had been saying for years that every step he took to end disunion and to destroy slavery was done in the name of "Union." Thus the party reached out to every constituency when delegates chose to campaign not as Republicans but as the "National Union Party." Most significantly, the new label meant that Union was no longer the optional goal of emancipation; the Union party was unequivocally the party of emancipation and of black soldiers.

The linkage was especially meaningful to one man sitting in the gallery. William Lloyd Garrison watched with tears in his eyes, grateful for the applause that came after egalitarian comments, especially moved that standing cheers followed the emancipation plank. Here at last was a national party commitment to end throughout the nation the institution that for over three decades he had been fighting. Lincoln's party had brought the nation to this grand moment.[25]

Lincoln knew the value of nurturing that gratitude even while committing himself further to equal liberty. Garrison was invited to the White House, and the president told him that he had insisted that the party commit to the emancipation amendment. Secretary of War Stanton gave Garrison a long interview, and congressmen left the floor of Congress to come and thank him for his efforts. Growing numbers of abolition publications told readers that Lincoln's reelection was indispensable to the cause of black freedom; they also pointed out how much Fremont had conceded to Democrats and to Copperheads. Once filled with idealism, challenging the status quo, excoriating the political constitutional system for its sell-out to expediency, the Garrison wing of the abolitionists now supported the established party system and the national government. But this was hardly a surprising switch, nor was it a betrayal of ideals as they gained influence. The governments they had challenged endorsed slavery and wrapped that endorsement in the constitutional logic of *Dred Scott* and the politics of racist popular sovereignty. By 1864 *Dred Scott* was anathema, not the law of the land, and the Democratic party offered racist rebuttals to challenge the government in power. Garrison and his allies knew very well which party marched toward equality.[26]

The real issue was no longer that of institutions versus idealism. It was what utilization of government power sustained by what degree of popular support would provide the greatest degree of freedom for blacks. Garrison and his supporters opposed the Fremont movement because it might result in the election of Democrats. The choice was not between the greatest imaginable equality and halfway measures; it was between moving forward and jumping backward. Phillips insisted that as an agitator his job was to assert the most advanced principles and the means to achieve them, to make politicians fear the consequences of falling short of the ideal. He had hoped that Fremont might push Lincoln to the Left, might even lead the Republicans to choose a less cautious emancipator. But once Fremont's "Radical Democracy" became more Democratic than radical, Republicans had little need to steer to the Left, especially while the war was going well. Large numbers of abolitionists agreed; they were content with the direction, if not the speed, of the administration.[27]

Had they been able to predict the future clearly, however, they would have been troubled at how wide the Republicans were now reaching for support. Safe on the Left, Lincoln's party reached to the Right as well. The Union party label was an indication, but the vice-presidential nomination revealed it even more clearly. Since almost every New England county had gone for Lincoln in 1860 defections there were not likely, but the border states, with their ancient attachment to slavery and their hopes for Union, were more problematic. Lincoln's understanding that the war was political as well as military included a recognition that a party with the broadest sectional appeal would not only gain voters but would promise people deeper in the South that there was room for them too.

Lincoln sent word to Nicolay, who was in Baltimore, that he "wish[ed] not to interfere about V.P.," and he repeated that to John Hay. Other Republicans in Baltimore thought that Lincoln wanted Andrew Johnson, and as the first ballot began the military governor of Tennessee and the state's former senator had 200 of the necessary 260 nominating votes. By the time the first ballot was over Johnson gained enough ballots to sweep easily to the nomination.[28]

At the time Johnson's rhetoric did not suggest an equal balance between conservatives and liberals. The Tennessean had spoken of hanging traitors and had favored both emancipation and the use of black troops. He was known as an active and vigorous military governor operating under Lincoln's reconstruction plan. Still, a vice-president from Tennessee instead of Maine would be a better magnet for the border states, even with Johnson's militant reputation. In the simmering struggle between president and Congress over reconstruction Johnson's presence on the ticket cleverly provided a bold voice for Lincoln's more conservative option, a voice so bold that some radicals saw Johnson as a friend. Even George Strong, New York's impassioned patrician Republican, preferred Johnson over the other candidates. Such support further strengthened the Republican campaign.[29]

The party unity of mid-1864 built on several factors. Optimism about the war was fundamental. Grant's newly launched offensive portended warmaking that would overwhelm the weakened South, and Sherman led a western army that had prevailed triumphantly at Chattanooga. Word was leaking out that Grant's advance was especially bloody, but this cast only a small cloud, for few people believed that the rebels could replace such casualties. There was some intraparty bickering about reconstruction policy, but most Republicans still believed that the president welcomed their input and would compromise. Even opponents in his party wanted to ride the president's coattails. Lincoln was so popular among Republicans that David Davis, his convention manager four years earlier, stayed in Illinois and told the president that his nomination was assured. It was. On the first ballot Lincoln received 506 votes of the 528 cast. Militant radicals from Missouri gave 22 votes for Grant but quickly made the nomination unanimous. Lincoln's National Union Party as it left the convention on 8 June 1864 was ready for a triumphant march to victory in the fall.

14

★ ★ ★ ★ ★

LOUISIANA AND REELECTION:
JUNE TO NOVEMBER 1864

By early June Lincoln and his party had achieved apparent unity in facing the national election. But events in Louisiana indicated the instability of the forces that mixed conservative means with radical ends. General Banks, clearly the designated "master" in the Bayou State, began a process that caused people to choose sides. Perhaps Lincoln had wanted to avoid division in Louisiana and hence had waited, hoping that unity among the Unionist factions would somehow turn up. But now Banks moved and the argument was on.

When Banks organized elections in February 1864 he picked former congressman Michael Hahn as his candidate for governor, but the election revealed a bitter split among Louisiana Unionists. Shortly after getting Lincoln's authorization to control events Banks had met with Durant, who was leading the radical Unionists in New Orleans, to work out procedures. Both men were as prepared to quarrel as to negotiate. Durant wanted a constitutional convention to be followed by elections for state officials; Banks wanted to elect the state officials first and then hold a constitutional convention. Indeed he had ordered an election for that convention to take place in early April, just two months after choosing the state officials. This difference soon grew until by election day, 22 February, the two groups, one led by Hahn and the other by Benjamin Flanders, Durant's man, were calling each other names in public. Most damaging, some of Hahn's supporters were stirring the caldron of racism, claiming that the Durant/Flanders forces were for racial equality and that they believed that "the black race is superior to the white race."[1]

At stake were two visions of how far to go, when to set forth, and how fast to proceed. Both factions wanted to expand black rights and to create a Republican coalition that would be led by city professionals, merchants, and white laborers. Blacks would gradually be added when prejudiced whites discovered blacks' capabilities and also when they needed their votes.[2] Flanders argued that hard core conservatives could not be conciliated. Only by setting up a strong and advanced standard and fighting for it with army support could the changes that the state needed be attained. "There is no middle ground in a revolution," one Flanders supporter proclaimed; there must be radical change, implemented vigorously. Meeting with black leaders, radicals spoke of having blacks of all classes work together for their rights, of constitutions based "on the broad basis of human rights." Implicit in the radical position was the belief that the defeated Southern populace would relent in their opposition to change when faced with a firm resolve to demand change. Their support for new directions was indicated when Durant sent a letter to Lincoln introducing the two black men who were on their way to the president to argue for full equality. Radicals thus insisted on protecting black rights, conceding as little as possible to conservative sentiment.[3]

Hahn and Banks were more sensitive to the immediate need for the broadest support possible. Banks was influenced by military as well as civilian needs. He knew the importance of persuading the majority of the people of Louisiana that change did not mean chaos, that they could adapt to the world that the war had created. Hahn's moderates also felt the power of conservatism in the state. They thought that the situation was fluid and that demanding too much change would create a dangerous reaction. As Banks wrote to Lincoln, "The history of the world shows that revolutions which are not controlled and held within reasonable limits produce counterrevolutions." Moderates were struck by the distance Louisiana had traveled in three years—every slave in the state now free, schools being set up to educate a black population that had suffered decades of oppression. They demanded emancipation and they spoke of a future where blacks might vote. But as Banks explained to his friend Congressman George Boutwell, "If the policy proposed be too conservative or too radical it will bring a counter-revolution." The progress that had been made might be imperiled unless the people could be persuaded that change would move at a speed that they could accommodate, that much, even most, of their lives would continue unshaken.[4]

Ironically, despite their division over the pace of progress, both factions of the Free State group wanted to end slavery and perhaps to expand the suffrage to include the educated free blacks of Louisiana. Durant's group spoke more radically and insisted on their revolutionary goals but in fact were not advancing much more toward them than Hahn's and Banks's people were. Only a few of Durant's allies urged full black suffrage, and Hahn's agenda included votes for part of the black population. But the election passions had evoked race-baiting rhetoric and further secured a split in Louisiana Unionist ranks, a split that would later exacerbate the conflict between Lincoln's Louisiana policies and those of his Congressional opponents.

Although both radicals and moderates shared essentially the same program, Lincoln favored Hahn, or more specifically, he favored Banks's policies. He did not explain fully why. Certainly having made Banks master was a commitment that recognized the need to give a free hand to the military while the war continued. Moreover, the president's conservatism endured. Given a choice between a policy that balanced constituencies and respected the force of convention, a policy that fit change within boundaries of custom and one that did not, Lincoln chose the former. The election results suggested the wisdom of that choice: Hahn's election as governor showed that voters preferred the less radical of the two liberal alternatives. The election also revealed conservative strength: Flanders came in third, behind a conservative Unionist candidate. Louisiana voters had had enough dramatic change.

But Lincoln was working quietly, again, for change. As the constitutional convention gathered, the president wrote Hahn with some "suggestions," influenced partly by the arrival in Washington of the two black representatives who had been endorsed by Flanders and Durant. The two black men visited Lincoln with their petition for full equal suffrage for all blacks. The next day Lincoln wrote Hahn to urge that a new constitution should include provisions that the vote be given to "the very intelligent, and especially those who have fought gallantly in our ranks." Ever sensitive to the political environment, the president made this suggestion "for your private consideration" and "not to the public."[5]

The careful quality and tone of Lincoln's letter to Hahn has led some historians to underestimate the extent of the president's efforts to achieve equality.[6] Two points are especially noteworthy in that regard. First, Lincoln included in his list of potential voters not just the free *gens de couleur* of New Orleans; soldiers were added to the president's list, soldiers who had been recruited from the fields and the plantations as well as from among free blacks. Lincoln's view of who deserved and needed to vote was expanding. Second, the president was pushing actively for expanded equal liberty. Although Lincoln emphasized the private nature of his "suggestion" Hahn believed that it was designed to nudge wavering Louisianans toward greater protections for blacks. And the president had added to Hahn's authority two days after writing the letter by giving him the powers of military governor of the state.[7]

Hahn used his own authority and the president's influence when the constitutional convention began in May. He showed the letter to various politicians at the meeting, suggesting that the Union power might be available to support constitutional changes. The result was a constitution that authorized immediate, uncompensated emancipation, education for children of both races, enrollment in the state militia without racial bars, and equal access to courts; it also granted the legislature the power to give the vote to blacks. Hahn tried to gain immediate suffrage for blacks, especially the free blacks of New Orleans, but this move was too extreme even for the liberal Unionists. Many of them thought that the whole constitution would be rejected if provisions for full equality were included. Their reasons for worry were understandable; even in this convention, some delegates spoke of slavery as a "perfect, humane" and "satisfactory" system of labor. Indeed, the provision granting legislative power to enfranchise blacks in the future passed only when a conservative spokesman was called off the convention floor to talk with General Banks. Taking advantage of the delegate's absence, liberals passed the measure.[8]

The constitution satisfied Lincoln, who thought that it treated poor blacks better than did the constitution of Illinois. There was little else at the moment to be pleased with: War still raged; Sherman was still trying to take Atlanta; Grant had bogged down before Petersburg; Confederate armies were active in the Shenandoah Valley, Tennessee and Missouri; the March to the Sea was in the future. Yet in the most politically spotlighted state in the South, emancipation, civil rights, and education had come to black Americans. Despite abiding conservative feelings, Louisiana had produced reforms unthinkable only a few years before.[9]

Lincoln wielded the patronage power prominently when the constitution was sent to the electorate. He told Banks to "let the civil officers in Louisiana, holding under me, know that [ratification] is my wish, and to let me know at once who of them openly declare for the constitution, and who of them, if any, decline so to declare." Banks sent Lincoln a list of the votes of every local treasury official when the election was over.[10]

Given the traditions of slavery and racism in Louisiana the constitutional convention could claim major accomplishments. But its measures satisfied neither important members of Congress nor some partisans on the scene in the Bayou State. Still angry at having lost to Hahn and thus being excluded from power, Flanders and Durant began a campaign to persuade congressmen and senators that Lincoln's government offered too little protection to the freedmen and too much latitude to former rebels.

To a degree they were right. Lincoln's expanding visions of liberty, broad though they were, remained restricted to his essentially political-constitutional ideals. He wanted a considerable number of blacks to vote; he favored civil rights for blacks and supported educational opportunities. His background as a lawyer and as a politician had prepared him to define these activities as basic for popular government. That they had now come to a slave society that had challenged the government and denied such imperatives marked a significant transformation.

But he did not foresee a similar revolution in economic relationships in the South. He was concerned about the ability of former slaves to become free disciplined laborers immediately and was ambiguous about the better path to follow. Should blacks serve as apprentices before launching out on their own, getting a basic education but working under white direction? Or, should they set forth unimpeded, making whatever contracts they could, becoming the free laborers of Northern ideals? Such ambiguity characterized wartime reconstruction as Republicans offered these options. Lacking a clear plan, Lincoln felt little compulsion to insist on a particular option. The result was that in economic relations "liv[ing] themselves out of their old relation to each other" clearly gave whites a better life than it brought blacks.[11]

Lincoln avoided dealing with that injustice directly because military needs for control over freedmen remained the foremost wartime imperative. Furthermore, General Banks was arguing that his policies were benefiting the blacks as well as sustaining his military goals. Banks defended his labor policies as a response to freedmen's wishes and as a necessary step toward full freedom. He said that he had asked freedmen in the rural regions what they wanted most; their answer had been safe and secure families, education, an end to whipping, and wages for their work. He claimed his rules for free labor were temporary and based on a belief that without slavery large plantation farming would erode and thus opportunity for freedman to buy land would grow. The "immediate and ultimate objective of the labor system of Louisiana," Banks said, was to encourage the freedmen to become owners of land. Thomas Conway, later to become head of the Freedmen's Bureau in Louisiana, claimed in early 1865 that Banks's program was displacing the power of plantation owners and making land available to blacks.[12]

But Banks was propagandizing for self-protection. Part of his justification was true, but freedmen had legitimate complaints. Although slavery was gone and the region of freedom was expanding daily, the army regulations of 1863 remained and continued to emphasize discipline and reliable labor. Free labor for black men in Louisiana, as in the rest of the South, still looked much different from free labor for white men. Black leaders and their white allies protested this situation in Louisiana, and the echoes, because of efforts by Flanders and Durant, were heard in Washington even as military failures forged a mood of anger and frustration.[13]

By late June an anti-Lincoln riptide was beginning to rise as a result of the war news. As the Republican convention ended, the casualty reports from Grant's Wilderness campaign were leaking out. They were ambiguous at first, and Grant's fighting spirit and the advances of his army cast the numbers in a positive light for many people. Lee's army was taking heavy casualties, and Grant had failed initially in other campaigns only to triumph ultimately. Yet as days passed and casualties in the tens of thousands piled up, Northern spirits faded. Sherman offered no cause for optimism, either. He was forcing Confederate Joe Johnston's army to retreat toward Atlanta but so slowly that the public began to doubt that progress was being made at all. Gold prices, always a sign of public sentiment, went up as morale dipped.

The divisions between the congressional radicals and the president grew. Returning from the Republican convention, congressional leaders had put the finishing touches on the Wade-Davis bill, and it passed by large margins. In the House the vote was seventy-three to fifty-nine; in the Senate eighteen to fourteen; only one Republican congressman from a Northern state voted against the bill. Congress strongly endorsed demands that 50 percent of the past voters in each state, not Lincoln's preferred number of 10 percent, were needed to begin reconstructing the South, that blacks receive protection for newly found rights, and that only those Southerners who could take an oath of past and future loyalty would govern the conquered South.[14]

Some congressmen believed that the president would sign the measure. During most of the debate, which stretched from February into July, Lincoln had kept silent about his reactions. Legislators had general hints about Lincoln's stance, but they continued to believe the president's assurances that his plan was not exclusive, that their plans filled in specifics to his general ideas. For his part, absorbed in Louisiana details, Lincoln did not need a public quarrel over general policy. Furthermore, since it was election season neither Lincoln nor Congress was interested in provoking a party split. Hopes guided expectations concerning the president's response.

Yet Lincoln pocket-vetoed the bill, and thus set back congressional involvement in the reconstruction process. The president offered several reasons for the veto. The bill had come to him "less than one hour before the *sine die* adjournment"—by implication too short a time for him to study it carefully. With that reason, he dissembled since he signed other bills that had come at the same time. He could have asked for and received more time from Congress. Furthermore, legislators had been debating this bill for over three months, and Lincoln was hardly ignorant of its contents. His more respectable reason was that he opposed setting aside "the free State constitutions and governments already adopted and installed in Arkansas and Louisiana"; doing so would discourage loyal citizens from taking further actions. Events had proceeded so far in Louisiana and in Arkansas that the president refused to redo what had been done. Perhaps wearied by the two-year-long Louisiana fight Lincoln could not face starting all over again. The president also doubted that Congress could end slavery within a state by legislation. He thought that a constitutional amendment was necessary, and the Republican platform had promised one. Despite these doubts the president still announced that "the system for restoration contained in the bill [was] one very proper plan for the loyal people of any State choosing to adopt it." He simply was "unprepared . . . to be inflexibly committed to any single plan."[15]

Lincoln set up a strange situation by his veto. Taken at his word the reconstruction process would have followed two paths. His proposals would be operative in two states and state governments would be passing laws that severely limited freedmen. Apprenticeship programs were possible, and these might place blacks under the supervision of former masters. Protests against reimpositions of slavery under new names would have been directed to state courts. Meanwhile, Congress would have been providing federal guarantees for freedmen in other states and establishing a federal enforcement mechanism. In "Lincoln's states" government would rest on the initial consent of 10 percent of previous voters; in "Congress' states" 50 percent would provide the initial constituency. The constitutions in the president's states would have been written by people who could swear only future loyalty; congressional constitutions would have been written by men who swore to past and future loyalty.

As a logical exercise Lincoln's explanation made legislators angry; as a practical guideline it made them furious. A month after Lincoln's veto Wade and Davis issued their "manifesto," filled with attacks on the president and his policies. In part the manifesto was political—efforts were under way to replace Lincoln as party nominee with John C. Fremont—but it also showed how strongly legislators favored a reconstruction plan that protected loyal freedmen and that provided a foothold for more change in the postwar South.

Lincoln's plan and his veto proclamation left the choice to the states themselves; if they decided to implement the congressional plan he would support them. Much of the legislators' frustration rested on Lincoln's dubious suggestion that a state might choose the more restrictive congressional path over his more lenient reconstruction option. They were hardly pleased with offering choices to past masters and rebels, allowing them to decide how much liberty former slaves would have.

The protest focused on the ultimate authority for reconstruction. Wade and Davis spent several paragraphs objecting to the fact that Lincoln had vetoed the law and then announced that he would implement it. That was "plenary dictatorial power," they charged. "A more studied outrage on the legislative authority of the people has never been perpetuated." Wade and Davis were infuriated by Lincoln's assumption of military authority—the effort to expand his authority as war director to the position of peacetime authority or "dictator."[16]

The manifesto resonated furiously for a time, for it was a strong and shocking challenge; politicians do not easily attack their party's candidate in the midst of an election. Furthermore, the manifesto built on real differences over who should rule reconstruction and how much protection freedmen would claim, differences that promised a long fight and suggested a deeply divided party.

And the war news remained bloody and frustrating. Grant had hit Lee hard in the Wilderness, at Spottsylvania Courthouse, at Cold Harbor, and at Petersburg, but the advances were drenched in over 60,000 casualties. On an average, every twenty-four hours in the East approximately 2,000 men were killed, wounded, or missing. Not only was Sherman moving glacially, he had been beaten at Kennesaw Mountain. Lincoln's reelection fortunes seemed to be spiraling downward. "Most seriously perturbed by what I hear from independent trustworthy sources about the increasing prevalence of discouragement, and aspirations for peace 'at any price,'" George Strong wrote 6 August. "Our slow progress, wretched finances, and difficulty recruiting can be endured or remedied; but if the national backbone become diseased and degenerate into cartilage or gelatin we are a lost people." Men the president respected, politically experienced Thurlow Weed and Henry Raymond, chairman of the Republican party, were bringing him similar news that he would lose the election. Some advisers urged him to contact the rebels to discuss ending the war. Horace Greeley had been pushing this course for some time; during July and August he had been drawn into discussions with alleged Confederate agents to discuss terms. Lincoln was suspicious but told Greeley to investigate their authority and their intentions; Lincoln's terms were Union and abolition. The agents turned out to be fraudulent. By late August Republican leadership was desperate. Raymond proposed a ploy that he thought would recoup lost ground: Let Lincoln contact Jefferson Davis and offer peace on the basis of Union alone, saying nothing about emancipation. Davis would reject this, Raymond reasoned, and that would undermine public confidence in the South and would strengthen Northern determination.

The president toyed with the idea. He even drafted the suggested memo—a frequent practice when he was pondering options. That Raymond should want such a letter was another blow, but he echoed the views of Weed and Seward. On 23 August Lincoln so despaired that he asked cabinet members to sign, sight unseen, this memo: "This morning, as for some days past, it seems exceedingly probable that this Administration will not be reelected. Then it will be my duty to so co-operate with the President elect as to save the Union between the election and the inauguration; as he will have secured his election on such ground that he cannot possibly save it afterwards."[17]

The man with whom Lincoln thought he would have to cooperate was Gen. George McClellan. The Democratic party was gathering for its convention in Chicago as Lincoln prepared the memo. Northern morale was at its lowest point, and Jackson's party capitalized on that mood by listening to "Peace Democrats" who saw nothing but failure in the past four years and who thought that recognizing that failure made more sense than perpetuating it. Although the party platform expressed gratitude to soldiers and sailors for their sacrifices, promised them protection and care, and avowed "unswerving fidelity to the Union under the Constitution," it had had enough of war. "Justice, humanity, liberty and the public welfare demand that immediate efforts be made for a cessation of hostilities with a view to an ultimate convention of the States, or other peaceable means, to the end that at the earliest practicable moment peace may be restored on the basis of the Federal Union of the States." The convention chose as McClellan's running mate George Pendleton of Ohio, known for his association with Vallandigham. Conspicuous by its absence was any mention of sustaining or expanding emancipation. No one doubted that a McClellan victory meant a reversal of the momentum of freedom for blacks, a reversal that would have made meaningless the reconstructed Union that Lincoln and other Republicans were arguing about.[18]

Such a reversal, to Lincoln, meant that the Union could not be saved. If the general won on the Democratic platform of peace in exchange for Union without emancipation, the North would lack the power to compel the South to agree even to unite. Lincoln wrote to several correspondents—who argued that Union without emancipation was the most viable policy—that without black troops he could not save the Union. He reminded Charles Robinson, editor of a Democratic pro-war newspaper, "Take from us, and give to the enemy, the hundred and thirty, forty or fifty thousand colored persons now serving us as soldiers, seamen, and laborers, and we can no longer maintain the contest." He drafted a letter to Isaac Schermerhorn, declaring, "Any different policy in regard to the colored man, deprives us of his help, and this is more than we can bear. . . . This is not a question of sentiment or taste, but one of physical force, which may be estimated as horse-power and Steam-power are measured and estimated. Keep it and you can save the Union. Throw it away, and the union goes with it." These statements echoed words he had written publicly to Conkling in August 1863: "If [Blacks] stake their lives for us, they must be prompted by the strongest motives—even the promise of freedom. And the promise being made, must be kept."

Yet Lincoln did not make public the letters to Robinson or Schermerhorn. He did have private meetings in which he spoke of these feelings—he even showed the Robinson draft to Wisconsin visitors. And on 25 August when Henry Raymond came to the White House to follow up his letter about the memo to Davis, Lincoln and "the stronger half of the Cabinet," as Nicolay called it, rejected that option. To contact Davis would mean "ignominiously surrendering" the election to McClellan. But Lincoln did not wave these linkages between emancipation and Union in the public's face. The party platform contained these ideas, but the president apparently did not want to trumpet them in this dark time. Still, Lincoln and his party clearly were committed to Union and to emancipation and to the belief that the two were linked indissolubly by the need for black soldiers. It was a potentially dangerous political linkage in a time of low Northern morale.[19]

But Sherman changed things and Sheridan followed suit. On 2 September Atlanta fell, and the news boosted Northern spirits. Within two weeks Sheridan had battered Jubal Early in the Shenandoah Valley; the Union momentum was back on track. Admiral Farragut's early August victories in Mobile Bay now seemed part of a turn for the better in fortunes, not just a single bright spot in the gloom. Grant's tenacious grip on Lee, even though the siege near Petersburg continued, was seen as a sign of action, not inertia.

Democrats scrambled to compensate for the changed environment. When McClellan wrote his letter accepting the Democratic nomination he retreated rapidly from immediate negotiations for peace. "The re-establishment of the Union in all of its integrity is and must continue to be the indispensable condition of any settlement," he wrote. He invoked dead comrades, sacrificed to save the whole nation; he linked the Union with constitutional rights; he asserted that "no peace can be permanent without Union." Indeed McClellan had retreated so far that several pro-peace Democratic newspapers declared that there was little difference between Lincoln and his opponent. Vallandigham canceled a speaking tour, and several of his midwestern supporters met in Cincinnati to consider new nominations.[20]

Democratic self-destruction did nothing to restrain Republican campaigning. Again and again the Chicago platform was proclaimed to be "The Great Surrender to the Rebels in Arms," as a widely circulated pamphlet announced. Democrats were "base and infamous men" who had "undertaken the ignoble task of excusing the traitors." The Chicago convention was "controlled by the most notoriously disloyal men in the country." Charges were reprinted that "there is a mutual understanding between [Democratic leaders] the Seymours, the Woods, Vallandigham and the rebels." To document the charge, Joseph Holt, judge advocate general of the army, produced a report on "Secret Societies" in the Northwest, which allegedly were composed entirely of Democrats organized to commit treasonous acts against the government. Holt charged that there were five hundred thousand of these conspirators, many of them officers in the rebel army. The Union Congressional Committee published ten thousand copies of the report for circulation to Union Leagues, and Republican newspapers published summaries of it, linked with accusations about Democrats. Holt's report gave credibility to earlier charges of widespread Democrat disloyalty. and added more authority to a treason trial that Governor Morton had generated in Indianapolis in an attempt to uncover and publicize suspicious activities of a local Democrat named Dodd. All this linked opposition to Lincoln with disloyalty to the nation and helped build Union party majorities.[21]

Lincoln's role in bitter and dubious campaigning is hard to decipher. He had doubted earlier conspiracy charges made in June. After having John Hay look into them the president dismissed the alleged conspiracy as "a mere political organization with about as much malice and as much puerility as the Knights of the Golden Circle." Yet the official nature of the Holt report, published in October, and the support that Stanton gave to Holt's activities suggest that the president at least knew the political value of tarring Democrats with disloyalty. He did nothing to stop the activities of his close subordinates.[22]

The administration did much more than engage in negative campaigning. Stanton was particularly vigorous. He supported requests for furloughs so that the soldiers could come home and vote for Lincoln; soldiers with other inclinations could foresee some problems in visiting home. He dismissed quartermaster officials who campaigned for McClellan. He and Holt carefully checked to see that anti-Lincoln newspapers and their editors did not get patronage jobs or government contracts. The president also played his cards politically. Actively encouraging the soldier vote, he wrote to Sherman asking that the general allow troops to return and vote in the important October Indiana election. He asked Meade and Sheridan to furlough Pennsylvania soldiers and told Rosecrans in Missouri to make sure that his men voted. He watched the navy, asking Welles to help the New York party chairman get sailor and seamen votes. He supported the practice of deducting political contributions from the salaries of officeholders and from the income of government contractors. And he courted newspaper editors such as James Gordon Bennett of the influential *New York Herald* with White House invitations and a publicized ambassador's nomination, which Bennett could graciously decline while gaining the social prestige he coveted. Bennett's paper, which had called the President "a joke," changed sides and endorsed Lincoln in 1864.[23]

In addition politics shaped the cabinet of 1864 just as it had in 1860–61. Late in June patronage struggles in New York revealed a wrestling for position in the coming contest. When the widely respected John Cisco resigned as assistant treasurer in the city Chase tried to put his own man, a former Democrat, in the post. But New York's senior senator Edwin Morgan protested: "It is in my judgment discreet, to appoint a Republican at New York at this time." Lincoln had already acquiesced in the appointment of two former Democrats that Chase had nominated in New York City. The party there was, he told the secretary, "at the verge of open revolt." "It will really oblige me," Lincoln said, if someone acceptable to Morgan could be appointed. Chase demurred and then talked Cisco into withdrawing his resignation, suggesting that his will and not the president's would control treasury patronage. To emphasize the point the secretary offered his own resignation.

Chase threw this gauntlet down at the wrong time. Lincoln was an incumbent president just renominated by his party and facing a difficult election. Chase's gambit to get the nomination had floundered; it was no time to challenge his party's leader. Lincoln jumped at the resignation, telling Chase that "you and I have reached a point of mutual embarrassment in our official relations which it seems cannot be overcome, or longer sustained, consistently with the public service." He recognized Chase's "ability and fidelity," but it was time to settle in which direction party workers would march. They marched with Lincoln; only one cabinet member, Stanton, even bothered to bid Chase farewell, and Welles reported that the president was supported by the cabinet "without an exception."[24]

Lincoln did not flaunt his victory. After appeasing Ohio by designating a former governor, who refused the offer, as Chase's successor Lincoln reached out to Congress and replaced Chase with Maine's widely respected senator William Fessenden. Fessenden, chairman of the Senate Finance Committee, had criticized Seward; he would suit the more radical congressmen. To placate the senator Lincoln promised to let him control officeholding in the Treasury Department with the caveat that "in filling vacancies he will strive to give his willing consent to my wishes in cases where I may let him know that I have such wishes." Furthermore, the president put in writing his "view" that the full cabinet should be consulted frequently "in questions affecting the whole country" and "that nothing should be done particularly affecting any department without consultation with the head of that department." With Fessenden as secretary of treasury, the threat to Lincoln's influence was greatly minimized. Fessenden was clearly a party man, had no aspirations for higher office, and had just witnessed Lincoln's will in action.[25]

Throughout the summer campaign politics continued to involve the cabinet, and Lincoln shuffled places to attract constituencies and to send messages to the nation. Political imperatives trumped administrative efficiency and Montgomery Blair was a case in point. He ran his department so competently that Lincoln remarked, "War does not seem to add to the difficulties of the Post Office Department." The postmaster general managed to turn a $10 million deficit in 1861 into a surplus of over $861,000 by 1865. Secession helped by eliminating postal routes, but Blair was active, cutting payments to railroads, eliminating unnecessary post offices, ending the franking privileges of postmasters. Meanwhile, he met the increased outpouring of mail (including parcels of food, clothing, photographs, and other mementos) to and from the front by setting up army post offices that operated well. And working with his friend, "Big Ben" Holladay, he reorganized mail delivery to the West, establishing the Overland Mail route to carry passengers and mail to the region.[26]

Yet Blair had become the lightning rod for congressmen who

wanted Lincoln to be more radical. Seward had been attacked for years to no avail, but Blair gradually emerged as an alternate scapegoat. His family was recognized as a major political force, and "The Blairs" became an epithet, standing for the political influence wielded by Francis Preston Blair, Sr., and his two sons, Frank and Montgomery. Rumors that the family had significant influence over Lincoln added resentment to envy.

The Blairs had made important enemies. They had alienated Fremont after an early friendship, and in Missouri the enmity had grown into a split among Republicans, the more radical men supporting Fremont. The Blairs also alienated Maryland radicals by challenging Henry Winter Davis in the state. This made Davis's friends Blair's enemies. Meanwhile, Montgomery Blair had accused radical Republicans of wanting miscegenation and had written to William Lloyd Garrison, urging separation of the races after the war. Frank Blair had come back from the army to attack Chase in two speeches in February 1864. By late 1863 the Union League of Philadelphia was electing everyone in the cabinet, except Blair, as an honorary member of the organization. And the Union party convention in Baltimore had slapped the Blairs twice, first by including a platform plank urging unity within the cabinet, which was widely seen as a thrust at the postmaster general, and second by seating the radical anti-Blair Missouri delegation. By late summer party chairman Raymond was urging Blair's ouster, and Sen. Henry Wilson warned Lincoln that Blair would cost the party tens of thousands of votes.[27]

Lincoln liked Blair but recognized that, unlike the president, he took politics personally as well as passionately. Lincoln once had told his adviser, "It is much better not to be led from the region of reason into that of hot blood by imputing to public men motives they do not avow." Blair's capacity for making enemies out of opponents had reached the point where the postmaster general would have to go. "You have generously said to me more than once, that whenever your resignation could be a relief to me, it was at my disposal," Lincoln wrote on 23 September 1864. "The time has come." The president expressed full satisfaction with Blair "personally and officially," and spoke of "uniform kindness unsurpassed by any friend," but political reality required a change.[28]

The nature of that reality was suggested when Fremont withdrew from the race just six days before Lincoln wrote Blair. Fremont claimed that he dropped out because, although Lincoln's administration was a failure in every way, McClellan's election would be a disaster for Union and for emancipation. Senator Chandler claimed that he had been negotiating between Fremont and Lincoln to arrange an exchange of exits; Blair thought he was "a peace offering to Fremont and his friends." Whatever the source, Lincoln believed that he had the most to gain by appealing to the party Left. Blair was let go, and the Republican party stood united against the Democrats.[29]

Several factors built that unity. Military victory was the major factor. Opposition to Lincoln grew when the war went badly; it faded when Union armies won. Sherman's advances were reflected in state victories in Indiana, Ohio, and Pennsylvania in October, and from that point Republican momentum grew. Men who had been attacking the president or sulking in their tents joined the campaign—Chase spoke for Lincoln, so did Blair (explaining that his resignation had been his father's idea—a sacrifice for the cause). Henry Winter Davis and Ben Wade joined in the chorus, harmonizing with Sumner and Henry Wilson. Republican governors, controlling most Northern states, combined to rally their popularity and patronage for the Lincoln cause. And the soldiers, voting either in the field, as the laws of nineteen states provided, or furloughed to vote at home as was necessary in the others, gave Lincoln an estimated 78 percent of their ballots. Lincoln would have won without their votes. In perhaps two states, New York and Connecticut, their ballots made a difference in the outcome.

But successful soldiers bearing recent victories were of vital importance symbolically, which may have been Lincoln's reason for attaching so much importance to the Indiana totals and soldier voting there. A loss in the Indiana state election in October, Lincoln said, "would go far towards losing the whole Union cause." Sherman sent soldiers he could spare home to the Hoosier State, and they helped carry it for Union candidates. Ohio and Pennsylvania state races in October also featured soldier voting, and word spread that the men who were risking their lives on battlefields were voting for Lincoln's party. They were also endorsing the most controversial of his policies. Maryland voted on a state constitution that disenfranchised prorebels and, more important, ended slavery in the state. The president avowed that he would trade a victory for the Constitution for a loss in the presidential canvass. Soldier votes swung the election in favor of the Constitution. And Lincoln carried Maryland.[30]

Soldiers may have been influential in the voting in a more subtle way. Commanders with Lincoln's permission sent troops to places where trouble was expected because of the dubious loyalty of the neighborhoods. New York City draft riots gave the army an excuse to police the polls in that city and to provide, according to General Butler, the first honest election in decades. It was also an election where soldiers watched as voters balloted. Baltimore saw soldiers near the polls, and Lincoln outpolled McClellan with 84 percent of the vote. Yet ballots more than intimidation shaped the outcome, for McClellan carried New York City with 68 percent of the votes.[31]

It was a Lincoln landslide in the nation as a whole. He won by the largest popular-vote percentage in thirty-two years. His 55 perecent was surpassed only twice in the nineteenth century, by Jackson in 1828 and by Grant in 1872. Lincoln's electoral college majority stood at 212 to Mc-Clellan's 21. Nineteen of the twenty-three Northern states that had voted in 1860 gave the president more votes in 1864 than he had won four years earlier; three of the remaining four were so safely Republican that the difference was meaningless. Lincoln's overall total increased over 340,000 votes, and the overall number of votes in loyal states increased by 145,500. Republicans gained congressional seats, too. In the House they would outnumber Democrats by over one hundred, 149 to 42, and in the Senate 42 to 10. Only one state, New Jersey, chose a Democratic governor, but Lincoln's party regained control over state legislatures it had lost in 1862. It was a huge victory in the midst of a war that had cost tens of thousands of lives, hundreds of millions in taxes, had portended huge transformations in race relations—and it was still going on. Northerners had clearly demonstrated that they endorsed the war, Lincoln, and the party he led.[32]

But the victory was not only for a party; it was for a process, for the system of self-government—the polity itself. Participation in that process had been widespread again. Almost 78 percent of those eligible had voted, and they had done so by assembling in camps and at civilian balloting places, of course, but also by traveling back home, packing the trains that headed North as the voting day approached. Despite the huge numbers of soldiers who had to stay in the field, others who could not vote because of restrictive state laws, and so many now in their graves, Northern voting totals in this election had increased, and electioneering was as energetic as it had ever been.

Confederates watched the Northern elections eagerly, hoping that this impassioned politicking would inflict damaging wounds to Union aims. If George McClellan, even though he was General McClellan, won, both North and South would discover a weakened Northern will and an implicit mandate for peace. There was some concern also that European nations would try mediation again if Lincoln lost. But these options vanished. Grant wrote Stanton, summarizing the consequences: "The election having passed off quietly, no bloodshed or riot throughout the land, is a victory worth more to the country than a battle won. Rebeldom and Europe will so construe it." Francis Lieber wanted to call it "The Great and Good Election of 1864." George Strong believed that the vote further secured the democratic process. Just as the Gunpowder Plot in Britain had failed to destroy parliamentary government in that country, so the successful holding of an election in this country and the result were signs that republican government endured and even flourished.[33]

Lincoln knew that the process of self-government was the most significant prize of the contest. Speaking to a serenade on 10 November 1864 the president noted, "It has long been a grave question whether any government, not too strong for the liberties of its people, can be strong enough to maintain its own existence, in great emergencies." The rebellion itself was the ultimate challenge to that government, and an election that divided and "partially paralyzed" the loyal people increased the risk. Yet "we can not have free government without elections; and if the rebellion could force us to forego, or postpone a national election, it might fairly claim to have already conquered and ruined us." But the election had been held, and that "demonstrated that a people's government can sustain a national election, in the midst of a great civil war. Until now it has not been known to the world that this was a possibility. It shows also how sound and how strong we still are."[34]

Ironically, that strength was measured also by the fact that Lincoln's victory, though substantial, was not total. Although Democrats lost by large margins, compared with other election results of the century, they remained a viable party. In the bloc of states from Illinois east to Connecticut McClellan and his party won almost 48 percent of the vote—indeed they increased party percentages by 1.4 percent over 1860. The Republican margins of victory actually went down in some crucial states—Pennsylvania, New York, Indiana, New Hampshire, and Maine. Overall the Democratic party kept the loyalty of its voters throughout the years from the mid-1850s into the late-nineteenth century. They were a minority, but as Joel Silbey has observed, "a respectable minority." They were well-positioned to offer an alternative to the Republicans in future elections. The Democratic message, protecting civil liberties, proclaiming governmental laissez faire, protesting economic as well as governmental concentrations of power, still kept its place in the polity. Unfortunately, so did racism. Nevertheless, by affirming the value of continued elections in the midst of the nation's grandest, most divisive and impassioned war, Lincoln had helped to preserve the environment in which debates on these issues would endure. That meant that the first principle of the conflict, the idea that government by ballot would prevail and carry through, continued to be affirmed in action as well as in ideals. The people of the Union not only talked of self-government; they walked in its paths.[35]

Lincoln strengthened the electoral system in the largest sense and in the smallest as well. His modest and fundamentally decent personal style abided throughout the war. He continued to favor "short statutes of limitation in politics." Although it struck Lincoln as "singular" that, not personally vindictive himself, he should be involved in campaigns where there was much bitterness, his own political speeches and official acts never included personal attacks. He was implacable in fighting the war and would be demanding in peace, but he never encouraged Northerners to hate the Confederate enemy. In small ways, such as in honoring the request to have "Dixie" played when crowds came to celebrate Lee's surrender, or in larger ones, such as rejecting malice after the war was over, he looked to reconcile rather than to embitter the people. That style mirrored his dealings with politicians in the North. Lincoln's policies were at stake in elections, but not Lincoln the man. For him the personal and the political were best separated. He seldom spoke of "my policy"—a stark contrast to the two of his successors who took politics personally and thus inspired impeachment. He scolded one politician: "You have more of that feeling of personal resentment than I. Perhaps I have too little of it; but I never thought it paid. A man has no time to spend half his life in quarrels. If any man ceases to attack me I never remember the past against him."

Lincoln carried over this attitude in the day-to-day business of the administration. One day Stanton turned down a congressman's request, supported by Lincoln, for a favor, calling the president "a damned fool." When the congressmen scuttled back to Lincoln with this remark the president asked, "Did Stanton say I was a damned fool?" "Yes he did, sir; and repeated it." Lincoln paused and then said, "If Stanton said I was a damned fool, then I must be one, for he is nearly always right and generally says what he means. I will step over and see him." Lincoln also avoided taking personal offense at legislators who challenged him. George Julian fought Lincoln over Fremont's proclamation and later over reconstruction but still insisted that "Mr. Lincoln had no resentments." The president stayed personally friendly with Charles Sumner even in the midst of a bitter clash over reconstruction policy. Sumner escorted Mrs. Lincoln into the inaugural ball on 6 March 1865, less than a week after he had stalemated the president's most important measure.[36]

Yet Lincoln's electoral victory, reflecting his personal and public political genius, did not end the reconstruction question. The political and constitutional system had been endorsed, and the promise was clear that blacks would join the society and perhaps the polity. The circumstances of their citizenship remained obscure, however, and that obscurity kept alive the conflict between Lincoln and Congress. Once again, Louisiana provided the most significant arena for the conflict.

1865

★ ★ ★ ★ ★

The President very quietly rode down to the Capitol in his own carriages, by himself, on sharp trot, about noon either because he wished to be on hand to sign bills, or to get rid of marching in line with the absurd procession—the muslin temple of liberty and pasteboard monitor.

I saw him on his return, at three o'clock, after the performance was over. He was in his plain two horse barouche, and looked very much worn and tired; the lines indeed of vast responsibilities, intricate questions, the demands of life and death cut deeper than ever upon his dark brown face; yet all the old goodness, tenderness, sadness and canny shrewdness underneath the furrows. . . . By his side sat his little boy of ten years. There were no soldiers, only a lot of civilians on horseback, with huge yellow scarves over their shoulders, riding around the carriage. (At the inaugural four years ago he rode down and back again surrounded by a dense mass of armed cavalrymen eight deep, with drawn sabres, and there were sharpshooters stationed at every corner of the route.)

—Walt Whitman, 4 March 1865

15

★ ★ ★ ★ ★

THE RECONSTRUCTION
PROPOSITION:
DECEMBER 1864 TO APRIL 1865

Just as the military situation had shaped national elections, so it also influenced directions in Louisiana. On the national stage Union forces were advancing, but in the Bayou State reversals were the rule. Banks, on whom rested the best chances for Lincoln's policies, was successful in shaping elections and the convention in New Orleans; in the field he failed. Even as the state's constitutional convention was meeting Banks was retreating from an ill-fated expedition into the Red River country where he had been bested by rebel general Richard Taylor, despite outnumbering the Confederates. He had gained nothing from the effort except the intense anger of the population in northwestern Louisiana, reacting to the destruction of civilian property as his army, foraging with little control, withdrew to the southern part of the state. Banks lost the military command of the Gulf through this failure. Despite Lincoln's support of Banks's new government in New Orleans, the president's first priority was the military. Edward Canby replaced Banks, who was demoted to commander of New Orleans. Had he stayed there he might have provided protection for Hahn's government, but frustrated by his demotion and eager to restore his position in Lincoln's eyes, Banks got Canby's permission to visit Washington in October. It would be April 1865 before he returned.[1]

Meanwhile, black protests against the land policy of the army continued. Their leaders were not convinced that soldiers favored equality. White leaders might speak of equal liberty; army provost marshals, however, the men responsible for day-to-day administration, ran the program to meet the needs of planters and the army. As 1864 turned to 1865 the most outspoken blacks in New Orleans were listing curfews and restrictions on travel as signs that "all the important prohibitions imposed upon the slave, are also enforced against the freedmen." Some were beginning to reach out for the hands of former slaves. "We regard all black and colored men as fellow sufferers," one of the *gens de couleur* announced at a December 1864 mass meeting. They asked Gen. Stephen Hurlbut, commanding in Banks's absence, to change the restrictions, but Hurlbut renewed them in March 1865. The black leaders protested that the system perpetuated dependency and would make it impossible for blacks to prove their capacity for freedom. The general responded by attacking the leadership, and Thomas Conway tried to undercut the *New Orleans Tribune*, the voice of black protest, by setting up a rival paper. The *Tribune* replied by accusing Conway of ignorance of black aspirations. Black militance was increasing in New Orleans, but Hurlbut was unconcerned.[2]

He and his superior, General Canby, had minimal interest in black liberty and saw the civilian government as an obstacle to their basic business of maintaining order. Hurlbut put Hugh Kennedy, a conservative, in charge of the New Orleans police force and reminded black leaders that their freedom depended on army determinations of their needs. Hurlbut seems to have been unwilling to stay out of the way of the civilian government that the constitution had created. When the convention voted to arrest a bitterly critical journalist for his attacks on their constitution-making efforts, Hurlbut stepped in and freed the man. He interfered when the convention voted itself large salaries and also when the new government requested a loan to the state from a local bank. Governor Hahn protested to Lincoln that with Banks gone the new commander's policies undercut reform and he asked that some blacks be made eligible to vote to supplement the numbers supporting his government. Without Banks or someone like him, Hahn warned, "we must break down in our efforts to build up a loyal State government here."[3]

Lincoln scolded Hurlbut for his interference with the new state government, explaining that such meddling with the loyal government was exactly what the rebels wanted. The general's actions threatened "the liberty promised to the black man by the new constitution." Such interference was "gratuitous hostility" toward the government on which vital hopes for the Union rested. Lincoln insisted that the military in the region uphold the decisions of the civil government, unless there was direct obstruction of military activity. The president clearly was interested in securing education, civil rights, and the possibility of voting for some freedmen, but he still gave priority to military matters. Even though his letter to Hurlbut showed a rare display of anger, Lincoln said that in military matters the commander was "master." On the important issue of the future Southern economy, the president preserved the wartime status quo. The labor regulations fell within the purview of the army, and Lincoln did not interfere with them. Curiously, he kept Banks in Washington, where he could lobby for Lincoln's government in Louisiana but not protect it.[4]

But Lincoln's focus was now in Washington; he could not watch every place all the time, even a place as significant as Louisiana. In the capital, policies for the entire South, indeed the entire nation, needed to be shaped and that, the president recognized, required working with Congress on writing the official death warrant for slavery.

Slavery died throughout the war in many ways. Union armies had been enforcing the Emancipation Proclamation each day after 1 January 1863. They had plenty of help from the slaves who rushed to Union protection as soon as those armies appeared and then joined the advances, which enlarged the territory of freedom with every forward step. West Virginia's 1863 constitution gradually eliminated slavery in that new state. And in states being reconstructed under Lincoln's plan the institution was outlawed. Arkansas began the process in March 1864; Louisiana followed in September, and in February 1865 Tennessee emancipated its slaves.[5]

Meanwhile, for the first time in sixty years, Congress was debating a constitutional amendment. The last time the document had been revised was in 1804 so that electoral votes for president and vice-president could be distinguished; the constitutional loophole had almost allowed Aaron Burr to become president in 1801. Congressional debate this time was over no mere loophole; at stake was the freedom of 4 million people and a federal arrangement that gave states control over their own race relations and public safety. When the Constitution was written the entire federal system had been shaped by the fact that six states would not join any union that did not protect their human property. The nation now was engaged in the greatest war in its history because eleven slave states by 1861 had determined to leave that Union. And still some states in the Union sent to Congress legislators to defend the right of states to control their own destiny in this matter. An amendment to end slavery was so dramatic that Democrats denied that amending the Constitution in such a fundamental way could ever be constitutional.[6]

Unpersuaded by the Democrats, Congress acted. Public pressure was too strong for emancipation to be chilled by Democratic legal logic, and Republicans rebutted arguments that the amendment process could not meet the demands of war and the ideals of freedom. Abolitionists, especially leading women such as Elizabeth Cady Stanton and Susan B. Anthony, had been building public momentum for months for a measure to end slavery permanently, not just in the heat of war. A petition drive of fall 1863, financed by the American Anti-Slavery Society, had rallied over two thousand men, women, and children to circulate petitions. Within two months one hundred thousand signatures had been gathered on a petition brought to Senator Sumner; three hundred thousand more would follow by summer 1864.[7]

Interestingly, it was a slave-state senator, John Henderson of Missouri, who introduced the first emancipation amendment in January 1864. Although clear evidence is lacking, it would not be surprising if Lincoln had put him up to it, for the president continued to believe that border-state challenges to slavery would deal a heavy blow to the rebellion. Sumner quickly jumped into the arena the next month, displaying the Anti-Slavery Society's huge petition. He offered his own amendment, which would have been even more expansive than the final measure. Sumner wanted to premise emancipation on the idea that "all persons are equal before the law, so that no person can hold another as a slave." It was an idea that might have outlawed clearly any discriminatory acts, not just slavery, and he hoped that his own committee on slavery would get the measures. But the Senate was more cautious. The majority thought that the Judiciary Committee, headed by Lyman Trumbull, would be sounder. Sumner thus stood aside for a time and let Trumbull shape the measure. Two months later Trumbull's committee produced wording drawn from the Northwest Ordinance—"Neither slavery nor involuntary servitude, except as a punishment for crime whereof the party shall have been duly convicted, shall exist within the United States, or any place subject to their jurisdiction." The president may have felt a special satisfaction about this because he had been pointing to that ordinance since 1854 as a symbol of hostility to slavery by the Framers of the Constitution.[8]

Meanwhile, Lincoln was at work. After the Senate passed the amendment by the necessary two-thirds majority it went to the House, and the president let it be known he favored it. He did not directly take part in the lawmakers' discussions, but he called in the chairman of the Republican National Committee, Senator E. D. Morgan, to make an emancipation amendment "the key-stone" of the party platform. Republicans would be campaigning that year in behalf of abolition.[9] Yet party unanimity could not swing enough votes to carry the amendment: Sixty-six Democrats checkmated ninety-three Republicans and two Democrats, and on 15 June 1864 the amendment failed in the

House. The emancipation amendment would have to wait until the elections were over.[10]

Reelected by large majorities, Lincoln moved again in December for action by Congress. He did not need to hurry since the elections had produced large enough Republican majorities to guarantee passage when these new congressmen assembled in December 1865. Furthermore, he could have called a special session of this new Congress any time after his inauguration to pass the measure. But Lincoln had the war on his mind and firmly believed that attacking slavery undermined the rebellion. The weight of congressional majorities, including Democratic votes, and especially the passage of the amendment by slave states would further erode the morale of the Confederacy. As he told Missouri Democrat James Rollins, "I am very anxious that the war be brought to a close at the earliest possible date. . . . I don't believe this can be accomplished as long as those fellows down South can rely on the border states to help them; but if the members of the border states would unite, at least enough of them to pass the . . . amendment . . . they would soon see that they could not expect much help from that quarter."[11]

Lincoln lobbied other Democrats, too. He appealed to their traditional self-image as the party of the people by pointing to the huge majority that had voted for Republicans and their platform. "It is the voice of the people now, for the first time heard upon the question." And he spoke again of the need for "unanimity of action . . . in a great national crisis. . . . No approach to such unanimity is attainable, unless some deference shall be paid to the will of the majority, simply because it is the will of the majority."[12]

He spoke in the currency congressmen liked best. Congressman Julian recalled that "the success of the measure had been considered very doubtful, and depended upon certain negotiations . . . the particulars of which never reached the public." Lincoln's two secretaries thought "it is not unlikely that [influences] of more selfish interest . . . were not entirely wanting." Congressman Ashley, who managed the amendment in the House, thought it was appropriate to ask Lincoln to make a deal with Senator Sumner: If the senator would call off his attacks on a New Jersey railroad monopoly, Democrats from that state could be influenced to support emancipation. Lincoln said he could not influence Sumner with such assurances—but only because of Sumner's peculiar commitments, not because this kind of trading was not right.

Democrats accepted the combination of rhetoric and horse trading partly because they also could count votes, recognizing that continuing to be a proslavery party was a political disadvantage. New issues promised better results. Even Vallandigham said, "The man who cannot get out of old ruts now, had better not attempt to travel," and Congressman Samuel Cox, during debate on the amendment, noted that "powder and ball" had made the issue of slavery "abstract." "Throw . . . off the *proslavery* odium," he urged. Playing on these feelings, still sensitive to ongoing war imperatives, and morally opposed to slavery, Lincoln used all of his resources to help Congress pass the Thirteenth Amendment. Seventeen Democrats joined 102 Republicans on 31 January 1865 and voted to end slavery everywhere in the United States. Eight Democrats helped out by not voting. Once the measure had passed congressmen sent it to Lincoln for his signature. The Constitution does not require that presidents sign amendments, but legislative leaders somehow forgot that Lincoln was not needed.[13]

The president and congressional Republicans were at one on emancipation but they remained divided over reconstruction. Almost every Republican congressman believed that Congress should control reconstruction and had voted overwhelmingly for the Wade-Davis bill based on that premise. Lincoln conceded some congressional responsibility but insisted on his prerogatives in wartime. Within the Congress were men with radical ideas that went beyond Lincoln's program. Influenced by the Louisiana dissidents, they were urging suffrage for blacks as well as whites and elimination of regulations that controlled the labor of freedmen and women. The most radical men wanted a transformation of Southern society that would require confiscation of the property of large landowning whites and redistribution to the freedmen. These were extreme positions for the time, and the majority of Congress stopped short of confiscation and equal suffrage. Still, radical men such as Sumner and Wade in the Senate and Thaddeus Stevens in the House were positioned to fight strongly against Lincoln's plans and especially against recognition of his Louisiana government. Sumner could filibuster, and Stevens, as chairman of the Ways and Means Committee and then of the Committee on Reconstruction, had significant leverage.[14]

In the aftermath of the election, however, both branches of government moved toward compromise. Lincoln might have used the impressive margin of his reelection to insist that his policy prevail, but he did not. Congressmen saw Lincoln's mandate and recognized the benefits of flexibility. Also helping the spirit of the compromise was the recent experience of working for the Thirteenth Amendment. Lincoln further reached out by replacing two known conservatives in the cabinet, Blair and Bates, with more radical men. On 6 December he raised Chase to chief justice of the Supreme Court, an appointment that promised egalitarian interpretations of antislavery laws.

Congress responded with some moderation of its own. It sent two bills on reconstruction to the Judiciary Committee chaired by moderate James Wilson of Iowa, not to the Committee on Territories where Henry Davis presided. Radical congressman James Ashley approached Lincoln to offer a bill that would recognize the presidential government in Louisiana in return for black suffrage there. When Lincoln objected to this as too strong Ashley changed the bill to permit only black servicemen to vote. The president also expressed concern over a provision that seemed to give Congress the power to emancipate, and Ashley dropped this idea.[15]

The harmony was soon interrupted. After the Christmas recess Ashley returned with a bill that seemed to resurrect the Wade Davis bill—it called for a 50 percent voter requirement for government-making in Arkansas and Louisiana, and it required equality of civil rights for all citizens in the reconstructed states. Perhaps afraid that the bill was going to unravel compromise with Lincoln, moderates in Congress backed away from Ashley's new bill; without their votes no reconstruction bill could pass. At the same time the lawmakers could not agree on accepting the governments Lincoln had approved. The Senate persuaded a majority to favor Lincoln's plans, but five radical senators, led by Sumner, filibustered that prospect to death. The result was impasse. Lincoln's reconstruction would proceed without a congressional alternative. Yet without being seated in Congress Louisiana, Arkansas, and the other states attempting reunion were in limbo; either Lincoln or Congress would have to yield to release them.[16]

Lincoln was now prepared to seek and provide a new vision. His years as politician and lawyer, as participant in the debate and conversation that a healthy constitutional process nurtured, established his commitment to reasoning together. Personally secure enough that losing an argument did not threaten his identity, he was able to separate his private needs from his political goals. Before the war the combination of these qualities had guided and fed his commitment to open discourse. But the war had expanded these qualities and changed him deeply.

In his First Inaugural Address he had presented a brief for the Northern position, showing that the South was wrong, the North right. His lawyer's skills and adversarial talents made him the defender of right, the powerful challenger to the injustice of slavery and the crime of secession. These skills were imperative in the crisis of disunion. Although they divided the house, they also gathered the material and emotional resources for the struggle to come and continued to do so in the heat of war.

But now, the nation was at last facing peace at the end of a long war, and much had happened. Lawyer Lincoln had become president and statesman, seeking a path that would combine equal justice with reunion and reconciliation. In the past four years he had seen how events had controlled him and the nation that he and the people had struggled to preserve. The war had become "astounding," vast: half-a-million dead young men, grief-shattered families throughout the nation; Willie, the favorite son, dead, and agony in the White House; 4 million free, men, women, children, chains now shattered, free after hopeless centuries of slavery; vast fields, busy cities, quiet villages destroyed; new economic paths charted with unknown costs and consequences ahead; 1 million men in arms, touched by fire, soon coming home, changed forever, changed utterly. Prewar hubris, surety, self-righteousness had been chastened by this.

Thus on 4 March 1865, in his Second Inaugural Address, the president carefully opened conversation with Congress and the country about the meaning of Reconstruction, seeking a peace that responded to the changes around them. The president had his eyes on other issues, defining the purposes of the war, shaping the meaning of peace. But Reconstruction was inescapably entwined with those questions, and it is probable that Louisiana specifically was on his mind. The most memorable of his lines—"with malice toward none; with charity for all; with firmness in the right, as God gives us to see the right"—echoed in word and idea the promises of "doing nothing out of malice" and yet doing "all I can to save the government," vows he had made to a Louisiana correspondent over two-and-a-half years earlier.[17]

The society that admires so much the subtle and compassionate Lincoln of the Second Inaugural has forgotten that Lincoln was thinking about reconstruction as he wrote the speech. Even though he sought reconciliation, by showing the limitations of both North and South he was trying to establish a policy and a direction that would secure the results of the war with much more than an absence of malice.

Yes, he spoke of the guilt of both North and South for slavery and thus for responsibility for the war. The peroration, perhaps the most well-remembered words of the speech, "with malice toward none, with charity for all," certainly suggested that moral absolutes would serve the nation poorly now. Yet Lincoln was not implying that the Union should forgive and forget; he was not urging that the prodigal be welcomed without question, without stipulations, and without judgment.

The white South had much to explain and to answer for. It had been willing to "make war rather than let the nation survive." The North "would accept war rather than let it perish." Even though both sections "read the same Bible, and pray to the same God, and each evokes His aid against the other," it was "strange" that "any men should ask a just God's assistance in wringing their bread from the sweat of other men's faces." Clearly the core of the conflict was slavery, and God was punishing both sections for allowing slavery to endure. It would be a "true and righteous judgment" if the war continued "until every drop of blood drawn with the lash shall be paid by another drawn with the sword."

Yet if both sides were being punished that did not mean that the North should be paralyzed because it was also guilty; even the sinful might have a stone or two worth casting. Lincoln asked Northerners to "strive on to finish the work we are in . . . with firmness in the right, as God gives us to see the right." They were to "bind up the nation's wounds," and since he had mentioned wounds drawn by the lash and by the sword, the wounds of slavery as well as of war needed care. The nation's goal was not only peace but "a just and lasting peace, among ourselves and with all nations."[18]

Lincoln clearly had spoken of continuing the struggle against slavery, but he had done so in a conciliatory manner that allowed both sides of the reconstruction dialogue to agree. He had placed the blame for the conflict on the South but had pointed out the responsibilities that Northerners shared and that he and Congress and the wider polity must assume. The tone of the speech conveyed the feeling that people seldom knew the will of God and the ways of fate, that firmness in the right depended on being able to see the right, and that in times such as they faced a search for answers to the issues and flexibility in finding them would bring the best result.

But in Louisiana a conservative reaction was beginning that prompted Lincoln to greater efforts to work with congressional reformers. On 4 March 1865, the very day of Lincoln's inauguration, J. Madison Wells took office as governor after Hahn resigned to become a senator. Despite suspicions over his background as a Red River planter, Wells had been put on the ticket to attract the support of Unionists outside New Orleans. He had managed to hide his conservative views, but with Hahn gone and Banks in Washington, Wells struck quickly. He appointed a mayor for New Orleans, Hugh Kennedy, who began replacing the supporters of Hahn and Banks in the police force, in city offices, and in judgeships. Many of these men were former rebels and Copperheads, and Wells gave statewide appointments to people of similar background. He appointed conservatives as judges in district courts and packed police juries with rural planters or even with active Confederates, throwing out Banks and Hahn men. Protests began in the city as liberals called rallies and asked for military support to protect the gains of reconstruction.

Although Louisiana reconstruction was in danger, elsewhere Union forces moved inexorably to victory. Sherman had reached Savannah and the sea just before Christmas 1864, ending a march that eviscerated the Deep South, destroying property, soldiers, and morale. During January and February he moved north into South Carolina; Columbia was destroyed, and Charleston fell on 17 February. The juggernaut advanced north again, heading toward the rear of Lee's beleaguered Army of Virginia. Before the Confederates, Grant's bountifully supplied army grew in men and in confidence, and Lee's army, eroded by desertions, could no longer protect the capital of the Confederacy—surrender was inevitable. A doomed rebel government did the unthinkable: They voted to permit blacks to fight for the Confederacy and then within five days adjourned for the last time. Richmond fell, and Lincoln went to see the city his armies had sought for four years. Freed slaves crowded around him, shouting that he was the emancipator and the protector of their freedom. The president conferred with generals on the scene, visited Davis's "white house," and returned to Washington. Louisiana was on his mind. The day after leaving Richmond he wrote a short note to General Banks, sending him back to New Orleans. Perhaps provoked by Wells and Kennedy, Lincoln was considering a change in policy.[19]

With the war practically over he faced the inescapable question of what to do in victory. The earlier stalemate with Congress, shelved when legislators had adjourned in March, demanded some resolution. Union victory provided greater room for congressional action and greater need for it. Lincoln had noted in his annual message of 6 December that "the Executive power itself would be greatly diminished by the cessation of actual war." Studying the situation in Louisiana, the president, shortly after this message, appointed a commission to investigate and report to him. Relying on Stanton, whose soldiers gave him the most complete data on events in the Southern states, Lincoln had sent commissioners south to confirm or deny the secretary of war's belief that moderation was not generating adequate loyalty.[20]

As peace spread through sections of the South the wartime military imperatives lost importance, were less necessary to weaken rebel will. Grant and Sherman had taken care of that. Thus Lincoln could consider imposing requirements on, as well as seeking the approval of, the white Southern population. And some specifics of his plan had become questionable, however. During the war Lincoln had promised to recognize state governments chosen by 10 percent of the voters of 1860. In wartime this was good strategy—let that small number have a government to operate, offices to distribute, favors to dispense, resources to control, and others might be drawn to them, from the Confederacy. After the war 10 percent was clearly too low a number to depend on for a stable government. Although Lincoln stuck to this figure in Louisiana, other states might require more solid numbers. (Indeed even Andrew Johnson accepted the idea of majority rule when he took over.) Conversely, the congressional demand that an iron-clad oath be imposed for those voters who wished to make constitutions in the defeated South might be too demanding in peacetime. How many Southerners could take it? How many would dare to do so? Nevertheless, some security for loyalty was needed, and the proposal that blacks vote offered to provide some of it. Here was another area where compromise between Lincoln and the legislators might have been compelled by circumstances.[21]

The situation was fluid and called for serious and careful thought about which direction Lincoln would take. By 11 April, in responses to serenades the day before, the president signaled that he had reached a decision. He was calculating the public impact of his words. But by going public he was doing several things. He was informing the nation where he stood, yet more important, he was opening negotiations in an arena that gave his opponents an advantage. He was listing his "demands" in a way that would make retreat difficult, and the stance he took bespoke flexibility and concession toward more advanced positions. He announced that he wanted to avoid irreconcilable theoretical debates. The question of the actual status of the seceded states in constitutional law, whether they were in or out of the Union, he had "*purposefully* forborne any public expression upon"; such theoretical discussion could serve only to divide the Republican party and its supporters. He wanted to focus on getting the states back "safely at home"; then people could speculate on what kind of place they had come from. The president also conceded that people were troubled by the limitations of the process in Louisiana. Too few people seemed to be represented by the new government; only twelve thousand people made up the constituency. Yet these people had sworn their allegiance to the Union, adopted a constitution that outlawed slavery, set up schools for both races, and were able to confer the vote on blacks. His preference was to give the vote to "the very intelligent [blacks] and . . . those who serve our cause as soldiers." But the government was committed to Union, to emancipation, to "nearly all the things the nation wants." Accepting this government and its accomplishments would encourage men in Louisiana to argue for it, build on it, and "ripen it to complete success." Blacks had gained steps toward the franchise that brought them closer than they had ever been. Could they come as close under another plan, one that had to begin again? It was a rhetorical question, but it also offered the chance for Congress to offer an option.[22]

Lincoln was reaching for grounds for agreement. He pointed out that no congressman had objected to his December 1863 proposal. Every cabinet member but one had agreed with the plan he had submitted and that one (everyone knew it was Chase though Lincoln did not name him) had asked that the president drop his suggestion that freedmen be apprenticed as a stage in their freedom. Chase had also asked that Lincoln expand his Emancipation Proclamation to include areas of Louisiana as well as of Virginia that had been excepted in January 1863. The president publicly noted that the new Louisiana constitution applied emancipation everywhere in the state and that no mention was made of apprenticeship.[23]

Conceding the continuing opposition in Congress to his plan he noted again that Congress controlled who would join its membership. Although he continued to argue for a government that sought readmission under his plan, he publicly announced his flexibility. "As bad promises are better broken than kept, I shall treat this as a bad promise, and break it, whenever I shall be convinced that keeping it is adverse to the public interest." He also reiterated his December statement that his was not the only acceptable plan and noted that other states had such varied conditions that the Louisiana proposal offered only general guidelines. "No exclusive and inflexible plan can safely be prescribed as to details and collatterals. . . . In the present 'situation' as the phrase goes, it may be my duty to make some new announcement."[24]

Lincoln put himself on record as willing to change and to negotiate without giving away negotiating strength. He provided a strong argument for accepting Louisiana's government and for overriding congressional objections to it. At the same time he had signaled the nation and Congress that new directions impended, and by stating his position publicly, he had offered congressional opponents the chance to get their way if they could successfully rebut his arguments.

Which way was Lincoln going? Congressional opponents insisted that they were the best defenders of freedmen's rights, that Lincoln was the conservative, hewing to the past by stopping short of full suffrage and by allowing whites of dubious loyalty to control the fate of undoubtedly loyal blacks. Sumner for one believed that Lincoln might move backward. But Chase was happy to see the president openly endorsing votes for some blacks, perhaps a sign that Lincoln was moving to the Left. In fact it was the first statement in the nation's history by a chief executive to endorse black voting; clearly, the president needed to compromise only with the position staked out by his congressional opponents. Lincoln was sending signals about his new paths in many ways. He invited Sumner to stand on the balcony with him when he gave his speech. The senator demurred but Lincoln gave other signs. He sought the advice of men more radical than he was. He had asked Stanton to prepare an executive order to set up military governments in former Confederate states, and Stanton was known to be a proponent of expanded suffrage. His new attorney general James Speed agreed with Stanton, and the two men met with Lincoln the day after the speech, emerging from the meeting with the belief that the chief executive was going to be more aggressive in his reconstruction policy. The evidence is strong that Lincoln was moving closer to Congress, not away, closer to expanded rights for blacks and to greater protection of those rights.[25]

John Wilkes Booth's murder of Lincoln on Good Friday 1865 destroyed any chance of knowing how close. There remained in Congress a minority of men, about twenty-five in the House, fewer than ten in the Senate, who wanted a more radical solution than Lincoln had committed himself to. Thaddeus Stevens, James Ashley, George Julian in the House and Charles Sumner, Ben Wade, Zachariah Chandler in the Senate were working for full suffrage for the freedmen; for confiscation of the land of rebels, distributing it to the blacks whose toil had made the land productive; and for depriving former rebel leaders of citizenship. But the majority in Congress, the Republican majority with Lincoln as the party leader, had not yet moved that far. They were advocating emancipation everywhere; the Thirteenth Amendment, on its way to the states for ratification, ensured that. They had passed and the president had signed the Freedmen's Bureau bill. The measure created in the War Department a Bureau of Freedmen's Affairs led by a commissioner who was to "adjust and determine all questions concerning persons of African descent" and to make rules to provide for them. The freedmen would be allowed to rent for three years farm land that was abandoned or that had been sold to or confiscated by the federal government and might purchase "such title . . . as the United States can convey" after their three years of work.[26]

At this stage some of the majority were pushing for national civil rights for the freedmen, but that measure had not yet become law; black suffrage was only discussed. Lincoln had endorsed it in a limited way, fought for it in Louisiana but had settled for something less—the provision that allowed the state legislature, someday, to provide that vote. But the radical men were not in charge; they were reduced to hoping that, as Ben Butler put it, "the rebels will behave so outrageously as to awaken the Government and the North once more."[27]

Subsequently, former rebels, encouraged by Lincoln's successor, fulfilled Butler's hope. Governments established under Johnson's reconstruction policy did end slavery, repudiated the Confederate debt, and repealed ordinances of secession. But they gave blacks almost no equality before the law and reimposed labor regulations that mirrored slavery. A vast wave of unpunished violence against freedmen who "forgot their manners" showed how little the defeated South welcomed even the moderate measures that Lincoln had urged.[28]

The martyred president had tried to implement a policy that folded emancipation and the promise of suffrage for the educated and veteran blacks into the established political-constitutional order as much as possible. He had hoped that men like himself, politicians, lawyers, officeholders, would adopt the changes that war had made necessary. Lincoln perhaps believed that by sharing his experience with and commitment to the processes of the polity they might grow, as he had grown, to see how the process at its best represented ideals of equal justice and the rule of law. If they did not, as his last days had shown, he was ready to require that they try. Lincoln's reconstruction policies promised continuing evolution.

But in Louisiana that evolution was in peril. The best hope to maintain it lay in the hands of Banks, returning from Washington. He arrived 21 April, and a week later a huge meeting gathered to urge the ouster of Wells and his appointed mayor. Banks quickly had Kennedy removed from office and replaced him with Boston Brahmin Samuel Quincy, former colonel of a black infantry troop. A large meeting of 17 May endorsed Banks's action and heard speeches advocating black suffrage, disfranchisement of rebel officers, and division of lands to assist ordinary farmers and workers in becoming independent free laborers. Conservative feelings still were strong, however. Despite the rhetoric of equality, when resolutions were passed black suffrage was not clearly included, and little was said about dividing the land. Yet for all its abiding conservatism this pro-Banks assemblage represented freedmen's interests far better than the Wells-Kennedy forces had. Meanwhile, Wells and Kennedy set off to Washington to protest Banks's actions to the president. Lincoln would hardly have welcomed their visit.[29]

But the nation had a new president, and Andrew Johnson ignored warnings from Banks and other supporters of expanded equality. Johnson supported Wells and Kennedy, removed Banks from his position as commander, and pardoned former rebels in order to sustain the conservative momentum. Although he would later be challenged by men even more conservative than himself, Wells exulted that Banks's (and Lincoln's) days and reforms were over. He wrote his wife that "the South will never regret [Johnson] being President. . . . We shall not again be troubled with Yankee adventurism—Banks is the last and he is for ever killed off—this is as it should be with all wretches who would thake [sic] their arms and dance with negroes at their balls."[30]

In the struggle between the past and the future, conservatism and reform, ideals and institutions, the Louisiana tide had turned away from Lincoln's wartime direction even as the president himself sought a new policy. Lincoln had wanted to achieve the ideal of equal liberty under law by expanding freedom within the context of existing traditions. He tried to demonstrate that the existing polity could be rescued from slavery, not by waging a war of ideals against institutions, Union against liberty, but by proving that liberty and equality were linked to self-government and that government could act to expand as well as to ensure both. In an ideal republic perhaps that demonstration would have succeeded without contradictions, advancing without having to retreat and emerging without compromises.

But this was a great Civil War, fought to preserve the republic and the best of its institutions. First, it had to be won or there would be no ideal republic, no demonstration that popular government was strong enough to preserve itself, no destruction of slavery, the foundation of disunion and war. Thus throughout the war Lincoln worked to sustain the army and to enlist Southern supporters, predominantly white Southern supporters at first and then hesitantly, hoping for a biracial coalition, blacks. But with peace at hand he was beginning to understand how potentially volatile such a coalition might be. Pressures grew to retreat from advances made in the war. Andrew Johnson would succumb to them, but Abraham Lincoln made a different choice. Having worked to save the Union he was prepared to advance the ideals that it had been established to preserve, ideals that applied now to blacks as well as to whites. A government of the people was prepared by war to confirm and then to elaborate in the future the proposition that all men are created equal.

Great crowds began to gather in front of the White House, and loud calls were made for the President. The band stopped playing, and as he advanced to the centre window over the door to make his address, I looked out, and never saw such a mass of heads before. It was like a black, gently swelling sea. The swaying motion of the crowd, in the dim uncertain light, was like the rising and falling of billows—like the ebb and flow of the tide. . . . Close to the house the faces were plainly discernible, but they faded into more ghostly outlines on the outskirts of the assembly; and what added to the weird, spectral beauty of the scene, was the confused hum of voices that rose above the sea of forms. . . . It was a grand and imposing scene. . . . The moment the President appeared at the window, he was greeted with a storm of applause . . . a lamp was brought, and little Tad at once rushed to his father's side, exclaiming: "Let me hold the light, Papa! let me hold the light!"

Mrs. Lincoln directed that the wish of her son be gratified, and the lamp was transferred to his hands. The father and son standing there in the presence of thousands of free citizens, the one lost in a chain of eloquent ideas, the other looking up into the speaking face with a proud, manly look, formed a beautiful and striking tableau.

—Elizabeth Keckley, *Behind the Scenes or Thirty Years
a Slave and Four Years in the White House*, 1865

16

★ ★ ★ ★ ★

CONCLUSION

The Lincoln presidency did not end through the operation of the political-constitutional system. There was no joyous ritual, no abiding process that had gone on for generations. It was the first assassination of a president in history. A single bullet erased the decision by the people of the Union that Abraham Lincoln should be their president. It was stunning, an awful repudiation of the system that helped define them as a people, that they had been fighting for over the last four years, that had cost them such blood and treasure.

Yet the process endured. Reacting to the murder of the president newspapers throughout the country spoke of the need to "let law and order resume their sway," as the *San Francisco Chronicle* noted. "The law must reign supreme," the *Philadelphia Evening Bulletin* declared, "or in this great crisis chaos will overwhelm us, and our own maddening feeling bring upon us national wreck and ruin which traitor arms have failed to accomplish." More specifically there was admiration and recognition for a system that could overcome even assassination. "When Andrew Johnson was sworn in as President," the Reverend Joseph Thompson told a New York audience, "the Statue of Liberty that surmounts the dome of the Capitol and was put there by Lincoln, looked down on the city and on the nation and said 'Our Government is unchanged—it has merely passed from the hands of one man into those of another.'"[1]

The words reflected part of a larger legacy. The Union was saved, and thus the political-constitutional process endured—the nation would change governments, settle controversies, and debate alternatives at the polls, in legislative halls, and in courtrooms, not on bloody battlefields. It would be a nation whose size and diversity gave it wealth and opportunities for its citizens and huge potential influence in the world. Future autocrats would have reason to fear that influence, just as future immigrants would be drawn to it. Its power would not always be used well. Native Americans who "obstructed" national mission, foreign governments deemed "un-American" had reason to fear and to protest against invasions of their rights and the destruction of their people. But within the nation itself, because of what it stood for and fought for and preserved, there remained a conscience that could be appealed to in the name of the ideals it symbolized and had demonstrated in its greatest war. Saving the Union had meant killing slavery.

Slavery was dead. Its power to divide the Union, to erode and destroy constitutional and political debate was over. No longer was the highest court in the land able to rule that under the Constitution black people had no rights that white people had to respect and that no political party legally could say otherwise. No longer could men, women, and children be bought and sold: treated as things without ties to each other, without the capacity to fulfill their own dreams. The Thirteenth Amendment, ending slavery throughout the nation and moving through the states toward ratification, ensured that. And in the van of that amendment came protection for civil rights and suffrage. Blacks were promised that they would enter the political arena and the constitutional system—this time as participants, not as objects.

This more perfect Union was achieved chiefly through an extraordinary outreach of national authority. Certainly Lincoln extended presidential power beyond any limits seen before his time—the war demanded that; Congress agreed, the Supreme Court acquiesced, and the people sustained his power. If one compares Lincoln's use of power with executive actions before 1861, popular and even scholarly use of a word such as "dictatorship" makes limited sense. Lincoln had produced, as Edwin S. Corwin observes, "a complete transformation in the President's role as Commander in Chief." Yet war was about the expansion of power, and Congress also stepped forward, expanding national power, extending its authority. Even state governments reached further than precedent admitted, increasing expenditures, strengthening their police powers over health, morals, and safety, and establishing new regulatory agencies to shape the economy.[2]

After the war public pressures demanded a return to peacetime boundaries. Executive authority in most areas, once the fight between Johnson and Congress was settled, rapidly contracted. A few outbursts of presidential influence showed that the White House was still occupied. Grant fought senators bitterly over the Santo Domingo Treaty and presided over an effective Treaty of Washington, which resolved claims against the British for building rebel raiders. Hayes sent federal troops to settle labor protests and worked for civil service reforms. Garfield, Arthur, and Harrison also kept busy; Cleveland's vetoes showed signs of vigor. Generally, however, the presidency declined in power. With the exception of Grant a series of one-term presidents did little to inspire demands that they stay in office. For the rest of the century no president came within miles of Lincoln's power or even close to Polk or Jackson, for that matter. By 1886 Woodrow Wilson was able to write that national government in the United States was "congressional government." M. Ostrogorsky, telling foreign audiences about America, described a lawmaking environment in which "after the [civil] war the eclipse of the executive was complete and definitive"; Lord Bryce told British and American audiences in 1894 that "the domestic authority of the President is in time of peace small." These late-nineteenth-century images may have inspired Theodore Lowi to assert in 1992 that "by 1875 you would not know there had been a war or a Lincoln."[3]

But Lord Bryce had added a caveat about the president's domestic authority: In time of war, "especially in a civil war, it expands with portentous speed." Clearly it had been thus with Lincoln. Despite calls to retreat from the vast domains of Civil War there is a sense in which Lincoln's legacy of power in the presidency survived the retreat. Certainly presidential authority, like the national authority with which it was connected, diminished when the war was over. But national power was still available after Appomattox and for the fundamental purpose that had called it forth originally: to destroy slavery and its vestiges. The fight between Congress and Lincoln's successor has obscured the fact that congressional Republicans were acting in the same cause for which Lincoln had acted. They were not recapturing power lost to the president; they were claiming power that they had shared increasingly with Lincoln.

Before Lincoln died many of the more radical Republicans had been attacking him for moving too slowly toward emancipation and then for yielding too much to military necessity and Southern loyalists. After early statements of satisfaction with Johnson they quickly came to their senses as Johnson proved not only to be slower than Lincoln to march to their goals but also to be a bitter racist obstructionist. Thus they fought against Johnson and for goals that Lincoln had espoused and had used his power to try to achieve: civil rights, education, suffrage for the freedmen. The army, which had been the major instrument of Lincoln's expanding egalitarianism and which looked to its commander in chief for direction, shifted its allegiance to Congress. Soldiers such as Grant, whom Lincoln had charged with leading the army to save the Union, did not think it incongruous to support Congress in its battle to preserve the gains of war. And when legislators moved to weaken executive power over the army with the Tenure of Office and the Command of the Army acts, they were trying to save Lincoln's legacy by weakening Johnson.[4]

Although President Grant retreated on other issues, he tried to protect former slaves from white Southerners' efforts to restore as much of the prewar South as they could. Grant sent troops into Louisiana, Mississippi, North Carolina, and South Carolina to effect the Force Acts and to destroy the Ku Klux Klan. A vocal element in the Republican party continued to push for federal intervention in the South in the form of national civil rights and suffrage-enforcement laws well into the 1890s. Despite retreating from the broadest definitions of federal power when it interpreted the Civil War amendments, the Supreme Court struck down laws that kept blacks off juries, and that denied Chinese Americans equal chances to work, and it upheld federal power to protect blacks from political violence. The Justice Department prosecuted thousands of election officers under this power. Local juries usually acquitted their white neighbors, but the national prohibition remained. Because of the Lincoln presidency the constitutional system carried promises of equality, and the processes to bring those promises to life endured. One hundred years after Lincoln had been awakened by the Kansas Nebraska Act to the dangers of slavery to the constitutional system, blacks and whites would see the United States Supreme Court strike down inequality in that system (that case would, interestingly enough, also involve Kansas).[5]

Not every element, even in that reformed constitutional system, promised equal justice. The Union that Lincoln and his forces had saved remained a Union of states. Lincoln's respect for those states, demonstrated in his commitment to reconstruct them rather than to allow Congress to govern territories and in his insistence that only a constitutional amendment, ratified by states, would secure slavery's death, strengthened later arguments that states should control the fate of their citizens, old and new. Lincoln's abiding insistence that the Constitution guided his actions meant that black equality could be hindered or denied by constitutional claims of states' rights and local self-government. Brutal racism could find shelter in such legal arguments.[6]

Yet the triumph and the irony of his administration resided in Lincoln's commitment to the Constitution; without that there would have been no promises to keep to 4 million black Americans. Because so many Americans cherished the Union that the Constitution forged, they made war on slave masters and their friends, on a government that Alexander Stephens claimed rested "on the great truth that the negro is not the equal of the white man; that slavery . . . is his natural and normal condition."

Without the president's devotion to and mastery of the political-constitutional institutions of his time, in all probability the Union would have lacked the capacity to focus its will and its resources on defeating that Confederacy. Without Lincoln's unmatched ability to integrate egalitarian ends and constitutional means he could not have enlisted the range of supporters and soldiers necessary for victory. His great accomplishment was to energize and mobilize the nation by affirming its better angels, by showing the nation at its best: engaged in the imperative, life-preserving conversation between structure and purpose, ideal and institution, means and ends.

NOTES

PREFACE

1. Dudley Taylor Cornish, *The Sable Arm: Black Troops in the Union Army, 1861–1865* (Lawrence: University Press of Kansas, 1987), pp. 262, 265, 288.

2. I define the political-constitutional system as the structure of rights and powers that the Constitution establishes, the ideals underlying the Declaration of Independence, and the discussion and debate over them that defines and redefines their meaning and relationship.

3. Richard Neustadt, *Presidential Power and the Modern Presidents: The Politics of Leadership from Roosevelt to Reagan* (New York: Free Press, 1990), p. 11, chap. 3.

4. As quoted in Thomas Brown, *Politics and Statesmanship: Essays on the American Whig Party* (New York: Columbia University Press, 1985), pp. 10–11. On the politics of the era generally, see Robert Kelley, *The Cultural Pattern in American Politics: the First Century* (New York: Knopf, 1979). On the Whigs, see Daniel Walker Howe, *The Political Culture of the American Whigs* (Chicago: University of Chicago Press, 1979), and Rush Welter, *The Mind of America, 1820–1860* (New York: Columbia University Press, 1975), pp. 190–218. Writing after the Lincoln-Douglas debates, the pro-Republican *Illinois Journal* observed that Lincoln's speeches "are stamped with the impress of a sincerity and candor which appeals at once to the higher and noble faculties of the mind, and wins over the better feelings and affections of our nature. . . . They, in effect, are in advance of the age . . . and thus contain those elements which . . . [carry] them beyond the present and makes them useful and beautiful in the future" (14 Nov. 1858, p. 1).

CHAPTER 1
THE STATE OF THE UNION: 1860

1. See Theodore H. White, *The Making of the President, 1960* (New York: New American Library, 1960), p. 1, for a brilliant evocation of the meaning and the feel of an American election. Jean Baker, *Affairs of Party: The Political Culture of Northern Democrats in the Mid-Nineteenth Century* (Ithaca, N.Y.: Cornell University Press, 1983), describes voting. Eric Foner, *Free Soil, Free Labor, Free Men: The Ideology of the Republican Party before the Civil War* (New York: Oxford University Press, 1970), describes the Republican vision.

2. Phillip Shaw Paludan, *A Covenant with Death: The Constitution, Law and Equality in the Civil War Era* (Urbana: University of Illinois Press, 1975); Russell B. Nye, *Fettered Freedom: Civil Liberties and the Slavery Controversy* (Lansing: Michigan State University Press, 1963); William Gienapp, *The Origins of the Republican Party, 1852–1856* (New York: Oxford University Press, 1987), pp. 300–303.

3. W. Dean Burnham, *Presidential Ballots, 1836–1892* (Baltimore: Johns Hopkins University Press, 1955), pp. 236–43.

4. Howard Cecil Perkins, ed., *Northern Editorials on Secession*, 2 vols. (New York: Appleton Century Crofts, 1964), 1: 158–237, 510–13, 520–24; G. Fisher Sidney, "Legalized Secession," *Philadelphia North American*, 31 Dec. 1860; Harold M. Hyman, *"A More Perfect Union": The Impact of the Civil War and Reconstruction on the Constitution* (New York: Knopf, 1973), chaps. 3, 4, and 8.

5. *The United States on the Eve of the Civil War as Described in the 1860 Census* (Washington, D.C.: U.S. Civil War Centennial Commission, 1963), pp. 1–2; *Statistical History of the United States from Colonial Times to the Present* (Stamford, Conn.: Fairfield, 1965), pp. 62–63.

6. Kenneth Stampp, *The Peculiar Institution* (New York: Vintage Books, 1956), pp. 220 et passim; James Oakes, *Slavery and Freedom* (New York: Knopf, 1990); Orlando Patterson, *Slavery and Social Death: A Comparative Study* (Cambridge, Mass.: Harvard University Press, 1982).

7. *United States on the Eve of the Civil War*, pp. 22–37, 67; *Statistical History of the United States*, p. 547; George Rogers Taylor, *The Transportation Revolution, 1815–1860* (New York: Holt, Rinehart and Winston, 1951), pp. 185–86.

8. Roy P. Basler, ed., *The Collected Works of Abraham Lincoln*, 8 vols. (New Brunswick, N.J.: Rutgers University Press, 1953), 3: 471–82, 3: 48–50 (hereafter *Collected Works*).

9. Ibid., p. 58.

10. See Richard Franklin Bensel, *Yankee Leviathan: The Origins of Central State Authority in America, 1859–1877* (Cambridge: Cambridge University Press, 1990), pp. 60–64, 78–85, for discussion of Northern economic reasons for contesting secession. Charles Warren, *Bankruptcy in United States History* (Cambridge, Mass.: Harvard University Press, 1935), p. 97.

11. See discussion in Phillip Shaw Paludan, *"A People's Contest": The Union and Civil War, 1861–1865* (New York: Harper & Row, 1988), Prologue and sources cited there.

12. Harold Hyman and William Wiecek, *Equal Justice under Law: Constitu-*

tional Development, 1835–1875 (New York: Harper & Row, 1982), pp. 192–99; Paul Finkleman, *An Imperfect Union: Slavery, Federalism and Comity* (Chapel Hill: University of North Carolina Press, 1981); Don E. Fehrenbacher, *The Dred Scott Case: Its Significance in American Law and Politics* (New York: Oxford University Press, 1978) pp. 444–45; James McPherson, *Battle Cry of Freedom* (New York: Oxford University Press, 1988), pp. 179–80. These works agree that a decision against Northern state antislavery laws was possible. For the argument against that position, see Phillip S. Paludan, "Lincoln and the Rhetoric of Politics," in Lloyd Ambrosius, ed., *A Crisis of Republicanism: American Politics during the Civil War Era* (Lincoln: University of Nebraska Press, 1990), p. 92, n. 23.

13. "Declaration of the Immediate Causes Which Induce and Justify the Secession of South Carolina from the Federal Union," as quoted in Robert Johannsen, ed., *Democracy on Trial* (Urbana: University of Illinois Press, 1988), pp. 156–58.

14. Henry Flanders, "British Strictures on Republican Institutions," *North American Review* (July 1859): 104–9; Phillip S. Paludan, "The American Civil War Considered as a Crisis in Law and Order," *American Historical Review* 77 (Oct. 1972): 1013–34.

15. Michael Holt, "The Politics of Impatience: The Origins of Know Nothingism," *Journal of American History* 60 (Sept. 1973): 323–31; Ronald G. Walters, *American Reformers: 1815–1860* (New York: Hill and Wang, 1978), pp. 3–11; David Brion Davis, *The Slave Power Conspiracy and the Paranoid Style* (Baton Rouge: Louisiana State University Press, 1970); Tyler Anbinder, *Nativism and Slavery: The Northern Know Nothings and the Politics of the 1850s* (New York: Oxford University Press, 1992), pp. 268–69; Ray Allen Billington, *The Protestant Crusade, 1800–1860* (Chicago: Quadrangle, 1964), pp. 262–88. Anbinder doubts that anxieties of the prewar period were primarily responsible for the rise of Know Nothingism but does not argue the point persuasively.

16. David Potter, *The Impending Crisis, 1848–1861* (New York: Harper & Row, 1976), chap. 26; Gienapp, *Origins of the Republican Party*. I rely extensively on these works for my discussion of prewar politics.

17. *Collected Works*, 1: 108–15.

18. Ibid., 271–79; Stephen B. Oates, *With Malice toward None: The Life of Abraham Lincoln* (New York: Mentor, 1978), pp. 13, 75, 77.

19. *Collected Works*, 1: 74, 126, 260; 2: 3, 5, 7–9, 11, 14, 121–30, 136, 156.

20. Ibid., 3: 242–43, 7 Oct. 1858. Taney, quoted from *Dred Scott* opinion in Stanley Kutler, ed., *The Dred Scott Decision: Law or Politics* (Boston: Houghton Mifflin, 1967), p. 15.

21. Lewis Perry, *Radical Abolitionism: Anarchy and the Government of God in Antislavery Thought* (Ithaca, N.Y.: Cornell University Press, 1973).

22. For antislavery constitutionalism before 1846 see William Wiecek, *The Sources of Antislavery Constitutionalism, 1760–1848* (Ithaca, N.Y.: Cornell University Press, 1977). Foner, *Free Soil*, pp. 73–102, describes the range of Republican interest in reconciling constitutional history with antislavery politics.

23. *Collected Works*, vol. 2, 16 Oct. 1854.

24. Ibid., 2: 222, 1 July 1854?, 4: 24, 6 Mar. 1860, 4: 438, 4 July 1861; Rich-

ard Hofstadter, "Lincoln and the Self Made Myth," in *The American Political Tradition and the Men Who Made It* (New York: Knopf, 1948), pp. 92–134; Foner, *Free Soil*; Gienapp, *Origins of the Republican Party*; Gabor Boritt, *Lincoln and the Economics of the American Dream* (Memphis: Memphis State University, 1978).

25. For one of several either/or conceptions of Lincoln's views, see Mark Neely, Jr., *Abraham Lincoln Encyclopedia* (New York: McGraw-Hill, 1982), p. 70. See bibliographical essay for discussion of historians' confusion over Lincoln's relation to the Declaration and the Constitution.

26. *Collected Works*, 3: 400–403.

27. Ibid., 2: 406, 26 June 1857.

28. Ibid., 3: 18, 21 Aug. 1858.

CHAPTER 2
ASSEMBLING THE CAST

1. Allan Nevins, *The Emergence of Lincoln*, 2 vols. (New York: Charles Scribner's Sons, 1950), 2: 457–58; Philip Klein, *President James Buchanan* (University Park: Pennsylvania State University Press, 1962), p. 402; *New York Times*, 4 Mar. 1861; *New York Herald* 5–6 Mar. 1861; *New York Tribune*, 5–6 Mar. 1861; Elbert B. Smith, *The Presidency of James Buchanan* (Lawrence: University Press of Kansas, 1975), pp. 190–92.

2. Mark W. Summers, *The Plundering Generation: Corruption and the Crisis of the Union, 1849–1861* (New York: Oxford University Press, 1987), pp. 239–60.

3. Smith, *Presidency of Buchanan*, p. 151; David Potter, *The Impending Crisis, 1848–1861* (New York: Harper & Row, 1976), pp. 519–21.

4. Howard Cecil Perkins, ed., *Northern Editorials on Secession*, 2 vols. (New York: Appleton Century Crofts, 1964), 1: 126, 136, 147, 152; Kenneth Stampp, *And the War Came: The North and the Secession Crisis, 1860–61* (Chicago: University of Chicago Press, 1964), pp. 61, 73, 177, 220–22.

5. James McPherson, "The Hedgehog and the Foxes," in *Abraham Lincoln and the Second American Revolution* (New York: Oxford University Press, 1990), pp. 114–15; Richard Current, *The Lincoln Nobody Knows* (New York: Hill and Wang, 1958), pp. 9–11.

6. On Lincoln's preparation, see Harold M. Hyman, *"A More Perfect Union": The Impact of the Civil War and Reconstruction on the Constitution* (New York: Knopf, 1973). "Lincoln had been the man-to-see-in-Springfield when one wished something done or not done in Illinois. Events proved that he was able to transfer eastward the experience gained from midwestern politicking. He understood power, loved politics, and comprehended the need to exert the latter to employ the former" (p. 58).

7. For a similar point about Lincoln's character, see Jacques Barzun, "Lincoln's Philosophic Vision," Fortenbaugh Memorial Lecture, Gettysburg College, 1982, pp. 18–19; William H. Herndon and Jesse W. Weik, *Abraham Lincoln: The True Story of a Great Life* (New York: D. Appleton, 1920), pp. 226–27.

8. *Collected Works*, 3: 511–12; 5: 479; 6: 326–27; James G. Randall, *Lincoln the*

President, 4 vols. (New York: Dodd, Mead, 1945-1954), 1: 4; John Nicolay and John Hay, *Abraham Lincoln; A History*, 10 vols. (New York: Century, 1890), 4: 468-69; Hans J. Morgenthau and David Hein, *Essays on Lincoln's Faith and Politics* (Lanham, Md.: University Press of America, 1983), pp. 29-38.

9. I follow Richard Current's exposition of Lincoln's fatalism in *Lincoln Nobody Knows*, pp. 71-75; *Collected Works*, 2: 255.

10. Nicolay and Hay, *Lincoln*, 9: 340. John Hay wrote of Montgomery Blair, "What have injured him are his violent personal antagonisms and indiscretions," in Tyler Dennett, ed., *Lincoln and the Civil War in the Diaries and Letters of John Hay* (New York: Dodd, Mead, 1939), pp. 219-20, 239.

11. Stampp, *And the War Came*, p. 182.

12. *Collected Works*, 1: 113-14, 501-3 ; Lawrence Frederick Kohl, *The Politics of Individualism: Parties and the American Character in the Jacksonian Era* (New York: Oxford University Press, 1989), pp. 157-63; Rush Welter, *The Mind of America, 1820-1860* (New York: Columbia University Press, 1975), 192-95; Major Wilson, "Lincoln and Van Buren in the Steps of the Fathers: Another Look at the Lyceum Address," *Civil War History* 29 (Sept. 1983): 197-211.

13. *Tribune Almanac for 1861* (New York: Tribune Assoc., 1861-1865), pp. 16-17.

14. These are rounded figures that include Virginia, North Carolina, Tennessee, and Arkansas along with Maryland, Delaware, Kentucky, and Missouri within a projected confederacy.

15. David Herbert Donald, *Charles Sumner and the Coming of the Civil War* (Chicago: University of Chicago Press, 1960), pp. 365-68; James McPherson, *The Struggle for Equality* (Princeton, N.J.: Princeton University Press, 1964), pp. 33-38; Stampp, *And the War Came*, pp. 208-12.

16. Nevins, *Emergence of Lincoln*, 2: 338-39; W. C. Harris, ed., *Zachariah Chandler: An Outline Sketch of His Life and Public Services* (Detroit: Post and Tribune Co., 1880), pp. 192-93; Kenneth Stampp, "Lincoln and the Secession Crisis," in *The Imperiled Union: Essays on the Background of the Civil War* (New York: Oxford University Press, 1980), p. 181. On Republican campaign rhetoric, see Ronald Formisano, *The Birth of Mass Political Parties: Michigan, 1827-1861* (Princeton, N.J.: Princeton University Press, 1971), pp. 266-70.

17. *Collected Works*, 4: 128.

18. Nicolay and Hay, *Lincoln*, 3: 254; David Potter, *Lincoln and His Party in the Secession Crisis* (New Haven, Conn.: Yale University Press, 1962), p. 139.

19. *Collected Works*, 4: 135, 29 Oct. 1860, 4: 138, 10 Nov. 1860.

20. Ibid., pp. 151-53, 15 Dec. 1860.

21. Lincoln to James T. Hale, 11 Jan. 1861, *Collected Works*, 4: 172.

22. Ibid., pp. 134-62. Robert W. Johannsen, *Lincoln, the South and Slavery: The Political Dimension* (Baton Rouge: Louisiana State University Press, 1991), calls Lincoln's words here "half hearted" (pp. 120-21).

23. I follow Potter, *Impending Crisis*, pp. 525-54, on the compromise measures in Congress.

24. Glyndon Van Deusen, *William Henry Seward* (New York: Oxford University Press, 1967), pp. 247, 242-49; Edward McPherson, *The Political History of the United States of America, during the Great Rebellion* (Washington, D.C.: Philp

and Solomons, 1865), pp. 52–66; James McPherson, *Battle Cry of Freedom* (New York: Oxford University Press, 1988), pp. 252–57; Potter, *Impending Crisis*, pp. 529–35.

25. Potter, *Impending Crisis*, pp. 533–34; Martin Duberman, *Charles Francis Adams, 1807–1886* (Stanford, Calif.: Stanford University Press, 1968), pp. 231–36.

26. *Collected Works*, 4: 149–51, 154, 155, 172, 183.

27. *Collected Works*, 4: 152, 160, 168–69, ca. Jan. 1861.

28. Potter, *Impending Crisis*, pp. 550–52.

29. "The Question of the Hour," *Atlantic Monthly* 7 (Jan. 1861): 120–21; Stampp, *And the War Came*, pp. 141–53.

30. James McPherson, *Battle Cry of Freedom*, pp. 254–57; Edward McPherson, *Political History of the Great Rebellion*, p. 37.

31. See James McPherson, *Abraham Lincoln and the Second American Revolution*, pp. 30–31. Lord Charnwood, *Abraham Lincoln* (New York: Garden City Publishers, 1917), and Harry Jaffa, *Crisis of the House Divided: An Interpretation of the Issues in the Lincoln Douglas Debates* (Chicago: University of Chicago Press, 1959), pp. 408–9, note that Lincoln's election was a danger to slavery and suggest that peace as well as war would have freed the slaves.

32. See Johannsen, *Lincoln, the South*, pp. 121–22 for Southern fears of Lincoln's election.

33. Harry Carman and Reinhard Luthin, *Lincoln and the Patronage* (New York: Columbia University Press, 1943), is the standard on all aspects of the patronage under Lincoln but lacks a context that links patronage to other elements of politics and self-government in the mid-nineteenth century. For the passion of the culture for its politics, see William Gienapp, "Politics Seems to Enter into Everything," in Stephen Maizlish, ed., *Essays on American Antebellum Politics, 1840–1860* (College Station: Texas A & M University Press, 1982); Walter Dean Burnham, "The Changing Shape of the American Political Universe," *American Political Science Review* 59 (1965): 7–28; and Jean Baker, *Affairs of Party: The Political Culture of Northern Democrats in the Mid-Nineteenth Century* (Ithaca, N.Y.: Cornell University Press, 1983).

34. Phillip S. Paludan, "The American Civil War Considered as a Crisis in Law and Order," *American Historical Review* 77 (Oct. 1972): 1013–34; Carman and Luthin, *Lincoln and the Patronage*, pp. 110–29.

35. Paul Van Riper and Keith A. Sutherland, "The Northern Civil Service: 1861–1865," *Civil War History* 11 (Dec. 1965): 351–69. Montgomery Meigs estimated that "at least one fifth of the able bodied men of the North were enlisted or employed in the immediate service of the army, and . . . another fifth were employed in furnishing them with material and subsistence" (pp. 362–63). See also Mark Neely, Jr., *Abraham Lincoln Encyclopedia* (New York: McGraw-Hill, 1982), pp. 232–34.

36. See Lincoln to Gov. William Sprague (R.I.), 10 May 1861, *New York Tribune*, 13 Mar. 1861, as quoted in Carman and Luthin, *Lincoln and the Patronage*, pp. 70–71. For linkage between legislators and executive appointments, see also Leonard White, *The Jacksonians: A Study in Administrative History, 1829–1861* (New York: Free Press, 1954), pp. 104–23. In 1848 Congressman Abraham Lin-

coln wrote the secretary of the treasury to complain about not being consulted over local appointments within Illinois and about appointments of Illinois citizens to posts elsewhere (*Collected Works*, 2: 32).

37. Kenneth Stampp, *America in 1857: A Nation on the Brink* (New York: Oxford University Press, 1990), pp. 60–63.

38. Van Deusen, *Seward*, p. 336.

39. "Speech at Yates County, Oct. 29, 1844," Baker, ed., *Works of Seward*, 3: 270, as quoted in Major Wilson, *Space, Time and Freedom: The Quest for Nationality and the Irrepressible Conflict* (Westport, Conn.: Greenwood, 1974), p. 215.

40. These paragraphs rely on ibid., chap. 9, and on Van Deusen, *Seward*, chap. 14.

41. William H. Freehling, *Road to Disunion:* vol. 1, *Secessionists at Bay* (New York: Oxford University Press, 1990), pp. 360–63; Frederick Blue, *Salmon P. Chase: A Life in Politics* (Kent, Ohio: Kent State University Press, 1987), pp. 42–43. Chase reluctantly supported Harrison in 1840, believing that the Whigs could be pushed toward antislavery ideas. But as soon as Tyler ascended to the office, Chase began his commitment to political antislavery.

42. Blue, *Chase*, p. 32.

43. Jacob Schuckers, *The Life and Public Services of Salmon Portland Chase* (New York: Appleton, 1874), p. 48; Eric Foner, *Free Soil, Free Labor, Free Men: The Ideology of the Republican Party before the Civil War* (New York: Oxford University Press, 1970), p. 76.

44. Foner, *Free Soil*, p. 77.

45. Blue, *Chase*, p. 236; David Donald, ed., *Inside Lincoln's Cabinet: The Civil War Diaries of Salmon P. Chase* (New York: Longman's, Green, 1954), p. 6.

46. Blue, *Chase*, pp. 211–12.

47. Burton J. Hendrick, *Lincoln's War Cabinet* (Boston: Little, Brown, 1946), pp. 65–70.

48. Hendrick, *Lincoln's War Cabinet*, pp. 59–60, alleges that a deal for Indiana votes in Chicago secured Interior for Smith. Willard King, *Lincoln's Manager: David Davis* (Cambridge, Mass.: Harvard University Press, 1960), effectively challenges that allegation. See Lincoln to Colfax, 8 Mar. 1861, *Collected Works* 4: 278, for suggestion of Lincoln's personal interest in Smith.

49. Hendrick, *Lincoln's War Cabinet*, pp. 43–50; Nevins, *Emergence of Lincoln*, 2: 234–60; Marvin Cain, *Lincoln's Attorney General: Edward Bates of Missouri* (Columbia: University of Missouri Press, 1965).

50. Hendrick, *Lincoln's War Cabinet*, pp. 71–78; John Niven, *Gideon Welles: Lincoln's Secretary of the Navy* (New York: Oxford University Press, 1973), pp. 303–23. On Weed in New York, see Summers, *Plundering Generation*, pp. 261–80.

51. Hendrick, *Lincoln's War Cabinet*, pp. 51–52.

52. King, *Lincoln's Manager*, pp. 162–68; Van Deusen, *Seward*, pp. 249–50; Erwin Stanley Bradley, *Simon Cameron: Lincoln's Secretary of War* (Philadelphia: University of Pennsylvania Press, 1966), pp. 163–74; Lincoln to Cameron, 31 Dec. 1860, 3 Jan. 1861, 13 Jan. 1861, *Collected Works*, 4: 165–81.

53. Summers, *Plundering Generation*, pp. 267–70.

54. Nicolay and Hay, *Lincoln*, 3: 369.

55. Benjamin Thomas, *Abraham Lincoln* (New York: Knopf, 1952), pp. 232–35; Nevins, *Emergence of Lincoln*, 2: 439–46; Stephen B. Oates, *With Malice toward None: The Life of Abraham Lincoln* (New York: Mentor, 1978), pp. 212, 214–20, 231–34; Randall, *Lincoln the President*, 1: 256–72.

CHAPTER 3
TO SUMTER

1. *Collected Works*, 4: 170, 3 Jan. 1861; Benjamin Thomas, *Abraham Lincoln* (New York: Knopf, 1952), pp. 231–32; Stephen B. Oates, *With Malice toward None: The Life of Abraham Lincoln* (New York: Mentor, 1978), pp. 211–25.

2. *Collected Works*, 4: 156–58; Glyndon Van Deusen, *William Henry Seward* (New York: Oxford University Press, 1967), pp. 240–41.

3. Van Deusen, *Seward*, pp. 245–46.

4. Quoted by David Potter, George Knoles, ed., in "Why the Republicans Rejected Both Compromise and Secession," *The Crisis of the Union: 1860–1861* (Baton Rouge: Louisiana State University Press, 1965), pp. 100–101.

5. David Potter, *The Impending Crisis, 1848–1861* (New York: Harper, 1976), p. 522, makes a similar point about the differences between 1860–61 and previous compromises.

6. *Collected Works*, 4: 215, 204–5, 194–96, 236–37.

7. Ibid., p. 240.

8. Ibid., pp. 262–71.

9. Howard Cecil Perkins, ed., *Northern Editorials on Secession*, 2 vols. (New York: Appleton Century Crofts, 1964), 2: 607–46.

10. Ibid., 2: 628–35.

11. Thomas calls Lincoln's inaugural "as indulgent as he could make it without renouncing his constitutional duties" (*Lincoln*, p. 247). Very helpful on Lincoln's first days in office is Don Fehrenbacher, "Lincoln's Wartime Leadership: The First Hundred Days," *Journal of the Abraham Lincoln Association* 9 (1987): 1–18.

12. On the Fort Sumter crisis I follow Potter, *Impending Crisis*, Chap. 20, though with greater emphasis on the border states. James McPherson, *Battle Cry of Freedom* (New York: Oxford University Press, 1988), p. 272, n. 78, summarizes the major historiographical perspectives on approaches Lincoln sought in the situation.

13. George Rogers Taylor, *The Transportation Revolution* (New York: Sharpe, 1977), p. 443, and David Donald, *Liberty and Union* (Lexington, Mass.: D. C. Heath, 1978), p. 5, provide data on travel time and distance.

14. Robert V. Bruce, "The Shadow of a Coming War," Twenty-eighth Annual Fortenbaugh Memorial Lecture, Gettysburg College, 1989. David Potter, *Lincoln and His Party in the Secession Crisis* (New Haven, Conn.: Yale University Press, 1962), emphasizes the extent to which Lincoln overvalued Southern unionism.

15. See *Collected Works*, 4: 159, 160, 164, for letters on the forts, and 4: 197–

201, for his appeals to Kentuckians. For similar views on Southern unionism, see Martin Duberman, *James Russell Lowell* (Boston: Beacon Press, 1966), pp. 202–3, and Glyndon Van Deusen, *Horace Greeley: Nineteenth Century Crusader* (Philadelphia: University of Pennsylvania Press, 1953), pp. 261–63.

16. The comparative importance of the two forts in the public mind may be seen in the fact that Perkins, *Northern Editorials on Secession*, lists five editorials that mention Pickens and provides eighty-four references to Sumter.

17. Howard K. Beale, ed., *Diary of Gideon Welles: Secretary of the Navy under Lincoln and Johnson*, 3 vols. (New York: Norton, 1960), 1: 11–12; Van Deusen, *Seward*, pp. 275–79.

18. *Collected Works*, 4: 254, 265–66.

19. Van Deusen, *Seward*, pp. 250–54, and John Nicolay and John Hay, *Abraham Lincoln: A History*, 10 vols. (New York: Century, 1890), 3: 368–72. Neither of these sources suggests that Seward's decision was affected by Lincoln's inaugural address, but the conjunction between the resignation and the speech raises the possibility.

20. *Collected Works*, 4: 249n.

21. The chronology of E. B. Long, *The Civil War Day by Day* (Garden City, N.Y.: Doubleday, 1971) is indispensable for the thirty-eight days between Lincoln's inauguration and the firing on Sumter.

22. *Collected Works*, 4: 279–80, 9 Mar. 1861.

23. *Collected Works*, 4: 284–85; Burton J. Hendrick, *Lincoln's War Cabinet* (Boston: Little, Brown, 1946), pp. 162–65.

24. Newspapers quoted in Kenneth Stampp, "Lincoln and the Secession Crisis," in Stampp, *The Imperiled Union: Essays on the Background of the Civil War* (New York: Oxford University Press, 1980), pp. 181, 298; Adams quoted in Van Deusen, *Seward*, p. 281.

25. Van Deusen, *Seward*, pp. 281–83. William Henry Seward Papers, Reel 188, Document 6501, Rush-Rhees Library, Rochester, N.Y.

26. Nicolay and Hay, *Lincoln*, 3: 391.

27. Potter, *Lincoln and His Party*, pp. 360–63; Hendrick, *Lincoln's War Cabinet*, p. 170.

28. Hendrick, *Lincoln's War Cabinet*, pp. 170–72; William Ernest Smith, *The Francis Preston Blair Family in Politics*, 2 vols. (New York: Macmillan, 1933), pp. 9–10; Welles, *Diary*, 1: 13–14.

29. Thomas, *Lincoln*, p. 540, citing George Plumer Smith to John Hay, 9 Jan. 1863; John Hay to Smith, 10 Jan. 1863, Lincoln papers, 97 reels, Robert Todd Lincoln Collection, Library of Congress.

30. *Collected Works*, 3: 321, 424–25. Compare Stampp, *Imperiled Union*, p. 179, and Potter, *Lincoln and His Party*, pp. 358–59.

31. *Collected Works*, 4: 324, 326; Long, *Civil War Day by Day*, p. 61.

32. Van Deusen, *Seward*, pp. 279–80; *Congressional Globe*, 36th Congress, 2d session, p. 1519.

33. Discussion of Lincoln's policy on Sumter too often depicts the South as a single entity—a flaw that William Freehling, *Road to Disunion*: vol. 1, *Secessionists at Bay* (New York: Oxford University Press, 1990), has done a great deal to

discredit. Lincoln's ongoing interest in Southern unionism and his attention to the pivotal role of the border states also suggest that the president knew of at least two Souths.

34. Perkins, ed., *Northern Editorials on Secession*, 2: 698–703.

35. *Collected Works*, 4: 350–51; Nicolay and Hay, *Lincoln*, 4: 44–63; Theodore Pease and James G. Randall, eds., *The Diary of Orville Hickman Browning*, 2 vols. (Springfield: Illinois Historical Society, 1925–33), 1: 475–76.

CHAPTER 4
CONGRESS ORGANIZES, LINCOLN ACTS

1. Allan Nevins, *War for the Union* (New York: Scribner's, 1959) 1: 79–81; William Brown, *Baltimore and the Nineteenth of April* (Baltimore, 1887); Gary Lawson Browne, *Baltimore in the Nation, 1789–1861* (Chapel Hill: University of North Carolina Press, 1980).

2. See Don Fehrenbacher, "Lincoln's Wartime Leadership," *Journal of the Abraham Lincoln Association* 9 (1987): 1–18.

3. *Collected Works*, 4: 331–32; Phillip Paludan, *"A People's Contest": The Union and Civil War, 1861–1865* (New York: Harper & Row, 1988), pp. 15–18; Kenneth Stampp, *And the War Came: The North and the Secession Crisis, 1860–61* (Chicago: University of Chicago Press, 1964), pp. 288–89; William Hesseltine, *Lincoln and the War Governors* (New York: Knopf, 1955), pp. 145–53.

4. *Collected Works*, 4: 340–44.

5. Ibid., 4: 331–32, 338–39, 346–47, 353–54.

6. Harold M. Hyman, *"A More Perfect Union": The Impact of the Civil War and Reconstruction on the Constitution* (New York: Knopf, 1973), chap. 5, undergirds much of my discussion of this issue. The precise terminology on suspension is "suspension of the *privilege* of the writ." The legal scholars of the war era emphasized the distinction between these words and the suspension of the writ itself. Though Congress was empowered to suspend the writ, the president could suspend the privilege of exercising it. See Horace Binney, *The Privilege of the Writ of Habeas Corpus* (Philadelphia: C. Sherman, 1862). I will use the shortened form "suspension of the writ."

7. Thomas Carlyle, "Horoscope," *Collected Works*, 12: 356–57.

8. William F. Duker, *A Constitutional History of Habeas Corpus* (Westport, Conn.: Greenwood, 1980). Duker argues that the power over suspension is essentially congressional but that the president may act in cases of "sudden attack."

9. Hyman, "*More Perfect Union*," pp. 65–77. Mark E. Neely, Jr., *The Fate of Liberty: Abraham Lincoln and Civil Liberties* (New York: Oxford University Press, 1991). I rely heavily on Neely's work although I will note disagreements when necessary.

10. Glyndon Van Deusen, *William Henry Seward* (New York: Oxford University Press, 1967), pp. 288–91.

11. "Arrested for Disloyalty" file, "Miscellaneous" Box, Record Group (RG) 59, National Archives, Washington, D.C.

12. Ibid. See also *Official Record of the War of the Rebellion*, series 2, vol. 2 (Washington, D.C.: GPO, 1880-1902). This latter volume contains many of the cases from the archives.

13. "Arrested for Disloyalty" file.

14. Ibid. Mayer wrote at least twice to Seward requesting that permission.

15. Ibid. Neither the material in the *Official Record* nor in the original documents contain evidence that the *Gazette* was allowed to resume mail circulation. Van Deusen, *Seward*, p. 290, is incomplete and misleading on this incident. James G. Randall, *Constitutional Problems under Lincoln* (Urbana: University of Illinois Press, 1951), pp. 477-510, provides the most detailed summary of newspaper suppression during the war.

16. See Neely, *Fate of Liberty*, pp. 20-31.

17. *Ex parte Merryman*, 17 Fed. Cases 144; Randall, *Constitutional Problems*, pp. 120-22, 160-61; Harold M. Hyman and William M. Wiecek, *Equal Justice under Law: Constitutional Development, 1835-1875* (New York: Harper & Row, 1982), pp. 238-41; Edward McPherson, *The Political History of the United States of America during the Great Rebellion* (Washington, D.C.: Philp and Solomon, 1865), pp. 154-55.

18. See Taney opinion in Edward McPherson, *Political History*.

19. On general issue of judicial review in the war, see Hyman, *"More Perfect Union"*; on *Merryman*, see pp. 81-98; Alfred Hinsey Kelly, Winfred A. Harbison, and Herman Belz, *The American Constitution: Its Origins and Development*, 6th ed. (New York: Norton, 1983), pp. 305, 311, 397-98; William Wiecek, "The Reconstruction of Federal Judicial Power," *American Journal of Legal History* 13 (1969): 333-59.

20. Phillip S. Paludan, *A Covenant with Death: The Constitution, Law and Equality in the Civil War Era* (Urbana: University of Illinois Press, 1975), pp. 95, 130-31; Sydney G. Fisher, "The Suspension of Habeas Corpus during the War of the Rebellion," *Political Science Quarterly* 3 (Sept. 1888): 454-88.

21. *Collected Works*, 4: 429-31, 4 July 1861.

22. Benjamin Thomas and Harold Hyman, *Stanton: The Life and Times of Lincoln's Secretary of War* (New York: Knopf, 1962), pp. 248-49; Neely, *Fate of Liberty*, pp. 40-43; Hyman, *"More Perfect Union,"* p. 221n.

23. Van Deusen, *Seward*, p. 291.

24. Randall, *Constitutional Problems*, chaps. 7-8; *Official Record of the War of the Rebellion*, series 2, vol. 2, 496-97; Neely, *Fate of Liberty*, pp. 231-35, passim; Herman Belz, *Lincoln and the Constitution: The Dictatorship Question Reconsidered* (Ft. Wayne, Ind.: Louis Warren Lincoln Library, 1984).

25. Neely, *Fate of Liberty*, pp. 40-50.

26. Joel Parker, "Habeas Corpus and Martial Law," *North American Review* 93 (Oct. 1861): 498.

27. Allan G. Bogue, *The Earnest Men: Republicans of the Civil War Senate* (Ithaca, N.Y.: Cornell University Press, 1981), pp. 26-28; Nevins, *War for the Union*, pp. 187-89.

28. Kelly, Harbison, and Belz, *American Constitution*, p. 301; Randall, *Constitutional Problems*, pp. 57–59.

29. "Suspension of the Privilege of the Writ of Habeas Corpus," *Opinions of the Attorneys General* 10 (1861): 82–83; *Collected Works*, 4: 428–30. I rely here on the argument of Michael Les Benedict in "The Constitution of the Lincoln Presidency and the Republican Era," in Martin Fausold and Alan Shank, eds., *The Constitution and the American Presidency* (Albany: State University of New York Press, 1991), pp. 45–62.

30. 2 *Black* 635 (1863).

31. John Nicolay and John Hay, *Abraham Lincoln: A History*, 10 vols. (New York: Century, 1890), 4: 375–84; Randall, *Constitutional Problems*, pp. 55–56; Bogue, *Earnest Men*, pp. 263–66; Leonard Curry, *Blueprint for Modern America: Non Military Legislation of the First Civil War Congress* (Nashville, Tenn.: Vanderbilt University Press, 1968).

32. *Congressional Globe*, 37th Congress, 1st session, 222–23; *Collected Works*, 4: 532, Browning, 22 Sept. 1861.

33. James McPherson, *Battle Cry of Freedom* (New York: Oxford University Press, 1988), pp. 354–56; Hyman, *"More Perfect Union"*; pp. 177–81; Randall, *Constitutional Problems*, chap. 12; Edward McPherson, *Political History of the Great Rebellion*, pp. 195–96.

34. Stephen Sears, *General George B. McClellan: The Young Napoleon* (New York: Ticknor and Fields, 1988), pp. 126–27.

35. Fred R. Shannon, *The Organization and Administration of the Union Army*, 2 vols. (Cleveland, Ohio: Arthur Clark, 1928), 1: 23–31; James G. Randall, *Lincoln the President*, 4 vols. (New York: Dodd, Mead, 1945–1954), 2: 54–56.

36. Michael Fellman, *Inside War: The Guerrilla Conflict in Missouri during the American Civil War* (New York: Oxford University Press, 1989).

37. Tyler Dennett, ed., *Lincoln and the Civil War in the Diaries and Letters of John Hay* (New York: Dodd, Mead, 1939), p. 183; *House Executive Document Number 94*, 37th Congress, 2d session, p. 34, as quoted in Randall, *Lincoln the President*, 2: 19–20; T. Harry Williams, *Lincoln and His Generals* (New York: Knopf, 1952), pp. 32–33. More sympathetic to Fremont is Andrew Rolle, *John Charles Fremont: Character as Destiny* (Norman: University of Oklahoma Press, 1991), and Nevins, *War for the Union*, vol. 1, chap. 16.

38. Nicolay and Hay, *Lincoln*, 4: 416–17.

39. James Rawley, *Turning Points of the Civil War* (Lincoln: University of Nebraska Press, 1974), pp. 36–38.

40. *Collected Works*, 4, 2 Sept 1861.

41. Ibid., 4: 549, 562–63, and 5: 1–2. Lincoln's removal of Fremont rested on grounds in addition to his proclamation (see letter to Browning, 22 Sept. 1861), but the proclamation was the precipitating incident (see letter to Samuel Curtis, 7 Oct. 1861).

42. James McPherson, *The Struggle for Equality* (Princeton, N.J.: Princeton University Press, 1964), pp. 73–74; Nevins, *War for Union*, 1: 339–41; Randall, *Lincoln the President*, 2: 21–22.

43. James McPherson, *Struggle for Equality*; Benjamin Quarles, *The Negro in the Civil War* (Boston: Little, Brown, 1969), pp. 68–69; Dudley Taylor Cornish, *The Sable Arm: Black Troops in the Union Army, 1861–1865* (Lawrence: University Press of Kansas, 1987), pp. 24–26.

44. *Collected Works*, 2: 255, 4: 426, 7: 23; Richard Current, "The Civil War and the American Mission," in Cullom Davis et al., eds., *The Public and Private Lincoln* (Carbondale: Southern Illinois University Press, 1979).

45. On the recognition question I have relied on Van Deusen, *Seward*; Norman Ferris, *Desperate Diplomacy: William Seward's Foreign Policy, 1861* (Knoxville: University of Tennessee Press, 1976); Peter Parish, *The American Civil War* (New York: Holmes and Meier, 1975), pp. 404–6; and Donald P. Crook, *The North, the South and the Powers, 1861–1865* (New York: Wiley, 1974), pp. 71–98.

46. Allan Nevins and Milton H. Thomas, eds., *The Diary of George Templeton Strong*, 4 vols. (New York: Macmillan, 1952), 3: 196–97.

47. *Collected Works*, 4: 376–80. The dispatch is analyzed somewhat differently and printed in full in Allen Thorndike Rice, ed., *Reminiscences of Abraham Lincoln* (New York: North American Review, 1888), pp. lv–lxix.

48. *Collected Works* 4: 62–64, 10 Dec. 1861; Crook, *North, South*, pp. 130–34; David Donald, *Charles Sumner and the Rights of Man* (New York: Knopf, 1970), pp. 31–39; James McPherson, *Battle Cry*, pp. 390–91.

49. Burton J. Hendrick, *Lincoln's War Cabinet* (Boston: Little, Brown, 1946), pp. 205–8; Randall, *Lincoln the President*, 2: 49–51, presents Lincoln in a more favorable light as do other writers on this episode.

50. Pollard quoted in James Rawley, *Turning Points of the Civil War*, pp. 91–93; Norman Ferris, *The Trent Affair* (Knoxville: University of Tennessee Press, 1977), p. 203.

51. John Stuart Mill, *The Contest in America* (Boston, 1862) as edited by Frank Freidel, *Union Pamphlets of the Civil War, 1862–1865*, 2 vols. (Cambridge, Mass.: Harvard University Press, 1967), 1: 326–44.

CHAPTER 5
FORGING THE RESOURCES OF WAR

1. Brian Holden Reid, "Historians and the Joint Committee on the Conduct of the War," *Civil War History* 38 (Dec. 1992): 319–41, provides helpful background on the committee.

2. T. Harry Williams, "The Attack upon West Point during the Civil War," *Mississippi Valley Historical Review* 25 (Mar. 1939): 491–504; *Collected Works*, 4: 438; Allan Bogue, *The Congressman's Civil War* (Cambridge: Cambridge University Press, 1989); Hans Trefousse, *The Radical Republicans: Lincoln's Vanguard for Racial Justice* (New York: Knopf, 1969), pp. 184–85

3. Quoted in Reid, "Historians and the Joint Committee," p. 319; John Nicolay and John Hay, *Abraham Lincoln: A History*, 10 vols. (New York: Century, 1890), 5: 150–51.

4. Burnside to McClellan, 5 Mar. 1862, 5 May 1862, in George B. McClel-

lan, *McClellan's Own Story* (New York: Webster, 1886), pp. 244–45; Marcus Cunliffe, *Soldiers and Civilians: The Martial Spirit in America, 1775–1865* (New York: Free Press, 1973), pp. 159–72; Russell Weigley, *Toward an American Army: Military Thought from Washington to Marshall* (New York: Columbia University Press, 1962), pp. 38–42; James Morrison, *"The Best School in the World": West Point, the Pre Civil War Years* (Kent, Ohio: Kent State University Press, 1986).

5. Bogue, *Congressman's Civil War*, pp. 101–2.

6. "General M. C. Meigs on the Conduct of the War," *American Historical Review* 26 (1921): 292; *Collected Works*, 5: 34.

7. *Collected Works* 1: 439, 12 Jan. 1848; Gabor S. Boritt, "Abraham Lincoln: War Opponent and War President," Fortenbaugh Lecture Series, Gettysburg College, 1987; James G. Randall, *Constitutional Problems under Lincoln* (Urbana: University of Illinois Press, 1951), pp. xiv–ix.

8. Stephen Sears, *General George B. McClellan: The Young Napoleon* (New York: Ticknor and Fields, 1988), pp. 131–32, 134, 141; Benjamin Thomas and Harold Hyman, *Stanton: The Life and Times of Lincoln's Secretary of War* (New York: Knopf, 1962), pp. 126–31. The following discussion of McClellan owes much to this volume.

9. Thomas Wentworth Higginson, "Regular and Volunteer Officers," *Atlantic Monthly* 14 (Sept. 1864): 348–51; William Tecumseh Sherman, *Memoirs of General W. T. Sherman*, 2 vols. (New York, 1892), 2: 381–409.

10. Sears, *McClellan*, p. 141. McClellan did take into his confidence a reporter from the *New York Herald*, however, to whom he gave a rather complete picture of his overall plans the next day, 14 January.

11. *Collected Works*, 5: 88, 1 Jan. 1862, for Lincoln's protection of McClellan; 5: 94, for his order that the general go before the committee.

12. Gerald Sorin, *Abolitionism: A New Perspective* (New York: Praeger, 1972), pp. 148–49; James McPherson, *The Struggle for Equality* (Princeton, N.J.: Princeton University Press, 1964); David Donald, *Charles Sumner and the Coming of the Civil War* (Chicago: University of Chicago Press, 1960) p. 388.

13. Intriguing is the fact that in the navy, blacks were already being used on ships and Secretary of the Navy Welles was not asked to stop it even when Cameron specifically mentioned naval practice. John Niven, *Gideon Welles: Lincoln's Secretary of the Navy* (New York: Oxford University Press, 1973), pp. 394–96.

14. McClellan to S. L. M. Barlow, 8 Nov. 1861, Barlow Papers, Huntington Library, San Marino, California; McClellan, *McClellan's Own Story*, pp. 487–89.

15. David Donald, *Charles Sumner and the Rights of Man*, (New York: Knopf, 1970), pp. 48–49; Marvin Cain, *Lincoln's Attorney General: Edward Bates of Missouri* (Columbia: University of Missouri Press, 1965), pp. 170–73.

16. Thomas and Hyman, *Stanton*, pp. 259–63; Sears, *McClellan*, pp. 143–46; Bogue, *Congressman's Civil War*, pp. 101–6; Trefousse, *Radical Republicans*.

17. Thomas and Hyman, *Stanton*, pp. 125–26, 138–42.

18. Ibid., pp. 146–49.

19. Ibid., pp. 164–65.

20. Ibid., pp. 152–54.

21. Herman Hattaway and Archer Jones, *How the North Won: A Military History of the Civil War* (Urbana: Illinois University Press, 1983), pp. 90–95.

22. *Collected Works*, 5: 118–25; Hattaway and Jones, *How the North Won*, pp. 93–97.

23. Bogue, *Congressman's Civil War*, pp. 44–47; Stephen B. Oates, "Abraham Lincoln: *Republican* in the White House," in John Thomas, ed., *Abraham Lincoln and the American Political Tradition* (Amherst: University of Massachusetts Press, 1986), pp. 104–8. I discuss Lincoln's more well-known interactions with Congress on reconstruction and emancipation later.

24. William R. Brock, *Conflict and Transformation: The United States 1844–1877* (Baltimore: Penguin, 1973), pp. 281–83; Harold M. Hyman, *"A More Perfect Union": The Impact of the Civil War and Reconstruction on the Constitution* (New York: Knopf, 1973), pp. 181–87; see especially Bogue, *Congressman's Civil War*, pp. 60–109.

25. Frederick Blue, *Salmon P. Chase: A Life in Politics* (Kent, Ohio: Kent State University Press, 1987), pp. 149–51. Economic measures of Congress are surveyed in Phillip Paludan, *"A People's Contest": The Union and Civil War, 1861–1865* (New York: Harper & Row, 1988), chaps. 5–6. More specialized studies will be cited as needed.

26. Irwin Unger, *Greenback Era, A Social and Political History of American Finance* (Princeton, N.J.: Princeton University Press, 1964), pp. 16–17; Jacob Schuckers, *The Life and Public Services of Salmon Portland Chase* (New York: Appleton, 1874), p. 229, chap. 35.

27. Paludan, *"People's Contest,"* pp. 180–84; Emerson Fite, *Social and Industrial Conditions in the North during the Civil War* (1910; rept., New York: Ungar, 1963) pp. 259–74; Reuben Kessel and Armen Alchain, "Real Wages in the North during the Civil War," *Journal of Law and Economics* 2 (1959): 95–113.

28. Schuckers, *Life of Chase*, pp. 293–311; Blue, *Chase*, pp. 157–64; David Gesche, "The New York City Banks and the Development of the National Banking System," *American Journal of Legal History* 23 (Jan. 1979): 33–38. Bray Hammond, *Sovereignty and an Empty Purse* (Princeton, N.J.: Princeton University Press, 1970).

29. See longer discussion in Paludan, *"People's Contest,"* pp. 114–15, 141–43.

30. Henry Steele Commager, ed., *Documents of American History*, 9th ed. (Englewood Cliffs, N.J.: Prentice-Hall, 1973), 1: 364–65; Eric Foner, *Free Soil, Free Labor, Free Men: The Ideology of the Republican Party before the Civil War* (New York: Oxford University Press, 1970).

31. Foner, *Free Soil*, pp. 19–21; Morton Keller, *Affairs of State: Public Life in Late Nineteenth Century America* (Cambridge, Mass.: Harvard University Press, 1977), pp. 162–64.

32. Paludan, *"People's Contest,"* pp. 134–35; Paul Gates, *Agriculture and the Civil War* (New York: Knopf, 1975).

33. *U.S. Statutes at Large*, vol. 12, p. 503.

34. *Collected Works*, 2: 124, 3: 471–82, 4: 36–53; Gabor Boritt, *Lincoln and the*

Economics of the American Dream, (Memphis: Memphis State University Press, 1978), p. 320, n. 6.

35. See two articles in *Mississippi Valley Historical Review* 32 (Sept. 1944): Robert S. Henry, "The Railroad Land Grant Legend in American History Texts," and Fred A. Shannon, "Comments on the Railroad Grant Legend." Stanley Engerman, "Some Economic Issues Related to Railroad Subsidies and the Evaluation of Land Grants," *Journal of Economic History* 32 (June 1972). Boritt, *Lincoln and Economics*, pp. 210–11.

36. Eric Foner, in *Free Soil*, quotes many western Republicans but fewer eastern ones about the free-soil image of the party. It may be that eastern Republicans had a slightly different emphasis from their western colleagues, a possibility that Foner does not explore.

37. David A. Nichols, *Lincoln and the Indians: Civil War Policy and Politics* (Columbia: University of Missouri Press, 1978).

38. I am indebted to discussions with my colleague Donald Worster for insights on the costs of Republican development ideals.

39. George Winston Smith and Charles Judah, eds., *Life in the North during the Civil War: A Source History* (Albuquerque: University of New Mexico Press, 1966), p. 224; Paludan, *"People's Contest,"* chap. 8; Max Lerner, ed., *The Mind and Faith of Justice Holmes* (New York: Modern Library, 1954).

CHAPTER 6
NORTHERN POWER EMERGES

1. Julia Ward Howe, *Reminiscences, 1819–1899* (Boston: Houghton Mifflin, 1899), pp. 273–76.

2. Ulysses S. Grant, *Personal Memoirs* (New York: World Publishing, 1952), pp. 150–61; James McPherson, *Battle Cry of Freedom* (New York: Oxford University Press, 1988), pp. 392–402.

3. I follow Peter Parish, *The American Civil War* (New York: Holmes and Meier, 1975), pp. 415–20; William Davis, *The Duel between the First Ironclads* (New York: Garden City Publishers, 1975); James McPherson, *Battle Cry of Freedom*, pp. 373–78; Herman Hattaway and Archer Jones, *How the North Won: A Military History of the Civil War* (Urbana: University of Illinois Press, 1983), pp. 127–32.

4. There were fifty-four ironclads of various sizes under construction in December 1862. See Adm. David D. Porter, *The Naval History of the Civil War* (Secaucus, N.J.: Castle, 1984), p. 266.

5. *Harper's Pictorial History of the Civil War* (Chicago: Star Publishing, 1866), Jan. 1862, p. 251; John Nicolay and John Hay, *Abraham Lincoln: A History*, 10 vols. (New York: Century, 1890), 5: chap. 13. The impact of the blockade on Union victory is the subject of debate. James McPherson, *Battle Cry of Freedom*, says that "it did play an important role in Union victory" (p. 382). Hattaway and Jones say that it "did not represent a major factor in the Confederacy's economic exhaustion" (p. 56). Parish, *American Civil War*, asserts that "it did not win the war but it established one of the conditions of eventual victory" (p. 423). These

assessments derive mostly from counting the amount of shipping that got through. An important consideration is also the question of its impact on Confederate morale—a less quantifiable factor.

6. John Niven, *Gideon Welles: Lincoln's Secretary of the Navy* (New York: Oxford University Press, 1973), chap. 19–20.

7. Stephen R. Wise, *Lifeline of the Confederacy: Blockade Running during the Civil War* (Columbia: University of South Carolina Press, 1988), pp. 8, 226 passim.

8. Howard K. Beale, ed., *The Diary of Gideon Welles*, 3 vols. (New York: Norton, 1960), 1: 61–69; Niven, *Gideon Welles*, pp. 402–15.

9. See the extensive description of the state of the cabinet in Welles, *Diary*, 1: 130–39, 16 Sept. 1862; David Donald, ed., *Inside Lincoln's Cabinet: The Civil War Diaries of Salmon P. Chase* (New York: Longman's, Green, 1954) pp. 191–92; Tyler Dennett, ed., *Lincoln and the Civil War in the Diaries and Letters of John Hay* (New York: Dodd, Mead, 1939), pp. 144–45; Martin Duberman, *Charles Francis Adams, 1807–1886* (Stanford, Calif.: Stanford University Press, 1968), pp. 387–88; Gideon Welles, *Lincoln and Seward* (1874; rept., Freeport, N. Y.: Books for Libraries, 1969); Allan Nevins, *War for the Union*, 4 vols. (New York: Scribner's, 1959), 3: 160; Edward Corwin, *The President: Office and Powers: 1787–1957*, 4th ed. (New York: New York University Press, 1957), pp. 233, 323.

10. Burton J. Hendrick, *Lincoln's War Cabinet* (Boston: Little, Brown, 1946), pp. 189–93; Glyndon Van Deusen, *William Henry Seward* (New York: Oxford University Press, 1967), pp. 274–75; Welles, *Diary*, 1: 6–8; Nevins, *War for the Union*, 4: 70–71.

11. Hattaway and Jones, *How the North Won*, p. 695, note that Lincoln's lack of administrative experience allowed him not to "immerse himself in the day to day details of decision making" on military matters. I think there is a larger significance to this fact—he operated in the same way in almost every matter affecting the war.

12. James McPherson, *The Struggle for Equality* (Princeton, N.J.: Princeton University Press, 1964), pp. 75–85.

13. Ibid., pp. 99–100.

14. Martin Duberman, *James Russell Lowell* (Boston: Beacon Press, 1966), pp. 210–13.

15. Christopher Breiseth, "Lincoln, Douglas and Springfield in the 1858 Campaign," in Cullom Davis et al., eds., *The Public and Private Lincoln* (Carbondale: Southern Illinois University Press, 1979), p. 118.

16. *Collected Works*, 5: 144–45, 152–53, 317–18.

17. Ibid., pp. 144–46. Lawanda Cox, *Lincoln and Black Freedom: A Study in Presidential Leadership* (Columbia: University of South Carolina Press, 1981), has an excellent discussion of the complexities of both emancipation and the reconstruction process. Lincoln could not know in 1862 all the complexities of the postwar world, but his conservative instincts surely made him sensitive to the entangled interweaving of ideas and institutions that had evolved over the decades in which the nation had protected slavery. He understood the power of racism, the impact of slavery on the slaves, and the reluctance of Americans to sup-

port extended outreaches of federal power. At the same time he retained a clear hope for freedom for all people and a willingness to do what he could to advance that cause.

18. James McPherson, *Struggle for Equality*, pp. 95–97.

19. Benjamin Thomas and Harold Hyman, *Stanton: The Life and Times of Lincoln's Secretary of War* (New York: Knopf, 1962), pp. 200–202; James W. Geary, *We Need Men: The Union Draft in the Civil War* (DeKalb: Northern Illinois University Press, 1991), pp. 7–8.

20. Hattaway and Jones, *How the North Won*, pp. 163–170; William McFeely, *Grant: A Biography* (New York: Norton, 1981); Grant, *Personal Memoirs*; Frederick Phisterer, *Statistical Record of the Armies of the United States* (New York: Scribner's, 1884), p. 213.

21. Grant, *Personal Memoirs*, pp. 29–30, 83–84.

22. James McPherson, *Struggle for Equality*, pp. 96–98.

23. *Collected Works*, 5: 219, 223–24.

24. G. S. Boritt, "The Voyage to the Colony of Linconia": The Sixteenth President, Black Colonization, and the Defense Mechanism of Avoidance," *Historian* 37 (1975): 622–23; George M. Frederickson, "A Man but Not a Brother: Abraham Lincoln and Racial Equality," *Journal of Southern History* 41 (Feb. 1975): 56–57; *Collected Works*, 5: 534.

25. *Collected Works*, 5: 370–75.

26. Boritt, "Voyage to the Colony." Black opposition to colonization is collected in James McPherson, ed., *The Negro's Civil War* (New York: Pantheon, 1965), pp. 77–97.

27. Eric Foner, *Free Soil, Free Labor, Free Men: The Ideology of the Republican Party before the Civil War* (New York: Oxford University Press, 1970), p. 271; Don Fehrenbacher, "Only His Stepchildren," in *Lincoln in Text and Context: Collected Essays* (Stanford, Calif.: Stanford University Press, 1987); V. Jacques Voegeli, *Free but Not Equal: The Midwest and the Negro during the Civil War* (Chicago: University of Chicago Press, 1967), pp. 44–45, 96–97, 24–25; Stephen B. Oates, *With Malice toward None: The Life of Abraham Lincoln* (New York: Mentor, 1978), pp. 289–90, 322–23, 358–59; Parish, *American Civil War*, pp. 240–42.

28. *Collected Works*, 5: 370–75; on the meaning of the frontier to Republicans, see Foner, *Free Soil*; Eugene Berwanger, *The Frontier against Slavery* (Urbana: University of Illinois Press, 1967).

29. Nevins, *War for the Union*, 2: 114–18, 146–49.

30. Henry Wilson, *History of the Antislavery Measures of the Thirty-seventh and Thirty-eighth United States Congresses* (Boston: Walker, Fuller, 1865); Louis Gerteis, *From Contraband to Freedman: Federal Policy toward Southern Blacks 1861–1865* (Westport, Conn.: Greenwood, 1973), pp. 13–17; James G. Randall and David H. Donald, *Civil War and Reconstruction* (Lexington, Ky.: Heath, 1969), pp. 372–73; *Collected Works*, 5: 128–39; Allan G. Bogue, *The Earnest Men: Republicans of the Civil War Senate* (Ithaca, N.Y.: Cornell University Press, 1981), pp. 188–96.

31. Margaret Leech, *Reveille in Washington, 1860–1865* (New York: Grosset & Dunlap, 1941), pp. 244–47.

32. Ibid., pp. 241–42; Leonard Curry, *Blueprint for Modern America: Non Military Legislation of the First Civil War Congress* (Nashville, Tenn.: Vanderbilt University Press, 1968), pp. 36–43; Fawn Brodie, *Thaddeus Stevens* (New York: Norton, 1966), p. 156; Michael J. Kurtz "Emancipation in the Federal City," *Civil War History* 26 (Sept. 1978): 250–67.

33. Wilson, *History of Antislavery Measures*, p. 109; James Rawley, *Turning Points of the Civil War* (Lincoln: University of Nebraska Press, 1974), pp. 129–30.

CHAPTER 7
LEAVING OLD MOORINGS: MCCLELLAN AND EMANCIPATION

1. George B. McClellan, *McClellan's Own Story* (New York: Webster, 1886), pp. 398, 407.

2. Johnston quoted in Archer Jones, *Civil War Command and Strategy: The Process of Victory and Defeat* (New York: Free Press, 1992), p. 62.

3. *Official Record of the War of the Rebellion*, Series 1, vol. 11, pt. 1, p. 61.

4. Hans Trefousse, *The Radical Republicans: Lincoln's Vanguard for Racial Justice* (New York: Knopf, 1969), pp. 196–98. Soldiers quoted in Stephen Sears, *George B. McClellan: The Young Napoleon* (New York: Ticknor & Fields, 1988), p. 231. See pp. 229–35 for debate over McClellan post-Seven Days.

5. *Collected Works*, 5: 306–307, 4 July 1862.

6. McClellan, *McClellan's Own Story*, pp. 159–60, 487–89.

7. T. Harry Williams, "Voters in Blue: Citizen Soldiers of the Civil War," *Mississippi Valley Historical Review* 31 (Sept. 1944): 187–204; Marcus Cunliffe, *Soldiers and Civilians: The Martial Spirit in America, 1775–1865* (New York: Free Press, 1973), pp. 318–34.

8. *Collected Works*, 5: 309–13; James G. Randall, *Lincoln the President*, 4 vols. (New York: Dodd, Mead, 1945–1954), 2: 68, 101–4. John Nicolay and John Hay, *Abraham Lincoln: A History*, 10 vols. (New York: Century, 1890), 5: 449–53, use the Harrison Landing letter to attack McClellan for challenging Lincoln, as does Kenneth P. Williams, *Lincoln Finds a General*, 5 vols. (Bloomington: Indiana University Press, 1949), 1: 248–50.

9. Allan Nevins, *War for the Union* (New York: Scribner's, 1959), 2: 462–63; Randall, *Lincoln the President*, 2: 290–91.

10. *Collected Works*, 5: 291–93.

11. Trefousse, *Radical Republicans*, pp. 168–202, passim; David Donald, "Devils Facing Zionwards," in Grady McWhiney, ed., *Grant, Lee, Lincoln and the Radicals* (New York: Harper & Row, 1964); Allan Bogue, *The Congressman's Civil War* (Cambridge: Cambridge University Press, 1989), pp. 132–39.

12. Tyler Dennett, ed., *Lincoln and the Civil War in the Diaries and Letters of John Hay* (New York: Dodd, Mead, 1939), p. 108; David Donald, *Charles Sumner and the Rights of Man* (New York: Knopf, 1970), p. 48.

13. Chandler quoted in Leonard Curry, *Blueprint for Modern America: Non Military Legislation of the First Civil War Congress* (Nashville, Tenn.: Vanderbilt

University Press,, 1968), p. 62; Trefousse, *Radical Republicans*, pp. 224–26; Dudley Taylor Cornish, *The Sable Arm: Black Troops in the Union Army, 1861–1865* (Lawrence: University Press of Kansas, 1987), pp. 53–55; Nicolay and Hay, *Lincoln*, vol. 6, chap. 5.

14. James H. Moorhead, *American Apocalypse: Yankee Protestants and the Civil War, 1860–1869* (New Haven, Conn.: Yale University Press, 1978), pp. 98–101.

15. James McPherson, *The Struggle for Equality* (Princeton, N.J.: Princeton University Press, 1964), pp. 110–11; Glyndon Van Deusen, *Horace Greeley: Nineteenth Century Crusader* (Philadelphia: University of Pennsylvania Press, 1953), pp. 284–86; Rachel Sherman Thorndyke, ed., *The Sherman Letters* (New York: Scribner's, 1894), pp. 156–57.

16. Allan G. Bogue, *The Earnest Men: Republicans of the Civil War Senate* (Ithaca, N.Y.: Cornell University Press, 1981), pp. 219–35; James G. Randall, *Constitutional Problems under Lincoln* (Urbana: University of Illinois Press, 1951), pp. 276–77.

17. *Collected Works*, 5: 420; Randall, *Constitutional Problems*, pp. 357–63.

18. *Collected Works*, 5: 328–31; Nicolay and Hay, *Lincoln* 6: 97–103.

19. Mary Francis Berry, *Military Necessity and Civil Rights Policy: Black Citizenship and the Constitution, 1861–1868* (Port Washington, N.Y.: Kennikat Press, 1977), pp. 41–45. James Geary, *We Need Men: The Union Draft in the Civil War* (De Kalb: Northern Illinois University Press, 1991), pp. 22–31.

20. Randall, *Constitutional Problems*, pp. 278–80; *Collected Works*, 5: 328–31.

21. Howard K. Beale, ed., *The Diary of Gideon Welles*, 3 vols. (New York: Norton, 1960), 1: 70–71; Gideon Welles, "History of Emancipation," *Galaxy* (Dec. 1872): 842–43; Stephen B. Oates, "Lincoln's Journey to Emancipation," in *Our Fiery Trial* (Amherst: University of Massachusetts Press, 1979), pp. 76–77.

22. *Collected Works*, 5: 336–38; John Hope Franklin, *The Emancipation Proclamation* (New York: Anchor, 1965), pp. 37–39. See also David Donald, ed., *Inside Lincoln's Cabinet: The Civil War Diaries of Salmon P. Chase* (New York: Longman's Green, 1954), pp. 95–100.

23. Benjamin Thomas and Harold Hyman, *Stanton: The Life and Times of Lincoln's Secretary of War* (New York: Knopf, 1962), pp. 231–40.

24. Nicolay and Hay, *Lincoln*, 6: 127–30; Chase, *Inside Lincoln's Cabinet*, pp. 98–100; Thomas and Hyman, *Stanton*, pp. 238–40. The latter authors argue that Lincoln was not persuaded at the cabinet meeting itself but came around the next day after a long discussion with Thurlow Weed, Seward's longtime associate and a political operator in his own right.

25. Herman Hattaway and Archer Jones, *How the North Won: A Military History of the Civil War* (Urbana: University of Illinois Press, 1983), pp. 208–11; Lincoln to Agenor-Etienne de Gasparin, 4 Aug. 1862, 5: 355–56.

26. Hay, *Diaries and Letters*, pp. 47–49. Lincoln told Welles that McClellan wanted to break Pope down "without regard of the consequences to the country" (Welles, *Diary*, 1: 113).

27. *New York Tribune*, 20 Aug. 1862.

28. *Collected Works*, 5: 388–89.

29. Ibid., pp. 342–43, 344–46, 350–51.

30. Ibid., pp. 388–89.

31. Ibid., pp. 419–25.

32. *Congressional Globe*, 2 July 1862, p. 3087, as quoted in Nicolay and Hay, 5: 443; Thomas and Hyman, *Stanton*, pp. 234–38; Cornish, *Sable Arm*, pp. 35–36; Berry, *Military Necessity*, pp. 38–41.

33. Thomas and Hyman, *Stanton*, pp. 230–40; Berry, *Military Necessity*, pp. 42–46.

34. Nicolay and Hay, *Lincoln*, 6: 440–50.

35. James McPherson, *Battle Cry of Freedom* (New York: Oxford University Press, 1988), pp. 540–45; *Historical Statistics of the United States* (Stamford, Conn.: Fairfield, 1965), p. 14; Frederick Phisterer, *Statistical Record of the Armies of the United States* (New York: Scribner's, 1884), p. 214.

36. This count is a rough one. I am using the 1860 census, and the slave population would have increased in three years by approximately 75,000 a year, using the increase in the number of slaves between 1850 and 1860 as a basis. Some counties in Louisiana were excluded from the 1 January proclamation as was western Virginia, but these areas held fewer slaves than those that the proclamation covered. See Ira Berlin, Barbara J. Fields, Thavolia Glymph, Joseph Reidy, and Leslie Rowland, *Freedom: A Documentary History of Emancipation, 1861–1867*, 3 vols. to date (Cambridge: Cambridge University Press, 1982–), 1: 67; Louis Gerteis, *From Contraband to Freedman: Federal Policy toward Southern Blacks, 1861–1865* (Westport, Conn.: Greenwood, 1973), p. 74.

37. *Collected Works*, 5: 433–36.

38. Quoted in Franklin, *Emancipation Proclamation*, pp. 57–60; Van Deusen, *Greeley*, pp. 286–88; Nevins, *War for the Union*, 2: 237–40; William Hesseltine, *Lincoln and the War Governors* (New York: Knopf, 1955), pp. 256–59.

39. Van Deusen, *Greeley*, pp. 287–88.

40. Walt Whitman, *Leaves of Grass* (New York: New American Library, 1955).

41. Ralph Waldo Emerson, "The Emancipation Proclamation," *The Works of Ralph Waldo Emerson*, 12 vols. (Boston: Houghton Mifflin, 1884), 4: 293–303.

42. Quoted in Joel Silbey, *A Respectable Minority: The Democratic Party in the Civil War Era, 1860–1868* (New York: Norton, 1977), pp. 85–86n, and see discussion of party racial rhetoric, pp. 80–85. Note also Jean Baker, "A Loyal Opposition: Northern Democrats in the 37th Congress," *Civil War History* 25 (June 1979): 146–48, demonstrating that the most unifying issue among Democrats was hostility to pro-Negro legislation. See also V. Jacques Voegeli, *Free but Not Equal: The Midwest and the Negro during the Civil War* (Chicago: University of Chicago Press, 1967), pp. 52–73.

43. *Tribune Almanac for 1863*, pp. 50–62; Voegeli, *Free but Not Equal*, pp. 61–64; John Sherman, *Recollections of Forty Years* (Chicago, 1895), p. 277; W. Sherman Jackson, "Emancipation, Negrophobia, and Civil War Politics in Ohio," *Journal of Negro History* 14 (Sept. 1980): 250–60.

44. *Collected Works*, 5: 503; Benjamin B. Curtis, *Executive Power* (Boston: Little, Brown, 1862); Joel Parker, "The Character of the Rebellion and the Con-

duct of the War," *North American Review* 95 (Oct. 1862): 500–533, are examples of the attacks on the proclamation. Rebuttals came from George William Curtis in *Harper's Weekly* 7 (3 Jan. 1863): 162; Charles Kirkland, *A Letter to the Hon. Benjamin P. Curtis* (New York: Latimer Bros. and Seymour, 1862), and George Livermore, *An Historical Research Respecting the Opinions of the Founders of the Republic on Negroes as Slaves, Citizens and Soldiers* (Massachusetts Historical Society, 1862–63). For Lincoln's attention to these last two, see *Collected Works*, 5: 544; Randall, *Lincoln the President*, 2: 169. Lincoln gave the pen used to sign the final proclamation to Livermore.

45. Welles, *Diary*, pp. 101–15; Burton J. Hendrick, *Lincoln's War Cabinet* (Boston: Little, Brown, 1946), pp. 292–318, *Collected Works*, 5: 481, 29 Oct. 1862. Some time later Lincoln told his secretaries that he had promised himself that if Lee got between the Army of the Potomac and Richmond, then he would fire McClellan (Nicolay and Hay, *Lincoln*, 6: 188). Lee's army achieved that on 3 November, and that may have been the main reason the president fired McClellan, but the political motives described here seem equally present. Lincoln knew when election day was.

46. Hattaway and Jones, *How the North Won*, pp. 262–65.

47. *Collected Works*, 5: 448, 468–69; E. B. Long, *Civil War Day By Day* (Garden City, N. Y.: Doubleday, 1971), p. 281.

48. McClellan, *McClellan's Own Story*, chap. 37; Sears, *McClellan*, 323–39; Hattaway and Jones, *How the North Won*, pp. 243–44, 263–67. U. S. Grant recalled late fall 1862 as a time when "voluntary enlistments had ceased throughout a greater part of the North, and the draft had been resorted to. . . . A backward movement . . . would be interpreted . . . as a defeat" (*Personal Memoirs* [New York: Library of America, 1990] pp. 295–96).

49. Hattaway and Jones, *How the North Won*, p. 266; Nicolay and Hay, *Lincoln*, 6: 173–95. Nicolay and Hay do not link Lincoln's political motives to the firing. They make no mention of proximity between the elections and the firing, explaining Lincoln's action in terms of military needs; other historians accept their emphasis. They do, however, note Lord Lyons's comments about New York politics. Their anti-McClellan bias has been mentioned—see Randall, *Lincoln the President*, 2: 68.

50. *Collected Works*, 5: 462, 470–71, 500, 504–5.

51. Randall, *Constitutional Problems*, chap. 18; Nicolay and Hay, *Lincoln*, vol. 6, chap. 14.

52. The message is in *Collected Works*, 5: 518–37.

53. James McPherson, *Battle Cry of Freedom*, pp. 562–63; Lawanda Cox, *Lincoln and Black Freedom: A Study in Presidential Leadership* (Columbia: University of South Carolina Press, 1981), pp. 9–11; Peter Parish, *The American Civil War* (New York: Holmes and Meier, 1975), p. 242. Harry Jaffa, on the other hand, respects the complexity of the December 1862 message, seeing in it a sophisticated understanding of the problem of slavery in a society believing in the rule of law, the consent of the governed, and the equality of all people. See Jaffa, "The Emancipation Proclamation," in Robert Goldwin, ed., *One Hundred Years of*

Emancipation (Chicago: Rand McNally, 1963), pp. 21–22. None of these sources links the message with reconstruction activity.

54. J. G. Randall, *Lincoln the President*, 2: 141–48, emphasizes the conservative quality of Lincoln's message.

55. Randall, *Lincoln the President*, 2: 145–48. Late in the war Lincoln wrote out a proposal for Congress that would have paid $200 million to rebel states for returning to the Union and an additional $200 million if the Thirteenth Amendment was ratified by 1 July 1866. His cabinet rejected the idea, Lincoln acquiesced, and it never went to Congress. See *Collected Works*, 8: 260–61, and Welles, *Diary*, 2: 237.

CHAPTER 8
CABINET CRISIS

1. Herman Hattaway and Archer Jones, *How the North Won: A Military History of the Civil War* (Urbana: University of Illinois Press, 1983), pp. 306–8.

2. V. Jacques Voegeli, *Free but Not Equal: The Midwest and the Negro during the Civil War* (Chicago: University of Chicago Press, 1967), pp. 62–63; Hans Trefousse, *The Radical Republicans: Lincoln's Vanguard for Racial Justice* (New York: Knopf, 1968), pp. 260–61.

3. Howard K. Beale, ed., *The Diary of Gideon Welles*, 3 vols. (New York: Norton, 1960), 1: 130–39, 16 Sept. 1862.

4. Welles, *Diary*, 1: 205, 23 Dec. 1862.

5. Glyndon Van Deusen, *William Henry Seward* (New York: Oxford University Press, 1967), pp. 335–40; Jean Baker, *Mary Todd Lincoln* (New York: Norton, 1987), p. 234.

6. Welles, *Diary*, 1: 130–39, 16 Sept. 1862.

7. Mark Neely, *The Fate of Liberty: Abraham Lincoln and Civil Liberties* (New York: Oxford University Press, 1991), p. 51; Welles, *Diary*, 1: 150.

8. Frederick Blue, *Salmon P. Chase* (Kent, Ohio: Kent State University Press, 1987), pp. 189–90; Welles, *Diary*, 1: 124–36; Benjamin Thomas and Harold Hyman, *Stanton: The Life and Times of Lincoln's Secretary of War* (New York: Knopf, 1962), pp. 253–54.

9. Blue, *Chase*, pp. 186–87.

10. Van Deusen, *Seward*, p. 344; David Donald, *Charles Sumner and the Rights of Man* (New York: Knopf, 1970), pp. 87–90.

11. *Diplomatic Correspondence, 1861* U.S. Govt., p. 74, as quoted in Burton J. Hendrick, *Lincoln's War Cabinet* (Boston: Little, Brown, 1946), pp. 325–27.

12. Joseph Medill quoted in Hendrick, *Lincoln's War Cabinet*, p. 327.

13. Hendrick, *Lincoln's War Cabinet*, pp. 323–48, provides most of the description of the events of the cabinet crisis. I follow him though occasionally deviate from his evaluations of evidence.

14. Francis Fessenden, *Life and Public Services of William Pitt Fessenden*, 2 vols. (Boston: Houghton Mifflin, 1907), 1: 233–53, contains the senator's recollection of the Senate "cabal" vs. Seward. Subsequent references to this event

rely heavily on this source; it must be consulted for the fullest picture of the event. Modern secondary sources rely too much on James G. Randall, *Lincoln the President*, 4 vols. (New York: Dodd, Mead, 1945-1954), 2: 241-49, and thus omit important information—especially about the constitutional visions that challenged for supremacy here. Welles, *Diary*, 1: 194-205, 19 Dec.-23 Dec. 1862, is also basic.

15. See Randall, *Lincoln the President*, 2: 242-43. Randall's interpretation of the story, like that of most scholars, places the burden of the crisis on legislators and on Chase's acting out of personal ambition. My account suggests that Lincoln, overburdened by his duties and inexperienced as an administrator, also contributed to the crisis.

16. Fessenden, *Life and Public Services*, 1: 242-43.

17. Welles, *Diary*, 1: 194-96.

18. Ibid., pp. 196-97; Fessenden, *Life and Public Services*, 1: 244-45.

19. Fessenden, *Life and Public Services*, 1: 247-48.

20. John Nicolay and John Hay, *Abraham Lincoln: A History*, 10 vols. (New York: Century, 1890), 6: 271.

21. Welles, *Diary*, 1: 201-2.

22. Jacob Schuckers, *The Life and Public Services of Salmon Portland Chase* (New York: Appleton, 1874), pp. 474-75; Blue, *Chase*, pp. 192-94; Nicolay and Hay, *Lincoln*, 6: 269-72; *Collected Works*, 6: 8-13.

23. Hendrick, *Lincoln's War Cabinet*, pp. 346-47, and Welles, *Diary*, 1: 201.

24. *Collected Works*, 6: 17, 26-28; Nicolay and Hay, *Lincoln*, 6: 300-313.

25. *Collected Works*, 6: 428-29.

26. Welles, *Diary*, 1: 205-11, 285, 320, 348, 351, 391; Donnal V. Smith, *Chase and Civil War Politics* (Freeport, N. Y.: Books for Libraries Press, 1972), pp. 63-64; David Donald, ed., *The Civil War Diaries of Salmon P. Chase* (New York: Longman's, Green, 1954), pp. 16-17, 149-51.

27. Welles, *Diary*, 1: 351-52, 30 June 1863; Allan Nevins, *War for the Union* (New York: Scribner's, 1971), 3: 149-50; Hendrick, *Lincoln's War Cabinet*, pp. 369-70.

28. Thomas and Hyman, *Stanton*, pp. 161-68.

CHAPTER 9
EMANCIPATION AND THE LIMITS OF DISSENT

1. Herman Hattaway and Archer Jones, *How the North Won: A Military History of the Civil War* (Urbana: University of Illinois Press, 1983), pp. 320-23.

2. James McPherson, *The Struggle for Equality* (Princeton, N.J.: Princeton University Press, 1964), pp. 117-21; David Donald, *Charles Sumner and the Rights of Man* (New York: Knopf, 1970), pp. 95-97.

3. William McFeely, *Frederick Douglass* (New York: Norton, 1991), pp. 215-16; Frederick Douglass, *The Life and Times of Frederick Douglass* (New York: Col-

lier's, 1962), pp. 353–55; John Hope Franklin, *The Emancipation Proclamation* (New York: Anchor, 1965), pp. 100–107.

4. Belle Becker Sideman and Lillian Friedman, eds., *Europe Looks at the Civil War* (New York: Orion Press, 1960), pp. 190–91; Richard Hofstadter, *The American Political Tradition and the Men Who Made It* (New York: Knopf, 1989), p. 131; Franklin, *Emancipation Proclamation*, p. 102.

5. See discussion in Alfred Hinsey Kelly, Winfred A. Harbison, and Herman Belz, *The American Constitution: Its Origins and Development* (New York: Norton, 1983), pp. 321–25. Harold M. Hyman, *"A More Perfect Union": The Impact of the Civil War and Reconstruction on the Constitution* (New York: Knopf, 1973), is also sensitive to these arguments.

6. Franklin, *Emancipation Proclamation*, pp. 86–87; Robert Warden, *An Account of the Private Life and Public Services of Salmon Portland Chase* (Cincinnati: Wilsatch, Baldwin & Co., 1874), pp. 513–15.

7. Harry Jaffa, "The Emancipation Proclamation," in *Equality and Liberty: Theory and Practice in American Politics* (New York: Oxford University Press, 1965), pp. 140–68; Harry Jaffa, *Crisis of the House Divided: An Interpretation of the Issues in the Lincoln-Douglas Debates* (Chicago: University of Chicago Press, 1959).

8. Thomas R. Kemp, "Community and War: The Civil War Experience of Two New Hampshire Towns," in Maris Vinovskis, ed., *Toward a Social History of the American Civil War: Exploratory Essays* (Cambridge: Cambridge University Press, 1990), pp. 43–46; William Walton, ed., *A Civil War Courtship: The Letters of Edwin Weller from Antietam to Atlanta* (New York: Doubleday, 1980), pp. 21–22; Allan Nevins, *War for the Union* (New York: Scribner's, 1960), 2: 462–63. The literature on conscription is analyzed in James W. Geary, "Civil War Conscription in the North: A Historiographical Review," *Civil War History* 32 (Sept. 1986): 208–28.

9. Mark Neely, *The Fate of Liberty: Abraham Lincoln and Civil Liberties* (New York: Oxford University Press, 1991), pp. 192–95.

10. Ibid., pp. 52–53; Harold Hyman and William Wiecek, *Equal Justice under Law: Constitutional Development, 1835–1875* (New York: Harper & Row, 1982), pp. 258–62; James G. Randall, *Constitutional Problems under Lincoln* (Urbana: University of Illinois Press, 1951), pp. 186–214.

11. Randall, *Constitutional Problems*, pp. 190–93; S. F. B. Morse, "The Constitution"; "The Draft, or Conscription Reviewed by the People," in Frank Freidel, ed., *Union Pamphlets of the Civil War* (Cambridge, Mass.: Harvard University Press, 1967), 1: 525–550, 2: 787–794.

12. Quoted in Nevins, *War for Union*, 2: 463; Benjamin Thomas and Harold Hyman, *Stanton: The Life and Times of Lincoln's Secretary of War* (New York: Knopf, 1962), pp. 279–80.

13. James G. Randall, *Lincoln the President*, 4 vols. (New York: Dodd, Mead, 1945–1954), 2: 291–92. On recruitment and organization of the army, see Fred R. Shannon, *The Organization and Administration of the Union Army*, 2 vols. (Cleveland: Arthur Clarke, 1926); Eugene Murdock, *One Million Men: The Civil War Draft in the North* (Madison: University of Wisconsin Press, 1971); and John

H. Geary, *We Need Men: The Union Draft in the Civil War* (De Kalb: Northern Illinois University Press, 1991).

14. Thomas and Hyman, *Stanton*, pp. 280-81; Randall, *Lincoln the President*, 2: 291-92; Nevins, *War for Union*, 2: 462-63.

15. Randall, *Constitutional Problems*, chap. 11.

16. Kemp, "Community and War, pp. 31-77.

17. For governors' reactions, see William Hesseltine, *Lincoln and the War Governors* (New York: Knopf, 1955), pp. 273-307.

18. Randall, *Constitutional Problems*, pp. 268-69; Randall, *Lincoln the President*, 2: 296-97; James McPherson, *Battle Cry of Freedom* (New York: Oxford University Press, 1988), pp. 608-9.

19. *Collected Works*, 6: 369-70, 391-92, 444-49.

20. Hesseltine, *Lincoln and the War Governors*, pp. 302-4; John Nicolay and John Hay, *Abraham Lincoln: A History*, 10 vols. (New York: Century, 1890), 7: 40-45.

21. E. B. Long, *Civil War Day by Day* (Garden City, N. Y.: Doubleday, 1971), p. 706; James McPherson, *Battle Cry of Freedom*, pp. 601-5. There is a conflict about the number of substitutes provided. McPherson follows Murdock, *One Million Men*, p. 356, and says 74,000 provided substitutes, but Mark Neely, Jr., *Abraham Lincoln Encyclopedia* (New York: McGraw-Hill, 1982), p. 70, says there were 117,986, and Peter Parish, *The American Civil War* (New York: Holmes and Meier, 1975), p. 143, lists 116,000 substitutes. Shannon's authoritative *Organization and Administration of the Union Army*, 2: 137, says, "For all practical purposes, it may be said that the two years of almost constant drafting and preparation for draft produced directly 170,000 men of whom nearly 120,000 were substitutes." If only the actual number of draftees who served are counted, then the draft did not produce many soldiers; but the purpose of the draft law was to provide men and not to target specific men identified in the enrollment process. It has seemed to me that including substitutes legitimately describes the results of the law. Neely counts the draftees and substitutes together but uses as the total Union forces that served in the war to reach a figure of 6 percent of all who served. I have used the figure of total soldiers available as of 1 January 1865—those who were present at the beginning of the last campaigns of the war, not including those who were once in but by then would have been out of the conflict. Even if the highest number of soldiers available, 1,000,516, is the benchmark, the draft—counting substitutes—provided 16 percent of those men.

22. Long, *Civil War Day by Day*, pp. 704-8.

23. *Collected Works*, 6: 446.

24. James McPherson, *Battle Cry of Freedom*, pp. 602-8; Eugene Murdock, "Was It a Poor Man's Fight?" *Civil War History* 10 (1964): 241-45; Hugh Earnhart, "Commutation: Democratic or Undemocratic?" *Civil War History* 12 (1966): 132-42; Kemp, "Community and War," pp. 61-66; W. J. Rorabaugh, "Who Fought for the North in the Civil War?" *Journal of American History* 73 (1986): 695-701.

25. *Collected Works*, 6: 78-79.

26. Hattaway and Jones, *How the North Won*, pp. 347-48, 378-84. On the

meaning of Jackson's death to the Confederacy, see Charles Royster, *The Destructive War: William Tecumseh Sherman, Stonewall Jackson, and the Americans* (New York: Knopf, 1991), chap. 5.

27. *Official Record of the War of the Rebellion*, series 2, vol. 5, 573ff. describes the Vallandigham case. See Frank Klement, *The Limits of Dissent: Clement Vallandigham and the Civil War* (Lexington: University of Kentucky Press, 1970), for background on the case. Phillip Paludan, *"A People's Contest": The Union and Civil War, 1861–1865* (New York: Harper & Row, 1988), pp. 239–43, is a recent interpretation.

28. Nicolay and Hay, *Lincoln*, 7: 228–38; Klement, *Limits of Dissent*.

29. Nicolay and Hay, *Lincoln*, 7: 340; Abraham Lincoln, "The Truth from an Honest Man" (Union League Pamphlet no. 31) as reprinted in Freidel, *Union Pamphlets*, 2: 739–43. This pamphlet includes the Democratic resolutions as well as Lincoln's reply, the famous "Corning Letter."

30. Howard K. Beale, ed., *The Diary of Gideon Welles*, 3 vols. (New York: Norton, 1960), 1: 306.

31. Neely, *Fate of Liberty*, pp. 223–24, explains Lincoln's sweeping assertion of power differently.

32. *Collected Works*, 6: 260–69, 300–306, 12 and 29 June 1863.

33. *Collected Works*, 6: 300–306, 29 June 1863.

CHAPTER 10
UNION POWER AFFIRMED

1. *New York Times*, 16 June 1863; *New York Herald*, 18 June 1863.

2. *Collected Works*, 6: 257–58, 10 June 1863, 6:40 P.M. I follow Herman Hattaway and Archer Jones, *How the North Won: A Military History of the Civil War* (Urbana: University of Illinois Press, 1983), pp. 399–404, T. Harry Williams, *Lincoln and His Generals* (New York: Knopf, 1952); and Benjamin Thomas and Harold Hyman, *Stanton: The Life and Times of Lincoln's Secretary of War* (New York: Knopf, 1962), pp. 270–73.

3. John Nicolay and John Hay, *Abraham Lincoln: A History*, 10 vols. (New York: Century, 1890), 7: 88; Thomas and Hyman, *Stanton*, p. 271.

4. *Collected Works*, 6: 282; Howard K. Beale, ed., *The Diary of Gideon Welles*, 3 vols. (New York: Norton, 1960), 1: 329, 336.

5. Thomas and Hyman, *Stanton*, pp. 272–73; Williams, *Lincoln and His Generals*, pp. 256–57; Hattaway and Jones, *How the North Won*, p. 404; Welles, *Diary*, 1: 344–48.

6. Frank A. Haskell, *The Battle of Gettysburg*, Bruce Catton, ed. (Boston: Houghton Mifflin, 1969), pp. 143–44.

7. Ibid., pp. 153–54.

8. Tyler Dennett, ed., *Lincoln and the Civil War in the Diaries and Letters of John Hay* (New York: Dodd, Mead, 1939), pp. 66–67.

9. I follow the judgment of Hattaway and Jones, *How the North Won*, pp. 424–26.

10. *Collected Works*, 5: 98-99.

11. Ulysses S. Grant, *Personal Memoirs* (New York: Library of America, 1990), pp. 223-24.

12. Allan Nevins, *War for the Union* (New York: Scribner's, 1971), 3: 55-56; Thomas and Hyman, *Stanton*, pp. 265-69; Hattaway and Jones, *How the North Won*, pp. 293-97, 343; Williams, *Lincoln and His Generals*, pp. 188-92.

13. Williams, *Lincoln and His Generals*, pp. 222-25; Grant, *Personal Memoirs*, pp. 231, 301.

14. Hattaway and Jones, *How the North Won*, pp. 410-12.

15. Grant, *Personal Memoirs*, p. 381; Lusk quoted in Henry Steele Commager, ed., *The Blue and the Gray* (New York: Fairfax, 1982), p. 643.

16. *Collected Works*, 5: 505-6, and 7: 41; Hattaway and Jones, *How the North Won*, p. 288; *Tribune Almanac and Political Register* (*New York Tribune* Association, 1864), pp. 37-38.

17. *Tribune Almanac and Political Register*, p. 38.

18. Phillip Paludan, *"A People's Contest": The Union and Civil War, 1861-1865* (New York: Harper & Row, 1988), pp. 140-41, 365-66; Eric Foner, *Reconstruction: America's Unfinished Revolution* (New York: Harper & Row, 1988), pp. 18-20; Nevins, *War for the Union*, 3: 254-57.

19. *Collected Works*, 6: 496; Nevins, *War for Union*, 3: 212-17; Paludan, *"People's Contest,"* pp. 143-44.

20. See Paludan, *"People's Contest,"* for general discussion of the economic background of the riots. The best work on the subject is Iver Bernstein, *The New York City Draft Riots* (New York: Oxford University Press, 1990). I follow his argument except where noted.

21. Gabor Boritt, *Lincoln and the Economics of the American Dream* (Memphis: Memphis State University Press, 1978), pp. 176-83, 217-21; *Collected Works*, 3: 459, 468, 473, 477-78; 4: 7-8, 12-13, 24-26, 203; Eric Foner, *Free Soil, Free Labor, Free Men: The Ideology of the Republican Party before the Civil War* (New York: Oxford University Press, 1970), passim; David Montgomery, *Beyond Equality, Labor and the Radical Republicans* (New York: Vintage, 1967), pp. 108-10.

22. Robert Sterling, "Civil War Draft Resistance in the Middle West," Ph.D. diss., Northern Illinois University, 1974, pp. 178-79, 259-74; Eugene Murdock, *One Million Men: The Civil War Draft in the North* (Madison: University of Wisconsin Press, 1971), pp. 83-90; Paludan, *"People's Contest,"* pp. 168-69, 192-94; James McPherson, *Battle Cry of Freedom* (New York: Oxford University Press, 1988), pp. 600-609; Matthew Gallman, *Mastering War: A Social History of Philadelphia during the Civil War* (Cambridge: Cambridge University Press, 1990); Grace Palladino, *Another Civil War: Labor, Capital and the State in the Anthracite Regions of Pennsylvania, 1840-1868* (Urbana: University of Illinois Press, 1990)

23. Bernstein, *Draft Riots*, pp. 59-60; Welles, *Diary*, 1: 369-73.

24. Bernstein, *Draft Riots*, pp. 60-67.

25. I follow Gabor Boritt's intriguing argument that Lincoln's economic philosophy undergirded his military efforts. See Boritt, *Lincoln and Economics*, chap. 18.

26. Boritt, *Lincoln and Economics*, pp. 273-74.

27. Nevins, *War for Union*, 3: 23–27, 224–26, and Paludan, *"People's Contest,"* pp. 139–46, chap. 7.

CHAPTER 11
THE MEANING OF WAR

1. Edward Hagerman, *The American Civil War and the Origin of Modern Warfare: Ideas, Organization, and Field Command* (Bloomington: Indiana University Press, 1988), pp. 67–68, 244–45; Herman Hattaway and Archer Jones, "Lincoln as Military Strategist," *Civil War History* 26 (Dec. 1980): 293–303.

2. For debate over Lincoln's abilities as military strategist, see T. Harry Williams, *Lincoln and His Generals* (New York: Knopf, 1952); Herman Hattaway and Archer Jones, *How the North Won: A Military History of the Civil War* (Urbana: University of Illinois Press, 1983), p. 687; Ulysses S. Grant, *Personal Memoirs* (New York: Library of America, 1990), pp. 361–62, 372–73. See *Collected Works*, 6: 466–84 (correspondence with Ambrose Burnside, Henry Halleck, and William Rosecrans, 16–27 Sept. 1863); Stephen Ambrose, *Halleck: Lincoln's Chief of Staff* (Baton Rouge: Louisiana State University Press, 1962).

3. Glyndon Van Deusen, *William Henry Seward*, (New York: Oxford University Press, 1967), pp. 211, 321; Donald P. Crook, *The North, the South and the Powers, 1861–1865* (New York: Wiley, 1974), pp. 227–45, 352–70.

4. Martin Duberman, *Charles Francis Adams, 1807–1886* (Boston: Little, Brown, 1961), pp. 293–303; Crook, *North, South*, pp. 258–62; Ephraim Douglas Adams, *Great Britain and the American Civil War*, 2 vols. (London: Longman's, Green and Co., 1925), 2: 119–31.

5. Benjamin Thomas and Harold Hyman, *Stanton: The Life and Times of Lincoln's Secretary of War* (New York: Knopf, 1962), pp. 286–89; David Donald, ed., *The Civil War Diaries of Salmon P. Chase* (New York: Longman's, Green, 1954), pp. 201–4; George Turner, *Victory Rode the Rails* (Indianapolis: Bobbs-Merrill, 1953), pp. 289–94.

6. Phillip Paludan, *"A People's Contest": The Union and Civil War, 1861–1865* (New York: Harper & Row, 1988), pp. 243–59; William Gienapp, "Politics Seems to Enter into Everything" in Stephen Maizlish, ed., *Essays on Antebellum Politics, 1840–1860* (College Station: Texas A & M University Press, 1982).

7. James W. Geary, *We Need Men: The Union Draft in the Civil War* (DeKalb: Northern Illinois University Press, 1991), pp. 104–8; Joel Silbey, *A Respectable Minority: The Democratic Party in the Civil War Era, 1860–1868* (New York: Norton, 1977), pp. 118–19, 147–48; Jean Baker, *Affairs of Party: The Political Culture of Northern Democrats in the Mid-Nineteenth Century* (Ithaca, N.Y.: Cornell University Press, 1983), pp. 338–39; Paludan, *"People's Contest,"* pp. 92–98.

8. Quoted in V. Jacques Voegeli, *Free but Not Equal: The Midwest and the Negro during the Civil War* (Chicago: University of Chicago Press, 1967), p. 179.

9. John Nicolay and John Hay, *Abraham Lincoln: A History*, 10 vols. (New York: Century, 1890), 7: 378–87.

10. *Collected Works*, 6: 406–10, 414, 423, 430; James G. Randall and Richard

M. Current, *Lincoln the President: Midstream*, 4 vols. (New York: Dodd, Mead, 1945–1954), 3: 256–62.

11. Nicolay and Hay, 6: 385–86n; Allan Nevins and Milton H. Thomas, eds., *The Diary of George Templeton Strong*, 4 vols. (New York: Macmillan, 1952), 3: 355.

12. Joseph Glatthaar, *Forged in Battle: The Civil War Alliance of Black Soldiers and White Officers* (New York: Free Press, 1990), pp. 136–42; James McPherson, *Battle Cry of Freedom* (New York: Oxford University Press, 1988), pp. 686–87.

13. I follow here Phillip Paludan, R. Gerald McMurtry Lecture, " 'The Better Angels of Our Nature': Lincoln, Propaganda and Public Opinion in the North during the Civil War," Ft. Wayne, Ind., Lincoln Museum, published 1993.

14. Frank L. Klement, *Dark Lanterns: Secret Political Societies, Conspiracies, and Treason Trials in the Civil War* (Baton Rouge: Louisiana State University Press, 1984), pp. 54–55; *Union Pamphlets of the Civil War, 1861–1865*, Frank Freidel, ed., 2 vols. (Cambridge, Mass.: Harvard University Press, 1967), 1: 1–14; Strong, *Diary*, 3: 303–7.

15. William Hesseltine, *Lincoln and the War Governors* (New York: Knopf, 1955), pp. 311–36.

16. Klement, *Dark Lanterns*, chap. 2. Klement does not make as much of the Lincoln connection as I do here; he also is less critical of the president than I.

17. Hesseltine, *Lincoln and the War Governors*, pp. 330–39; Allan Nevins, *War for the Union* (New York, Scribner's, 1971), 3: 177–79; Nicolay and Hay, *Lincoln*, 7: 375–77; Jean Baker, *Affairs of Party*, chap. 4.

18. Joel Silbey, *Respectable Minority*, pp. 118–19, 147–48, 155–62.

19. *Tribune Almanac and Political Register* (*New York Tribune* Association, 1964), p. 69.

20. *Collected Works*, 7: 48–49, 8 Dec. 1863; Peter Parish, *The American Civil War* (New York: Holmes and Meier, 1975), pp. 501–3. Allan Nevins calls the 1863 elections "one of the important turning points in the political history of the nation" (*War for Union*, 3: 155).

21. This is the major contention of Garry Wills, *Lincoln at Gettysburg: The Words that Remade America* (New York: Simon and Schuster, 1992), p. 38: "He altered the [Constitution] from within. . . . By . . . doing this, he performed one of the most daring acts of open-air sleight of hand ever witnessed by the unsuspecting. Everyone in that vast throng of thousands was having his or her intellectual pocket picked." Chapter 4 is entitled "Revolution in Thought."

22. Robert Bruce, "Lincoln and the Riddle of Death," Fourth Annual R. Gerald McMurtry Lecture, Ft. Wayne, Ind., Louis Warren Lincoln Library, 1981; *Collected Works*, 6: 16–17.

23. See James Boyd White, *Heracles' Bow: Essays on the Rhetoric and Poetics of the Law* (Madison: University of Wisconsin Press, 1985), chap. 1, for the ways in which larger stories can subsume and reconcile smaller antagonistic visions.

24. Harry Jaffa, *Crisis of the House Divided: An Interpretation of the Issues in the Lincoln-Douglas Debates* (Chicago: University of Chicago Press, 1959), explains Lincoln's integration of equality and democracy in the debates with

Douglas. Lincoln's reassertion of the linkage was given special meaning in wartime by the sacrifices of tens of thousands, deaths that moved that linkage closer to reality.

25. Wills, *Lincoln at Gettysburg*, pp. 146–47, argues the dubious proposition that the address was significantly a statement that the *national* government was now responsible for securing equality.

26. James M. McPherson, *Abraham Lincoln and the Second American Revolution* (New York: Oxford University Press, 1990), chap. 3, and Don E. Fehrenbacher, "The Paradoxes of Freedom," chap. 10 in *Lincoln in Text and Context* (Stanford, Calif.: Stanford University Press, 1987), discuss the meanings of negative and positive liberty in Lincoln's time.

27. Phillip S. Paludan, "The American Civil War Considered as a Crisis in Law and Order," *American Historical Review* 77 (October 1972): 1013–1034.

28. James McPherson, "Lincoln and Liberty," in *Abraham Lincoln and the Second American Revolution* (New York: Oxford University Press, 1990), pp. 62–63, 138.

CHAPTER 12
RECONSTRUCTION BEGINNINGS

1. *Harper's Pictorial History of the Civil War* (Chicago: Star Publishing, 1866), p. 269.

2. Richard West, *Lincoln's Scapegoat General: A Life of Benjamin F. Butler* (Boston: Little, Brown, 1965), pp. 149–52; Benjamin Butler, *Butler's Book* (Boston: A. M. Thayer, 1892), pp. 439–43; Joseph G. Dawson III, *Army Generals and Reconstruction: Louisiana, 1862–1877* (Baton Rouge: Louisiana State University Press, 1982), pp. 5–10.

3. *Butler's Book*, chaps. 9–10; Hans Trefousse, *Ben Butler: The South Called Him Beast* (New York: Twayne, 1957); Peyton McCrary, *Abraham Lincoln and Reconstruction: The Louisiana Experiment* (Princeton, N.J.: Princeton University Press, 1978), pp. 74–82.

4. Dawson, *Army Generals*, pp. 9–10.

5. *Collected Works*, 7: 52, 8 Dec. 1863; I rely throughout the following discussion on Eric Foner, *Reconstruction: America's Unfinished Revolution, 1863–1877* (New York: Harper & Row, 1988). For reconstruction as driven by war necessity, see Ted Tunnell, *Crucible of Reconstruction: War, Radicalism and Race in Louisiana, 1862–1877* (Baton Rouge: Louisiana State University Press, 1984), and Herman Belz, *Reconstructing the Union: Theory and Policy during the Civil War* (Ithaca, N.Y.: Cornell University Press, 1969), pp. 277–78.

6. On Louisiana, I follow Lawanda Cox, *Lincoln and Black Freedom: A Study in Presidential Leadership* (Columbia: University of South Carolina Press, 1981), Peyton McCrary, *Lincoln and Reconstruction*, and Tunnell, *Crucible of Reconstruction*; the amount and quality of this work on Louisiana is further reason to concentrate there. Phillips's comment is in Edward McPherson, *The Political History*

of the United States of America during the Great Rebellion (Washington, D.C.: Philp and Solomons, 1865), p. 412.

7. Foner, *Reconstruction*, p. 47; Tunnell, *Crucible of Reconstruction*, pp. 66–91.

8. Tunnell, *Crucible of Reconstruction*, pp. 26–32.

9. William F. Messner, "Black Violence and White Response: Louisiana, 1862," *Journal of Southern History* 41 (Feb. 1975): 19–23; Leon Litwack, *Been in the Storm So Long: The Aftermath of Slavery* (New York: Knopf, 1979), pp. 135–38, 148–49, 428.

10. Messner, "Black Violence," pp. 24–25.

11. Ibid., pp. 26–27.

12. McCrary, *Lincoln and Reconstruction*, pp. 83–84; Dudley Taylor Cornish, *The Sable Arm: Black Troops in the Union Army, 1861–1865* (Lawrence: University Press of Kansas, 1987), pp. 53–68; Lincoln to George Robertson, 20 Nov. 1862, *Collected Works*, 5: 502.

13. *Collected Works*, 5: 342–46, 26 and 28 July 1862, pp. 462–63, 504–5, 14 Oct. 1862, two letters of 21 Nov. 1862.

14. McCrary, *Lincoln and Reconstruction*, pp. 87–88; David Donald, ed., *Inside Lincoln's Cabinet: The Civil War Diaries of Salmon P. Chase* (New York: Longman's, Green, 1954), pp. 95–100.

15. McCrary, *Lincoln and Reconstruction*, pp. 95–101.

16. *Congressional Globe*, 37th Cong., 3d sess., 1030–1031; McCrary, *Lincoln and Reconstruction*, pp. 102–7; Belz, *Reconstructing the Union*, pp. 85–118.

17. McCrary, *Lincoln and Reconstruction*, pp. 108–11.

18. Cox, *Lincoln and Black Freedom*, pp. 49–50.

19. As quoted in J. Thomas May, "Continuity and Change in the Labor Program of the Union Army and the Freedmen's Bureau," *Civil War History* 17 (Sept. 1971): 245–54; McCrary, *Lincoln and Reconstruction*, pp. 271–72; James McPherson, *Struggle for Equality: Abolitionists and the Negro in the Civil War and Reconstruction* (Princeton, N.J.: Princeton University Press, 1964), pp. 240–45. For Grant's involvement with refugees, see Brooks Simpson, *Let Us Have Peace: Ulysses S. Grant and the Politics of War and Reconstruction, 1861–1868* (Chapel Hill: University of North Carolina Press, 1991), pp. 29–33. The basic works on the refugee problem include Ira Berlin et al., eds., *The Destruction of Slavery*, series 1 of *Freedom: A Documentary History of Emancipation, 1861–1867*, 3 vols. (Cambridge: Cambridge University Press, 1982–), John Eaton, *Grant, Lincoln and the Freedmen* (New York: Negro Universities, 1908), and Louis Gerteis, *From Contraband to Freedman: Federal Policy toward Southern Blacks, 1861–1865* (Westport, Conn.: Greenwood, 1973).

20. Whitelaw Reid, *After the War: A Tour of the Southern States, 1865–1866*, C. Vann Woodward, ed. (New York: Harper's, 1965), pp. 408–11.

21. *Collected Works*, 6: 287–89, 19 June 1863.

22. Ibid., pp. 364–65, 5 Aug. 1863.

23. Cox, *Lincoln and Black Freedom*, pp. 64–65, quotes Durant's letter.

24. *Collected Works*, 6: 546–53; Herman Belz, "The Etheridge Conspiracy of 1863: A Projected Conservative Coup," *Journal of Southern History* 36 (Nov. 1970): 549–67; Tyler

Dennett, ed., *Lincoln and the Civil War in the Diaries and Letters of John Hay* (New York: Dodd, Mead, 1939), pp. 130–31; McCrary, *Lincoln and Reconstruction*, pp. 175–78.

25. *Collected Works*, 7: 1–2.

26. Ibid., p. 2, n. 1.

27. "Lincoln aimed primarily at restoring states quickly by weakening the will of southern states to continue warring, rather than antagonizing them further and reinforcing their will to carry on the war" (Harold M. Hyman and William M. Wiecek, *Equal Justice under Law: Constitutional Development, 1835–1875* [New York: Harper & Row, 1982], p. 270).

28. *Collected Works*, 7: 54–56, 8 Dec. 1863.

29. Hay, *Diaries and Letters*, pp. 131–32.

30. *Collected Works*, 6: 365–66, and 7: 90–91.

31. Hay, *Diaries and Letters*, pp. 140–41. Banks's December letters to Lincoln are discussed in Cox, *Lincoln and Black Freedom*, pp. 67–72; McCrary, *Lincoln and Reconstruction*, pp. 200–203.

32. Lincoln to Banks (emphasis in original), *Collected Works*, 7: 89–90, 24 Dec. 1863.

33. Tunnell, *Crucible of Reconstruction*, pp. 41–47.

34. ibid., pp. 38–39.

35. Quoted in ibid., p. 78, and see pp. 36–38.

36. I follow Tunnell's criticism of McCrary on the radicalism of white Unionists in Louisiana. See also Cox, *Lincoln and Black Freedom*, pp. 76–77.

CHAPTER 13
LINCOLN AFFIRMED

1. Both Lincoln to Grant and Grant's reply are in *Collected Works*, 6: 324–25, and see Lincoln to Burnside, 6: 350, 27 July; George Agassiz, ed. *Meade's Headquarters, 1863–65: Letters of Colonel Theodore Lyman* (Boston: Atlantic Monthly, 1922), pp. 80–81.

2. T. Harry Williams, *Lincoln and His Generals* (New York: Knopf, 1952); Tyler Dennett, ed., *Lincoln and the Civil War in the Diaries and Letters of John Hay* (New York: Dodd, Mead, 1939), pp. 178–79.

3. Frederick Blue, *Salmon P. Chase: A Life in Politics* (Kent, Ohio: Kent State University Press, 1987), pp. 202–6. William Frank Zornow, *Lincoln and the Party Divided* (Norman: University of Oklahoma Press, 1954), is still the primary source for the 1864 election; I rely on it for evidence, not for interpretation. Peter Parish, *The American Civil War* (New York: Holmes and Meier, 1975), pp. 530–41; James Randall and Richard M. Current, *Lincoln the President*, 4 vols., *Last Full Measure* (New York: Dodd, Mead, 1945–1954), 4: chap.11, and John Nicolay and John Hay, *Abraham Lincoln: A History*, 10 vols. (New York: Century, 1890), 9: chaps. 3, 4, 11, 15, and 16, underlie my discussion of the election. Harry Carman and Richard Luthin, *Lincoln and the Patronage* (New York: Columbia University Press, 1943), is indispensable on how the president shaped politics.

4. Blue, *Chase*, pp. 216–22. Randall and Current, *Last Full Measure*, contains

a thorough description of the Chase movement but one that suffers from their vision of Lincoln alienated from radicals.

5. Phillips as quoted in James McPherson, *Struggle for Equality* (Princeton, N.J.: Princeton University Press, 1964), p. 260; *Collected Works*, 7: 55.

6. Louis Gerteis, "Salmon P. Chase, Radicalism and the Politics of Emancipation," *Journal of American History* 60 (June 1973): 42–62; Herman Belz, *A New Birth of Freedom: The Republican Party and Freedmen's Rights, 1861–1866* (Westport, Conn.: Greenwood, 1976), pp. 42–47.

7. Gerteis, "Salmon P. Chase." See discussion of debate in David Donald, *Charles Sumner and the Rights of Man* (New York: Knopf, 1970), pp. 174–78. Donald says that Sumner was indifferent as to which department controlled the agency.

8. Lincoln to Lorenzo Thomas, 28 Feb. 1864, to Alpheus Lewis, 23 Jan. 1864, *Collected Works*, 2: 145–46, 212.

9. James McPherson, *Struggle for Equality*, pp. 242–44; Belz, *New Birth of Freedom*, pp. 52–53.

10. Edward McPherson, *The Political History of the United States of America during the Great Rebellion* (Washington, D.C.: Philp and Solomons, 1865), pp. 317–19; Michael Les Benedict, *A Compromise of Principle: Congressional Republicans and Reconstruction, 1863–1869* (New York: Norton, 1974), pp. 80–83; Eric Foner, *Reconstruction: America's Unfinished Revolution* (New York: Harper & Row, 1988), pp. 39–41.

11. Harold Hyman and William Wiecek, *Equal Justice under Law* (New York: Harper & Row, 1982), pp. 269–75, emphasize the military focus of Lincoln's ideas and the features shared by Lincoln's proclamation and the Wade-Davis plan.

12. Herman Belz, *Reconstructing the Union: Theory and Policy during the Civil War* (Ithaca, N.Y.: Cornell University Press, 1969), pp. 200–205. Furthermore, the Wade-Davis bill granted no more rights to blacks than the Louisiana constitution was giving them. Indeed, Lawanda Cox has argued that the civil rights provided for under Wade-Davis were also less than in the Louisiana constitution (*Lincoln and Black Freedom: A Study in Presidential Leadership* [Columbia: University of South Carolina Press, 1981], p. 103).

13. Robert Warden, *An Account of the Private Life and Public Services of Salmon Portland Chase* (Cincinnati: Wilsatch, Baldwin and Co., 1874), p. 562; Nicolay and Hay, *Lincoln*, 8: 312–14.

14. Howard K. Beale, ed., *Diary of Gideon Welles: Secretary of the Navy under Lincoln and Johnson*, 3 vols. (New York: Norton, 1960), 1: 525–27, and 2: 17–18; Allan Nevins, *War for the Union* (New York: Scribner's, 1971), 4: 70–71.

15. Blue, *Chase*, pp. 214–16; Hay, *Diaries and Letters*, 18 Oct. 1863, pp. 100, 110.

16. Hay, *Diaries and Letters*, 18 Oct. 1863, pp. 100, 110.

17. David Donald, *Lincoln Reconsidered: Essays on the Civil War Era* (New York: Knopf, 1956), pp. 73–74.

18. *Collected Works*, 7: 120. Zornow, *Lincoln and the Party*, pp. 44–45, de-

scribes state activities. Hay, *Diaries and Letters*, pp. 152–53, describes Pennsylvania competitions.

19. Nicolay and Hay, *Lincoln*, 8: 319–20.

20. Blue, *Chase*, pp. 223–25; Zornow, *Lincoln and the Party*, pp. 49–54.

21. Chase to Lincoln, 22 Feb. 1864, Lincoln to Chase, 29 Feb. 1864, *Collected Works*, 7: 200–201, 212–13. Years later a Chase supporter declared that Chase in fact had known of the Pomeroy circular; see Randall and Current, *Last Full Measure*, pp. 107–9.

22. James McPherson, *Struggle for Equality*, pp. 264–70; Zornow, *Lincoln and the Party*, pp. 72–75; James B. Stewart, *Wendell Phillips: Liberty's Hero* (Baton Rouge: Louisiana State University Press, 1986), pp. 248–53.

23. Donald, *Sumner and the Rights of Man*, pp. 165–69.

24. James McPherson, *Struggle for Equality*, pp. 269–71; Phillip Paludan, *"A People's Contest": The Union and Civil War, 1861–1865* (New York: Harper & Row, 1988), pp. 250–52; Zornow, *Lincoln and the Party*, pp. 72–85; Edward McPherson, *Political History of the Great Rebellion*, pp. 411–14.

25. Edward McPherson, *Political History of the Great Rebellion*, pp. 403–7; James McPherson, *Struggle for Equality*, p. 271; Carman and Luthin, *Lincoln and Patronage*, pp. 259–60.

26. See George M. Frederickson, *The Inner Civil War: Northern Intellectuals and the Crisis of Union* (New York: Harper & Row, 1965), chap. 9 on "Meaning of Emancipation" for an implicit critique of Garrisonians for abandoning their anti-institutional positions.

27. James McPherson, *Struggle for Equality*, pp. 272–77.

28. *Collected Works*, 7: 376–78. James McPherson, *Battle Cry of Freedom* (New York: Oxford University Press, 1988), p. 717, reports that "two of the most thorough students" of the nomination process, Randall and Current, *Last Full Measure*, 4: 130–34 and Zornow, *Lincoln and the Party*, pp. 99–103, believe that Lincoln pushed for Johnson. This conclusion may have been affected by the fact that both these books also argue that Johnson followed Lincoln's policies and that both presidents were attacked by "unconditionals" or radicals.

29. Allan Nevins and Milton H. Thomas, eds., *The Diary of George Templeton Strong*, 4 vols. (New York: Macmillan, 1952), 3: 455. For the political machinations of the nomination of Johnson, see Glyndon Van Deusen, *Thurlow Weed: Wizard of the Lobby* (Boston: Little, Brown, 1947), pp. 307–8; Welles, *Diary*, 2: 45–51, and Donald, *Sumner and the Rights of Man*, pp. 169–71.

CHAPTER 14
LOUISIANA AND REELECTION

1. Lawanda Cox, *Lincoln and Black Freedom: A Study in Presidential Leadership* (Columbia: University of South Carolina Press, 1981), pp. 89–91; Fred Harvey Harrington, *Fighting Politician: Major General N. P. Banks* (Westport, Conn.: Greenwood, 1970), pp. 144–46.

2. Cox, *Lincoln and Black Freedom*, pp. 133–34. Cox speaks here of the goals

of Banks, Hahn, and Lincoln, but Flanders and Durant seem not to have differed from them on these points.

3. Peyton McCrary, *Abraham Lincoln and Reconstruction: The Louisiana Experiment* (Princeton, N.J.: Princeton University Press, 1978), pp. 227–29.

4. Ibid., pp. 224–27.

5. *Collected Works*, 7: 243, 13 Mar. 1864.

6. See for example Eric Foner, *Reconstruction: America's Unfinished Revolution* (New York: Harper & Row, 1988), pp. 49–50.

7. Lincoln to Hahn, 15 Mar. 1864, *Collected Works*, 7: 248.

8. Cox, *Lincoln and Black Freedom*, pp. 100–101; McCrary, *Lincoln and Reconstruction*, pp. 262–63.

9. Lincoln to Banks, 9 Aug. 1864, *Collected Works*, 7: 486–87; Foner, *Reconstruction*, pp. 49–50; McCrary, *Lincoln and Reconstruction*, pp. 245–53.

10. *Collected Works*, 7: 486, 9 Aug. 1864; Cox, *Lincoln and Black Freedom*, pp. 101–2.

11. Herman Belz, *A New Birth of Freedom: The Republican Party and Freedmen's Rights, 1861–1866* (Westport, Conn.: Greenwood, 1976), pp. 42–45; *Collected Works*, 6: 365, 387, and 7: 51, 55; Foner, *Reconstruction*, pp. 53–58; Willie Lee Rose, *Rehearsal for Reconstruction: The Port Royal Experiment* (New York: Vintage Books, 1967).

12. Cox, *Lincoln and Black Freedom*, pp. 131–34.

13. Leon Litwack, *Been in the Storm So Long: The Aftermath of Slavery* (New York: Knopf, 1979), pp. 377–79; Foner, *Reconstruction*, pp. 66–67.

14. The Wade-Davis bill is in Harold Hyman, ed., *The Radical Republicans and Reconstruction 1861–1870* (Indianapolis: Bobbs-Merrill, 1967), pp. 128–34. On the vote for the bill, see Mark Neely, Jr., *Abraham Lincoln Encyclopedia* (New York: McGraw-Hill, 1982), pp. 322–23. The most complete study of the bill is in Herman Belz, *Reconstructing the Union: Theory and Policy during the Civil War* (Ithaca, N.Y.: Cornell University Press, 1969), pp. 198–243, 251–66.

15. *Collected Works*, 7: 433–34. Belz, *Reconstructing the Union*, notes that during the full time that the bill had been under debate Lincoln had not tried to influence anyone in Congress.

16. "Wade-Davis Manifesto," in Hyman, ed. *Radical Republicans and Reconstruction*, pp. 137–47.

17. *Collected Works*, 7: 514, 517; Allan Nevins and Milton H. Thomas, eds., *The Diary of George Templeton Strong*, 4 vols. (New York: Macmillan, 1952), 3: 470. Nevins, *War for the Union*, 4: 92–93, discusses the Raymond proposal for negotiations with Davis without noting Lincoln's memo. John Nicolay and John Hay, *Abraham Lincoln: A History*, 10 vols. (New York: Century, 1890), 9: 218–21, argue that Lincoln wrote it out to show the absurdity of the idea. James McPherson, *Battle Cry of Freedom* (New York: Oxford University Press, 1988), pp. 770–71, suggests that Lincoln "almost succumbed to demands for the sacrifice of abolition as a stated condition of peace" but then pulled back.

18. Edward McPherson, *The Political History of the United States of America during the Great Rebellion* (Washington D.C.: Philp and Solomons, 1865), pp. 417–20.

19. *Collected Works*, 7: 499–501, 506–8, and 8: 1–2. James McPherson, "Lincoln and the Strategy of Unconditional Surrender" in *Abraham Lincoln and the Second American Revolution* (New York: Oxford University Press, 1990), p. 89, suggests that Lincoln was wavering in his commitment to emancipation as a condition of peace negotiations. I differ.

20. William Frank Zornow, *Lincoln and the Party Divided* (Norman: University of Oklahoma Press, 1954), pp. 136–40; Edward McPherson, *Political History of the Great Rebellion*, p. 421; James McPherson, *Battle Cry of Freedom*, pp. 775–76.

21. "The Great Surrender to the Rebels in Arms. The Armistice (Union Executive Congressional Committee, No. 4), in Frank Freidel, ed., *Union Pamphlets of the Civil War*, 2 vols. (Cambridge, Mass.: Harvard University Press, 1967), 2: 1016–1027; Frank L. Klement, *Dark Lanterns, Secret Political Societies, Conspiracies, and Treason Trials in the Civil War* (Baton Rouge: Louisiana State University Press, 1984), chap. 5.

22. Tyler Dennett, ed., *Lincoln and the Civil War in the Diaries and Letters of John Hay* (New York: Dodd, Mead, 1939), pp. 192–93; Klement, *Dark Lanterns*, pp. 138–50.

23. Benjamin Thomas and Harold Hyman, *Stanton: The Life and Times of Lincoln's Secretary of War* (New York: Knopf, 1962), p. 328; *Collected Works*, 8: 11, 24, 43; David Donald, "A. Lincoln: Politician," in Donald, *Lincoln Reconsidered: Essays on the Civil War Era* (New York: Knopf, 1956), pp. 75–81. See Howard K. Beale, ed., *Diary of Gideon Welles: Secretary of the Navy under Lincoln and Johnson*, 3 vols. (New York: Norton, 1960), 2: 97–98, 136–37, for a description of patronage operations in navy yards.

24. *Collected Works*, 7: 412–19; Burton J. Hendrick, *Lincoln's War Cabinet* (Boston: Little, Brown, 1946), pp. 442–51; Frederick Blue, *Salmon P. Chase: A Life in Politics* (Kent, Ohio: Kent State University Press, 1987), pp. 234–37; Welles, *Diary*, 2: 92–93.

25. Nevins, *War for the Union*, 4: 80–81; *Collected Works*, 7: 423.

26. William Ernest Smith, *The Francis Preston Blair Family in Politics*, 2 vols. (New York: Macmillan, 1933), 2: 90–111.

27. Hans Trefousse, *The Radical Republicans: Lincoln's Vanguard for Racial Justice* (New York: Knopf, 1969), pp. 277–79; Hendrick, *War Cabinet*, pp. 439–41; Smith, *Blair Family*, vol. 2, chap. 24–26.

28. Nicolay and Hay, *Lincoln*, 9: 340. John Hay wrote, "What have injured him are his violent personal antagonisms and indiscretions" (*Diaries and Letters*, pp. 219–20).

29. *Collected Works*, 8: 18; Welles, *Diary*, 2: 156–58. Welles says that Fremont's resignation was received the day before Blair's ouster. E. B. Long, *The Civil War Day by Day* (Garden City, N. Y.: Doubleday, 1971), puts the date of Fremont's withdrawal at 17 September, the day that the general told Republican officials. On the debate over why Fremont withdrew, see Nevins, *War for the Union*, 4: 105–8.

30. Nevins, *War for the Union*, 4: 136–37; James McPherson, *Battle Cry of Freedom*, pp. 803–5; Zornow, *Lincoln and the Party*, pp. 198–202; *Collected Works*, 8: 84.

31. Zornow, *Lincoln and the Party*, pp. 208–9; Benjamin Butler, *Butler's Book* (Boston: A. M. Thayer, 1892), pp. 753–73.

32. *Tribune Almanac and Political Register* (New York: Tribune Association, 1865), pp. 46–66.

33. Strong, *Diary*, 3: 514–15; *Collected Works*, 8: 100–102; Thomas and Hyman, *Stanton*, p. 334; Larry Nelson, *Bullets, Bayonets and Rhetoric: Confederate Policy for the United States Presidential Contest of 1864* (Tuscaloosa: University of Alabama Press, 1980).

34. *Collected Works*, 8: 96, 100–102.

35. Joel Silbey, *A Respectable Minority: The Democratic Party in the Civil War Era, 1860–1868* (New York: Norton, 1977), pp. 148–57; Philip Paludan, *"A People's Contest": The Union and Civil War, 1861–1865* (New York: Harper & Row, 1988), pp. 256–58. Mark Neely, Jr., *The Fate of Liberty: Abraham Lincoln and Civil Liberties* (New York: Oxford University Press, 1991), pp. 202–9, points to the ambiguous position of the Democratic party on Lincoln's civil liberty violations during the election; however, the Democratic platform of 1864, in which three of the six planks protest civil liberty violations, suggests little of that ambiguity. See Edward McPherson, *Political History of the Great Rebellion*, pp. 419–20.

36. Nicolay and Hay, *Abraham Lincoln*, 9: 337, 381; David Donald, *Charles Sumner and the Rights of Man* (New York: Knopf, 1970), 2: 205–6; Allen Thorndike Rice, ed., *Reminiscences of Abraham Lincoln* (New York: North American Review, 1888), pp. 56–60.

CHAPTER 15
THE RECONSTRUCTION PROPOSITION

1. Fred Harvey Harrington, *Fighting Politician: Major General N. P. Banks* (Westport, Conn.: Greenwood, 1970), pp. 159–63.

2. Ted Tunnell, *Crucible of Reconstruction: War, Radicalism and Race in Louisiana, 1862–1877* (Baton Rouge: Louisiana State University Press, 1984), pp. 84–87; Eric Foner, *Reconstruction: America's Unfinished Revolution* (New York: Harper & Row, 1988), pp. 62–67; Leon Litwack, *Been in the Storm So Long: The Aftermath of Slavery* (New York: Knopf, 1979), pp. 377–79.

3. Harrington, *Fighting Politician*, p. 166; Lawanda Cox, *Lincoln and Black Freedom: A Study in Presidential Leadership* (Columbia: University of South Carolina Press, 1981), pp. 112–14.

4. Lincoln to Hurlbut, 14 Nov. 1864, *Collected Works*, 8: 106–8. There is a clash of opinion over the meaning of the Hurlbut letter. See Cox, *Lincoln and Black Freedom*, pp. 112–15, versus Tunnell, *Crucible of Reconstruction*, pp. 48–49. I follow Tunnell. For the unchanged nature of labor control regulations see J. Thomas May, "Continuity and Change in the Labor Program of the Union Army and the Freedmen's Bureau," *Civil War History* 17 (Sept. 1971): 245–54, and Litwack, *Been in the Storm*, pp. 379, 413–15.

5. I follow the chronology of J. G. Randall and Richard Current in *Lincoln the President: The Last Full Measure* (New York: Dodd, Mead, 1955), chap. 13.

6. Lawanda Cox and John Cox, *Politics, Principle and Prejudice, 1865–1866* (New York: Free Press, 1963), p. 5; Samuel L. M. Barlow to Montgomery Blair, 10 Jan. 1865, Barlow Papers, Huntington Library, San Marino, Calif.

7. James McPherson, *Struggle for Equality* (Princeton, N.J.: Princeton University Press, 1964), pp. 125–27.

8. David Donald, *Charles Sumner and the Rights of Man* (New York: Knopf, 1970), pp. 148–50; *Collected Works*, 2: 240–41.

9. *Collected Works*, 7: 172–73, 8 Feb. 1864; Randall and Current, *Last Full Measure*, p. 307.

10. Edward McPherson, *The Political History of the United States of America during the Great Rebellion* (Washington, D.C.: Philp and Solomons, 1865), p. 258, lists the votes on the amendment.

11. Randall and Current, *Last Full Measure*, pp. 309–10.

12. *Collected Works*, 8: 149–50, 6 Dec. 1864.

13. Randall and Current, *Last Full Measure*, chap. 13; John Nicolay and John Hay, *Abraham Lincoln: A History*, 10 vols. (New York: Century, 1890), 10: chap. 4; Joel Silbey, *A Respectable Minority: The Democratic Party in the Civil War Era, 1860–1868* (New York: Norton, 1977), pp. 182–84; Allan Bogue, *The Congressman's Civil War* (Cambridge: Cambridge University Press, 1989), pp. 49–50, 161, n. 54.

14. Foner, *Reconstruction*, pp. 60–62; Donald, *Sumner and the Rights of Man*, pp. 197–209; Fawn Brodie, *Thaddeus Stevens: Scourge of the South* (New York: Norton, 1966), pp. 206–16.

15. Herman Belz, *Reconstructing the Union: Theory and Policy during the Civil War* (Ithaca, N.Y.: Cornell University Press, 1969), pp. 250–52.

16. Ibid., pp. 257–60.

17. Lincoln to Cuthbert Bullett, 28 July 1862, *Collected Works*, 5: 346.

18. Ibid., 8: 332–33.

19. Ibid., p. 386.

20. Ibid., pp. 151–52; Benjamin Thomas and Harold Hyman, *Stanton: The Life and Times of Lincoln's Secretary of War* (New York: Knopf, 1962), pp. 346–47.

21. Belz, *Reconstructing the Union*, pp. 299–300.

22. See Peyton McCrary, *Abraham Lincoln and Reconstruction: The Louisiana Experiment* (Princeton, N.J.: Princeton University Press, 1978), pp. 3–10, for the setting of the speech and a description and analysis that corresponds to my reading of its meaning, though without the emphasis here on negotiating with Congress.

23. Herman Belz, *A New Birth of Freedom: The Republican Party and Freedmen's Rights, 1861–1866* (Westport, Conn.: Greenwood, 1976), pp. 44ff., interprets the message more conservatively.

24. *Collected Works*, 8: 399–405.

25. McCrary, *Lincoln and Reconstruction*, pp. 10–11; David Donald, ed., *Inside Lincoln's Cabinet: The Civil War Diaries of Salmon P. Chase* (New York: Longman's, Green, 1954), pp. 265–69; Donald, *Sumner and the Rights of Man*, pp. 214–15; Thomas and Hyman, *Stanton*, pp. 353–57. For a conservative view of Lincoln's direction, see T. Harry Williams, *Lincoln and the Radicals* (Madison:

University of Wisconsin Press, 1941), pp. 370-73. Randall and Current, *Last Full Measure*, pp. 361-64, and Michael Les Benedict, *A Compromise of Principle: Congressional Republicans and Reconstruction, 1863-1869* (New York: Norton, 1974), pp. 98-99, are ambiguous.

26. "First Freedmen's Bureau Act," in Walter Fleming, ed., *Documentary History of Reconstruction*, 2 vols. (New York: Peter Smith, 1966), 1: 319.

27. Belz, *Reconstructing the Union*, p. 304.

28. George Rable, *But There Was No Peace: The Role of Violence in the Politics of Reconstruction* (Athens: University of Georgia Press, 1984); Dan T. Carter, *When the War Was Over: The Failure of Self-Reconstruction in the South, 1865-1867* (Baton Rouge: Louisiana State University Press, 1985), pp. 6-23; Foner, *Reconstruction*, pp. 119-23.

29. Tunnell, *Crucible of Reconstruction*, pp. 95-97; McCrary, *Lincoln and Reconstruction*, pp. 308-12.

30. Cox, *Lincoln and Black Freedom*, pp. 136-38.

CHAPTER 16
CONCLUSION

1. Allan Nevins and Milton H. Thomas, eds., *The Diary of George Templeton Strong*, 4 vols. (New York: Macmillan, 1952), 3: 584; Thomas Reed Turner, *Beware the People Weeping: Public Opinion and the Assassination of Abraham Lincoln* (Baton Rouge: Louisiana State University Press, 1982), p. 28.

2. Morton Keller, *Affairs of State: Public Life in Late Nineteenth Century America* (Cambridge, Mass.: Harvard University Press, 1977), pp. 18-19; Edward S. Corwin, *The President: Office and Powers, 1787-1957*, 4th ed. (New York: New York University Press, 1957), p. 227; Lance Davis and John Legler, "The Government in the American Economy, 1815-1902: A Quantitative Study," *Journal of Economic History* 26 (Dec. 1966): 514-27; Harold M. Hyman, *"A More Perfect Union": The Impact of the Civil War and Reconstruction on the Constitution* (New York: Knopf, 1973), pp. 300-325.

3. M. Ostrogorsky, *Democracy and the Organization of Political Parties*, 2 vols. (New York: Anchor, 1964), 2: 77; James Bryce, *The American Commonwealth*, abridged (New York: Macmillan, 1915), pp. 38-39; Martin Fausold and Alan Shank, eds., *The Constitution and the Presidency* (Albany: State University of New York, 1991), p. 45. Michael Les Benedict in this volume argues that the presidency was stronger than I have pictured it. He cites an 1895 assessment by Henry Ford Jones that "from Jackson's time to the present day . . . political issues have been decided by executive policy." Corwin, *President*, p. 28, cites these same words by Jones and doubts their accuracy.

4. See Brooks Simpson, *Let Us Have Peace: Ulysses S. Grant and the Politics of War and Reconstruction, 1861-1868* (Chapel Hill: University of North Carolina Press, 1991); Martin Mantell, *Johnson, Grant and the Politics of Reconstruction* (New York: Columbia University Press, 1973); Harold Hyman, "Johnson, Stanton and

Grant: A Reconsideration of the Army's Role in the Events Leading to Impeachment," *American Historical Review* 66 (1960): 85–100

5. See Donald Nieman, *Promises to Keep: African Americans and the Constitutional Order, 1776 to the Present* (New York: Oxford University Press, 1991), chap. 4.

6. Phillip Shaw Paludan, *A Covenant with Death: The Constitution, Law and Equality in the Civil War Era* (Urbana: University of Illinois Press, 1975); Michael Les Benedict, "Preserving the Constitution: The Conservative Basis of Radical Reconstruction," *Journal of American History* 61 (1974): 65–90; Hyman, *"More Perfect Union."*

BIBLIOGRAPHICAL ESSAY

The major argument of this book is that Lincoln respected equally the nation's institutions, manifested in the political-constitutional system, and its ideals, revealed in the Declaration of Independence. He saw those institutions as providing the process necessary to realize those ideals.

The current reigning opinion, strongly influenced by the struggles for equality of recent decades, differs. It emphasizes Lincoln's egalitarian goals and thus either asserts or strongly implies that his constitutional commitments were secondary. See Stephen B. Oates, *With Malice toward None* (New York: Harper & Row, 1977); James M. McPherson, *Abraham Lincoln and the Second American Revolution* (New York: Oxford University Press, 1990); Otto Olsen, "Abraham Lincoln as Revolutionary," *Civil War History* 24 (1978); Mark Neely, Jr., *Abraham Lincoln Encyclopedia* (New York: McGraw-Hill, 1982); and Garry Wills, *Lincoln at Gettysburg: The Words That Remade America* (New York: Simon and Schuster, 1992). Harry Jaffa, *Crisis of the House Divided: An Interpretation of the Issues in the Lincoln-Douglas Debates* (Chicago: University of Chicago Press, 1959), is more complex on the issue but still seems to separate ideals from institutions. The same can be said for Gary Jacobsohn, "Abraham Lincoln 'On This Question of Judicial Authority': The Theory of Constitutional Aspiration," *Western Political Science Quarterly* 36 (1983), which is, however, the first essay to focus directly on the relationship between the Constitution and the Declaration. Merrill Peterson, "'This Grand Pertinacity': Abraham Lincoln and the Declaration of Independence" (R. Gerald McMurtry Lecture, 1991, Fort Wayne, Indiana) says that Lincoln connected the Constitution with the Declaration and asserts the fundamental place of the Declaration's clause, "all men are created equal," in Lincoln's mature thought, but Peterson refrains from describing the connection.

The major historians who have written about Lincoln's constitutional views either have ignored or quickly passed over the relationship between those views and his respect for the ideals of the Declaration. James G. Randall, *Constitutional Problems under Lincoln* (Urbana: University of Illinois Press, 1951), for example, has no mention of the Declaration. Randall's *Lincoln the Liberal Statesman* (New York: Dodd, Mead, 1957), asserts that Lincoln's ideals were those of Jefferson and says that the Framers wanted slavery outside the constitutional system but spends most of its discussion of the "liberal" Lincoln arguing that he was no apostle of "laissez faire." Harold Hyman, in *"A More Perfect Union": The Impact of the Civil War and Reconstruction on the Constitution* (New York: Knopf, 1973), demonstrates that the president integrated his ideas of equality with his nationalism but argues that Lincoln sees the prewar Constitution as "flawed because it included slavery." At the same time Hyman, in Harold Hyman and William Wiecek, *Equal Justice under Law: Constitutional Development, 1835–1875* (New York: Harper & Row, 1982), says, without elaboration, that in 1857 Lincoln had said that the Declaration was part of the Constitution. In both works one finds the view that it took the Civil War to move Lincoln closer to abolitionists who for years had been speaking of a Constitution resting on the Declaration's ideals.

Mark Neely, Jr. *The Fate of Liberty: Abraham Lincoln and Civil Liberties* (New York: Oxford University Press, 1991), notes that Lincoln called the premise that "all men are created equal" "the fundamental principle on which our free institutions rest," but Neely also says that the Constitution was "an embarrassment to the antislavery cause." Don E. Fehrenbacher, in *Lincoln in Text and Context: Collected Essays* (Stanford, Calif.: Stanford University Press, 1987), refers in a footnote to the idea of "constitutional aspiration," which is similar to the position I am arguing, that the Constitution embodies the Declaration's ideals. Yet Fehrenbacher responds cursorily with a doubt that Lincoln agreed with that embodiment since the president accepted the necessity of the fugitive slave law once it had been incorporated into the legal system.

My argument for Lincoln as an integrator of ideals and institutions was provoked by constitutional theory as analyzed by Ronald Dworkin, *Law's Empire* (Cambridge, Mass.: Harvard University Press, 1986), and Sotirios Barber, *On What the Constitution Means* (Baltimore: Johns Hopkins University Press, 1984), the two major expounders of "constitutional aspiration," and by Charles Black, *Structure and Relationship in Constitutional Law* (Baton Rouge: Louisiana State University Press, 1969), James Boyd White, *When Words Lose Their Meaning: Constitutions and Reconstitutions of Language, Character and Community* (Chicago: University of Chicago Press, 1984), and *Heracles' Bow: Essays on the Rhetoric and Poetics of the Law* (Madison: University of Wisconsin Press, 1985). Harry Jaffa, *Crisis of the House Divided*, first demonstrated the value of theoretical analysis of Lincoln's thought.

The position taken in this book should also be distinguished from the radical critique of constitutionalism as simply politics and as one of the means whereby elites impose their hegemony on the masses and thus stifle equality. Hendrik Hartog summarizes this view as rejecting "Lincoln's . . . conception of the Constitution as an estate to be husbanded." My argument presents Lincoln's commitment to the Constitution as an insistence that only by preserving the values inherent in the constitutional system can the goals of equality be achieved. Hartog's statement, a summary of the views of several essayists, is in David Thelen, ed., *The Constitution and American Life* (Ithaca, N.Y.: Cornell University Press, 1988). For an assessment of those views and of critiques of them, see Herman Belz, "Constitutional and Legal History in the 1980s: Reflections on American Constitutionalism," *Benchmark* 4, no. 3 (Summer, 1990). I accept fully the idea that "the Constitution still matters—as a framework, as a statement of broad purposes, as a point of recurring reference, as a legitimation of further developments, as a restraint on the overbearing and the righteous," enunciated in Philip B. Kurland and Ralph Lerner, eds., *The Founders' Constitution*, 5 vols. (Chicago: University of Chicago Press, 1987), 1: ix.

GENERAL HISTORIOGRAPHY

"The Lincoln legend," Richard Hofstadter wrote in 1948, "has come to have a hold on the American imagination that defies comparison with anything else in political mythology." This remains true, as the popularity and number of Lincoln books since 1948 clearly reveals. As James McPherson observes, only Jesus and Shakespeare have had more books written about them. Lincoln matters not just to scholars who want to understand him but to a general public and to some specific interest groups who want to "get right with Lincoln" and so wrap themselves in his formidable reputation. To discuss this literature would require another book, at least. I shall resist the temptation to write that book here and discuss only a selected number of works that I have found most helpful, sources that will help interested readers begin their investigations.

David Donald's fine collection of essays, *Lincoln Reconsidered: Essays on the Civil War Era* (New York: Knopf, 1956), including his essay "Getting Right with Lincoln," explores much historiography, popular and scholarly. The best modern introduction to the various historiographic traditions is Don E. Fehrenbacher, in *Lincoln in Text and Context*, in which he describes "The Changing Image of Lincoln," "The Anti-Lincoln Tradition," "The Deep Reading of Lincoln" (psychoanalytical writings), and "The Fictional Lincoln." Fehrenbacher carries on a tradition of collected essays, including Donald's, which points the paths of Lincoln scholarship in ways that are fundamental for thinking about the Lincoln presidency: J. G. Randall, *Lincoln: The Liberal Statesman*; Norman Graebner, ed., *The Enduring Lincoln* (Urbana: University of Illinois Press, 1959); Richard N. Current, *The Lincoln Nobody Knows* (New York: Hill and Wang, 1958); Cullom Davis et al., eds., *The Public and Private Lincoln* (Carbondale: Southern Illinois University Press, 1979); Eric Foner, *Politics and Ideology in the Age of the Civil War* (New York: Oxford University Press, 1980); Stephen B. Oates, *Abraham Lincoln: The Man behind the Myths* (New York: Harper & Row, 1984); John L. Thomas, ed., *Abraham Lincoln and the American Political Tradition* (Amherst: University of Massachusetts Press, 1986); James M. McPherson, *Abraham Lincoln and the Second American Revolution*; Lloyd Ambrosius, ed., *A Crisis of Republicanism: American Politics during the Civil War Era* (Lincoln: University of Nebraska Press, 1990); and David Donald, ed., *Why the North Won the Civil War* (Baton Rouge: Louisiana State University Press, 1960). Richard Hofstadter, "Abraham Lincoln and the Self Made Myth," in *The American Political Tradition and the Men Who Made It* (New York: Knopf, 1989), is a significant and influential essay.

The most recent reviews of the Lincoln literature are Mark Neely, Jr., "The Lincoln Theme since Randall's Call: The Promises and Perils of Professionalism," *Papers of the Abraham Lincoln Association* (1979), and the bibliographic essay in Gabor S. Boritt, *Lincoln and the Economics of the American Dream* (Memphis: Memphis State University Press, 1978). Gabor Boritt, ed., *The Historian's Lincoln: Pseudohistory, Psychohistory, and History* (Urbana: University of Illinois Press, 1988), presents and analyzes most of the major Lincoln writings of recent years.

The most recent and most readable of the one-volume surveys of the Civil War era is James M. McPherson, *Battle Cry of Freedom* (New York, Oxford University Press, 1988). Peter Parish, *The American Civil War* (New York: Holmes and Meier, 1975), is filled with thoughtful analyses, as is William R. Brock, *Conflict and Transformation: The United States 1844–1877* (Baltimore: Penguin, 1973). The best of several recent one-volume surveys of the war are William Barney, *Battleground for the Union, 1848–1877* (Englewood Cliffs, N.J.: Prentice-Hall, 1990), David Donald, *Liberty and Union* (Lexington, Mass.: D. C. Heath, 1978), and Richard Sewell, *A House Divided, 1848–1865* (Baltimore: Johns Hopkins University Press, 1988). James Rawley provides a helpful overview in *Turning Points of the Civil War* (Lincoln: University of Nebraska Press, 1974), and in *The Politics of Union: Northern Politics during the Civil War* (Hinsdale, Ill.: Dryden, 1974).

LINCOLN AND THE PRESIDENCY

The basic Lincoln writings are John Nicolay and John Hay, *Abraham Lincoln: A History* (New York: Century, 1890), 10 vols., and James G. Randall, *Lincoln the President*, 4 vols., vol. 3 and 4 coauthored by Richard M. Current (New York: Dodd, Mead, 1945–1954). The best of the one-volume studies are Lord Charnwood, *Abraham Lincoln* (New York: Garden City Publishers, 1917), Stephen B. Oates, *With Malice toward None* (New York: Harper & Row, 1977), and Benjamin Thomas, *Abraham Lincoln* (1952; rept., New York: Modern Library, 1968).

The basic documents for Lincoln's life and presidency are Roy P. Basler, ed., *The Collected Works of Abraham Lincoln* (New Brunswick, N.J.: Rutgers University Press, 1953); the Abraham Lincoln Papers, 97 reels (Robert Todd Lincoln Collection), Library of Congress (containing incoming correspondence); Tyler Dennett, ed., *Lincoln and the Civil War in the Diaries and Letters of John Hay* (New York: Dodd, Mead, 1939); David Donald, ed., *Inside Lincoln's Cabinet: The Civil War Diaries of Salmon P. Chase* (New York: Longman's, Green, 1954); Howard K. Beale, ed., *Diary of Gideon Welles: Secretary of the Navy under Lincoln and Johnson*, 3 vols. (New York: Norton, 1960); Howard Beale, ed., *The Diary of Edward Bates*, (Washington, D.C.: GPO, 1933); and Theodore Pease and James G. Randall, eds., *The Diary of Orville Hickman Browning* (Springfield: Illinois State Historical Society, 1925–1933). E. B. Long, *The Civil War Day by Day* (New York: Doubleday,

1971), and Mark E. Neely, Jr., *The Abraham Lincoln Encyclopedia* (New York: Mc-Graw-Hill, 1982), are indispensable for the period and the man.

Lincoln's personality is discussed in all the biographies and collections of essays. In addition I have found helpful Hans J. Morganthau and David Hein, *Essays on Lincoln's Faith and Politics* (Lanham, Md.: University Press of America, 1983); Glen Thurow, *Abraham Lincoln and American Political Religion* (Albany: State University of New York Press, 1976); William Wolf, *The Religious Ideas of Abraham Lincoln* (New York: Seabury, 1963); Elton Trueblood, *Abraham Lincoln: Theologian of American Anguish* (New York: Harper & Row, 1973); Sidney Mead, "Abraham Lincoln's 'Last Best Hope of Earth': The American Dream of Destiny and Democracy," *Church History* 23 (March 1954); Jacques Barzun, "Lincoln's Philosophic Vision" (Fortenbaugh Memorial Lecture, Gettysburg College, 1982); Robert V. Bruce, "Lincoln and the Riddle of Death" (R. Gerald McMurtry Lecture, Fort Wayne, Ind., 1981); Charles Strozier, *Lincoln's Quest for Union: Public and Private Meanings* (New York: Basic Books, 1982); and William Herndon and Jesse Weik, *Abraham Lincoln: The True Story of a Great Life* (1889; rept., New York, D. Appleton, 1920). For the limitations of "Herndon's Lincoln," see David Donald, *Lincoln's Herndon* (New York: Knopf, 1948). Jean Baker, *Mary Todd Lincoln* (New York: Norton, 1987), is also illuminating on Lincoln.

The most recent analysis of the presidency under Lincoln is Michael Les Benedict, "The Constitution of the Lincoln Presidency and the Republican Era," in Martin Fausold and Alan Shank, eds., *The Constitution and the American Presidency* (Albany: State University of New York Press, 1991), which contains helpful discussion of other sources, especially those that speak of Lincoln's "dictatorship." The major works of that genre include Clinton Rossiter, *Constitutional Dictatorship: Crisis Government in the Modern Democracies* (Princeton, N.J.: Princeton University Press, 1948); Edward S. Corwin, *The President: Office and Powers, 1787–1957*, 4th ed. (New York: New York University Press, 1957); and James MacGregor Burns, *Presidential Government: The Crucible of Leadership* (Boston: Houghton Mifflin, 1965). Herman Belz, *Lincoln and the Constitution: The Dictatorship Question Reconsidered* (Fort Wayne, Ind.: Louis Warren Lincoln Library, 1984), and Benedict clear Lincoln of the charge of "dictator" as do the writings of Harold Hyman and Mark Neely. The question of Lincoln's vision and use of the executive office is debated in David Donald, "Whig in the White House," in *Lincoln Reconsidered*, and Stephen Oates, "Abraham Lincoln: *Republican* in the White House," in *Lincoln and the American Political Tradition*. The most helpful modern discussion of executive power is Richard Neustadt, *Presidential Power and the Modern Presidents: The Politics of Leadership from Roosevelt to Reagan* (New York: Free Press, 1990). Gabor Boritt, ed., *Lincoln, The War President* (New York: Oxford University Press, 1993), usefully collects lectures given at Gettysburg College's Fortenbaugh series on Lincoln and the Civil War.

Presidential authority is integral to surveys of constitutional history in the Civil War era. Three works stand out here: James G. Randall, *Constitutional Problems under Lincoln*; Harold M. Hyman, *"A More Perfect Union"*; and Harold Hyman and William Wiecek, *Equal Justice under Law*. Phillip S. Paludan, *A Covenant with Death: The Constitution, Law and Equality in the Civil War Era* (Urbana: University of Illinois Press, 1975), discusses constitutional thought in the war years. Carl B. Swisher, *The Taney Period,*

1836–64 (vol. 5 of the Holmes Devise, *History of the Supreme Court of the United States* [New York: Macmillan, 1974]), and David Silver, *Lincoln's Supreme Court* (Urbana: University of Illinois Press, 1956), cover the Supreme Court. William Wiecek, "The Reconstruction of Federal Judicial Power," *American Journal of Legal History* 13 (1969), explains the rise of judicial power in the war years as does Stanley I. Kutler, *Judicial Power and Reconstruction Politics* (Chicago: University of Chicago Press, 1968).

CIVIL LIBERTIES

The crucial issue of civil liberties in wartime is explored masterfully "from the ground up" in Mark Neely, Jr., *The Fate of Liberty*, and in works by Frank Klement, *The Limits of Dissent: Clement Vallandigham and the Civil War* (Lexington: University of Kentucky Press, 1970), and *Dark Lanterns: Secret Political Societies, Conspiracies, and Treason Trials in the Civil War* (Baton Rouge: Louisiana State University Press, 1984), in addition to treatments in general constitutional histories. William F. Duker, *A Constitutional History of Habeas Corpus* (Westport, Conn.: Greenwood, 1980), provides a helpful historical context. An older and still useful work is Sydney G. Fisher, "The Suspension of Habeas Corpus during the War of the Rebellion," *Political Science Quarterly* 3 (Sept. 1888). Frank Freidel, ed., *Union Pamphlets of the Civil War, 1861–1865*, 2 vols. (Cambridge, Mass.: Harvard University Press, 1967), contains many pamphlets debating Lincoln's authority over civil liberties as well as other subjects.

POLITICAL ENVIRONMENT OF THE LINCOLN ERA

The most valuable survey of the entire period of the disunion crisis and its resolution in 1865 is Allan Nevins's monumental *Ordeal of the Union*, 8 vols. (New York: Scribner's, 1947–1971). On the political culture of the period, see Robert Kelley, *The Cultural Pattern in American Politics: The First Century* (New York: Knopf, 1979); Lawrence Frederick Kohl, *The Politics of Individualism: Parties and the American Character in the Jacksonian Era* (New York: Oxford University Press, 1989); Rush Welter, *The Mind of America, 1820–1860* (New York: Columbia University Press, 1975); Daniel Walker Howe, *The Political Culture of the American Whigs* (Chicago: University of Chicago Press, 1979); Jean Baker, *Affairs of Party: The Political Culture of Northern Democrats in the Mid-Nineteenth Century* (Ithaca, N.Y.: Cornell University Press, 1983); Eric Foner, *Free Soil, Free Labor, Free Men: The Ideology of the Republican Party before the Civil War* (New York: Oxford University Press, 1970); Ronald Formisano, *The Birth of Mass Political Parties: Michigan, 1827–1861* (Princeton, N.J.: Princeton University Press, 1971); and William Gienapp, *Origins of the Republican Party 1852–1856* (New York: Oxford University Press, 1987). Descriptions of the extensive participation in politics of the mid-nineteenth century are found in William Gienapp, "Politics Seems to Enter into Everything," in Stephen Maizlish, ed., *Essays on American Antebellum Politics, 1840–1860* (Arlington: Texas A & M University Press, 1982), and Walter Dean Burnham, "The Changing Shape of the American Political Universe," *American Political Science Review* 59 (1965). The basic documents and statistics of wartime politics can be found in Edward McPherson, *Political History of the United States of America during the Great Rebellion* (Washington, D.C.: Philp and Solomons, 1865), and the *Tribune Almanac and Political Register* (New York: *New York Tribune* Association, 1860–1865).

The prewar sectional crisis in politics is discussed most recently from a viewpoint suspicious of Lincoln in Robert W. Johannsen, *The Frontier, the Union and Stephen A. Douglas* (Urbana: University of Illinois Press, 1989), and *Lincoln, the South and Slavery: The Political Dimension* (Baton Rouge: Louisiana State University Press, 1991). Tyler Anbinder, *Nativism and Slavery: The Northern Know Nothings and the Politics of the 1850s* (New York: Oxford University Press, 1992), and Michael Holt, *Political Parties and American Political Development from the Age of Jackson to the Age of Lincoln* (Baton Rouge: Louisiana State University Press, 1992), incorporate ethnocultural perspectives to explain political change. This work builds on writings that remain indispensable for seeing Lincoln in the context of prewar politics and constitutional argument: Kenneth M. Stampp, *The Imperiled Union: Essays on the Background of the Civil War* (New York: Oxford University Press, 1980); Don E. Fehrenbacher, *The Dred Scott Case* (New York: Oxford University Press, 1978); David Potter, *The Impending Crisis, 1848–1861* (New York: Harper & Row, 1976); Allan Nevins, *The Emergence of Lincoln*, 2 vols. (New York: Scribner's, 1950); Don Fehrenbacher, *Prelude to Greatness: Lincoln in the 1850s* (Stanford, Calif.: Stanford University Press, 1962); Robert W. Johannsen, *Stephen A. Douglas* (New York: Oxford University Press, 1973); and Roy F. Nichols, *The Disruption of American Democracy* (New York: Macmillan, 1948). On the Lincoln-Douglas debates see two thoughtful interpretive works, Harry Jaffa, *Crisis of the House Divided* and David Zarefsky, *Lincoln, Douglas, and Slavery* (Chicago: University of Chicago Press, 1990).

Work focusing more specifically on slavery, politics, and the Constitution clarifies the nature of the crisis that slavery provoked. See Paul Finkelman, *An Imperfect Union: Slavery, Federalism and Comity* (Chapel Hill: University of North Carolina Press, 1981); William Wiecek, *The Sources of Antislavery Constitutionalism, 1760–1848* (Ithaca, N.Y.: Cornell University Press, 1977); Lewis Perry, *Radical Abolitionism: Anarchy and the Government of God in Antislavery Thought* (Ithaca, N.Y.: Cornell University Press, 1973); Thomas Morris, *Free Men All: The Personal Liberty Laws of the North, 1780–1861* (Baltimore: Johns Hopkins University Press, 1974); Richard Sewell, *Ballots for Freedom: Antislavery Politics in the United States, 1837–1860* (New York: Norton, 1976); Russell B. Nye, *Fettered Freedom: Civil Liberties and the Slavery Controversy* (Lansing: Michigan State University Press, 1963); Robert Cover, *Justice Accused: Antislavery and the Judicial Process* (New Haven, Conn.: Yale University Press, 1975); James Rawley, *Race and Politics: Bleeding Kansas and the Coming of the Civil War* (Philadelphia: Lippincott, 1969); and Kenneth M. Stampp, *America in 1857: A Nation on the Brink* (New York: Oxford University Press, 1990). The most stimulating history of Southern reactions to the crisis, William Freehling, *Road to Disunion: Secessionists at Bay, 1776–1854* (New York: Oxford University Press, 1990), also contains a fine analysis of constitutional debate in Congress. George Forgie, *Patricide in the House Divided: A Psychological Interpretation of Lincoln and His Age* (New York: Norton, 1979), provides a stimulating perspective. Peter Knupfer, *The Union as It Is: Constitutional Union-ism and Sectional Compromise* (Chapel Hill: University of North Carolina Press, 1991), argues the value of compromise as a constitutional tradition.

The Fort Sumter crisis is analyzed and placed in context in Don E. Fehren-bacher, "Lincoln's Wartime Leadership: The First Hundred Days," *Journal of the Abraham Lincoln Association* 9 (1987), and in Potter, *Impending Crisis*, chapter 20. Robert V. Bruce, "The Shadow of a Coming War" (Fortenbaugh Memorial Lec-ture, Gettysburg College, 1989), and Gabor S. Boritt, "Abraham Lincoln: War Opponent and War President" (Inaugural Lecture of Robert C. Fluhrer Profes-sor, Gettysburg College, 1987), provide valuable assessments of Lincoln's views on war. James McPherson, *Battle Cry of Freedom*, summarizes the major perspec-tives on what Lincoln sought at Sumter. Most scholars now reject the idea that Lincoln deliberately pushed the Confederates into firing the first shot so that he could save his party. That argument was advanced most notably in Charles Ramsdell, "Lincoln and Fort Sumter," *Journal of Southern History* 3 (1937). Coun-terpositions, as well as subtle analyses of Lincoln's views, are David Potter, *Lin-coln and His Party in the Secession Crisis* (New Haven, Conn.: Yale University Press, 1962), and "Why the Republicans Rejected Both Compromise and Seces-sion," in George Harmon Knoles, ed., *The Crisis of the Union, 1860-1861* (Baton Rouge: Louisiana State University Press, 1965), and Kenneth Stampp, *The Imper-iled Union* (New York: Oxford University Press, 1980), pp. 162-90, and *And the War Came: The North and the Secession Crisis, 1860-61* (Chicago: University of Chi-cago Press, 1964). Richard Current, *Lincoln and the First Shot* (Philadelphia: Lip-pincott, 1963), agrees with Stampp. Useful background on the secession crisis is also provided in Philip Klein, *President James Buchanan* (University Park: Penn-sylvania State University Press, 1962), and Elbert Smith, *The Presidency of James Buchanan* (Lawrence: University Press of Kansas, 1975). Howard Cecil Perkins, ed., *Northern Editorials on Secession*, 2 vol. (New York: Appleton Century Crofts, 1964), is the basic gathering of sources. Phillip S. Paludan, "The American Civil War Considered as a Crisis in Law and Order," *American Historical Review* 77 (1972), and Arthur Bestor, "The Civil War as a Constitutional Crisis," *American Historical Review* 69 (1964), put the disunion crisis in constitutional context. The Baltimore riot is followed best in Gary Lawson Browne, *Baltimore in the Nation, 1789-1861* (Chapel Hill: University of North Carolina Press, 1980), and George Brown, *Baltimore and the Nineteenth of April* (Baltimore, 1887).

THE NATIONAL CONTEXT

For the United States in 1860 I have relied on two statistical syntheses, *The United States on the Eve of the Civil War as Described in the 1860 Census* (Washing-ton, D.C.: U.S. Civil War Centennial Commission, 1963), and *The Statistical His-tory of the United States from Colonial Times to the Present* (Stamford, Conn.: Fair-field, 1965), as well as on my own *"A People's Contest": The Union and Civil War, 1861-1865* (New York: Harper & Row, 1988), which is the basis for my argument about prewar anxieties and economic change. On the economy, see also George

Rogers Taylor, *The Transportation Revolution, 1815–1860* (New York: Holt, Rinehart and Winston, 1951), and Alfred Chandler, *The Visible Hand: The Managerial Revolution in American Business* (Cambridge, Mass.: Harvard University Press, 1977). Richard Franklin Bensel, *Yankee Leviathan: The Origins of Central State Authority in America, 1859–1877* (Cambridge: Cambridge University Press, 1990), is complex but useful on economic change in the era. The same can be said for Roger Ransom, *Conflict and Compromise: The Political Economy of Slavery, Emancipation, and the American Civil War* (Cambridge: Cambridge University Press, 1989). Susan Lee and Peter Passell, *A New Economic View of American History* (New York: Norton, 1978), summarize recent writings that evaluate costs and benefits of economic growth. Mark Summers, *The Plundering Generation: Corruption and the Crisis of the Union, 1849–1861* (New York: Oxford University Press, 1987), usefully connects the economic environment with politics.

The politics of, and within, the administration is studied best in Harry Carman and Reinhard Luthin, *Lincoln and the Patronage* (New York: Columbia University Press, 1943), and Burton J. Hendrick, *Lincoln's War Cabinet* (Boston: Little, Brown, 1946), as well as in the diaries of cabinet members already cited. Indispensable also are the biographies of Lincoln's cabinet members. The most useful of these are Glyndon Van Deusen, *William Henry Seward* (New York: Oxford University Press, 1967); Frederick Blue, *Salmon P. Chase: A Life in Politics* (Kent, Ohio: Kent State University Press, 1987); Jacob Schuckers, *The Life and Public Services of Salmon Portland Chase* (New York: Appleton, 1874); Robert Warden, *An Account of the Private Life and Public Services of Salmon Portland Chase* (Cincinnati: Wilsatch, Baldwin & Co., 1874); Benjamin Thomas and Harold M. Hyman, *Stanton: The Life and Times of Lincoln's Secretary of War* (New York: Knopf, 1962); Erwin Stanley Bradley, *Simon Cameron: Lincoln's Secretary of War* (Philadelphia: University of Pennsylvania Press, 1966); John Niven, *Gideon Welles: Lincoln's Secretary of the Navy* (New York: Oxford University Press, 1973); Marvin Cain, *Lincoln's Attorney General: Edward Bates of Missouri* (Columbia: University of Missouri Press, 1965); William Ernest Smith, *The Francis Preston Blair Family in Politics*, 2 vols. (New York: Macmillan, 1933); and Elmo Richardson and Alan Farley, *John Palmer Usher: Lincoln's Secretary of the Interior* (Lawrence: University Press of Kansas, 1960). Paul Van Riper and Keith A. Sutherland, "The Northern Civil Service: 1861–1865," *Civil War History* 11 (Dec. 1965), describes the other government employees of the war years. Leonard White, *The Jacksonians: A Study in Administrative History, 1829–1861* (New York: Free Press, 1954), sets the prewar context of cabinet activities. William Hesseltine, *Lincoln and the War Governors* (New York: Knopf, 1955), provides good background for the president's relationship with the states. David Donald, *Charles Sumner and the Rights of Man* (New York: Knopf, 1970), is excellent on both diplomacy and civil rights.

Helpful biographies and diaries of other public figures of the day also illuminate the presidency. Martin Duberman has two fine works, *Charles Francis Adams, 1807–1886* (Boston: Little, Brown, 1961), and *James Russell Lowell* (Boston: Beacon, 1966). Willard King, *Lincoln's Manager: David Davis* (Cambridge, Mass.: Harvard University Press, 1960), and Glyndon Van Deusen, *Horace Greeley: Nineteenth Century Crusader* (Philadelphia: University of Pennsylvania Press,

1953), describe two men who influenced Lincoln's presidency in different ways. Van Deusen, *Thurlow Weed: Wizard of the Lobby* (Boston: Little, Brown, 1947), is useful on wartime politics.

The Civil War Congress needs more study. The best work available includes two books by Allan Bogue, *The Earnest Men: Republicans of the Civil War Senate* (Ithaca N.Y.: Cornell University Press, 1981), and *The Congressman's Civil War* (Cambridge: Cambridge University Press, 1989), and Leonard Curry, *Blueprint for Modern America: Non Military Legislation of the First Civil War Congress* (Nashville, Tenn.: Vanderbilt University Press, 1968). Hans Trefousse, *The Radical Republicans: Lincoln's Vanguard for Racial Justice* (New York: Knopf, 1969), explores relations between Lincoln and these legislators. It is a fine counterbalance to T. Harry Williams, *Lincoln and the Radicals* (Madison: University of Wisconsin Press, 1941). Work on emancipation and civil rights legislation also reveals Congress at work. Brian Holden Reid, "Historians and the Joint Committee on the Conduct of the War," *Civil War History* 38 (Dec. 1992), is the place to start for investigators of that committee. Biographies of congressmen are imperative: Fawn Brodie, *Thaddeus Stevens* (New York: Norton, 1966), and Rachel Sherman Thorndyke, ed., *The Sherman Letters*, (New York: Scribners, 1894), are revealing about the interaction of war and lawmaking. Francis Fessenden, *Life and Public Services of William Pitt Fessenden*, 2 vols. (Boston: Houghton Mifflin, 1907), is especially good on the cabinet crisis of December 1862.

MILITARY STUDIES

The best introduction to the military history of the war is Herman Hattaway and Archer Jones, *How the North Won: A Military History of the Civil War* (Urbana: University of Illinois Press, 1983). Statistics about battles and losses and units are available in Frederick Phisterer, *Statistical Record of the Armies of the United States* (New York: Scribners, 1884). The organization of the army is described in Thomas and Hyman, *Stanton*, and in Fred R. Shannon, *The Organization and Administration of the Union Army*, 2 vols. (Cleveland: Clark, 1926). Thomas and Hyman, *Stanton*, provides an excellent discussion of the interactions of soldiers and civilian leaders during the war. Lincoln's relationships to his generals are the focus of T. Harry Williams, *Lincoln and His Generals* (New York: Knopf, 1952), and Kenneth P. Williams's magisterial *Lincoln Finds a General*, 5 vols. (New York: Macmillan, 1949–58). Helpful for overall strategy is Archer Jones, *Civil War Command and Strategy* (New York: Free Press, 1992), and Edward Hagerman, *The American Civil War and the Origin of Modern Warfare: Ideas, Organization, and Field Command* (Bloomington: Indiana University Press, 1988). Russell Weigley, *The American Way of War* (Bloomington: Indiana University Press, 1977), has a stimulating essay on Grant. The biographies of leading generals clarify the military side of the discussions that generals had with Lincoln. On McClellan, see two critics, Stephen Sears, *General George B. McClellan: The Young Napoleon* (New York: Ticknor and Fields, 1988), and Michael C. C. Adams, *"Our Masters, the Rebels": A Speculation on Union Military Failure in the East*

(Cambridge, Mass.: Harvard University Press, 1978), and one defender, Rowena Reid, *Combined Operations in the Civil War* (Annapolis, Md.: Naval Institute Press, 1978). On Fremont, the most recent work is Andrew Rolle, *John Charles Fremont: Character as Destiny* (Norman: University of Oklahoma Press, 1991). On Grant, see William McFeely, *Grant: A Biography* (New York: Norton, 1981), a work that is stronger on Grant the man than on Grant the soldier, and Brooks Simpson, *Let Us Have Peace: Ulysses S. Grant and the Politics of War and Reconstruction, 1861–1868* (Chapel Hill: University of North Carolina Press, 1991), which is concerned with the general's political sensitivity although helpful on his military talent. Sherman is seen best in Lloyd Lewis, *Sherman: Fighting Prophet* (New York: Harcourt, 1932), and most recently in John Marzalek, *Sherman: A Soldier's Passion for Order* (New York: Free Press, 1993). The memoirs of the three leading Union generals repay reading: George B. McClellan, *McClellan's Own Story* (New York: Webster, 1887); Ulysses S. Grant, *Personal Memoirs* (New York: Library of America, 1990); and William Tecumseh Sherman, *Memoirs of General W. T. Sherman* (New York: Library of America, 1990).

Other important aspects of the war that set the context for Lincoln's military decisions are Michael Fellman, *Inside War: The Guerrilla Conflict in Missouri during the American Civil War* (New York: Oxford University Press, 1989); Charles Royster, *The Destructive War: William Tecumseh Sherman, Stonewall Jackson, and the Americans* (New York: Knopf, 1991); Reid Mitchell, *Civil War Soldiers* (New York: Viking, 1988); Gerald Linderman, *Embattled Courage* (New York: Free Press, 1987); Marcus Cunliffe, *Soldiers and Civilians: The Martial Spirit in America, 1775–1865* (New York: Free Press, 1973); Russell Weigley, *Toward an American Army: Military Thought from Washington to Marshall* (New York: Columbia University Press, 1962); and "General M. C. Meigs on the Conduct of the War," *American Historical Review* 26 (1921). For navy activity, see William Davis, *The Duel between the First Ironclads* (New York: Garden City Publishers, 1975); John Niven's biography of Gideon Welles; and Victor Carrington Jones, *Civil War at Sea*, 3 vols. (New York: Holt, Rinehart, 1960–1962). An older, detailed volume by one of the participants is available: Adm. David D. Porter, *The Naval History of the Civil War* (Secaucus, N.J.: Castle, 1984). The crucial role of railroads in moving the army is explored in George Turner, *Victory Rode the Rails* (Indianapolis: Bobbs-Merrill, 1953).

DIPLOMATIC CONTEXTS

The best summary of wartime diplomacy is D. P. Crook, *The North, the South and the Powers, 1861–1865* (New York: Wiley, 1974). Van Deusen's *Seward* presents the secretary of state's foreign affairs ably. Norman Ferris, *Desperate Diplomacy: William Seward's Foreign Policy, 1861* (Knoxville: University of Tennessee Press, 1976), and Ferris, *The Trent Affair* (Knoxville: University of Tennessee Press, 1977), as well as Gordon Warren, *Fountain of Discontent: The Trent Affair and Freedom of the Seas* (Boston: Northeastern University Press, 1981), and Stuart Bernath, *Squall across the Atlantic: The American Civil War Prize Cases* (Los Angeles: University of California Press, 1970), provide fine background on their topics. On relations with Great Britain, start with Brian Jenkins, *Britain and the War for the Union*, 2 vols. (Montreal: McGill University Press, 1974); on France, see Lynn Case and Warren Spencer, *The United States and France: Civil War Diplomacy* (Philadelphia: University of Pennsylvania Press, 1970). Useful on public opinion is Donaldson Jordan and Edwin Pratt, *Europe and the American Civil War* (Boston: Houghton Mifflin, 1931). For the mission of the nation in the eyes of Republican leaders, see Major Wilson, *Space, Time and Freedom: The Quest for Nationality and the Irrepressible Conflict* (Westport, Conn.: Greenwood, 1974), and the essay by Richard Current, "The Civil War and the American Mission," in Davis, ed., *The Public and Private Lincoln*. Norman Graebner, "Northern Diplomacy and European Neutrality," in Donald, ed., *Why the North Won the Civil War*, is useful, too.

EMANCIPATION

The military aspects of emancipation are seen in two older works: Benjamin Quarles, *The Negro in the Civil War* (Boston: Little, Brown, 1969), and Dudley Cornish's excellent *The Sable Arm: Black Troops in the Union Army, 1861–1865* (Lawrence: University Press of Kansas, 1987). Mary Frances Berry, *Military Necessity and Civil Rights Policy: Black Citizenship and the Constitution, 1861–1868* (Port Washington, N.Y.: Kennikat Press, 1977), and Joseph Glatthaar, *Forged in Battle: The Civil War Alliance of Black Soldiers and White Officers* (New York: Free Press, 1990), analyze the relationships between black soldiering and freedom. Ira Berlin, Barbara J. Fields, Thavolia Glymph, Steven F. Miller, Joseph P. Reidy, and Leslie S. Rowland, *Slaves No More: Three Essays on Emancipation and the Civil War* (Cambridge: Cambridge University Press, 1992), provide essays based on *Freedom: A Documentary History of Emancipation, 1861–1867*, 3 vols. to date (Cambridge: Cambridge University Press, 1982–), the most important collection of material on the coming of emancipation. Louis Gerteis, *From Contraband to Freedman: Federal Policy toward Southern Blacks, 1861–1865* (Westport, Conn.: Greenwood, 1973), describes the degree of freedom freedmen in the South experienced. On Washington, D.C., see Constance McLaughlin Green, *Washington: Village and Capital, 1800–1878* (Princeton, N.J.: Princeton University Press, 1962); Margaret Leech, *Reveille in Washington, 1860–1865* (New York: Grossett and Dunlap, 1941); and Michael Kurtz, "Emancipation in the Federal City," *Civil War History* 26 (Sept. 1978).

Abolitionists during the Civil War are best studied in James McPherson, *The Struggle for Equality: Abolitionists and the Negro in the Civil War and Reconstruction* (Princeton, N.J.: Princeton University Press, 1964). James B. Stewart, *Wendell Phillips: Liberty's Hero* (Baton Rouge: Louisiana State University Press, 1986), is also a fine recent picture. Black experiences in the war are usefully collected in James McPherson, ed., *The Negro's Civil War* (New York: Pantheon, 1965). The only study that focuses on the Emancipation Proclamation is John Hope Franklin, *The Emancipation Proclamation* (New York: Anchor, 1965). Harry Jaffa, "The Emancipation Proclamation," in Robert Goldwin, ed., *One Hundred Years of*

Emancipation (Chicago: Rand McNally, 1963), is a thoughtful interpretation. Lincoln's progress toward emancipation is presented in Gideon Welles, "History of Emancipation," *Galaxy* (Dec. 1872), and Stephen Oates, "Lincoln's Journey to Emancipation," in Oates, *Our Fiery Trial* (Amherst: University of Massachusetts Press, 1979). Lincoln's racial views are explored in all the biographies but are more carefully considered in George M. Frederickson, "A Man but Not a Brother," *Journal of Southern History* 41 (Feb. 1975), and Don Fehrenbacher, "Only His Stepchildren," in *Lincoln in Text and Context*. Gabor Boritt, "The Voyage to the Colony of Linconia," *Historian* 37 (1975), imaginatively treats the colonization question. Congress' role in emancipation is described by a participant in the process in Henry Wilson, *History of the Antislavery Measures of the Thirty-seventh and Thirty-eighth United States Congresses* (Boston: Walker, Fuller, 1865). V. Jacques Voegeli, *Free but Not Equal: The Midwest and the Negro during the Civil War* (Chicago: University of Chicago Press, 1967), describes the racial biases that opposed black progress. William McFeely, *Frederick Douglass* (New York: Norton, 1991), supplemented by Douglass's own *Life and Times of Frederick Douglass* (New York: Collier's, 1962), and David Blight, *Frederick Douglass' Civil War* (Baton Rouge: Louisiana State University Press, 1989), and Waldo Martin, *The Mind of Frederick Douglass* (Chapel Hill: University of North Carolina Press, 1984), provide a rich portrait of the most influential black man of the age and his impact on Lincoln.

NORTHERN SOCIETY IN WAR

Paludan, *"A People's Contest,"* is the most recent survey and interpretation of Northern society at war. Emerson Fite, *Social and Industrial Conditions in the North during the Civil War* (1910; rept., New York: Ungar, 1963), is still helpful, as is Arthur Cole, *The Irrepressible Conflict, 1850–1865* (New York: Macmillan, 1934). The best introduction to the growing field of social history of the war is Maris Vinovskis, ed., *Toward a Social History of the American Civil War: Exploratory Essays* (Cambridge: Cambridge University Press, 1990). Catherine Clinton and Nina Silber, eds., *Divided Houses: Gender and the Civil War* (New York: Oxford University Press, 1992), is filled with useful insights.

Primary sources are invaluable in presenting the society at war; three in particular represent a sampling. Allan Nevins and Milton Halsey Thomas, eds., *The Diary of George Templeton Strong,* (New York: Macmillan, 1952), especially vol. 3, is a treasure of observations from the top of New York City society. George Winston Smith and Charles Judah, eds., *Life in the North during the Civil War: A Source History* (Albuquerque: University of New Mexico Press, 1966), gathers materials across all levels of the society. *Harper's Pictorial History of the Civil War* (Chicago: Star Publishing, 1866), follows the military forces but offers the picture that Northerners of the age saw of the conflict.

The economics of warmaking can be seen in the biographies of Secretary of the Treasury Chase; in Bray Hammond, *Sovereignty and an Empty Purse* (Princeton, N.J.: Princeton University Press, 1970); Paul Gates, *Agriculture and the Civil*

War (New York: Knopf, 1975); and Boritt, *Lincoln and Economics*. The impact of the war on workers is seen in Iver Bernstein, *The New York City Draft Riots* (New York: Oxford University Press, 1990); Matthew Gallman, *Mastering War: A Social History of Philadelphia during the Civil War* (Cambridge: Cambridge University Press, 1990); and Grace Palladino, *Another Civil War: Labor, Capital and the State in the Anthracite Regions of Pennsylvania, 1840–1868* (Urbana: University of Illinois Press, 1990). David Montgomery, *Beyond Equality: Labor and the Radical Republicans* (New York: Vintage, 1967), is the standard study.

Recruitment and the draft are thoughtfully considered in James W. Geary, *We Need Men: The Union Draft in the Civil War* (DeKalb: Northern Illinois University Press, 1991). Geary's "Civil War Conscription in the North: A Historiographical Review," *Civil War History* 32 (Sept. 1986), explores that literature. Eugene Murdock, *One Million Men: The Civil War Draft in the North* (Madison: University of Wisconsin Press, 1971), is also useful. The question of who fought in the war is analyzed in Murdock, "Was It a Poor Man's Fight?" *Civil War History* 10 (1964); Hugh Earnhart, "Commutation: Democratic or Undemocratic?" *Civil War History* 12 (1966); and William Rorabaugh, "Who Fought for the North in the Civil War?" *Journal of American History* 73 (1986).

The reactions of intellectuals to the war are considered thoughtfully in George M. Frederickson, *The Inner Civil War: Northern Intellectuals and the Crisis of Union* (New York: Harper & Row, 1965). Literary figures are assessed in Daniel Aaron, *The Unwritten War: American Writers and the Civil War* (New York: Knopf, 1973), and Edmond Wilson, *Patriotic Gore: Studies in the Literature of the American Civil War* (New York: Knopf, 1862). Wilson and Frederickson share a hostility to warmaking that distances them from the people they study. James Moorhead, *American Apocalypse: Yankee Protestants and the Civil War, 1860–1865* (New Haven, Conn.: Yale University Press, 1978), discusses the important role of religion in the war.

Wartime politics are discussed in the major biographies and studies of the presidency. For more specific information on Democrats, see Joel Silbey, *A Respectable Minority: The Democratic Party in the Civil War Era, 1860–1868* (New York: Norton, 1977), and Jean Baker, *Affairs of Party*. The election of 1864 needs a new study. The fullest work remains William F. Zornow, *Lincoln and the Party Divided* (Norman: University of Oklahoma Press, 1954), which sees a permanent split between the president and "Unconditional" Republicans. Harold M. Hyman, "The Election of 1864," in Arthur Schlesinger, Jr., ed., *History of American Presidential Elections* (New York: Chelsea House, 1971), is a more balanced evaluation. Larry Nelson, *Bullets, Bayonets and Rhetoric: Confederate Policy for the United States Presidential Contest of 1864* (Tuscaloosa: University of Alabama Press, 1980), discusses rebel hopes for the election. For thoughtful interpretations of the value and viability of partisan politics in North and South, see the debate between Eric McKitrick, "Party Politics and the Union and Confederate War Efforts," in William Chambers and Walter Dean Burnham, eds., *The American Party Systems* (New York: Oxford University Press, 1967), and Michael Holt, "Abraham Lincoln and the Politics of Union," in John L. Thomas, ed., *Lincoln and the American Political Tradition*.

RECONSTRUCTION

Eric Foner, *Reconstruction: America's Unfinished Revolution* (New York: Harper & Row, 1988), is the imperative beginning point for reconstruction study. The Southern context is provided in George Rable, *But There Was No Peace: The Role of Violence in the Politics of Reconstruction* (Athens: University of Georgia Press, 1984), and Dan T. Carter, *When the War Was Over: The Failure of Self-Reconstruction in the South, 1865–1867* (Baton Rouge: Louisiana State University Press, 1985). Congressional policymaking is thoroughly analyzed in Herman Belz, *Reconstructing the Union: Theory and Policy during the Civil War* (Ithaca, N.Y.: Cornell University Press, 1969); in Belz, *A New Birth of Freedom: The Republican Party and Freedmen's Rights, 1861–1866* (Westport, Conn.: Greenwood, 1976); in Michael Les Benedict, *A Compromise of Principle: Congressional Republicans and Reconstruction, 1863–1869* (New York: Norton, 1974); and in Lawanda Cox and John Cox, *Politics, Principle and Prejudice, 1865–1866* (New York: Free Press, 1963). Works already cited by Hyman and Wiecek, *Equal Justice under Law*; Hyman, *"A More Perfect Union"*; Trefousse, *Radical Republicans*; and Paludan, *A Covenant with Death* also discuss congressional reconstruction. David Donald, *Charles Sumner and the Rights of Man*, is also helpful. These works challenge earlier writings that depicted a bitter clash between Congress and the president. See Williams, *Lincoln and the Radicals*; William B. Hesseltine, *Lincoln's Plan of Reconstruction* (Chicago: Quadrangle, 1967); and William A. Dunning, *Essays on the Civil War and Reconstruction* (New York: Macmillan, 1904). Harold Hyman, ed., *The Radical Republicans and Reconstruction, 1861–1870* (Indianapolis: Bobbs-Merrill, 1967), provides the basic documents and a thoughtful introduction. See also Michael Les Benedict, "Preserving the Constitution: The Conservative Basis of Radical Reconstruction," *Journal of American History* 61 (1974), and Donald Nieman, *Promises to Keep: African Americans and the Constitutional Order, 1776 to the Present* (New York: Oxford University Press, 1991).

Louisiana is the subject of several fine works. Lawanda Cox, *Lincoln and Black Freedom* (Columbia: University of South Carolina Press, 1981), provides an excellent discussion of the complexities of both emancipation and the reconstruction process. Joseph G. Dawson III, *Army Generals and Reconstruction: Louisiana 1862–1877* (Baton Rouge: Louisiana State University Press, 1982), provides a military context. Peyton McCrary, *Abraham Lincoln and Reconstruction: The Louisiana Experiment* (Princeton, N.J.: Princeton University Press, 1978), and Ted Tunnell, *Crucible of Reconstruction: War, Radicalism and Race in Louisiana, 1862–1877* (Baton Rouge: Louisiana State University Press, 1984) are invaluable. Cox argues that Lincoln had a generally egalitarian policy; Tunnell sees Lincoln supporting the military. I think Cox inadequately distinguishes between the economic and the political aspects of Lincoln's egalitarianism. On Butler's activities, see Benjamin Butler, *Butler's Book* (Boston: A. M. Thayer, 1892); Richard West, *Lincoln's Scapegoat General: A Life of Benjamin F. Butler* (Boston: Little, Brown, 1965); and Hans Trefousse, *Ben Butler: The South Called Him Beast* (New York: Twayne, 1957). Banks's work in Louisiana can be followed in Fred Harvey Harrington, *Fighting Politician: Major General N. P. Banks* (Westport, Conn.:

Greenwood, 1970). The context of disorder in the region is seen in William F. Messner, "Black Violence and White Response: Louisiana, 1862," *Journal of Southern History* 41 (Feb. 1975); Leon Litwack, *Been in the Storm So Long: The Aftermath of Slavery* (New York: Knopf, 1979); and Gerteis, *From Contraband to Freedman.* For the connections between military policy and reconstruction, see J. Thomas May, "Continuity and Change in the Labor Program of the Union Army and the Freedmen's Bureau," *Civil War History* 17 (Sept. 1971). Louis Gerteis, "Salmon P. Chase, Radicalism and the Politics of Emancipation," *Journal of American History* 60 (June 1973), presents Chase's policy sympathetically. Whitelaw Reid, *After the War: A Tour of the Southern States, 1865–1866,* ed. C. Vann Woodward (New York: Harpers, 1965), and John Eaton, *Grant, Lincoln and the Freedmen* (New York: Negro Universities, 1908), provide contemporary context.

THE END OF THE PRESIDENCY

The assassination of Lincoln is the subject of Thomas Reed Turner, *Beware the People Weeping: Public Opinion and the Assassination of Abraham Lincoln* (Baton Rouge: Louisiana State University Press, 1982), and William Hanchett, *The Lincoln Murder Conspiracies* (Urbana: University of Illinois Press, 1983).

The consequences of the presidency may be assessed in Morton Keller, *Affairs of State: Public Life in Late Nineteenth Century America* (Cambridge, Mass.: Harvard University Press, 1977), the best recent study, and in late-nineteenth-century writings by James Bryce, *The American Commonwealth* (New York: Macmillan, 1915); M. Ostrogorsky, *Democracy and the Organization of Political Parties,* 2 vols. (New York: Anchor, 1964); and Woodrow Wilson, *Congressional Government: A Study in American Politics* (Boston: Houghton Mifflin, 1898).

INDEX

Abandoned Property Act, 263
Abolitionists: on emancipation, 144–45,
    299–300; on leadership, 262, 270, 272–73;
    and Lincoln, 88, 124, 129, 187, 262, 264,
    272; popularity of, 124–25; on slavery,
    103, 124–25
Adams, Charles Francis, 61, 90, 93, 123,
    218–19
Agriculture, Department of, 116
Alexander, Edward Porter, 167
Anderson, Robert, 57, 58
Andrew, John A., 155, 223
Anthony, Susan B., 144, 300
Antietam, battle at, 154
Arkansas, 161, 250, 281
Army of the Potomac, 138, 142, 149, 154,
    167, 197, 259, 261
Ashley, James, 143, 301, 303, 309

Baker, Edward, 97
Baltimore riot, 69, 70
Banks, Nathaniel: on black employment,
    245–46; as commander, 159, 244, 277,
    297, 310; on emancipation, 255, 279–80;
    on Louisiana, 247, 248, 252–54, 275, 276,
    278, 310
Barney, Hiram, 268
Bates, Edward, 15, 41, 104; on cabinet, 44,
    64, 92, 123, 168, 174, 175, 178, 180, 302;
    political experience of, 42; on slavery, 42
Beauregard, P. G. T., 199
Beecher, Henry Ward, 144, 155–56

Bell, John, 4–5
Belmont, August, 150
Bingham, John, 244
Black Americans: attacks on, 213; black
    codes and, 128; employment of, 212,
    245–46, 262–63, 280, 281, 310; free blacks
    in Louisiana, 238, 239, 264, 277, 298;
    Lincoln on, 19, 131, 165, 222–23, 247–48,
    263–64, 277, 279; militancy of, 298; in
    the military, xiii, 103, 144, 146–47, 148,
    153–54, 155, 170, 189, 209, 214, 222, 223–
    24, 227, 238–39, 241–42, 243, 284, 306;
    and property ownership, 238, 262–63,
    297–98, 309; rights, 276, 279, 297–98,
    309; suffrage, 254, 263–64, 266, 277, 303,
    308–9, 310. *See also* Emancipation; Rac-
    ism; Slavery
Blair, Francis P., Sr., 41–42, 64, 288
Blair, Frank, 41–42, 86, 288
Blair, Montgomery, 42, 63, 92, 102; and
    cabinet crisis, 173, 174, 178, 180; and
    Lincoln, 168, 175; politics of, 44, 262,
    287–88; as postmaster general, 41, 287–
    88; replacement of, 288–89, 302; on war,
    61, 64
Blockades, Northern, 71, 82, 89, 90, 122,
    210, 218
Booth, John Wilkes, 309
Border states, 125, 126, 127, 130, 133, 152,
    300
Bragg, Braxton, 219
Breckenridge, John, 4, 12

379

Britain. *See* Great Britain
Browning, Orville, 157
Buchanan, James, 22, 23, 29, 36–37, 59
Buckner, Simon Bolivar, 120
Buell, Don Carlos, 85, 99, 104, 129, 158, 159
Bull Run, battle at, 83
Burnside, Ambrose, 99, 160, 167, 197, 198–99
Butler, Benjamin, 289, 309; on blacks in military, 153, 238–39, 243; as commander, 153, 159, 234–35, 244–45; on slavery, 84, 241, 242

Cabinet: changes in, 105, 286–89, 302; criticism of, 171–174, 287–88; formation of, 36–45; politics in, 43–45, 267–68, 286, 287. *See also* Lincoln, Abraham, and cabinet
Cadwalader, George, 75
Cameron, Simon, 23, 43–44, 73, 85, 87, 103, 105, 123, 268
Campbell, John, 60
Canby, Edward, 297, 298
Carey, Henry, 114
Carlyle, Thomas, 72
Cass, Lewis, 37
Chancellorsville, battle at, 198
Chandler, Zachariah, 29, 97–98, 142–43, 144, 146, 288, 309
Channing, William Ellery, 11
Chase, Salmon, 178; appointment of, 37, 39; on blacks, 243, 262–63; complaints on cabinet, 41, 169, 173, 174, 180, 261; and election of 1863, 226; on emancipation, 130, 148–49, 170, 179, 188, 247; and Lincoln, 40–41, 108, 123, 168, 175, 176–77, 247, 261, 266–69; personal traits of, 40–41; political ambitions of, 73, 261–62, 266–70; political experience and beliefs of, 39, 40, 225, 226, 249; resignation offer, 176–77, 286–87; on slavery, 39, 41; as Supreme Court chief justice, 302; and war, 61, 64, 92, 102, 158; and war funding, 83, 109, 111–12
Chattanooga, Tenn., 219–21
Chickamauga, battle at, 219
Cisco, John, 286
Civil War: battles, 83, 86, 97, 120, 129, 138–39, 154, 167–68, 186, 198, 205–6, 209, 219–20, 282; casualties of, 66, 83, 129, 138, 139, 154, 186, 198, 205, 282; end of, 306; funding of, 83, 108, 109–10, 111–12; navy in, 120–22; preparation for, 65, 66, 70–71, 72–73, 80–84
Clay, Henry, 17, 115, 117, 125

Cobb, Howell, 37
Cochrane, John, 271
Collamer, Jacob, 171–72, 175
Colonization proposal, 130–33, 134, 151, 155, 165, 189
Committee on the Conduct of War, 104–5, 106, 139, 140
Confiscation Acts, 127, 145–46, 147, 235, 241–42
Confiscation of slaves, 127, 145–46, 147, 188, 235, 241–42
Congress, U.S.: on blacks in military, 144, 146, 241–42; on cabinet, 171–76; on conscription, 191, 193; and constitutional amendments, 231, 299–302; and economic development, 7, 113–15, 116; and education, 115; on emancipation, 127, 143, 145–46, 147, 166, 188, 241–42, 299–302; on habeas corpus, 191–92; on military leadership, 97–99, 104–5, 139, 140, 144; on reconstruction, 143–44, 264–66, 280–81, 282, 302–3; regional influence on, 6; on slavery, 31–34, 83–84, 133, 134–35, 148, 266; on Southern representation, 243–44, 248–49, 251; 38th, 109; 37th, 108–9, 113, 133; and war funding, 83, 108, 109–10, 111–12. *See also* Committee on the Conduct of War; Lincoln, Abraham, and Congress
Conkling, James, 224
Conscription, 146, 191–97, 226. *See also* Draft riots
Constitution, U.S.: amendments to, 231, 271, 299–302; and conscription, 194–95; interpretation of, 13–14; limitations of, 82, 108, 127; on rights, 54; and slavery, 12–13, 17–18, 39–40, 126; and Supreme Court, 12, 13, 17, 54, 77. *See also* Habeas corpus, writ of; Lincoln, Abraham, on the Constitution
Conway, Thomas, 279, 298
Cooke, Henry, 112
Cooke, Jay, 110, 112
Corning, Erastus, 199
Cox, Lawanda, 165
Cox, Samuel S., 248, 302
Crittenden, John J., 31, 83
Crittenden Compromise, 32, 33
Curtin, Andrew, 214
Curtis, Benjamin, 158

Dana, Charles, 208–9
Davis, David, 274
Davis, Henry Winter, 143, 265, 281, 282, 289, 303
Davis, Jefferson, 31, 66, 89, 192, 198, 199

Declaration of Independence, 18, 19, 126
Democratic party: and elections of 1862, 157, 190; and elections of 1863, 226–27; and elections of 1864, 283–84, 285, 290, 291; on emancipation, 299, 301–2; on equality, 271; on federal authority, 192, 194, 198; and Lincoln, 143, 199–202; racism of, 199, 221–22; Southern influence on, 6; and the Union, 222, 283–84, 285
Dix, John A., 214
Douglas, Stephen, 4, 5, 12, 17, 31
Douglass, Frederick, 103, 155, 183, 187, 270
Draft. See Conscription
Draft law, 194, 195, 196, 226
Draft riots, 213–14, 223, 289
Dred Scott, 12, 13, 54, 77, 135, 272
Durant, Thomas, 245, 246, 248, 253–54, 275, 276, 279, 280
Durrell, Edward, 254

Economy: Congress and, 7, 113–15, 116; prewar, 8–11; wartime, 210–12, 216, 219; and western development, 14, 116–17
Edmunds, James, 225
Elections of 1860, 3–5, 13, 14–15, 28, 239
Elections of 1862, 157, 167, 190
Elections of 1863, 220–21, 224, 226–27
Elections of 1864, 225–26, 259, 283–86, 289–91
Emancipation: abolitionists on, 270–71, 272, 300; constitutional amendment on, 299–302; in District of Columbia, 134–35; in Maryland, 289; Proclamation of, 147–48, 153, 154–56, 158, 186–89; response to, 151–52, 157–58, 168, 186–88, 189, 227–28; and Union army, 146–47, 152–53, 236, 264, 299, 301–2. See also Congress, on emancipation; Lincoln, Abraham, on emancipation
Emerson, Ralph Waldo, 156
England. See Great Britain
Equality, 18, 189, 310. See also Dred Scott; Lincoln, Abraham, on equality
Ericsson, John, 121
Etheridge, Emerson, 248–49
Ewing, Thomas, 157

Farragut, David, 142, 234, 284
Faxon, William, 122
Federal jobs, 35–36
Fessenden, William, 170, 174, 175, 287
Fifty-fourth Massachusetts regiment, 223
Flanders, Benjamin, 243, 244, 245, 246, 249, 253–54, 275, 277, 279, 280
Floyd, John B., 22

Foote, Andrew, 120
Foreign affairs, 62, 88–93, 133, 218–19
Forney, John, 225
Fort Donelson, 120
Fort Henry, 120
Fort Pickens, 59, 62, 63–64, 66
Fort Sumter, 55, 57, 58–60, 61, 62, 63–66
Foster, Stephen S., 124
Fox, Gustavus, 122
France, relations with U.S., 92, 219
Fredericksburg, battle at, 167
Freedmen's Bureau, 246, 263, 279, 309
Fremont, John, 86–87, 116, 130, 270–71, 272, 273, 288
Fry, James, 194

Garrison, William Lloyd, 17, 39, 124, 128, 187, 262, 270, 272, 273
Gettysburg, battle at, 205–6
Gettysburg Address, 89, 228–30
Gladstone, William, 218
Goodell, William, 124
Gordon, Nathaniel, 133
Grant, Ulysses S.: as commander in West, 120, 129, 142, 158, 185, 208, 220, 246; on election of 1864, 290; as general in chief, 259–61, 280, 284–85; on Lincoln, 260–61
Great Britain: on Confederacy, 89–90, 91–93, 142, 218; and U.S. relations, 89–93, 133, 218–19
Greeley, Horace, 15, 70, 114, 117, 144, 150, 156, 194, 283
Grierson, Benjamin, 209
Grimes, James, 98, 173, 175
Gwin, John, 60

Habeas corpus, writ of, 71–76, 79, 81, 82, 157, 191–92, 200
Habeas Corpus Act, 191–92
Hahn, Michael, 243, 244, 245, 246, 275, 276, 277, 278, 298, 305
Halleck, Henry: command in West of, 85, 99, 120, 142; as general in chief, 141, 149, 203, 204, 205, 206, 207–8, 210, 217; and Lincoln, 204, 205, 207–8, 210, 217, 218, 260; on slavery, 88
Haskell, Frank, 205–6
Hay, John, 26, 49, 106, 206, 249, 257
Henderson, John, 300
Hofstadter, Richard, 187
Holmes, Oliver Wendell, Jr., 118
Holt, Joseph, 153, 285, 286
Homestead Act, 114, 116
Hooker, Joe, 197–98, 203–4, 205, 206
Howard, Jacob, 173, 175
Howe, Julia Ward, 119

Hunter, David, 87, 130, 152–53, 236
Hunter, Robert, 60
Hurlbut, Stephen A., 63, 298

Immigration, 7, 212
Indiana, 289
Interior, Department of, 117
Internal Revenue Act, 116
Internal security operations, 73–75

Jackson, Andrew, 27
Jackson, Stonewall, 149
Johnson, Andrew, 83, 234, 273, 310
Johnston, Joseph, 138
Julian, George, 292, 301, 309

Kansas, 22
Keckley, Elizabeth, 313
Kennedy, Hugh, 298, 305, 310
Kentucky, 82–83, 87, 125

Lamon, Ward, 134
Lane, James, 143, 153
Lee, Robert E., 138, 149, 198, 199, 207
Legal Tender Act, 109, 226
Lieber, Francis, 153, 290
Lincoln, Abraham
—on black Americans, 19, 131, 165, 222–
  23, 247–48, 263–64, 277, 279
—on blacks in military, 148, 155, 189, 243,
  284
—and cabinet, 61, 108, 122, 123, 168, 169,
  170–77, 179–80, 267–68, 286–88
—as commander in chief, 58–59, 61, 63,
  64–66, 80, 81, 82, 99–100, 102–3, 108,
  139–41, 158–59, 160, 179, 197, 203–4,
  206, 208, 215, 217, 220, 236–37, 261
—and Congress, 80, 81, 82, 108, 133, 143,
  162–63, 166, 171–77, 187, 244, 250, 251,
  265–66, 280–81, 306, 308–9
—on the Constitution, 13, 17–18, 20, 35,
  53, 54, 56, 77, 78, 126, 158, 164, 179, 289
—and economic development, 116–17, 211
—education of, 16, 115
—and elections, 4, 15–16, 226, 285–86, 290
—on emancipation, 125–28, 129–30, 133,
  147–48, 151–52, 154, 155, 158, 163, 164,
  165–66, 170, 179, 188, 222, 236, 244, 247,
  249, 251, 284, 300–301, 302
—on equality, 18, 19, 20, 33, 52, 146–47,
  229, 277–78, 279, 311
—and expansion of executive power, 71,
  72–73, 76, 79–81, 230
—on foreign affairs, 88–93, 218
—inaugural addresses of, 52–57, 60, 303–5
—on labor, 115–16, 212–13

—on military leadership, 99–100, 102–3,
  140–41, 143, 149, 154, 159, 160, 197, 204,
  205, 206, 217–18, 259–61
—nomination of, 15–16, 226, 261, 271–72
—and patronage, 35–36, 278
—personal traits of, 15–17, 24, 25–26, 27,
  100, 292
—political beliefs of, 15, 16–17, 19, 55, 165,
  172, 215, 262
—political experience of, 24–25, 123
—on reconstruction, 143, 161, 236–37, 246–
  48, 250–51, 263–64, 265, 266, 280–81,
  298, 302, 304, 306–9
—rhetorical style of, xiv–xv
—on secession, 29, 30–31, 52, 53, 55, 150–
  51, 179, 230
—on self-government, 18–19, 53, 242, 250,
  291
—on slavery, xii–xiii, 17–18, 19, 30–31, 32,
  33, 34–35, 53, 56, 87, 150, 242, 305
—threats against, 52–53
—on the Union, xii–xiii, 34–35, 52, 53, 55–
  56, 150–51, 155, 163, 166, 179, 222, 236,
  237, 284
—on warfare, 100, 107–8
Lincoln, Mary, 106, 168
Logan, John, 222
Longstreet, James, 219
Louisiana: constitution of, 246, 247, 277,
  278; elections in, 243, 246–47, 248; free
  blacks in, 238, 239; liberation of New
  Orleans, 234–35; reconstruction in, 161,
  234–35, 238–49, 250, 251, 252–55, 263–64,
  276, 297–98, 305–6, 310; rejoining the
  Union, 161, 240, 243; slavery in, 240–41;
  Unionists in, 239–40, 242, 246, 248, 249,
  254, 275, 277, 278, 305
Lovejoy, Owen, 143
Lowell, James Russell, 34, 124–25
Lusk, Will, 209
Lyon, Nathaniel, 86

McClellan, George, 97; on blacks, 103, 144;
  as commander, 107, 108, 137–39, 144,
  149, 159; on emancipation, 98, 103, 140,
  141–42; and Lincoln, 101–3, 108, 137–38,
  139–40, 141, 143, 149, 154, 158, 159, 173;
  ousting of, 158, 159–60; personal traits
  of, 99, 101–2, 138; politics of, 104, 105,
  140, 141; as presidential candidate, 283,
  285, 290, 291; qualifications of, 84–85,
  100–101; on recruitment, 128
McClernand, John, 159, 208
McCormick, Cyrus, 211
McDowell, Irwin, 84, 104
McPherson, James, 34, 165

Mallory, Stephen, 120
Marx, Karl, 187
Maryland, 69, 70–71, 75, 78, 289
Mason, James, 91, 93
Meade, George, 205, 206, 207, 217–18
Medill, Joseph, 171
Meigs, Montgomery, 102, 107, 139
Mellin, William, 263
Merryman, John, 75
Militia Act, 146, 191, 242
Mill, John Stuart, 93
Morgan, Edwin D., 286, 300
Morgan, George, 122
Morrill Land Grant Act, 115, 116
Morrill Tariff Act, 114
Morton, Oliver, 224, 285
Mumford, William, 234
Murfreesboro, Battle of, 186

Napoleon III, 219
National Banking Act, 111, 112
National Union party, 272
Native Americans, 117
Navy, 120–22
Neely, Mark, 79
Nelson, Samuel, 60
New Mexico, 32
New Orleans, 234–35
New York City draft riots, 213–14, 223, 289
Nicolay, John, 49
Northup, Solomon, 238

Pacific Railroad Act, 116
Parish, Peter, 165, 227
Parker, Joel, 158
Patronage, 35–36, 278
Pemberton, John, 209
Pendleton, George, 283
Phelps, John, 150, 153, 241, 242
Phillips, Wendell, 17, 124, 128, 130, 189, 238, 262, 264, 270, 271, 273
Polk, James, 27
Pomeroy, Samuel, 175, 266, 268, 269
Pope, John, 149
Population, U.S., 6, 7, 219
Porter, David, 209
Porter, Fitz John, 104
Porter, Horace, 193
Prize Cases, 81

Quincy, Josiah, 223
Quincy, Samuel, 310

Racism, 17, 128, 132, 160, 165, 189–90, 212, 221, 222–23, 237–38, 255. See also Slavery
Railroads, 116, 220

Raymond, Henry, 282, 283, 288
Reconstruction: Congress and, 143–44, 264–66, 280–81; Johnson and, 310; in Louisiana, 161, 234–35, 238–49, 250, 251, 252–55, 263–64, 276, 297–98, 305–6, 310; Wade-Davis bill and, 266, 280–81, 302–3. See also Lincoln, Abraham, on reconstruction
Recruitment, 82, 84, 128–29, 142, 146, 190, 192, 195–96. See also Conscription
Republican party, 6, 27; agenda of, 104, 113, 271–72; on black rights, 143, 309; commitment of, 33–34, 284; on Democratic party, 285–86; and economic development, 113–14; and elections of 1862, 157, 167–68; and elections of 1863, 224, 227; and elections of 1864, 224, 225–26, 271–72, 273, 285–86, 290; and patronage, 35; radicals in, 142–43, 224, 270–71, 273; on secession, 29, 65; on slavery and emancipation, 18, 145, 271, 272; and Union League, 224–25, 285; on war, 128; and western policy, 116–17
Rosencrans, William, 186, 219, 246
Russell, John, 90, 93, 218–19

Saxton, Rufus, 153
Schurz, Carl, 1, 5
Scott, Winfield, 21, 61, 63, 84
Secession, 5–6, 34; impact of, 10; opinions on, 28–29, 64; threat of, 28, 51, 55, 64. See also Lincoln, Abraham, on secession
Self-government, practice of, 5–6, 13–14, 18–19, 53, 242, 250
Seven Days campaign, 138–39
Seward, William: appointment of, 37, 43; in Congress, 31, 32; on emancipation, 149, 170; on foreign affairs, 62, 89–93, 218; and Lincoln, 61, 73, 168, 169, 172, 174, 177, 180; opposition to, 170, 171, 172, 173, 175–76; personal traits of, 40; political experience and beliefs of, 37–38, 40, 49–50, 262; political power and aspirations of, 37–38, 49–50, 60, 73, 78, 88, 168–69, 267; resignation offer, 60, 172, 176; on secession, 51, 59, 178; on slavery, 38; and war, 61–62, 64, 65, 102, 142, 192, 220
Seymour, Horatio, 190, 194, 195
Shaw, Robert Gould, 223
Shepley, George, 235, 243, 248, 254
Sheridan, Philip, 219, 284
Sherman, John, 98, 112, 145, 157, 211, 246, 269
Sherman, William Tecumseh, 47, 185, 259, 280, 284, 289, 306

Shiloh, battle at, 129
Slavery: and black codes, 128; changing attitudes toward, 227, 240–41; confiscation of slaves, 127, 145–46, 147, 235, 241–42; congressional debates on, 31–34, 84; constitution and, 12–13, 17–18, 39–40, 299–301; in District of Columbia, 134; and the economy, 8; expansion of, 4, 31–33, 135; fugitive slave laws, 30, 32, 53, 72; military policy on, 88, 134; religious sentiment on, 144, 151–52; slave codes, 7–8; Supreme Court on, 4, 12, 13, 54. *See also* Emancipation; Lincoln, Abraham, on slavery
Slidell, John, 91, 93
Smith, Caleb, 42, 43, 64, 117, 168, 169, 174
Smith, Elbert, 23
Speed, James, 309
Springfield, Ill., 9–10
Stanley, Edward, 244
Stanton, Edwin, 78, 138, 178, 180; administrative skills of, 106–7, 168; on black suffrage, 309; on cabinet problems, 170, 174, 176, 267, 287; and Congress, 106; and Lincoln, 105, 168, 180, 205, 208, 217; personality traits of, 105; politics of, 225, 226, 286; on recruitment, 128–29; on war, 122, 137, 149, 220
Stanton, Elizabeth Cady, 270, 300
States' rights, 72, 164, 221, 266, 282
Stevens, Thaddeus, 43, 134, 143, 145, 302, 309
Stoddard, William O., 225
Stone, Charles, 104, 105
Stowe, Harriet Beecher, 238
Strong, George Templeton, 11, 90, 95, 223, 274, 282, 291
Sumner, Charles: on foreign affairs, 92; and Lincoln, 142, 270, 289, 292; on Seward, 170, 173, 175; on slavery and emancipation, 4, 29, 103, 187, 223, 263, 300, 309; on war, 142–43
Supreme Court: on conscription, 194; and constitutional questions, 12, 13, 17, 54–55, 77; Lincoln on, 54–55, 250; on presidential authority, 81; on slavery, 4, 12, 13, 54

Taney, Roger, 12, 13, 17, 39, 75–77, 79, 194
Tariffs, 113–14
Taxes, 83, 111
Taylor, Richard, 297

Tennessee, 161, 250
Thirteenth Amendment, 299–302
Thomas, George, 219, 263
Thomas, Lorenzo, 246
Tilton, Theodore, 155
Treason, 73–75, 199
Treasury Department, 109–10, 263
Trent affair, 91–93
Trumbull, Lyman, 29, 31, 65, 168, 175, 300
Tunnell, Ted, 253–54

Union army, advantage of, 209–10, 215–16, 219
Unionists, Southern, 58–59, 264; in Louisiana, 239–40, 242, 246, 248, 249, 254, 264, 275, 277, 278, 305; in Virginia, 64–65, 178
Usher, John, 117

Vallandigham, Clement, 78, 199, 201, 202, 226–27, 237, 285, 302
Vicksburg, Miss., 206, 207, 208–9
Virginia, 64–65, 71, 161–62

Wade, Benjamin, 98, 102, 106, 107, 143, 265, 280, 281, 282, 289, 302, 309
Wade-Davis bill, 266, 280–81, 302, 303
Walker, Francis, 114
War Department, 105; problems in, 85, 102; and recruitment and conscription, 85, 128–29, 196; War Board, 106
Wayne, James, 78
Weed, Thurlow, 23, 43–44, 170, 282
Weld, Angelina Grimke, 145
Weller, Edwin, 190
Welles, Gideon: on cabinet problems, 169, 170, 173, 174, 175, 176, 180, 267, 287; Lincoln and, 123, 168; personal traits of, 43, 44; as secretary of navy, 121–22, 123, 168; on war, 64
Wells, J. Madison, 305, 310
West, policy on, 114, 116–17
West Virginia, 161–62, 178–79
Wheeler, Joseph, 186
Whig party, 27, 55, 71
Whitman, Walt, 156, 295
Wilkes, Charles, 91, 92
Wilson, Henry, 135, 223, 288, 289
Wilson, James, 303
Wilson's Creek, battle at, 86
Woodyard, George, 226
Wycliffe, Charles, 153

Yates, Richard, 211, 224